Sergei N. Pozdniakov · Valentina Dagienė (Eds.)

Informatics in Schools

Fundamentals of Computer Science and Software Engineering

11th International Conference on Informatics in Schools: Situation, Evolution, and Perspectives, ISSEP 2018
St. Petersburg, Russia, October 10–12, 2018
Proceedings

Springer

Editors
Sergei N. Pozdniakov
Saint Petersburg Electrotechnical University
St. Petersburg, Russia

Valentina Dagienė
Vilnius University
Vilnius, Lithuania

ISSN 0302-9743 ISSN 1611-3349 (electronic)
Lecture Notes in Computer Science
ISBN 978-3-030-02749-0 ISBN 978-3-030-02750-6 (eBook)
https://doi.org/10.1007/978-3-030-02750-6

Library of Congress Control Number: 2018958307

LNCS Sublibrary: SL1 – Theoretical Computer Science and General Issues

This Springer imprint is published by the registered company Springer Nature Switzerland AG
The registered company address is: Gewerbestrasse 11, 6330 Cham, Switzerland

Lecture Notes in Computer Science 11169

Commenced Publication in 1973
Founding and Former Series Editors:
Gerhard Goos, Juris Hartmanis, and Jan van Leeuwen

More information about this series at http://www.springer.com/series/7407

Preface

This volume contains the papers presented at the 11th International Conference on Informatics in Schools: Situation, Evolution and Perspectives (ISSEP 2018). The conference was held at the St. Petersburg Electrotechnical University LETI, Russia, during October 10–12, 2018.

ISSEP is a forum for researchers and practitioners in the area of informatics education, in both primary and secondary schools (K12 education). It provides an opportunity for educators to reach the goals and objectives of this subject, its curricula, and various teaching/learning paradigms and topics, possible connections to everyday life, and various ways of establishing informatics education in schools. This conference also has a focus on teaching/learning materials, various forms of assessment, traditional and innovative educational research designs, the contribution of informatics to the preparation of individuals for the 21st century, motivating competitions, and projects and activities supporting informatics education in schools. The ISSEP series started in 2005 in Klagenfurt, with subsequent meetings held in Vilnius (2006), Torun (2008), Zurich (2010), Bratislava (2011), Oldenburg (2013), Istanbul (2014), Ljubljana (2015), Münster (2016), and Helsinki (2017). The 11th ISSEP conference was hosted by the St. Petersburg Electrotechnical University LETI, Faculty of Computer Science and Technology. The conference received 74 submissions. Each submission was reviewed by at up to four Program Committee members and evaluated on its quality, originality, and relevance to the conference. Overall, the Program Committee wrote 159 reviews and 79 reviews were prepared by external reviewers. The committee selected 30 papers for inclusion in the LNCS proceedings, leading to an acceptance rate of 40%. The decision process was made electronically using the EasyChair conference management system. ISSEP was federated with a teacher conference for K12 teachers. The conference was geared toward teachers from St. Petersburg, although teachers from other regions also participated. The decision to federate the teacher conference and ISSEP was made so as to bring the results of computer science education research closer to practising K12 teachers. We would like to thank all the authors who responded to the call for papers, the members of the Program Committee, the external reviewers, and last but not least the members of the Organizing Committee.

August 2018

Sergei N. Pozdniakov
Valentina Dagienė

Organization

Program Committee

Conference Co-chairs

Valentina Dagienė	Vilnius University, Lithuania
Sergei Pozdniakov	St. Petersburg Electrotechnical University, Russia

Steering Committee

Andreas Bollin	University of Klagenfurt, Austria
Andrej Brodnik	University of Ljubljana, Slovenia
Valentina Dagienė	Vilnius University, Lithuania
Yasemin Gülbahar	Ankara University, Turkey
Arto Hellas	Helsinki University, Finland
Juraj Hromkovič	Swiss Federal Institute of Technology Zurich, Switzerland
Ivan Kalas	Comenius University, Slovakia
George A. Papadopoulos	University of Cyprus, Cyprus
Sergei Pozdniakov	St. Petersburg Electrotechnical University, Russia
Françoise Tort	ENS Paris-Saclay, France

Program Committee

Erik Barendsen	Radboud University Nijmegen and Open Universiteit, The Netherlands
Liudmila Bosova	Moscow Pedagogical State University, Russia
Christian Datzko	SVIA-SSIE-SSII, Basel, Switzerland
Ira Diethelm	Oldenburg University, Germany
Michalis Giannakos	Norwegian University of Science and Technology, Norway
Bruria Haberman	Holon Institute of Technology, Tel Aviv, Israel
Peter Hubwieser	Technical University Munich, Germany
Petri Ihantola	Tampere University of Technology, Finland
Kirill Krinkin	St. Petersburg Electrotechnical University LETI, Russia
Tiina Korhonen	University of Helsinki, Finland
Peter Micheuz	University Klagenfurt and Gymnasium Völkermarkt, Austria
Mattia Monga	Università degli Studi di Milano, Italy
Violetta Lonati	Università degli Studi di Milano, Italy
Fedor A. Novikov	ITMO University, St. Petersburg, Russia
Ralf Romeike	University of Erlangen (FAU), Germany

Yuri B. Senichenkov	St. Petersburg State Polytechnic University, Russia
Giovanni Serafini	ETH Zrich, Switzerland
Maciej M. Syslo	Nicolaus Copernicus University, Toru, Poland

Organizing Committee

Mikhail Kupriyanov	St. Petersburg Electrotechnical University, Russia
Sergei Pozdniakov	St. Petersburg Electrotechnical University, Russia
Liudmila Bosova	Moscow Pedagogical State University, Russia

Additional Reviewers

A. Alekseeva
A. Chukhnov
V. Dolgopolovas
F. Faiella
N. Grgurina
U. Hauser
M. Ivanovic
E. Jasut
T. Jevsikova
U. Jung
F. Kalelioglu
M. Kesselbacher
T. Kohn
S. Pasterk
Y. Peryazeva
I. Posov
E. Reci
Y. Shichkina
J. Staub
G. Stupurien
M. Winczer

Sponsoring Institutions

St. Petersburg Electrotechnical University LETI
Publishing house BINOM. Knowledge Laboratory

Contents

Role of Programming and Algorithmics in Informatics for Pupils of All Ages

Exploring Control in Early Computing Education

Ivan Kalas[1(✉)], Andrej Blaho[1], and Milan Moravcik[2]

[1] Comenius University, 842 48 Bratislava, Slovakia
{kalas, blaho}@fmph.uniba.sk
[2] Edix, Bratislava, Slovakia
milan.moravcik@gmail.com

Abstract. In the paper we reflect on how our design research approach in the current development allows us to study the increasing cognitive complexity of *different levels of control* which pupils conduct when they program Emil, a virtual character on the screen. In our earlier work we outlined conceptual framework for primary programming, which recognised three different levels of control: (a) *direct manipulation*, (b) *direct control* and (c) *computational control (i.e. programming)* an actor. In the present research we managed to get deeper into the complexity of control by identifying four instead of three of its levels. Based on our close collaboration with three design schools we have also found that it is more productive to project and analyse learning progression of pupils connected with control within two-dimensional grid, where the first dimension is control itself and the second explores the way how the control is represented. Along this dimension we have identified five distinct levels of representation: (a) *none*, *(b) as internal record*, (c) *as external record*, (d) *as internal plan for future behaviour*, and finally (e) as *external plan for future behaviour*. In our paper we explain the grid of control by presenting selected tasks from different environments of Emil, our new approach to educational programming for Year 3 pupils.

Keywords: Primary programming · Program as record · Program as plan Levels of control · Control/representation grid of cognitive demand

1 Background

Through giving instructions, young children gain mastery over their world. They create and control things to execute their orders. They set them in motion, make them do things, and "boss them around". How could this not satisfy a 3 years olds' craving for omnipotence!

E. Ackermann, 2012 in [1]

S. N. Pozdniakov and V. Dagienė (Eds.): ISSEP 2018, LNCS 11169, pp. 3–16, 2018.
https://doi.org/10.1007/978-3-030-02750-6_1

Actual interest in educational programming emphasizes the need to implement it for every pupil from early primary stage. This is based on the perception of programming as an important new skill for everybody. And naturally, it also motivates researchers to study which *computational constructs*[1] and *computational practices* to introduce in lower primary school, so that systematic and appropriate interventions for sustainable educational programming are being built.

In our current project we draw on the design principles and pedagogy of the ScratchMaths intervention for Years 5 and 6 of the primary schools in England [4] but move our focus to lower primary pupils and pre-Scratch programming: our goal is to identify *computational constructs* and *computational practices* developmentally appropriate for lower primary pupils[2] and better understand how to break them into productive gradations of suitable small steps[3]. We are developing new programming environments for pupils to discover, explore and adopt these *constructs* and *practices* through thoroughly designed activities supplemented with regular all-group discussions.

In our work we are inspired by Papert's position on programming as an opportunity to experience and explore powerful ideas [5] and encourage pupils to perceive programs as instruments to do that, as objects to think with and think about. We have also adopted Blackwell's view [6, p. *v*] that pupils[4] program whenever they stop … *directly manipulate observable things, but specify behaviour to occur at some future time.* Blackwell [ibid] continues by formulating two reasons that make programming hard: (a) loss of the benefits of *direct manipulation* and (b) introduction of notational elements to represent abstraction. Another inspiration for our endeavour in understanding how pupils *control things to execute their orders…* see [1], is Clayson when he mentions *computational control* [7, p. 2.34]: *Of course, we want to computationally control the filling of design object parts…* referring to our capacity to explicitly control certain effect by expressing our intension in our own program, thus using programming as an instrument to develop and explore better understanding of certain effect or relation.

In fact, in this paper we focus our attention entirely on studying control, namely, finding out in which steps pupils can learn how to plan future behaviour(s) of an actor, how they can learn to externally represent their plans and work with them: read them

---

[1] Here we borrow from [2] the dimensions of their computational thinking framework, however as we explained in [3] we prefer to broaden the dimension of *computational concepts* into *computational constructs*, i.e. concepts plus associated *computational procedures* (e.g. a sequence of steps as a *concept* and acting it, interpreting, filling in a missing step, comparing two sequences, modifying a sequence etc. as some of related *computational procedures*); and also, we consider *control* – the way how pupils give orders to a sprite or a programmable toy – to be one of the key Brennan's and Resnick's *computational practices*.

[2] Aged 5 to 10.

[3] By suitable steps we mean gradations of tasks which support all pupils in exploring these constructs and practices and constructing their true and sustainable understanding. We strive to do so despite the fact these *concepts* and *practices* are often wrongly considered trivial.

[4] We deliberately narrowed Blackwell's view from all non-professional programmers to pupils.

and envisage what they do, analyse them and compare, explain, modify, simplify and share, simply think with them and think about them.

In our previous work, see [8], we identified three levels of control with growing cognitive demand that pupils exploit[5] when they control physical or virtual programmable devices. These are (a) *direct manipulation*, (b) *direct control* or *direct drive* and (c) *computational control*. We can think of moving from one level to the higher one as increasing the distance – in a symbolic or real way – between the device to be controlled and the pupils who control it. In the following chapter we illustrate this with two well-known instruments: Bee-Bots and Scratch.

2 How the Learners Control in Early Programming

To clarify our perception of the levels of control, let us select two typical representatives of programming tools in early computing education: (a) Bee-Bots, simple physical programmable toys for very young learners; and (b) Scratch, currently the most successful and influential virtual programming environment for older pupils and after-school or out-of-school programming activities. We will characterise different levels of control by examining how they manifest in these tools.

2.1 Controlling Bee-Bots

Bee-Bots are widespread physical programmable floor robots with five basic control buttons (move forward and backward by a constant distance, turn left and right by 90° and GO), plus extra buttons for Clear and Pause, well verified as a productive digital technology for pupils aged 5 to 7 or so. It is a well-known practice of the lower primary teachers in many countries, see our analytical survey [9], to integrate Bee-Bots into early computing but also in various cross-curricular activities, often starting by young learners moving the robot by hand through a constructed context (a ZOO, a house, a street, a town etc.) on the carpet – thus exploiting *direct manipulation* control. Next step is to press a navigation button to make it move a fixed distance forward or backwards, or turn left or right, then running that command by pressing the GO button – conducting a kind of *direct drive* control[6].

In the sequence of growing cognitive demand, see [10], pupils then incrementally collect (i.e. record) '*one button – one step*' bits of planning while moving the robot in parallel by hand on the carpet, thus physically interpreting the command by themselves. When the intended goal is reached, pupils move the Bee-Bot back to its initial position and initial heading and press GO.

[5] With occasional deflections, see our comment on controlling Bee-Bots later in the paper.

[6] There is a deflection though from basic *direct drive* strategy in Bee-Bots. If we want to give it a single command then run it, we have to press an arrow key, then press GO, then before the following command is pressed, Clear the memory. Otherwise the next command would be added at the end of the previously recorded steps. This makes *direct drive* with Bee-Bots less straightforward and we in our Bee-Bot pedagogy recommend advancing from *direct manipulation* to *incremental recording of the program*, as described above.

Finally, pupils working in groups start planning the steps of the toy in advance, without moving it by hand. From that moment they start *controlling* the robot *computationally*.

It is significant for this paper and specific for Bee-Bots that the program pupils built can easy be re-run by repeatedly pressing GO. And yet, learners cannot see the program or access it in any other way, thus they cannot exploit it as an object to think with. Sometimes experienced educators bypass this 'limitation'[7] by having pupils construct the program both by pressing the buttons and building the program on the carpet using paper cards, see [9, p. 62].

A step towards building explicitly represented program which pupils can work with, i.e. read, analyse or modify is provided e.g. by Blu-Bots or Pro-Bots.

2.2 Controlling Sprites and Stage in Scratch

In Scratch environment the term 'control' is mostly used in the context of *computational drive*, referring either to:

- the Control category of blocks, including **repeat**, **forever**, **if**, **ifElse**, and **repeat until** C blocks; **wait** and **wait until** stack blocks; and three blocks to control clones, i.e. referring to standard CS concept of *the order in which commands are executed*, or
- the More blocks category when Scratch scripts are used to control external hardware such as LEGO WeDo, PicoBoard, InO Bot and others.

In the context of educational programming and research, where we want to better understand the learning processes of pupils developing their computational thinking, all three levels of control can be identified when working with Scratch:

- we *directly manipulate* a sprite when we 'manually' switch its costume in the Costumes tab or drag[8] it in the stage (not in the player mode) etc.
- we *directly control* a sprite or the stage when we click an isolated block in the scripts area, such as **next costume** (block with no input), **move 30 steps** (block with a number input) or **switch backdrop to** *backdrop* (block with a drop-down menu of all alternatives) etc., thus directly executing the corresponding command,
- we *computationally control* a sprite, multiple sprites or a stage, if we build one or several scripts, either **incomplete** (with no event block atop) or **complete**, and either click the script or trigger the corresponding event. In that way we run (and can re-run, debug, modify or delete) a future behaviour description which we previously planned and constructed.

Although technically we can consider an isolated block to be a 'short incomplete script' and ignore differences between the two levels of control, in our educational context we see clear and important distinctions here. In the ScratchMaths pedagogical framework

[7] Although we consider it developmentally appropriate affordance of Bee-Bots.

[8] Note that such dragging (we call it 'meta dragging') is in Scratch indicated by a shadow rim around a sprite.

of 5Es, see [12] or [4], we encourage learners to explore a new block in isolation, incrementally building the insight into the *programming constructs* in behind, only then exploit it as an instrument in their thinking about, planning, or discussing a future behaviour, see Fig. 1.

3 Method

In this paper we focus on exploring cognitive complexity embedded in control, one of the key practices of educational programming, which pupils conduct when they program a virtual sprite or sprites in the screen. To achieve that goal, it is natural that we employ design research methods, see [13] or [14], as far as:

- we want to learn how demanding different levels of control are for primary pupils and how to implement them in regular school context so that everybody can experience them. To achieve that, however, we need new programming environments (which we failed to find among the existing ones[9]) to be used as our research instruments,
- if we are to design such instruments in an appropriate way, we must better understand the cognitive transformation of pupils when they are discovering and exploring various *constructs* and *practices*, and understand which gradations of the tasks will scaffold them in adopting those *constructs* and *practices* as their own.

In our research the decision to apply the design research approach with its numerous small iterations immediately deployed in the real classes, evaluated and exploited in the following design and development cycle in our three design schools proved to be highly productive. We will present our resulting theory[10] of how to classify and understand the control in Emil environments in the next part. Before that, we will briefly present some more details of how we proceed in the project.

In our iterative design we are closely working with three primary schools[11] and five classes, working in total with about 90 pupils. At the end of the first year of the project we have completed the intervention for Year 3 (pupils aged 8 to 9). It consists of 12+ lessons with corresponding teacher materials, three software worlds or environments (connected into one common navigation interface) called Emil the Collector, Emil the Caretaker and Emil the Collagist, plus pupils' workbook with worksheets attached to most of the units of tasks and several supplementary sheets with extension unplugged activities to solve either at school or at home as homework.

Pupils always work in pairs using one tablet or laptop. The basic pedagogical principle is that software does not provide usual feedback – pupils are always encouraged by the teacher to discuss the solution and come to common agreement on whether they solved the task correctly or not. Both members of the pair fill in their own

---

[9] Having analysed and explored many alternatives.

[10] In its current, not final state as this is on-going process. We comment on this issue in the closing remarks.

[11] We refer to them as the *design schools*, see more details in [11].

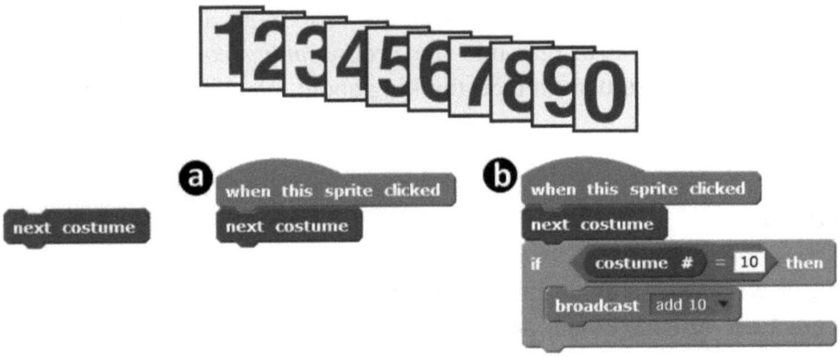

Fig. 1. In our ScratchMaths module 4 which focuses on place value, see [12], we use multiple sprites with ten costumes displaying digits from 1 to 9 to 0. A learner can ‘manually’ switch the costume in the Costumes tab, then explore the **next costume** block in isolation (making use of the fact that costumes can be iterated in endless loop), then exploit it in a script, first with no interaction, see (a), then broadcasting a message to a higher order digit, see (b).

worksheet. After solving a unit of tasks all pairs meet “on the carpet” in front of the teacher and a common big screen and they discuss the tasks and the strategies they applied. The discussion is moderated by the teacher, discussing the computational constructs and practices involved. Both working in pairs then discussing with the whole group are the most productive moments of “learning together”. The tasks and the discussions (the questions asked by a teacher) are the key element of our pedagogy.

In our initial iterations we usually develop first one or two units of tasks and visit our design schools where we run the lesson[12] repeatedly in several classes. The team is present, observing the process and talking to pupils and the teacher, then discussing our notes and taking decisions for the next iteration. This usually results in transforming the initial unit(s) of tasks into more and more detail gradation of units of tasks, after several months becoming extended to ten or even more units of repeatedly trialled tasks.

After the first year of iterations well considered and trusted sequence of *computational constructs* and *pre-constructs* for Year 3 intervention has crystallised, together with a series of the *design principles* that inform our development and a series of *powerful ideas* which pupils experience, explore and construct in the units of tasks (see [11], while the focus of this paper is studying control, the key *computational practice*). At present we have already started developing the sequel intervention for Year 4.

4 Studying Control and Representation

Since the beginning of our design and development work in 80s we have always tried to keep the principle that the actual programming of an actor[13] should be preceded by activities when the learners give isolated commands which the actor immediately

[12] Currently the lessons are already run by the class teachers themselves, with our continuous support.

[13] i.e. planning its future behaviour.

carries out. We often included a functionality which automatically recorded these commands and somehow made them visible – to make it possible to reflect on the previous steps[14].

All versions of Logo[15] support (or supported) a way how to run a single command, some versions collecting and providing these commands in a history. As explained above, we refer to these different approaches as (a) *direct control* and (b) *computational control* and consider the later one claiming higher cognitive demand on the learners than the former one – based on our long-term experience as well as the recent observations, and in harmony with Blackwell [6] who considers the *loss of the benefits of direct manipulation*[16] being one of the main reasons *why programming is hard.* Working with very young children, see [15] or [9], and encouraged by [5] we learned that the most natural introductory level of programming – to precede *direct control* itself – is taking the 'physical' actor by hand[17], or identifying ourselves with it and 'act' the solution. We refer to this basic level of control as *direct manipulation*, coined by Shneiderman [16] and frequently used also in the domain of human-computer interfaces, where it is defined as… *an interaction style in which the objects of interest … are visible and can be acted upon via physical, reversible, incremental actions whose effects are immediately visible on the screen* [17], a definition well acceptable in our domain as well.

When starting our current development, we relied on this categorisation of the levels of control of increasing cognitive demand as one of the key design principles. However, analysing the tasks and data collected in numerous iterations with the pupils in our design schools[18] resulted in two important findings:

- we can better understand various aspects of control if we refine it to consist of four different levels, three levels introduced above, with one additional – *indirect manipulation*, see Fig. 2 – inserted in between *direct manipulation* and *direct control*,
- we can get much deeper in understanding and supporting learning processes in educational programming at the primary stage, when we study two important issues of computing together: *dimension of control* and *dimension of representation* of the corresponding computational process and the relations between them.

4.1 Dimension of Control

Let us characterise this dimension of computing by explaining its four levels in the context of Emil the Collector and Emil the Caretaker environments.

---

14 As a preparation for later perciving programs to be objects to think about and think with.

15 Including Scratch, as explained in 2.2 How we control in Scratch.

16 Blackwell does not distinguish between *direct manipulation* and *direct control.*

17 Which in the case of virtual actor would correspond to what we call 'meta dragging' by mouse.

18 Which regularly led to modifying or reorganizing the tasks, adding new ones and removing others, transforming a task into a whole new unit of tasks.

Fig. 2. In the first environment pupils control Emil by clicking a position in his actual row or column whereto they want him to float. In the first seven units of tasks Emil immediately carries out each command, if possible.

Direct Manipulation. Emil is a virtual character living in his stage, thus directly manipulating him (in the Scratch style) would mean dragging Emil by mouse 'above' the task[19] to be solved. This, however, is not possible, thus the lowest level of control is not applicable in our programming environments of Emil.

Indirect Manipulation. There is no way to move Emil by dragging him to another position. However, we can click a position[20] in his stage thus indicating where we want him to float, see Fig. 2. At the beginning pupils usually start clicking neighbouring positions of Emil. However, later units of tasks introduce new constraints which gradually increase the need to optimise the number of clicks. These restrictions encourage pupils to apply only 'far clicks': if any position in actual Emil's row or column is clicked, he will float there and collect all objects on his way. We tend to distinguish such control from *direct manipulation* because learners do not act directly upon Emil. More than that, it also increases the distance (both in real and symbolic way) between the object which is controlled and the person who controls it. Thus, we propose to call this level of control *indirect manipulation.*

For example, in the task E4 (i.e. 4th task of unit E) illustrated in Fig. 2 pupils are asked to control Emil to collect the biggest amount possible, without picking up the button – however, applying only four clicks. In this unit pupils will have already completed adopting the practice of 'far clicks' as they have to minimize the number of clicked positions, because each position clicked becomes 'used up' in that task, until we click the Next or Again or Previous button.

Direct Control. When pupils start working with Emil the Caretaker, the 'distance' between him and them increases even more: no click in the stage is possible any more. Instead, the arrow buttons (and soon also all other action buttons) will appear on the right, see Fig. 3. Clicking any of them means giving a command to Emil who immediately reacts – either by doing it (moving by one position or toggling the light in a house on/off or other action) or by demonstrating he cannot carry that command out.

[19] We sometimes refer to this as 'meta dragging'.

[20] with several constraints, which pupils will eventually discover by exploring – no diagonal clicks are allowed, no clicks behind a missing possition and several other constraints.

We consider such control in Emil more powerful than *indirect manipulation*. In fact, it is not manipulation any more – unlike in the previous level, each command issued now acts directly upon Emil and has unambiguous meaning and effect in the stage.

Computational Control. The highest level of control is planning future behaviour in advance. In our intervention, this level is always indicated by Emil sleeping in his stage, expecting us to think about the problem and formulate its solution as a plan of future steps (moves, actions etc.), see Fig. 4. When the planning is completed, we wake Emil up by clicking him – only then he starts carrying the steps out.

4.2 Dimension of Representation

When trying to refine the theory of four levels of control in programming with Emil in lower primary years after almost final iteration of our *design – develop – deploy – use – evaluate – analyse – formulate theory* design research cycles we were not contented with the resulting categorization of the tasks. Figure 4 shows an example of two different ways how *computational control* is represented and manifests itself in first two environments of Emil Year 3. We struggled with categorisation of the levels of control referring to the tasks of both Emil the Collector and Emil the Caretaker environments.

At that moment we realised our units of tasks and resulting progression of corresponding cognitive demand – in the context of control – can be better understood and categorised if we start characterising them from two different perspectives, the first one being the control itself (as presented above), the second dimension being the way how the process (steps taken to solve a problem) is *represented*[21]. In the units of tasks of our two environments under discussion we identified five *levels of representation*, let us present them one by one.

No Representation. When pupils start solving tasks of the first four units of Emil the Collector conducting *indirect manipulation*, the steps are not represented or preserved in any way. In the next two units a small move towards *representation by internal records* (see below) is taken by greying each position which pupils click to make Emil float there. They also discover here that greyed positions cannot be clicked again. This new constrain motivates pupils to optimise their solutions without being asked to use as few clicks as possible.

As Internal Record. Starting with unit G, see Fig. 5 for an example, each click – a signal for Emil to float there immediately – is numbered and greyed, thus creating an unambiguous history of the moves. Additionally, maximum number of clicks (i.e. moves) is defined by a stock of numbers on the left (while each click removes corresponding number from there). In that way, the exact history of the moves is kept within Emil's stage, the reason why we refer to this representation an *internal record* of

[21] As we discuss later, the second dimension gives different categorisation of the tasks then the *control* dimension by itself. When we use both dimensions in one grid, see Fig. 6, each of the resulting 20 combinations (positions) has a meaningful interpretation in educational programming.

Fig. 3. In the second environment, pupils directly control Emil by clicking the arrow or other action buttons on the right – with Emil carrying out each click directly (in first four units). The task here is to control Emil so that he lights up all houses. Each command is simultaneously recorded in the panel above the stage. In part 5.2 we will refer to such representation of the behaviour as its *external record.*

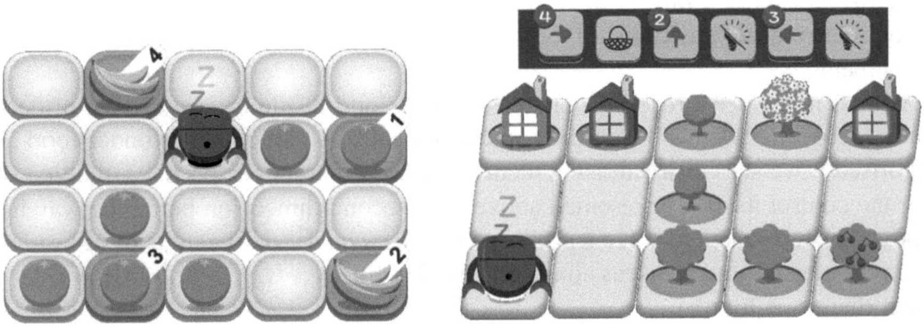

Fig. 4. *Computational control* level in Emil the Collector and Emil the Caretaker. Both formats of plans are already familiar to pupils as the same notation has been used in the *direct control* levels of these environments already, serving as a record of the steps and actions.

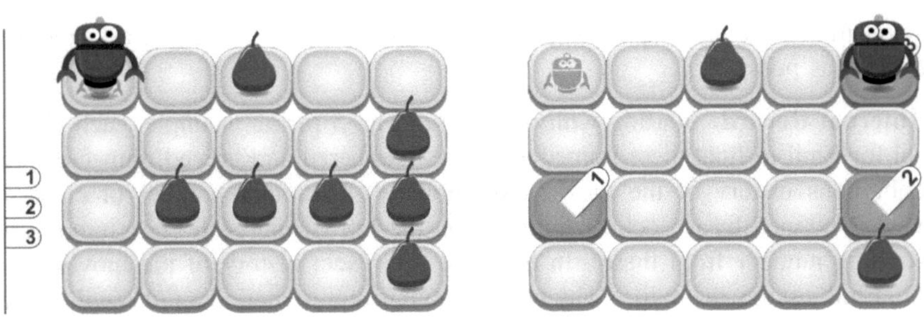

Fig. 5. The task here is to collect as many pears in a box as possible. Pupils will discover that the number of clicks (i.e. moves) is limited and each click is recorded within Emil's stage.

the process. An unexpected benefit of this decision is discussed in the concluding chapter.

As External Record. In Emil the Caretaker we encourage the progression in the context of control by moving from the *indirect manipulation* into *direct control* (see above) and from the very beginning building a record of the steps (moves and actions) in a separate panel above Emil's stage, see Fig. 3 and also Fig. 4 on the right.

As Internal Plan. In the first environment with Emil, in the final two units, Emil is initially displayed sleeping (in the second environment the same signal comes much earlier). The opening task asks pupils to first *plan* the whole journey then *wake Emil up* – he will start running the plan step by step. The plan itself is represented in an identical way to the earlier internal record, see Fig. 4 on the left.

As External Plan. The highest level along the dimension of representation comes when sleeping Emil waits until we construct the plan to be followed – and the plan is externally represented in the panel above his stage. In that way, the program of a future behaviour becomes an object to think with, discuss, analyse, and modify (in thoroughly restricted way until last units of the tasks of the second environment and in the third one).

5 Findings and Discussion

Resulting control/representation grid characterizes two dimensions in progression of cognitive demand in developing basic programming constructs with Emil. Surprisingly, each of its positions has a meaningful instantiation in educational programming at KS1 and KS2. While the goal of the educational programming is to reach the lower right position of the grid – where an *external plan* of a future behaviour is interpreted by an agent in a *computational way* – all other positions have meaningful interpretations as well. For example, programming a Bee-Bot would fit in the lower left corner of the grid (as the program is not accessible to the learner in any other way than running it by pressing the GO button, i.e. from the learner's perspective it is not represented at all). On the other hand, if 5 or 6-year-old pupils interpret by hand a program for Bee-Bot built of printed paper cards on the carpet, see [9, p. 62], they conduct an *external plan* in a *direct manipulation* way – the upper right position of the grid.

Using the grid of control/representation has provided us with an effective means to categorise the tasks of the first two environments of Emil, see the result in Fig. 6. It illustrates that in Emil the Collector the progression of cognitive demand goes from *indirect manipulation/no representation* to *indirect manipulation/internal record* to *computational control/internal plan*, while Emil the Caretaker starts at *direct control/external record* and progress to *computational control* with *external plan*. Our conviction that the grid – when progressing from left to right and from top to bottom – correctly corresponds to increasing cognitive demand in lower primary programming is based on regular observations and iterative design and development of the units of the tasks for pupils in our design schools and naturally needs further research.

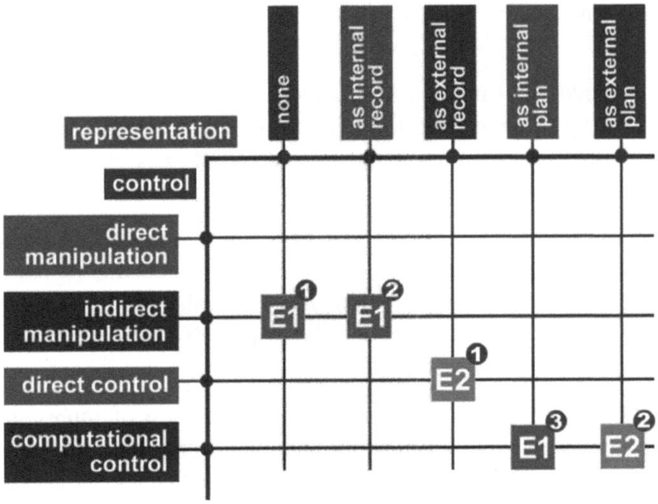

Fig. 6. Two-dimensional structure of increasing cognitive demand of the tasks in Emil the Collector (E1) and Emil the Caretaker (E2). The positions of three labels of E1 (from left to right and downwards) characterise three major steps in the gradation of the tasks in Emil the Collector, ditto with two labels of E2. This classification resulted from our analysis of the tasks after final iteration of working with the pupils in our design schools

When pupils were solving *indirect manipulation/internal record* tasks in our design class, see e.g. tasks in Fig. 7, they were asked to record their solutions in their worksheets. When invited to the carpet to discuss that unit of tasks, the teacher asked them how many pears they managed to collect, their answers ranged between 4 and 7. As it is possible to collect six pears but not seven, teacher asked the 'seven' pairs to demonstrate their solutions. At that moment several pupils ran back to their seats to fetch their worksheets – so that they could read their solution and recapitulate them in the teacher's computer in front of others, an unexpected moment for us as the pupils themselves discovered the value of the programs as records and effectively initiated their transition to thinking of a program as of an executable plan.

Our understanding of control in early programming and how it relates to the way of the representation of corresponding computational process has evolved considerably since the beginning of the Emil design research and development. Presently, we are approaching the final iteration of Emil the Collagist and we admit that a new *computational construct*[22] which pupils start exploring in this final environment for Year 3 may lead to further refinement of our perception of different levels of representation. Next stage[23] of this development will extend our effort both upwards to Year 4 but also downwards into Years 1 and 2. We believe that these extensions will provide us with many more opportunities to verify and refine our perception of the two dimensions of computing: control and representation.

[22] In [11] we refer to it more precisely as a *pre-construct.*

[23] To start in October 2018.

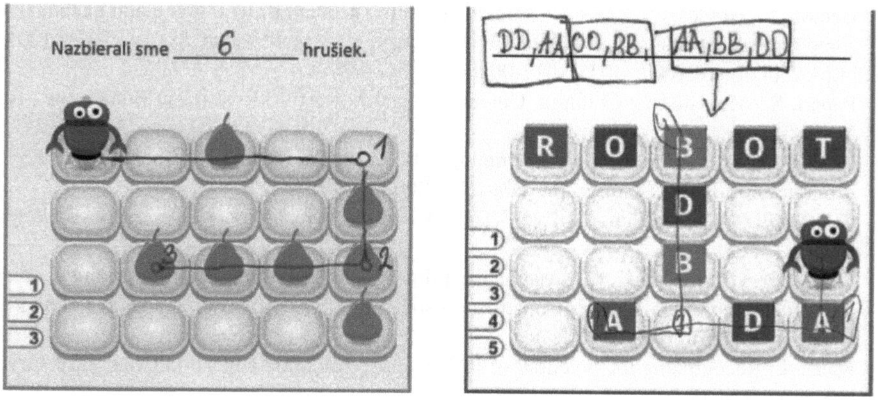

Fig. 7. The task on the left is about collecting as many pears as possible in the box, while there are only three clicks available, as signalled by three numbers at the left side. The task on the right asks pupils to collect as many pairs of identical letters in the box as possible, with no single letters collected. These scans of the pupils' worksheets illustrate their own strategies how to record the solutions.

In this paper we wanted to share our transformational experience in understanding the cognitive demand of programming in lower primary years, our strongest experience ever resulting from the consistent design research approach, based on regular and systematic work with the pupils of our five design classes. In numerous iterations we have deepened our insight into the relation between levels of control and levels of representation of the processes pertaining to the tasks in the two environments with Emil for primary pupils. This experience helped us identify the second (out of four) levels of control and five levels of representation and classify the tasks from the perspective of this control/representation grid.

Acknowledgments. The authors would like to thank Indicia, non-for-profit organisation funding our project, all the teachers and pupils from our design schools for their invaluable contributions to the design and development of Emil intervention, and Celia Hoyles, Richard Noss and James Clayson for exciting discussions about the issue of control in educational programming.

References

1. Ackermann, E.: Programming for the natives: what is it? What's in it for the kids? In: Proceedings of Constructionism: Theory, Practice and Impact, Athens, 10 p. (2012). [CD-ROM]
2. Brennan, K., Resnick, M.: New frameworks for studying and assessing the development of computational thinking. In: Proceedings of the 2012 Annual Meeting of the American Educational Research Association, Vancouver, Canada, (2012)
3. Kalas, I., Benton, L.: Defining procedures in early computing education. In: Tatnall, A., Webb, M. (eds.) WCCE 2017. IAICT, vol. 515, pp. 567–578. Springer, Cham (2017). https://doi.org/10.1007/978-3-319-74310-3_57

4. Benton, L., Hoyles, C., Kalas, I., Noss, R.: Bridging primary programming and mathematics: some findings of design research in England. Digit. Exp. Math. Educ. **3**(2), 115–138 (2017). https://doi.org/10.1007/s40751-017-0028-x
5. Papert, S.: Mindstorms: Children, Computers, and Powerful Ideas. Basic Books, Inc., New York (1980)
6. Blackwell, A.F.: What is programming? In: 14th Workshop of the Psychology of Programming Interest Group, pp. 204–218 (2002)
7. Clayson, J.: A Computational Eye: Visual Modelling with Python. Deep Springs College, Bishop (2015)
8. Kalas, I.: On the road to sustainable primary programming. In: Proceedings of the Constructionism in Action: Constructionism, pp. 184–191. Suksapattana Foundation, Bangkok, (2016)
9. Kalas, I.: Recognizing the potential of ICT in early childhood education. Analytical survey, 148 p. UNESCO IITE, Moscow (2010)
10. Moravcik, M., Pekarova, J., Kalas, I. Digital technologies at preschool: class scenarios. In: Proceedings of 9th WCCE: IFIP World Conference on Computers in Education, Bento Goncalves, 10 p. (2009). [CD-ROM]
11. Kalas, I.: Programming in lower primary years: design principles and powerful ideas. Submitted to Constructionism, Vilnius, (2018)
12. Benton, L., Saunders, P., Kalas, I., Hoyles, C., Noss, R.: Designing for learning mathematics through programming: a case study of pupils engaging with place value. Int. J. Child Comput. Interact. **16**, 68–76 (2018). https://doi.org/10.1016/j.ijcci.2017.12.004
13. diSessa, A.A., Cobb, P.: Ontological innovation and the role of theory in design experiments. J. Learn. Sci. **13**, 77–103 (2004)
14. Nieveen, N., Folmer, E.: Formative evaluation in educational design research. In: Plomp, T., Nieveen, N. (eds.) Educational Design Research, pp. 152–169. SLO – Netherlands Institute for Curriculum Development (2013)
15. Moravcik, M., Kalas, I.: Developing software for early childhood education. In: Addressing educational challenges: the role of ICT. In: IFIP Working Conference, Manchester, 12 p. MMU (2012). [CD-ROM]
16. Shneiderman, B.: Direct manipulation: a step beyond programming languages. Computer **16**(8), 57–69 (1983)
17. Sherugar, S.M., Budiu, R.: Direct manipulation: definition. NN/g (2016). www.nngroup.com/articles/direct-manipulation. Accessed 31 May 2018

Autonomous Recovery from Programming Errors Made by Primary School Children

Martina Forster[1], Urs Hauser[1], Giovanni Serafini[1], and Jacqueline Staub[1,2](✉)

[1] Department of Computer Science, ETH Zürich, Universitätstrasse 6, 8092 Zürich, Switzerland
martfors@student.ethz.ch,
{urs.hauser,giovanni.serafini,jacqueline.staub}@inf.ethz.ch
[2] Pädagogische Hochschule Graubünden, Scalärastrasse 17, 7000 Chur, Switzerland

Abstract. Programming classes offer unique opportunities to learn both semantic and syntactic precision, even for primary school children without prior knowledge in computer science. In order to make students progress autonomously, programming languages and environments need to be chosen with care to their didactic quality. This paper introduces four classes covering the majority of what we call structural programming errors. These mistakes are either syntactical errors or the result of invocations that do not match the signature of any user-defined command, and therefore prevent the execution of a program. Furthermore, we present a methodology that allows for detecting as many structural programming errors as possible, and show how we integrated this methodology in our Logo programming environment for primary schools. Finally, we reflect on an evaluation we carried out at school that confirms the didactic benefits of the chosen approach.

1 Introduction

This paper introduces the idea of what we call a *structural programming error* and discusses a methodology that allows for detecting as many of such errors as possible early on, while writing Logo code in introductory programming classes. A structural programming error occurs whenever (i) a program cannot be parsed according to a given language specification due to a syntax error or (ii) a program fails to execute because a call does not match the signature of any user-defined command. In the latter case, it is not possible to decide whether the mistake has a syntactic explanation (the programmer simply misspelled an existing command) or if the error is of semantical nature (the programmer speculates about the availability of some command that, in fact, does not exist).

Moreover, the paper describes how we integrated the proposed methodology into our existing XLogoOnline [1] programming environment and how it supports primary school children in rapidly locating and identifying frequent mistakes. In our intention, the proposed approach is expected to facilitate autonomous recovery from programming errors and therefore to smoothen independent learning.

S. N. Pozdniakov and V. Dagienė (Eds.): ISSEP 2018, LNCS 11169, pp. 17–29, 2018.
https://doi.org/10.1007/978-3-030-02750-6_2

1.1 Computer Science Is Rapidly Becoming a School Subject

The introduction of computer science as a mandatory school subject is currently experiencing a sudden and promising acceleration. This phenomenon is not circumscribed to the subjective experience in our country, but it is supported by several concrete initiatives like "Computer Science For All" in the United States [2], "Programma il futuro" in Italy [3] and the well known "National curriculum in England: computing programmes of study" [4], to only cite some of them. There eventually seems to be a general consensus that the importance of computer science for society, research, and economy finally requires a dedicated subject for all children attending the compulsory school.

In his *Mindstorms* book, Papert predicts and justifies the need for programming classes at school by observing how "our culture is relatively poor in models of systematic procedures" and thereafter inferring that "without the incentive or the materials to build powerful, concrete ways to think about problems involving systematicity, children are forced to approach such problems in a groping, abstract fashion" [5]. Nowadays, the contribution of computer science to general and therefore to school education is subsumed with the concept of algorithmic (or computational) thinking.

Our center for computer science education has more than fourteen years of experience in introducing primary school children and their teachers to computer science. The so-called *Logo school projects* represent one of our core activities. They usually take place on-site at school, last up to 20 lessons and are distributed over several weeks. Together with regional partners, we were able to visit more than 200 schools and to teach more than 10 000 children and teachers. Such a project mainly pursues two objectives: firstly, we aim at introducing the pupils to the way computer scientists use to think when they face an algorithmic problem. To this end, we teach children how to draw geometric shapes by writing Logo programs. Starting with a reduced set of instructions, they learn how to stepwise refine the language by applying modular design. Second, we train the hosting primary school teachers and prepare them for taking over the programming classes [6].

1.2 The Paradox of Teaching Programming in Half-Classes

Teachers, at least in our country, advocate for programming lessons in half-classes of 10 to 12 pupils instead of full classes, and argue that otherwise a pedagogically adequate and didactically differentiated fostering of the specificities of each pupil would not be possible. The question is undoubtedly controversial, but the problem is hard to deny. We face a paradoxical scenario: children interacting with a computer receive direct and individual feedback; and yet they seem to need more personal support by the teacher than, e.g., children who are solving math exercises with pencil and paper.

The theory of constructive alignment [7] implicitly allows for an explanation of the depicted paradox and indirectly suggests the approach that can lead to its resolution. This theory says that teachers who conceive learning materials should (i) define the educational objectives they are pursuing, (ii) develop learning activities and materials that allow for attaining those objectives, and (iii) prepare summative assessments that measure how the learning outcome matches the original educational goals or at least a sample of them. Moreover, the theory states that teachers necessarily have to align the three above aspects by design. Computer Science teachers are even expected to choose a programming language that allows for reaching the learning objectives and to opt for a programming environment that actively supports the learners and empowers them to systematically identify mistakes and to autonomously recover from them. The programming environment is a crucial element of the learning process, and has therefore *to be explicitly constructively aligned* with all the other three aspects.

2 Related Work

In the literature, different solutions have been proposed that address the struggles children face with structural programming errors. We highlight three common approaches: (i) reducing syntactic errors, (ii) simplifying syntax, and (iii) error diagnosis. In this section, we illuminate how these approaches address the problem of novices who struggle coping with errors autonomously.

2.1 Reducing Errors

In visual programming languages, such as Snap! [8], Blockly [9], App Inventor [10] or EasyLogo [11], errors are reduced by making children snap command blocks with semantic meaning. Blocks only fit in ways that comply with the underlying language specification, which eliminates syntax errors altogether. Runtime errors, however, can still occur. Scratch blocks are failsafe, meaning they try to recover from errors rather than failing and showing error messages or hints to programmers [12].

2.2 Simplifying the Language

Languages with small vocabularies and simple grammars are less susceptible for mistakes. Logo's keywords, for example, are simple two-letter abbreviations for terms originating from natural languages like English. Working with such short commands, the risk for typos reduces. This makes Logo a suitable language for young audiences such as primary school children [6]. Python is another showcase programming language that is widely used in high school education and comes with a simple and small syntax. Thanks to its dynamic type system, Python allows for high flexibility and eliminates static type errors entirely [13]. Remaining errors can be resolved by providing purposeful diagnostics.

2.3 Error Diagnosis

Once an error occurred, diagnostics are the only support autonomous programmers receive. Professional diagnosis tools (e.g. Clang [14] for C++ or C) pinpoint errors by highlighting the affected range and the exact error location using colors, carets and coordinates. Moreover, they provide information about the cause of the error and fix-it hints. For beginning programmers, we need to keep an eye on how to present errors – novices are prone not to pay attention to long, redundant or overly detailed error messages [15]. Learning from errors, however, is considered good practice in general education [16]. Pupils who commit errors and receive corrective feedback deepen their understanding and learn how to handle mistakes [17–20].

We consider autonomous error recovery a crucial skill that needs to be taught as part of general education. Rather than preventing novice programmers from making structural mistakes, we help them understanding the exact cause of errors and teach them how to cope using purpose-built diagnostics and inline hints.

3 What Structural Errors Do Beginners Make?

We want to build diagnostics that help novices to locate and resolve structural defects in their Logo code and, to this end, we were interested in first establishing what errors beginning programmers make in the early stage of them learning a new language. In this section, we present four classes of structural errors that are covered by our diagnostics.

3.1 Four Error Classes Cover the Vast Majority of All Structural Errors

To detect what errors beginning programmers make, we ran a large-scale user study with 180 primary school children, aged 11 and 12. They spent their very first two hours programming in our labs and, after a 5-minute theoretical introduction to Logo's movement commands, they started solving exercises. We collected a trace of all 5040 submissions and investigated what structural mistakes they faced. Out of 6500 errors, we distilled four major categories of errors.

Towards the beginning, pupils got acquainted with the platform and made deliberate errors in what we call *exploration phase*. Once this phase was over, pupils settled in to programming but still made occasional mistakes, mostly around erroneous invocations of built-in commands.

Exploration. Children do not know what happens within a computer. They treat it as a magic black box and first need to discover that computers lack human intelligence by exploring its boundaries. A few such examples include:

1. Wordy and descriptive instructions (as if they were talking to a human)
2. Commands in their native language (`forward 100` becomes `geradeaus 100`)

3. Misread characters that are substituted by optically similar ones (e.g. using the letter 'O' in `fd 1OO` rather than real digits: `fd 100`)
4. Entirely random strings by mashing on the keyboard (`hvgfghfzffzugo8zt7`)

Programming in a language with formal syntax and rigorous structure requires precision. The experience pupils gain during this initial phase is therefore valuable for building an intuition and demystifying how the language constructs work.

Program Invocation By this stage, pupils have been exposed to many examples from a workbook but not yet been formally introduced to the concept of arguments or program design. We see this reflected in three types of errors:

1. **Missing spaces:** Students struggle to grasp the difference between `fd 100` and `fd100`. This purely syntactical error shows that students are not aware of the significance of whitespace in programming.
2. **Incorrect number of arguments:** Students provide too many or too few arguments as in: '`fd`' or '`fd 100 100`'. This error, by contrast, is semantic and shows how operators are used without being fully understood yet.
3. **Typos:** Most built-in Logo commands are based on English terms like *forward* or *repeat*. Our target group is at the early stage of learning English and so we noticed many incorrect spelling variations. For example: `repead`, `repat`, `reapeat`, `repaet` and `repet` (sorted in descending frequency) were all common misspellings of the keyword `repeat`. Pupils tried several alternatives, while a simple inline hint would have sufficed to put them back on track.

These three types of errors tie back to the broader topic of parameterized commands and program decomposition, which pupils will be exposed to later in the curriculum. With more expertise, the rate of these errors should decrease, however, locating these subtle defects remains notoriously hard and makes them worthy candidates for our diagnosis tool.

Program Declaration. In later stages of programming, children will learn to design programs modularly. They assign names to sequences of commands, and thus introduce new purpose-built commands. Errors within the body of such commands fall into the class of faulty program invocations. Program signatures, on the other hand, lead to new opportunities for errors such as:

1. Missing or extraneous keywords *to* or *end* (`to to abc end`)
2. Misspelled keywords *to* or *end* (`to abc emd`)
3. Missing program name (`to end`)
4. Missing colon before parameters (`to abc a :b end`)
5. Missing parameter name (`to abc : :b end`)

If a program call cannot be matched with the signature of any user-defined command, the blame can be put either on the caller or the definition-side. Following common design conventions, we trust program declarations over invocation sites, which assumes that all program signatures are correctly specified.

Brackets. Logo uses matching pairs of square brackets to unambiguously identify the beginning and end of code blocks, for example in repetition and conditionals. In reality, children produce code where either or both brackets are missing, as in `repeat 4 [fd 100`, or they choose the wrong kind of bracket: `repeat 4(rt 90)`. This is a common error which becomes increasingly difficult to resolve as pupils start nesting multiple code blocks.

3.2 Challenges in Design

Language ambiguities place a major burden on diagnosis tools. In Logo, there is no strict requirement for brackets around arguments. Therefore, in case of nested commands with extraneous or missing arguments, we cannot know which of the commands the argument was intended for. For example: Using command '`fd`' (that takes one argument) and command '`mod`' (that takes two), we build the following ambiguous program, which has two interpretations: `fd mod 5 3 7`.

(a) `fd (mod 5 3) 7`
(b) `fd (mod 5 3 7)`

Either we understand it as '`fd`' that was illegally given two arguments or '`mod`' that illegally received three. Without brackets, we cannot know and react by reporting overly generic error messages. To prevent this, the language would need to be clearly specified and must not allow for ambiguities.

In the next section, we will explain how we extended our programming environment such that it recognizes, localizes and reports all classes of errors mentioned in this section, while also providing actionable hints whenever possible.

4 Checking for Structural Errors Early On

In this section, we explain how we extended XLogoOnline with additional error checking mechanisms that detect mistakes in both built-in and user-defined commands and control structures. While pinpointing and reporting an arbitrary number of flaws, we also provide useful hints on how errors could be resolved. In the following, we first sketch the state of error detection we started from and then describe how adding parser rules allows to map even syntactically-incorrect programs into a parse tree. Last, we explain how to detect errors in program calls by trying to match them against compatible program signatures.

4.1 State of Error Detection Prior to Our Modification

Language-specific constructs like Logo's movement commands are defined in *grammars* that contain two sets of grammatical rules: (i) *lexer rules*, that group sequences of characters into tokens such as numbers or strings and (ii) *parser rules* that organize tokens into a tree structure which reflects syntactical structures in a form suitable for execution. Whenever the parser successfully builds a

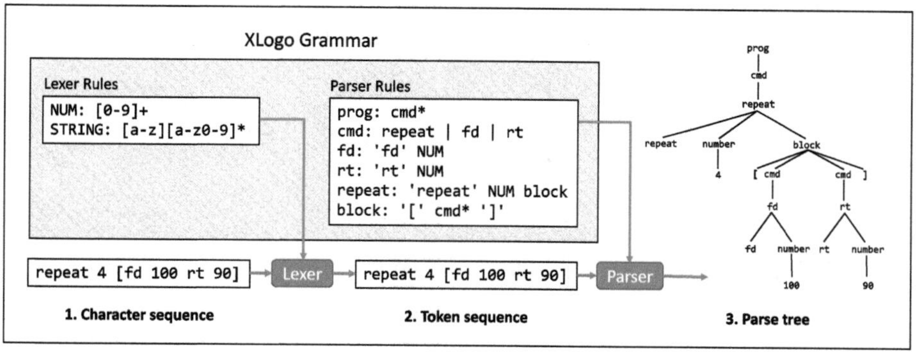

Fig. 1. Example of a reduced grammar for a subset of Logo. The parser successfully turns a sequence of characters into a parse tree. Prior to our extension, the grammar only had 'positive' rules that match against valid syntactical elements.

parse tree (see Fig. 1), all underlying built-in language constructs are guaranteed to be free of syntactical defects.

In error cases like missing or extraneous arguments, the parser cannot retrieve a program's syntactical structure. Instead, it crashes and fails to generate a parse tree. Error detection is affected by this in two ways:

1. **Identifying multiple errors requires repeated parsing:** Every error causes the parser to stop. Thus, without repeated parsing, it is not possible to identify more than one error in a single pass through the code.
2. **Poor classification quality:** In '`repeat [rt 90] 4`' the expression 4 is provided at the wrong position. The parser crashes trying to match `[rt 90]` against a number. At that point, it is ignorant of the subsequent expression. Therefore, it cannot distinguish the example from '`repeat [rt 90]`', where the expression is missing entirely. The two errors are fundamentally different and deserve to be classified individually.

4.2 Extending the Grammar to Detect Failure States

To overcome these issues, we extended the grammar with extra parser rules which cover typical error cases involving built-in commands, program declarations or bracket errors. Additional rules allow the parser to successfully retrieve the syntactic structure of faulty Logo programs. Special markers are retained in the parse tree to denote the location of errors and are presented to the user in a later stage. Figure 2 shows a case where a defective program is parsed and the resulting parse tree contains a special marker at the respective error location. Note how the parser contains three rules related to the 'fd' built-in, each flagged with an associated error case.

By adding extra rules to our grammar, parse trees can be constructed despite them containing structural errors which are ordinarily not allowed. An important

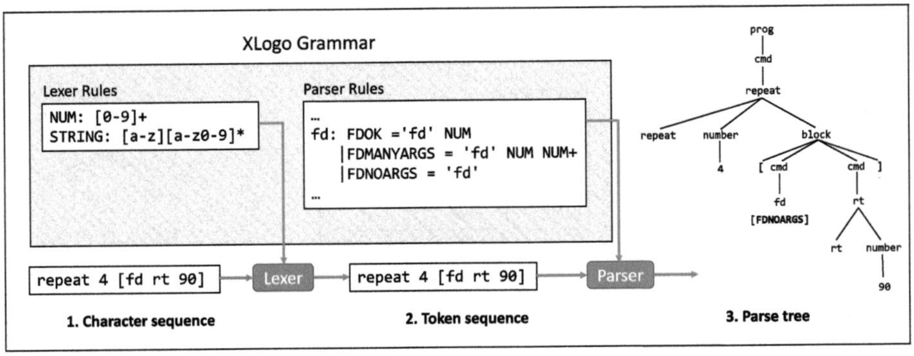

Fig. 2. Parser rules are enhanced with additional error cases that flag syntactic errors while building the parse tree.

point to note is how this approach allows us to successfully parse programs containing an arbitrary number of errors, without aborting the parsing process.

Logo also allows students to extend the language by defining new commands. Detecting errors in invocations to user-defined commands is not possible by extending parser rules, since new rules cannot be added dynamically. In the next section, we will address this limitation by collecting program signatures to be compared against.

4.3 Collecting Program Signatures to Match Against

A program is made up of a declaration and a body. By using the program name and parameter definitions we have a signature which fully specifies how the command expects to be invoked. Without prior indexing of all program declarations, it is not possible to tell whether a given program invocation matches any of the defined signatures. In the following example we see three Logo programs, each with one program declaration and one program call. Only the program on the left is correct, while the middle one invokes a non-existent program named 'foo' and the one on the right calls a program with matching program name but too few arguments and therefore does not match the declared program signature (Table 1 and Fig. 3):

Since we cannot check program calls on-the-fly, we first need an indexing pass. We process the entire program code and perform checks for all built-in commands (as in Sect. 4.2). As we read through the program code, we additionally collect all program calls and signatures and, in a second pass, validate whether program calls can be matched with one of the user-declared programs.

With this last stage, it is possible to check the invoked program calls against their actual declarations and inform the programmer in case of errors. Unmatched program calls are analyzed for typos and missing spaces by calculating the edit distance to all available commands and showing a hint in case of satisfying similarity. Further, we report missing or extraneous arguments. This

Table 1. Invocations can be interpreted differently depending on surrounding context. In order to validate program calls, we also need to know all user-defined modules and their program signatures.

to foo
  fd 100
end
 	
# CORRECT 	
foo
	to bar
	  fd 100
	end
	
	# NO SUCH PROGRAM
	foo
		to foo :n
		  fd 100
		end
		
		#NOT ENOUGH ARGS
		foo

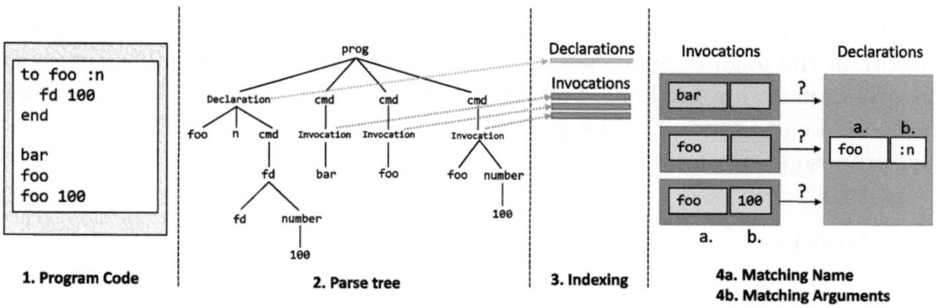

Fig. 3. Identifying errors in program calls to user-defined modules. After building the parse tree, the program is indexed and program invocations are matched against available program signatures.

simple and effective mechanism is surprisingly inexpensive to run while the pupil types and allows to validate programs on-the-fly even before the program has been run.

5 How Do Diagnostics Aid with Preventing Runtime Errors?

We wanted to know whether our diagnostics empower novices to actively prevent runtime errors before they occur. For this, we conducted a classroom experiment with primary school children whom we introduced to programming in Logo. The children received a worksheet with two erroneous Logo programs whose execution results in runtime errors. The task was to localize all errors and propose working fixes without running the program. One half of the class was working with the enhanced error diagnostics proposed in this work, the other had no support. Our results show that children working with enhanced diagnostics outperform their classmates at successfully preventing runtime errors.

Hypothesis: *Novices equipped with diagnostic support locate and resolve a greater number of errors before execution than novices who face the same issues without diagnostics.*

5.1 Subjects and Context

We introduced a class of 37 primary school pupils aged 10 to 12 to programming. For ten weeks, the children spent two hours per week learning about Logo's basic movement commands, repetition, modular design, and parametrization. During the first nine programming sessions, all the pupils used a lean version of XLogoOnline with no support for runtime error detection. During our last two-hour programming session, we performed our experiment. The class was divided into two groups: (i) a control group (N = 17), which received absolutely no support and (ii) an experimental group (N = 20), which received diagnostic support in the form of error messages and inline hints. After familiarizing with the environment for one hour, both groups received an exercise sheet containing erroneous Logo programs. The pupils were asked to first locate the errors and then propose a solution to them.

5.2 Exercises

We crafted two faulty Logo programs (see Appendix) which contain (i) misspelled program calls, and (ii) misspelled keywords. Those core errors were carefully disguised by shuffling in uncommon but syntactically- and semantically-correct Logo code snippets. Both errors are interpreted as program calls and, importantly, are not detected by both the old and the new parser. Our new diagnosis tool checks whether program calls can be matched with existing program signatures or, otherwise, it issues error messages and inline hints. We evaluated what impact the availability of diagnostics has on children's error prevention rates.

5.3 Results

For every task, we first validated whether the children correctly identified the error (e.g. by marking or explaining the cause of it) and second, whether they found a solution that fixes the underlying issue. Comparing the results, we found the experimental group to consistently outperform the control group in both locating and resolving errors. In Fig. 4, we find the ratio of children successfully handling errors with diagnostics (in black) to be significantly higher than without (in grey).

Moreover, during the familiarization phase, we noticed how errors related to well-known concepts seemed to be easier to master than errors related to concepts that were only just introduced. We generally think of programming learning as a two-dimensional process: while novices' programming skills are widened with new concepts, they also deepen prior knowledge. This entails that during their learning, children have differing levels of expertise for distinct programming

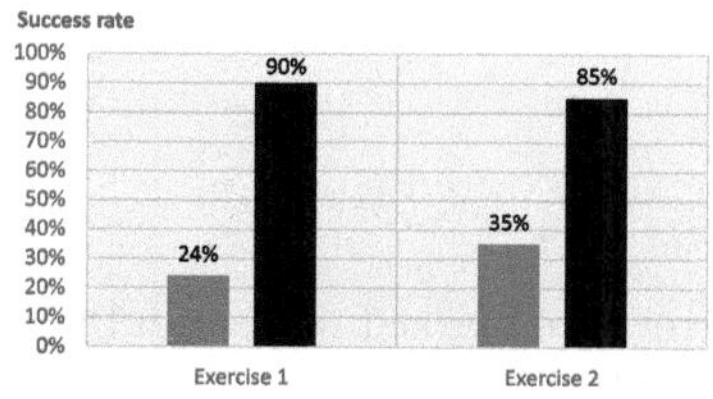

(a) Identifying errors.

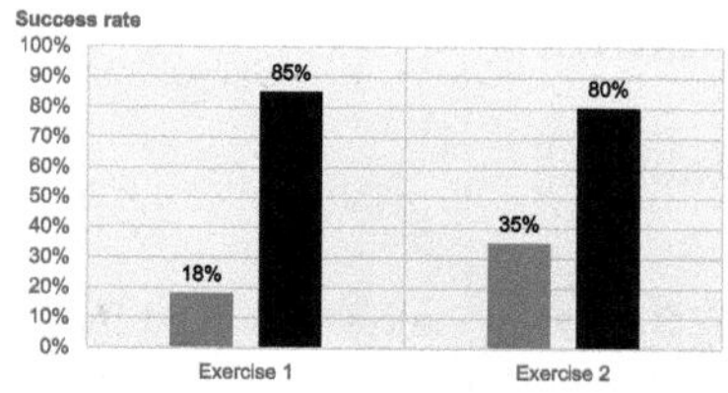

(b) Resolving errors.

Fig. 4. The experimental group (black) outperformed the control group (grey) at both identifying and resolving errors in all exercises

concepts. In our curriculum, children start by stringing together built-in movement commands. Later, they learn about repetition and program design and, only after ample time to practice, do we tackle the concept of parametrization. In our experiment, the exercises cover built-ins and program design respectively, both of which have been covered several weeks prior to our experiment.

6 Conclusion

Novice programmers are confronted with a wide range of different errors. Some of them fall in the category of what we call *structural errors*. Those cover (i) all syntactic errors and (ii) the subset of semantic errors that contain corrupt program calls which cannot be matched with any declared program signature. In this paper, we propose a methodology that provides novices with tailored diagnostics for structural errors and show how we integrated it into our programming environment for primary schools. Using our error messages and hints, children are able to actively prevent runtime errors without external support. Even primary school children are empowered to work at their own pace and recover from errors autonomously. This alleviates pressure from the teachers and provides a basis for more sustainable and effective programming classes.

Not all errors, however, are structural. In order to make children recover from semantical errors, that cannot be detected by any computer, children need to develop debugging strategies and require tools that are adequate to their age and abstraction skills. Such a debugger is the focus of a promising project we are currently carrying out.

Appendix

See Table 2.

Table 2. Actual exercises solved in our study. Errors are marked red (note: this information was not provided to the pupils). While our control group was solving the exercise blindly, our diagnosis tool provided the experimental group with detailed information and hints.

	Program code (error indicated in red)	Error message

1	`to quatsch`
	`fd 100 rt 90 repeat 3 [fd 100 rt 90]`
	`blablabiblu`
	`end`
	
	`to blablabliblu`
	`fd 20 setpc 7 right 20 bk 70 setpc 5`
	`left 20 repeat 7 [forward 10+5] fd 100`
	`end`
		Control group:
		No error message.
		
		Experimental group:
		There is no program with the name: blablabiblu
		Did you mean: blablabliblu

2	`to quatsch`
	`fd 150 right 90 left 45 bk 300`
	`repaet 4 [fd 100 rt 90]`
	`end`
		Control group:
		No error message.
		
		Experimental group:
		There is no program with the name: repaet
		Did you mean: penpaint
		Did you mean: repeat

References

1. Hromkovič, J., Serafini, G., Staub, J.: XLogoOnline: a single-page, browser-based programming environment for schools aiming at reducing cognitive load on pupils. In: Dagiene, V., Hellas, A. (eds.) ISSEP 2017. LNCS, vol. 10696, pp. 219–231. Springer, Cham (2017). https://doi.org/10.1007/978-3-319-71483-7_18
2. Smith, M.: https://obamawhitehouse.archives.gov/blog/2016/01/30/computer-science-all. Status as of 15 June 2018
3. https://programmailfuturo.it/progetto/descrizione-del-progetto. Status as of 15 June 2018
4. https://www.gov.uk/government/publications/national-curriculum-in-england-computing-programmes-of-study/, 15 June 2018
5. Mindstorms, S.P.: Children, Computers, and Powerful Ideas, 2nd edn. Basic Books, New York (1993)
6. Hromkovič, J., Kohn, T., Komm, D., Serafini, G.: Combining the power of Python with the simplicity of Logo for a sustainable computer science education. In: Brodnik, A., Tort, F. (eds.) ISSEP 2016. LNCS, vol. 9973, pp. 155–166. Springer, Cham (2016). https://doi.org/10.1007/978-3-319-46747-4_13

7. Biggs, J.: Enhancing teaching through constructive alignment. High. Educ. **32**(3), 347–364 (1996)
8. Harvey, B., et al.: Snap! (build your own blocks). In: Proceedings of the 45th ACM Technical Symposium on Computer Science Education. ACM (2014)
9. Fraser, N.: Ten things we've learned from Blockly. In: Conference: 2015 IEEE Blocks and Beyond Workshop (Blocks and Beyond) (2015)
10. Wolber, D.: App inventor and real-world motivation. In: Proceedings of the 42nd ACM Technical Symposium on Computer Science Education. ACM (2011)
11. Salanci, L.: EasyLogo - discovering basic programming concepts in a constructive manner. Constructionism 2010, Paris. http://edi.fmph.uniba.sk/~salanci/EasyLogo/index.html
12. Maloney, J., Resnick, M., Rusk, N., Silverman, B., Eastmond, E.: The Scratch programming language and environment. ACM Trans. Comput. Educ. **10**, 4 (2010). Article 16
13. Grandell, L., et al.: Why complicate things?: introducing programming in high school using Python. In: Proceedings of the 8th Australasian Conference on Computing Education, vol. 52. Australian Computer Society Inc. (2006)
14. Lattner, C., et al.: https://clang.llvm.org/diagnostics.html. Status as of 15 June 2018
15. Kohn, T.: Teaching Python programming to novices: addressing misconceptions and creating a development environment. Doctoral thesis (2016)
16. Metcalfe, J.: Learning from errors. Annu. Rev. Psychol. **68**, 6.1–6.25 (2016)
17. Gartmeier, M., Bauer, J., Gruber, H., Heid, H.: Negative knowledge: understanding professional learning and expertise. In: Proceedings of Vocation and Learning 2008, pp. 87–103. https://doi.org/10.10007/s12186-008-9006-1
18. Oser, F., Spycher, M.: Lernen ist schmerzhaft. Zur Theorie des negativen Wissens und zur Praxis der Fehlerkultur. Weinheim; Beltz (2005)
19. Kummerfeld, S.K., Kay, J.: The neglected battle fields of syntax errors. In: ACE 2003 Proceedings of the Fifth Australasian Conference on Computing Education, Adelaide, vol. 20, pp. 105–111 (2003)
20. Kornell, N., Metcalfe, J.: The effects of memory retrieval, errors, and feedback on learning. In: Applying Science of Learning in Education. VA Benassi (2013)

Effects on the School Performance of Teaching Programming in Elementary and Secondary Schools

Angélica Herrera Loyo(✉)

ABZ, ETH Zürich, Zürich, Switzerland
angelica.herrera@inf.ethz.ch

Abstract. The aim of this report is to describe some aspects of teaching programming to teenagers from 10 to 13 years old. The examples, data and impressions were taken from some courses given in public and private schools in Mexico, Switzerland and Colombia. The paper is organized as follows: It starts with a description of the didactic proposal of ABZ-ETHZ under which the courses were given. Then the observations and reflexions are described with respect to several considerations: (a) The ubiquitous recreational and social use that children and young people make of the technology, (b) their motivation for programming, (c) reading and writing in language acquisition and ((d) strengthening and applying mathematics as a decisive aspect of the ability to think logically.

Keywords: Computational thinking · Teaching programming
LOGO · Logical thinking

1 Specific Aspects of the Didactic Proposal of ABZ-ETHZ: Introductory Courses in Programming

Introductory workshops into programming could target children from the age of ten. The exercises involved in these workshops were designed with the intention of helping children grasp the central concepts of programming in an implicit, experimental and entertaining way. This means that the concepts should not be taught in an abstract way and be memorized meaninglessly, nor that there are any simple or single answers. On the contrary, the workshops promote deeper thinking, a systematic and constructive approach to finding efficient solutions to the proposed problems [2]. This work environment is based on four aspects: analysis, creativity, discipline and concentration. The language used is LOGO, a free software designed for educational purposes.

1.1 The Thematic Structure of the Proposal

(1) To Familiarize Students/children with the Language and encourage them to master the basic commands. This first goal can be achieved in a session of two hours. Very early on in the course children will learn how important it is to

S. N. Pozdniakov and V. Dagienė (Eds.): ISSEP 2018, LNCS 11169, pp. 30–41, 2018.
https://doi.org/10.1007/978-3-030-02750-6_3

be accurate when typing commands and before long, they will realize that they themselves are creating new commands that can be reused to solve increasingly complex problems. Already in this session students begin to understand the concept of programming. We know that in LOGO a turtle uses simple commands, such as `fd 100`, in which the turtle moves forward by 100 pixels (`fd` is an abbreviation of the command `forward`) or `bk` , which makes it go backward. By advancing the turtle, a line is drawn. Students have sufficient commands to create images or geometric figures. The syntax of this language is very basic but teaches students precision, spatial orientation, and logical thinking.

(2) The Command Repeat. In this lesson pupils implicitly understand the concept of loop or cycle; they find out for themselves that instructions which are repeatedly used can be programmed with a code without having to write them again. They are pleased to see that they have a command at their disposal which makes their work more efficient. At the same time, however, the structure demands that a complex figure can be broken down into simpler ones, for which routines are written which can then be assembled into more complex routines. This process requires analytical thinking.

(3) Name and Run Programs. In LOGO it is possible to type in an instruction sequence, give it a name and then execute it. By doing so, students become familiar with the concepts of input, execution and exit. They learn to reuse these programs as pieces in order to create other programs. They will thus practice the concept of modular programming.

(4) Draw Circles and Regular Polygons. In this lesson the students strengthen their spatial orientation and reinforce the calculation of angles. Their knowledge of geometry as well as their adding and subtracting skills will be enhanced. Some find that they do not know how to do simple mental arithmetic and are in need of internalizing it. On the other hand, while dealing with the circle, which is an interesting geometric figure, they find out that its programming properties are far from simple. However, at such times they can be offered playful exercises, such as drawing mandalas and flowers using colors.

(5) Programs with Parameters. This theme is a first approach to the notion of variables, which in computing is often complex. To the students the parameter is initially a value that is fixed in the design of the program. Later they realize that also non-fixed parameters may be chosen to run a program. In this way they are given the possibility to work more efficiently and reuse the programs more easily.

(6) Animations. Can increase the motivation of the learners but at the same time, the previous lessons should be reviewed.

1.2 Exercises and Tasks

Both the book and the notebook contain exercises for the students to learn the above-mentioned concepts almost by themselves. Each block of exercises is preceeded by explanations and questions that invite learners to think for themselves. In the book, pedagogical suggestions are made to teachers to put students on the right track so as to prepare them for the workshops. In general, the proposal suggests that only explanations should be given which induce thought and reflexion, and that giving full answers should be avoided. For example, if `repeat 4 [fd 100 rt 90]` results in a square of 100 in length, how could we make a triangle? If necessary a second question could be phrased: "How many sides does a triangle have?" The students begin to think logically and to observe a language, which is in principle a formula. In this context though, they are using and interpreting it to achieve a specific goal.

1.3 Work Dynamics

In teaching programming both, discipline as well as creativity, are important aspects to ensure that students are motivated and learn to solve problems in an implicit way. While they are doing the exercises, they realize that with discipline they get better results. However, creativity should always be a constant. If they practice something in which their ideas and intellect are not challenged, their motivation for programming will decrease. It is recommended to keep a balance between these two aspects. To achieve this, the thematic structure should be combined with its playful and its reflexive side. In addition, the work dynamics[1] take into account the pace of each student but also add an ingredient of competitiveness. The respect for the individuality of the students generates self-confidence and at the same time encourages them to be competitive in their ability to solve exercises. Although the time factor puts them under pressure, they are concentrated for a longer period of time than in other classes and they try to work efficiently and systematically paying attention to the accuracy of the language.

2 Observations and Reflections Made in the Programming Workshops in Schools in Mexico, Switzerland and Colombia

The results and impressions of the workshops in Mexico, Switzerland and Colombia are presented descriptively and qualitatively. In Mexico the courses were held in a public elementary school, in a private high school[2] and at the Swiss College

[1] We mean this a whole: how the workshop develops and how it is conducted.

[2] In September 2015 the Spanish edition of Introduction to programming with LOGO written by Juraj Hromkovic was presented. The institution which sponsored this edition was the CIMAT (Mathematics Research Center), which also organized a programming course for a group of 25 children from first and second year of high school in the city of Guanajuato in Mexico.

of Mexico City. In Switzerland they were held in a public school in the Canton of Schaffhausen and in Colombia in a public school of the city of Medellin.

All courses had a duration of about 20 h.

The data were obtained by a questionnaire, where some questions were answered at the beginning, as for example if they had access to a computer at home. Other questions had to be answered at the end of each day on a scale from 1 to 10, as for example if the exercises were easy to solve. Finally at the end of the course they had to answer few questions more, as for example if programming was fun on a scale from 1 to 3.

2.1 The Use of Computers and New Technologies at School and in the Family

In most schools they have proper computer rooms and access to the internet. The activities the children realize in these computer rooms are among others: to gather information from the internet, to fill out questionaires for the proper school, to solve exams online, to train with basic courses for storing and presenting information digitally, and in some cases they also use the computer room to play video games.

The characteristics of the group confirm that none of the courses that the teenagers had taken on a computer so far, had been about programming. Furthermore, they show that the use of social networks and the recreative activities, such as video games are omnipresent in their lives (see Fig. 1).

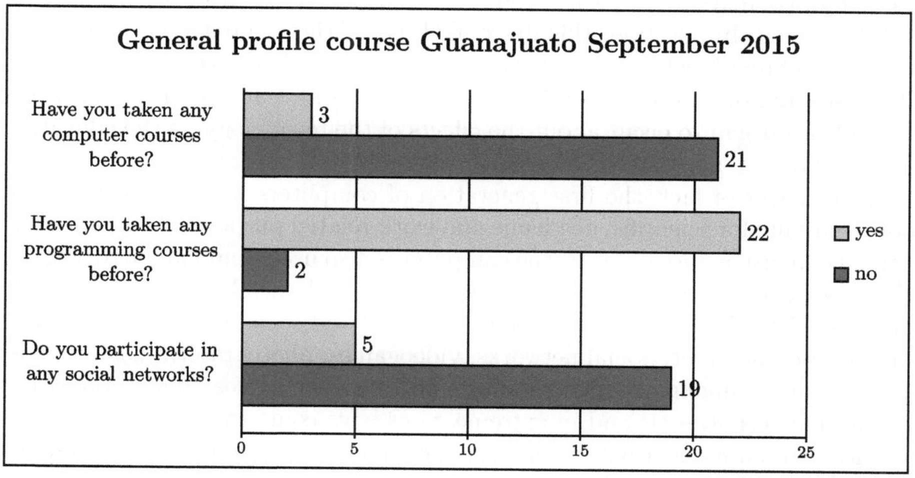

Fig. 1. Information about prior experience

Many politicians and educational institutions are mainly concerned with providing infrastructure, such as computers, networks, the internet and above all, computer rooms. Schools, however, have not been able to take advantage of the newly-provided technology; on the contrary, they have merely suffered under their implementation. This is basically due to two factors. On the one hand, schools often lack a clear sense of purpose. On the other hand, teenagers are accustomed to using computers for entertainment and communication in social networks, which means that the computer is used in this context only for specific purposes. Most of the time, computer activities performed at school are elementary and related to the handling of a specific piece of software, such as word processing, spreadsheets or slides presentations. They learn how to open and save a document, how to create a folder and so on. In their free time, many children use applications, play games and are constantly connected to the network.

It is interesting to compare the current uses of the computer with the vision described 50 years ago in a magazine for children[3]. They explain how a computer works and which utility is beneficial for the user. The computer is described as a tool created by and for man and that its potential lies in the fact that it is possible to "program" it. It is a machine which can do calculations, save, sort, compare data, and take decisions according to a prescribed condition. However, it is also stated that the computer is not able to make its own decisions, but only carries out processes and routines which we regard as boring, wearisome, complicated and far from interesting. According to the magazine, the main effect of this great tool is that people will have more time to think.

It all started in the 80's when the use of the computer spread to became to be an indispensable tool in many homes. It was a tool for work as well as for recreational activities and social communication. The use of the computer in the household, compared with other equipment (such as TV), was soon generalized and diversified. In addition, this diversified use of the computer gave access to new forms of relationships and interactions between individuals and institutions. This impacted our society in different ways. It was also at this time that some ambivalence began to occur about the effects of the technology on the education of teenagers.

As a matter of fact, the first generation of computers was designed to be a tool essentially for scientific, academic and work-related purposes. Now, however, with its expansion and ubiquity, the computer is also used -and maybe to an even greater extent- for consumption, entertainment and social communication. It cannot be denied that at present the recreational and social use of the computer is in fact predominant. Social networks, videogames, photography, music videos, private videos, among others, are known to represent a great distraction from educational activities [1] and in extreme cases have come to cause situations of violence and harassment within the school community. To counter this, students are required to become autonomous and creative users, who can think and make decisions for themselves.

Reaching a certain degree of autonomy is seen as the ultimate goal in the process of growing up, learning and, therefore, in the process of education. The latter is subsequently associated with the behaviour of the individual, which involves

[3] Pestalozzi Kalendar 1974.

a reflexive attitude and a sense of responsibility for the world that surrounds the young person (in this case the technology and its countless applications)[4]. In this sense, we note that it is not the new technology in itself that creates negative effects on young people, but rather the uses and applications which they themselves make. People without proper knowledge of the technology will most probably not be aware of the full potential it can provide.

2.2 About the Motivation and Interest in Programming

According to our experience in the workshops, we can say that students at that age can easily be motivated for programming and that it stimulates their interest. Although the differences are very subtle, "cases" of apathy or disinterest are more frequent in groups of students who are on average older than 13 or who have begun adolescence. Students aged between 10 and 13 can be motivated more easily and they are also capable of maintaining a constant level of interest during the workshop.

In Fig. 2 we see that first-year students of secondary school (students who are 12 years old) find programming slightly more fun than students in their second year. This difference is due to the fact that one student (adolescent) showed no interest right from the beginning. However, it is evident that what is difficult is not necessarily boring. We also see that in general, programming is considered to be more fun than easy, see Figs. 2 and 3.

Although in the courses in Mexico and Colombia girls and boys express roughly the same level of interest, we can observe that girls tend to be a little less interested than boys. In the case of Switzerland, however, boys and girls show the same motivation and interest and the performance in the final test shows no gender bias. In this case, there is probably more equality in the treatment and education of boys and girls, and this also applies to the opportunities offered [6] in schools and families. It could be that in the case of Mexico and Colombia teachers and parents choose different recreational activities or tasks for boys than for girls, and thus create some bias.

2.3 Literacy and Their Ability to Think, Analyze and Express Themselves Accurately and Logically

The ability to communicate accurately is not promoted by the recreational and social use of new technologies. Writing short messages and chatting has changed the rules of written communication. Currently the messages exchanged have few

[4] According to Piaget [5], there are two phases in human development (although they are expressed in relation to moral behaviour). The first is known as the heteronomous phase and the second as the autonomous phase. This means, that in the first phase the child accepts the rules of the world as something given, as something concrete and explicit. In the second phase, the young person agrees with and understands consciously the way rules are formed and participates in the world that surrounds him or her.

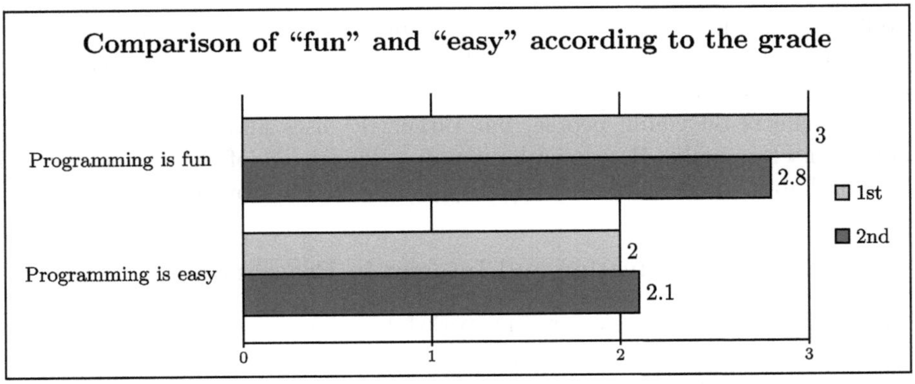

Fig. 2. Perceptions of programming according to the grade on a scale from 1 to 3

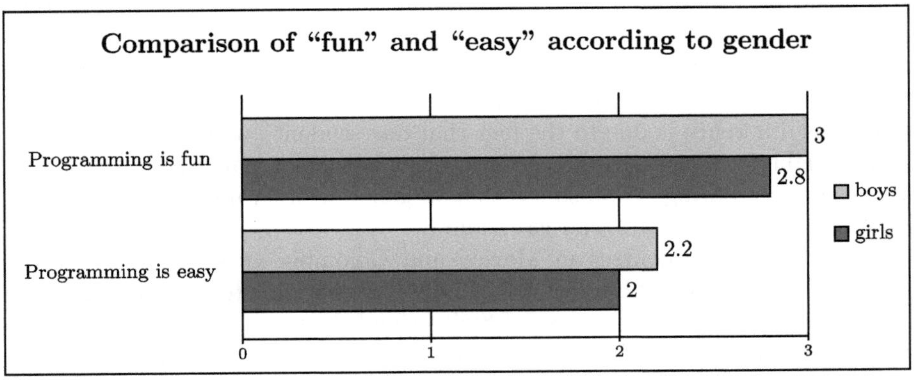

Fig. 3. Perceptions of programming according to gender on a scale from 1 to 3

words and may be accompanied by short animations, leaving much to the interpretation of each person. In direct communication between people the language may to a certain extent be deficient but it does not affect because there is always a cultural context. Precise and logical explanations are not necessary, since connotations or interpretations can always be adapted to the circumstances. In computer programming this is very different: There is hardly any room for incorrectness. It is necessary to learn to design, code, and debug computer programs using a formal language.

Programming languages are formal languages designed to encode processes that a machine can interpret. In order to understand these types of languages, children are required to be precise in their use of symbols. They also need to be coherent and adhere to the rules of syntax and semantics consistently.

One of the most notable differences between classes in Mexico, Switzerland and Colombia was the domain of literacy. In classes with deficiencies in reading and writing instructions it was observed, especially at the beginning of the course, that they had difficulties solving the exercises efficiently without getting distracted. In these cases they were given individualized attention, in two consecutive steps: First they were monitored to read instructions and write the solution (the program) and second, they were asked to solve the follow-up exercise on their own and show it to the teachers.

Although this seems hard work, especially with groups of 25 students, after the first session, many students with initial difficulties were able to work on their own. They were grateful for the personal attention they were given and reveleated their motivation by showing their achievements in the learning process.

In Switzerland we observed only a few isolated cases that needed this support. In general it was evident that they could concentrate for longer periods and had a better mastery of literacy. The most extreme case was the experience in the school of Medellin. In this group the concentration time was very short, and they found it hard to keep reading the instructions on their own. It was also evident that they were not used to write and to express themselves in written form. In this group we observed a lack of precision in thinking and expressing their ideas.

In the Public School in Mexico we observed a greater diversity among the groups. There were students who stood out, average students and isolated cases with difficulties in concentrating or reading. They were used to writing but committed grammatical errors. We observed, especially in public schools, that they are bare accustomed to making additions or subtractions mentally.

In general, the problems or deficiencies we observed are very diverse. Here are two different examples that could be common in different schools.

Case A: Dyslexia A student (in Medellin, Colombia) at the beginning of the course behaved very restlessly and tried to draw attention by showing distress. When reviewing his exercises we noticed that he had written the same program about ten times only that he had sometimes confused the command `rt 90` with `rt 09`. The student had not noticed the difference. He had executed the program several times and did not observe any discrepancy, he had only seen that sometimes it worked and sometimes it did not. Only after showing the student each of his programs pointing out the crucial detail did he become calmer because he understood that he had not always observed the distinction of the position of the digits. He realized his mistake and began to do the exercises with interest.

Case B: Following and Giving Instructions in A logical Order A student first correctly did an exercise step-by-step in which she wrote a program for a square and then used this as a subprogram to perform a vertical column of squares. Then she was asked to write a program to produce a horizontal row of squares. In doing so, she tried to proceed similarly, but after having drawn each square she forgot to locate the turtle properly.

```
to cuadrado10
repeat 4 [fd 10 rt 90]
end

to filacudrados10
repeat 11 [cuadrado10]
end
```

We see in her program that **cuadrado10** is called as a subprogram but the turtle is not located in the proper position to allow a easy repetition. Besides this, when the task was to make 10 squares, she gave the instruction to repeat the subprogram 11 times. These may seem to be very obvious mistakes, but when she ran the program she did not achieve the desired figure. In order to correct her program she had to follow the instructions mentally to detect the missing commands and erroneous instructions.

This two cases show that in the programming courses it is possible to detect students who need special attention and to locate their difficulties. Then, with a few helpful instructions the students are able to solve the encountered problems on their own. Sometimes the reasons for their problems are that their literacy is not sound. And this can be the reason why students are not able to concentrate on doing this type of exercises.

2.4 Teaching Programming with Regard to the Strengthening the Students' Understanding of Mathematics

In mathematics at a basic level children should practice and understand the four basic arithmetic operations: Addition, subtraction, multiplication and division. At the same time, the teaching of mathematics should in principle intend to promote logical reasoning. There is an ongoing discussion about the primacy of rote learning and discovering things by understanding. Should a student learn the multiplication as a recipe or should he or she be given time to discover a proper recipe for him- or herself? There does not seem to be a perfect solution and many students struggle to master the basic operations after learning them one way or another.

In our courses we could observe that the children practice the basic operations as a by-product and that they realize that mathematics has an immediate use: At some stage of the course students have to use parameters, that is, variables which define specific attributes, such as the lengths of some lines or how many times a pattern is repeated or to locate the turtle. In doing so, they use basic calculations [4].

Some students do the necessary calculus in their head, other notice that these calculations can be done directly by the computer. But for this, the student must first understand the necessary calculus and then express it in a formula. They thus notice that the instructions can be expressed in different ways. This seems interesting and gives them the opportunity to be creative. In this way children may discover an affinity for numbers.

For example: With the command fd 100 the turtle advances hundred units and draws a line of 100 in length. But with the command bk 100 the turtle also draws a line of the same length, with the difference that the turtle moves in the opposite direction. On the other hand, if the child uses the command fd -100 he or she obtains the same result by using bk 100. In practice, the command fd -100 is not used frequently.

Programming offers child two possibilities: One is to make the calculations themselves and the other is to learn to use the symbols in order to give instructions to the computer. This distinction becomes clear in the following example.

We asked the students to draw an octagon. Some of them decided (a) to do the calculations for the measurement of angles by hand while others (b) gave the instructions through a division.

Option (a) `repeat 8 [fd 100 rt 360/8]`

Option (b) `repeat 8 [fd 100 rt 45]`

Either option gives the children the opportunity to exercise basic operations and to become familiar with them. In any case, the child develops a practical sense to use the computer and if their program is efficient, they will develop computational thinking.

What we observed was that the children often began to write their programs using commands with fixed units, with little chance to reuse them and without using symbols for operations. During the course, they learned to write instructions as formulas. Later, they solved more complex exercises and used the different operations with ease.

In the course given at the public school in Medellin the students encountered difficulty using loops and reusing programs as subprograms. Therefore, their programs, although written with a lot of creativity, tended to be very long. It seems that they were not conscious of the utility of the computer as a tool to automate jobs. One possible explanation for this could be that they used computers mainly for recreational and social purposes. As the course went on, they became more skill full and developed greater awarness.

On another occasion, in the private school in Guanajuato, the students had to draw a house composed of a square with a triangle above. One of them used the command repeat instead of a subprogram to create the square, (see the program of case (a) below). To draw the triangle above he had to turn the turtle the correct angle, advance the turtle to draw one side of the roof, turn by 120 degrees and draw the remaining side. This shows that the student reflected upon several things: First he started the drawing in one of the two vertices, where the square and the triangle meet, a choice which simplifies the program. Next, he chose to start horizontally with the square, which implies that after turning 4 times the turtle comes back in a horizontally position again. Finally, he had to calculate the angle by which the turtle turns. This is often a difficult task, since first he has to turn by the interior angle and then by the exterior angle of the triangle. It also requires the knowledge that in a triangle the interior angles measures 180°.

Case (a):

```
to casa :nc
rt 90 repeat 4 [fd :nc rt 90] <60
fd :nc
rt 120 fd :nc
end
```

The program casa2 of case (b) draws the same figure, but is achieved the triangle with the command repeat, turning by 120 degrees in each step.

Case (b):

```
to casa2 :lado
rt 90
repeat 4 [fd :lado rt 90]
repeat 3 [fd :lado lt 120]
end
```

In both solutions the students have to reflect on the measurements of certain angles. In order to get a set of instructions that correctly draws the figure, they have to use a certain amount of mathematics. If they are not sufficiently familiar with the concepts, it is a good incentive to reflect on them, and if they are already familiar, they will be able to practice them.

We observed that the children who have basic math skills perform usually better in the courses. The examples above give us a good hint for this to be so: Students with these skills are quicker in realizing relationship between the involved angles and they are also faster in doing the necessary calculations. However, the course sustains a good level of powerful motivation: each completed program, each set of instructions which correctly draws a given figure provides incentive to carry on and to tackle the next problem. Therefore, even pupils who have difficulty performing basic calculations will be in a position to exercise these operations and receive immediate feedback and recognition for their performance.

3 Concluding Remarks

One of the most important arguments of the proposal to teach programming in basic education is: to give children the opportunity to learn and solve problems on the basis of their analysis, and at the same time to favour the acquisition of certain skills, such as abstraction, modularity and logical thinking.

An important aspect of teaching programming is to increase the time of concentration in an activity which requires them to think. There is a diversity of factors which can prevent children from concentrating: (a) Family factors or more generally the socio-cultural context, (b) school factors, such as teacher competence and access to good teaching materials, and also (c) the personality and the abilities of each student [3].

(a) A positive family factor, which covers the basic needs, such as food, security and affection, improves the ability to concentrate. This could be seen as a socioeconomic context which guarantees access to resources, to culture and, therefore, to a stress-free family environment. (b) It lies in the ability of the teacher to not only transmit information, but also to develop the learning skills of the students. For this, the teachers need to think about what and how to teach, so that their students can learn well. With regard to this, their commitment, workload and the operation of the school as an institution is of great importance. (c) The third factor mentioned above is the personality or character of the child, whose reactions will always depend on the circumstances. With this in mind, the proposal to teach programming hinges on the commitment and willingness of the school authorities, the capacity of the teachers and above all, on the experience and motivation of the students. In this proposal the opportunity to program is seen as a trigger factor that helps the child achieve results and deal with situations of failure and error. We also believe that teaching programming to children with problems at school could bring about a change in attitude towards school.

The premise by which we consider teaching programming as a meansbring about a better school performance is that through an induction process it is possible to develop a cognitive progress. This process starts by observing examples or specific problems, finding different solutions and making generalizations. If approached in this way, students at a more advanced level will learn to make deductions. The experience or knowledge that children acquire should be very specific and enable them to acquire the material step by step. Thus, children go through the experience of suggesting and creating solutions which can then be put to the test immediately. When programming, the student realizes what it means to internalize, automate, assemble and reuse instructions (in a program). The efficiency and complexity of a solution will automatically teach them to think algorithmically.

To summarize, the general thesis of this proposal is to challenge the status of the sociocultural context of children, improve cognitive abilities that modify the superficial use of the new technology and to promote the acquisition of concrete tools to be proactive.

References

1. Burbules, N.C.: Education: Risks and Promises of the New Information Technologies. Granica editions (2014)
2. Juraj, H.: Introduction to Programming with LOGO Spanish edition, translated from German to Spanish by Angelica Herrera Loyo. Cimat Newton Editing and Educational Technology, Mexico (2015)
3. Méndez-Ramírez, O.: Quality of education and school performance in sixth grade students of Monterrey, Mexico. Iberóforum. Journal of Social Sciences of the Universidad Iberoamericana, July–December, pp. 52–78 (2011)
4. Papert, S.: The Children's Machine Rethinking School in the Age of Computers, 1st edn. Editorial Polity Press, Barcelona, Spain (1995)
5. Piaget, J.: The Moral Judgement of the Child. Kegan Paul, Trench, Trubner and Co., London (1932)
6. Training Course "Introduction to programming with Logo" for primary school teachers, taught by Giovanni Serafin on 28 October 2015, ABZ ETH Zurich, Switzerland

A Case Study on the Effect of Using an Anchored-Discussion Forum in a Programming Course

Jean-Philippe Pellet[1,2(✉)], Gabriel Parriaux[1], and Tristan Overney[2]

[1] University of Teacher Education, Lausanne, Switzerland
{jean-philippe.pellet,gabriel.parriaux}@hepl.ch
[2] École polytechnique fédérale de Lausanne, Lausanne, Switzerland
tristan.overney@gmail.com

Abstract. In the context of a programming course taught to college freshmen, we give an account of the switch from a classical, Moodle-based discussion forum to MIT's NotaBene (NB) platform. One of the defining features of NB is to anchor each discussion thread to a given rectangular zone freely highlightable in any of the course's PDF documents. In doing so, it forces a precise contextualization of every post–be it to a slide from the lectures, to a sentence from the instructions in the exercises, or to lines of code in the given exercise keys. We hypothesize that this feature lowers the contextualization effort needed to ask a question, thus strengthening students' engagement and, ultimately, understanding of the matter. Using historical data on three years of giving the same course, we first examine and classify the students' interventions with both the traditional and the NB-based approach to see if the questions significantly differ qualitatively or quantitatively. We also quantify the contextualization effort needed in both approaches. Finally, we discuss our teacher experience with both platforms and make recommendations on the choice such a discussion forum in a programming course.

Keywords: Discussion forum · Contextualization
Anchored comments · Teaching of programming

1 Introduction

All courses require an understanding by the students of the matter being taught. Whether the course is given in the form of a series of lectures, of group or project work, of exercises, etc., very often, not all concepts required to be mastered by the students can be acquired in the presence of the teacher or assistants. Moreover, time and human resources are limited: if every question students had could be asked in the teacher's presence, most probably, not all could be answered. Besides, students may prefer asking questions in writing rather than orally. This leads many teachers who use learning-management systems like Moodle to make available some sort of forum, bulletin board, or other discussion systems which

S. N. Pozdniakov and V. Dagienė (Eds.): ISSEP 2018, LNCS 11169, pp. 42–54, 2018.
https://doi.org/10.1007/978-3-030-02750-6_4

allow asynchronous, written interactions between students and staff. Those interactions may be part of prescriptive work assigned by the teacher or be simply available to the students who wish to make use of it without any obligation to participate. Another motivation for such a system is that teachers may want to encourage student to interact with each other, ask and answer questions, thus encouraging learning based on cognitive conflict [4].

In this paper, we are interested in the form that this forum may take technically in the context of an introductory programming course taught to college freshmen at the Swiss Federal Institute of Technology in Lausanne (EPFL). In an effort to encourage students to ask questions about the matter they do not understand, we seek a system that lowers the engagement effort and avoids some of the downsides of a traditional forum system. One early observation we made is that the *contextualization effort* is important when asking a programming question in a traditional, Moodle-style forum: students often copy significant portions of code before asking a question related to it, or, when failing to do so, must be asked to provide more details. Our experience shows that most questions are easily linked to a precise concept, or even to a precise piece of code, that appears either in the lecture slides, in the exercise statements, or in the exercise keys—all of which are readily available to all students and staff, thus being easily referenceable.

For several years, we had been using Moodle's built-in forum solution. Our interest was sparked when we stumbled upon MIT's *NotaBene* (NB) platform[1]. Its main functionality is to allow a teacher to distribute PDF files while allowing members to privately or collectively annotate portions of the PDFs. This system thus links each private annotation or shared discussion thread to a precise rectangular zone of a PDF file. As such, it can be used in place of a discussion forum and, because each interaction is linked to such a zone, automatically provides the needed context for the question.

We were greatly interested in the effect of using NB instead of the Moodle forum and collected data on usage of the Moodle and NB solutions on three years giving the almost exact same programming course. We found several concerns relevant, summed up in the following research questions:

(1) *Which platform is more engaging for the students to ask questions?*
As an indicator for this, we propose to count the number of interventions on the two platforms and compare them after normalizing them by the number of students. The results are shown in Subsect. 4.1.
(2) *Which platform makes the effort of writing and reading questions lower?*
Here, we compare the lengths of the posts made by students in the two platform and we try to isolate the part of the post that is needed to explain the context of the question, hypothesizing that NB's anchored discussion will reduce the contextualization effort. The results are discussed in Subsect. 4.2.
(3) *Does the nature and the depth of the question change depending on the used platform?*
The platforms, by their design and through the way students use them, may lead students to ask different kinds of questions. We propose a classification

[1] http://nb.mit.edu.

for the nature of these questions and discuss potential differences and their distribution in Subsect. 4.3.

The upcoming Sect. 2 lists related work. Section 3 explains the full context in which data was collected, details how, and discusses how it was processed and classified. We then divide Sect. 4 into subsections as shown above to attempt to answer our research questions in light of the obtained data; finally, we conclude in Sect. 5.

2 Related Work

Recently, anchored-discussion forums have been developed and discussed from a variety of needs and points of view.

In [12], the author makes a short review of several systems—one of which is NB—improving online discussion by focusing on 3 aspects: (a) extracting information from large discussions; (2) situating the discussion in its context; (3) more finely control delivery and notification settings. In a wider context, [10] inspects how learner–instructor feedback can be gathered efficiently by the means of NB-like anchored discussion forums.

Some of the most closely related work was done by the authors of NB themselves [14], who detail its deployment in 49 classes in 10 institutions. They are interested in the design of a forum/discussion tool like NB according to students' and instructors' practice. Their most important conclusions, based on log data, questionnaires, and focus-group interviews are: (a) students like to interleave reading with annotations and questions, progressively abandoning paper for online reading; (b) students combine responses to "geographically close" discussion threads (especially in social sciences); (c) instructors express a large interest in tools that encourage feedback and discussion; (d) student-to-student feedback can be far faster than feedback from staff members.

Other authors have explored the benefits of anchoring student feedback to course material. [7] shows a collaborative video-annotation system that overlays translucent red circles on the slides whenever a student asks a clarification about a geographically related concept. This yields a view of "muddy points" in the lecture, allowing instructors to determine visually where the problematic concepts are and to answer questions efficiently. [11] proposes a system where not only text comments can be collectively deposited on documents, but also voice and "gestural comments", and suggest ways to make the audio annotation easily accessible. [13] shows a visual discussion forum system used in an edX MOOC on an introduction to programming in Python. The authors argue for the need for a domain-specific implementation making it easy to discuss and visualize code and program state during execution. [3] discusses the improvement of textbooks by depositing and visualizing anchored collective annotations, showing which parts of the text are unclear and would need rewriting.

On related topics, [9] details the extension of NB to handle annotations on videos. The author specifically discusses the need of choreographers and the need to determine the duration of visibility of the comment thread with respect to the video feed. In [6], the author shows how students, when using the anchored-discussion system Open Rev for assignments in astrophysics, tended to prefer traditional reading assignment outside of the platform but preferred discussing them on the platform. Finally, [5] discusses a system allowing multiple references to parts of documents as well as to timestamps in video feeds, and shows how it reduces the overhead compared to other systems.

Despite the number of related publications, the work presented here has the unique property of inspecting data collected for the very same course in very similar conditions over three years, thus allowing valid comparisons along several quantitative metrics.

3 Context and Methodology

In order to answer our research questions, we collected and analyzed forum posts from 3 consecutive years of giving the same course to college freshmen at EPFL. The course was an introduction to programming consisting of a one-hour weekly lecture followed by a two-hour programming-exercise session in computer rooms. Slide decks, distributed prior to the lectures as PDF files, were presented during the lectures. Exercise statements were given as PDF files (and possibly some base code as text files); exercise keys were given both as PDF files and as text files. The semester lasted 14 weeks.

The forum system used in the first two years was the forum module of Moodle. In year 3, it was NB. (Moodle continued to be used, albeit without the forum part, to better structure weekly material distribution. For the sake of simplicity, we now write "Moodle" to refer to the Moodle's *forum* and not to the whole platform.) Apart from that, we took care to change as little as possible to the course and exercises so as to keep very close conditions for the students and obtain data that can be compared. In particular, changes to the slide decks and to the exercise statements were minimal (occasional typos and slide reorderings).

Two exams were given: a midterm and a final exam. Over the 3 years, all 6 exams were different, although they all tested the same concepts. For that reason, we did not compare scores and grades on the exams.

All staff–student interaction going through the course forum was collected over those 3 years. Staff consisted of the main instructor and about one teaching assistant per 15 students in the class. As the main instructor does not have an office or other office hours at EPFL, the forum was always recommended as the preferred and only means of asynchronous interaction between students and staff. Course interactions absent from the data collection detailed here consist solely of the occasional, in-lecture question and of all synchronous questions and answers between students and staff that happened orally during the exercise sessions. The occasional questions asked by email were systematically redirected to the forum so as to ensure a consistent data collection.

Each of our 3 datasets consists of a sequence of **threads**, each consisting of a sequence of **posts**. Forum threads (on Moodle and NB alike) are almost always started by a student asking a question. Typically, a staff member answers the question. Other students can answer the question, too, if they so wish. The thread can then either stop, be concluded by a "thank you" post, or be continued with a follow-up question by the original poster or by another student.

In order to better analyze and classify the posts, we have first split each of them into **units of meaning** (UoMs) [8]. This accounts for the fact that a single post may ask several questions, provide an answer to a question and then ask a second one, act as "thank you" post while still asking a question, etc. Splitting into UoMs acts as a normalization step—some students naturally make two posts when asking two questions; some others combine them into one—and allows us to apply a more fine-grained classification.

Each UoM was then classified as either:

(a) a **question** from a student;
(b) an **answer** from a **staff** member;
(c) an **answer** from an **another student**; or
(d) a **concluding remark** from a student (of the type "thank you", "I now understand", "This helps", etc.).

We were also interested in the possible differences in the nature of the questions asked on Moodle and on NB. To try and answer this, we further classified each student question according to how "deep" it was. The following categories are inspired by a categorization along the cognitive dimension proposed by [8], simplified to follow the critical thinking categories proposed by [2]. (The first category below, 0., was added by us to reflect this special case we were seeing in our data.)

0. **Logistic:** not pertaining to course content per se, but related to *organizational and technical issues* that are not part of programming concepts. Examples are questions on the format of the exam, on the availability of the exercise keys, or on how to solve network connectivity issues with one's devices.
1. **Elementary:** prompting an answer that restates a concept *discussed in the lectures*, well described in the slides, and considered *relatively easy*. No further understanding is required to answer it than reading the slides and possibly slightly generalizing one of the code examples in them. Examples are "I don't understand the loop variable", "why must I use parentheses to call this function?" or "what is the constructor of this object?" Typically, they pertain to concepts students are expected to grasp if they read the slides carefully.
2. **Deep:** prompting an answer that requires a somewhat deeper understanding of the concept than what is presented in the slides and which cannot be directly read from the course material, but which *requires experimenting with the code practically to acquire*. Examples are "how do I initialize this variable to make sure the loop ends?", "why must I write a nested loop here?" or "why mustn't I pass these parameters in that method call?" These questions usually arise from the need to combine *several base concepts together* while solving a programming exercise and typically reflect the understanding gained by students the exercise session that would be difficult to obtain from reading the course slides alone.

3. **Inference:** such questions go beyond what would be strictly needed to solve all exercises and demonstrate, in the way they are formulated, an understanding of base concepts and a questioning about the *extension, generalization, or universal applicability* of some aspect. Examples are "so this means that if I wanted to, say, sort the array, I cannot do it in a single loop", "how can you allocate memory correctly if you don't know the size of your dynamic array in advance?" or "how can this data structure know how to compare its elements if it allows the insertion of arbitrary objects?"
4. **Strategy:** such questions are rare; they denote a very good understanding of a series of concepts of the course and pertain to *higher-level questioning* about the relevance of a global design decision, the merits of object orientation, the way a given programming language implements an algorithmic concept, etc. An example could be, "is the object-oriented idea to hide data in an object and prevent access to its fields still valid if we use a style where all fields are immutable?"

Conceptually, the four latter levels 1. through 4. can roughly be mapped to levels of the Anderson–Krathwohl taxonomy [1] as follows: 1. → remembering and understanding; 2. → applying; 3. → analyzing; 4. → evaluating.

Obviously, the classification of the above examples can only be reasonably determined with the knowledge of what the course material covers and of which concepts are expected to be masted, which others to be identified with no practical applications, and which others yet are not mentioned at all. Our classification was thus done by two coders: (1) the course instructor (and first author of this paper) and (2) the head TA (last author). These are the two people who know the course material best: the instructor designed the slides, the exercises, the keys, and the exams; the head TA carefully read and dry-ran all exercises and exams. The head TA, however, has more superficial knowledge of the exact set of base concepts clearly explained in the course slides vs. the concepts that are expected to be acquired in the exercises, and this can make it harder for him to apply the classification criteria described above. The resulting coders' agreement is discussed in the section below with the results.

4 Results and Discussion

As previously mentioned, we observed 3 datasets of three years of giving the same course. The first 2 datasets come from the forum module built into Moodle; the third comes from NB.

4.1 Basic Metrics: Threads, Posts, and UoMs

Table 1 shows basic information for our forum data.

First, note that the number of students varies from one year to the other. In 2012 especially, two sections were taking the class together. The difference between 2013 and 2014 is explained by normal fluctuations. Then, whatever

Table 1. Basic metrics for our datasets. A normalized "density" (i.e., count divided by number of students) is shown in parentheses for the last 3 rows. The highest rates are typeset in boldface.

Year (Platform)	2012 (Moodle)	2013 (Moodle)	2014 (NB)	Total
Students	297	171	113	581
Threads	71 (0.24)	41 (0.24)	60 (**0.53**)	172
Posts	254 (0.86)	104 (0.60)	160 (**1.42**)	518
UoM	279 (0.94)	112 (0.65)	163 (**1.44**)	554

the metric is—"density" of threads, posts, or UoMs—participation, prior to any classification, seems to be roughly twice as important with NB than with Moodle. Considering the derived metric of posts per thread (between 2.5 and 3.6) yields no dependence to the chosen platform. Another derived metrics, UoMs per post (Moodle: 1.08–1.10; NB: 1.02), tells us that students tended to ask questions slightly more "atomically" with NB; i.e., there were fewer cases of multiple UoMs per post. This tends to make it easier to answer questions, as answering a post containing multiple UoMs usually implies additional text indicating which part of the post is being answered where.

Based on this, we answer our research question *"Which platform is more engaging for the students to ask questions?"* with: NB seems to yield roughly twice as many posts as Moodle. Assuming, given that the course content and delivery stayed the same, that students have a relatively constant level of (non)-understanding, we allow ourselves to directly equate a higher number of posts with a higher positive engagement and a greater willingness to ask about aspects that were not understood.

4.2 Length of Posts and Contextualization Effort

Before moving on to the classification of the UoMs, we think it interesting to discuss the length of the forum posts (in terms of number of characters). A longer post can be an indicator for several underlying phenomena: a longer question could be more detailed, more articulate; it could reveal a higher contextualization effort when the question has to refer to specific parts of the lecture or of an exercise; it could be formulated differently as a result of the way a platform presents its user interface, leading to a more formal style (salutations, signature)... At any rate, a longer post takes more time to be read and usually to be written.

As one of the differentiating features of NB is to have anchored discussions, we decided to determine, for each post, the part of it that was needed to provide **context** for the actual question. This context includes sentences like "I was solving exercise X and...", "In the code of method Y", or any copy-pasted code or console output. In general, there may be several such parts in a post, and, in a single post, several UoMs may share such context parts (this is why we determine the context length for each post and not for each UoM).

Table 2. Comparison of the mean lengths of posts, isolating the contextualization length. The last row shows the mean fraction of the post dedicated to contextualization. The figure following the ± sign represents the standard deviation.

Year (Platform)	2012 (Moodle)	2013 (Moodle)	2014 (NB)
Total Length	873 ± 873	424 ± 774	161 ± 124
Context Length	602 ± 838	76 ± 139	19 ± 50
Core Question Length	270 ± 184	240 ± 178	141 ± 102
Context Fraction	$.48 \pm .34$	$.19 \pm .23$	$.08 \pm .16$

Table 2 shows the results of the mean lengths, listing the total length of the posts, the length of the context parts, and the difference—the length of the core question actually being asked once context is set.

We see that Moodle yields, on average, much longer posts—statistically significantly so as reported by a Welch two-sample t-test ($t(df = 150) = 7.73, p \approx 1.5 \times 10^{-12}$). The standard deviations for Moodle post lengths are also much larger, reflecting the fact that student sometimes copy large chunks of code to provide context for a question. This happens much less frequently with NB. Also note that in 2013, remarks by the instructor to try and limit copy-pasted code only to relevant portions yielded somewhat shorter posts than in 2012.

Copying and pasting large chunks of code might seem like a good idea as the posters feel like they are providing every possible relevant context, but in practice, the readers have to do an important amount of reading, parsing, and comparing of the code with what they know of the exercise statement or of the code they have themselves written. While, for the instructor, a quick visual pattern-matching strategy is often enough to locate where, relative to the exercise being solved, the pasted code comes from, it remains difficult to distinguish the parts that were written or modified by the posters themselves from the parts that were potentially provided in the initial exercise statement. Often, in problematic code, the devil hides in the details, and finding that precise devil is at least linearly more complicated with respect to the length of the post.

Again, with NB, the context parts are about an order of magnitude smaller (and again, statistically significantly so: $t(df = 141.5) = 6.72, p \approx 4.1 \times 10^{-10}$). Not only smaller, but also, again, more predicable (smaller standard deviation).

All this seems to indicate that questions are both easier to write and easier to read with NB than with Moodle because of the sheer length of the post. Note, however, that the length of the context parts does not in itself faithfully represent the whole contextualization effort for the writer. Indeed, in Moodle, a student can right away access the forum activity and ask a question immediately. In NB, first, the PDF where the question should reside must be opened on NB, and a relevant rectangular zone from it must be selected to anchor the question. We did not quantify this effort. It can either be an additional effort (when students must look for the relevant PDF or portion) or, as the authors of NB suggest [14], a lesser burden, if we assume that questions arise most probably when the relevant PDF is being read and already displayed before the eyes of the students, thus saving them from having to open a separate, disconnected browser window to reach the forum activity as they would do in Moodle.

It is interesting to note, however, that the contextualization effort does not, in itself, account for the whole difference in post length between NB and Moodle. The "Core Question Length" column, obtained by subtracting the context length from the total length, still shows a significant difference between NB and Moodle ($t(df = 206.9) = 6.11, p \approx 4.9 \times 10^{-9}$). The lengths of the non-context parts of the post are still a little less than twice more important. Part of this is due, as announced, to the more formal style used in Moodle than in NB (where salutations and signatures are often skipped altogether). We did not try to quantify this part: if salutations and signatures are easy to spot, other stylistic changes are more difficult to isolate numerically.

Finally, it is worth mentioning that some questions (for instance, strategy) are difficult to attach to a very precise part of a PDF as they pertain to several notions, exercises, or code excerpts at the same time. For those questions, the NB need to anchor them could imply an additional effort to find a (somewhat meaningful) anchor place rather than just freely asking away without context.

Based on this, we answer our research question *"Which platform makes the effort of writing and reading questions lower?"* with: NB yields much shorter posts that include, as expected, a much smaller textual part describing the needed context, owing to the anchored-discussion design.

4.3 Question Depth

Without further classification, we now know that using NB yielded more questions, which were both shorter and required a smaller contextualization effort. Our next interest lies in the nature of the questions: were they significantly different?

In order to answer this, all student questions were classified according to the categories described in Sect. 3. Interrater divergences did not surface in the splitting of posts into UoM or in the initial categorizations of UoMs according to the (a)–(d) criteria on p. 5; neither were there disagreements in the classification of questions as either logistic (level 0 on p. 5) or non-logistic (i.e., as belonging to one of the 4 following levels). There were disagreements, however, on the precise level (1 to 4) assigned to non-logistic questions. Because we had 2 raters and the ratings are ordered, we chose Spearman's ρ rank correlation coefficient to measure that. This yielded $\rho = 0.54$ on the 188 considered UoMs, with perfect agreement on about 64% of them (120 out of 188).

While this may at first seem like a low agreement, first note that this measure focuses on the part of classification where there were disagreements; i.e., on the 188 UoM which needed to be classified on levels 1 to 4. There was no disagreement on the other 366 classified UoMs. A large part of the disagreement can be explained by the fact that the definition of our levels required a very precise idea of what concepts were presented in the lecture and what others were expected to be acquired in the exercise sessions. The two raters were the instructor and the head TA: the instructor had a more precise knowledge of the repartition of the concepts underlying the questions. After discussion on the classification of the 68 UoMs where there was disagreement, the head TA rejoined the instructor's classification 48 times, the instructor changed his 18 times, and on 2 occasions, a third option was chosen. Except for these two data points, the disagreement was never more than one level apart.

Table 3 shows the repartition of UoMs into the 4 general types (a)–(d) defined earlier. We see that the part of student questions among all UoMs remains roughly the same around 43%. Staff answered questions slightly more frequently with NB than with Moodle and, accordingly (since no question ever went completely unanswered), students answered questions less frequently. In fact, with NB, only one student ever answered a question, contrary to the Moodle years. This a priori surprising finding can be explained, we believe, by the absence of mail notifications showing whole post content when new questions were asked on NB, contrary to Moodle. The mail notification setting can be changed on NB, but defaults to none, which seemed to negatively impacts student answers for us. Finally, conclusions were also slightly less frequent with NB than with Moodle. Although the differences are subtle, they are still significant as shown by a χ^2 test of homogeneity (we compared all Moodle data on both years to the NB data on the last year: $\chi^2(df = 3) = 13.66, p \approx 0.0034$).

Table 3. Initial classification of UoMs into questions, answers, and conclusions. Shown are the fractions of each category and year, with the absolute number in parentheses.

Year (Platform)	2012 (Moodle)	2013 (Moodle)	2014 (NB)	Combined
Num. of UoMs	279	112	163	554
(a) student questions	.41 (113)	.42 (47)	.45 (73)	.42 (233)
(b) staff answers	.40 (112)	.47 (53)	.50 (81)	.44 (246)
(c) student answers	.06 (17)	.04 (4)	.01 (1)	.04 (22)
(d) conclusions	.13 (37)	.07 (8)	.05 (8)	.10 (53)

Let us now inspect the distribution of the levels 0 to 4 in student questions in Table 4. This corresponds to a further breakdown of all UoMs represented by the *(a) student questions* row from Table 3. First, we see from the Logistic question level that the rate in the second Moodle year is especially high. In large parts, this can be explained by questions pertaining to a network connectivity issue in the computer rooms used for the exercise session. The rest of the distribution of parts shows a preponderance of elementary questions (slightly more with NB), a varying part of deep questions, quite a few more inference questions during the first Moodle year, and almost inexistent strategy questions. At this point, it may seem appropriate to mention that the course was given to future civil engineers and not future computer scientists: the former, while being interested in getting a good grade at the course, are not primarily interested in programming. This may explain the relative lack of inference and strategy questions, although the lack of comparable data for a similar course given to computer scientists prevents us from numerically validating this claim.

Table 4. Further classification of questions according to their level. Shown are the fractions of each category and year, with the absolute number in parentheses.

Year (Platform)	2012 (Moodle)	2013 (Moodle)	2014 (NB)	Combined
Num. of questions	113	47	73	233
0. Logistic	.12 (14)	.36 (17)	.19 (14)	.19 (45)
1. Elementary	.39 (44)	.45 (21)	.49 (36)	.43 (101)
2. Deep	.31 (36)	.17 (8)	.26 (19)	.27 (62)
3. Inference	.17 (19)	.02 (1)	.05 (4)	.10 (24)
4. Strategy	.01 (1)	0	0	.00 (1)

Do these numbers reveal a different distribution of the question levels? A Wilcoxon rank-sum test shows that this data does not provide enough evidence again the hypothesis that the distribution of questions is different between the Moodle case and the NB case ($W = 6348.5, p \approx 0.26$). This lets us answer our research question *"Does the nature and the depth of the question change depending on the used platform?"* with: No, not significantly—over the 3 years where data was collected, students basically had questions that were of a similar level, independently of the platform used to allow them to ask questions.

5 Conclusion

In the context of an introductory programming course, we have tested two platforms proposing asynchronous communication facilities: on the one side, Moodle's forum module; on the other side, NB's anchored-discussion system. Data was collected over three years of giving the almost exact same course and allows us to numerically compare several indicators revealing that, on average and in the described context of the given course:

- students are about twice as likely to write questions on NB than on Moodle;
- using NB yields shorter posts that are easier to write and read, with a much lower contextualization effort;
- despite the previously mentioned differences, students do not ask questions of a significantly different nature.

Besides these conclusions, there are less quantitative aspects of the two compared platforms that are worth mentioning, both from the instructor's and the students' points of view. For instance, students are used to using Moodle in other courses and are familiar with it. Even when the instructor deposited the course

PDFs on NB in the third year, NB links were posted to the main page of the course to Moodle, which offers a richer, more structured interface (and allows for many other activity types). Thus, students and staff had to switch back and forth between two platforms, each with its own separate login system. This was seen by some students as a disadvantage, albeit by a minority of them. One other technical point is that NB uses a custom PDF renderer which rasterizes the PDF files at a fixed, relatively low resolution. On high-resolution screens, they tended to be shown in a blurry way. Finally, user interaction with NB on tablets was sometimes cumbersome.

Based on all this, we have decided to stick with NB for now, but surely different instructors will weigh those aspects differently and decide whether using a different platform for questions, however more engaging it may be, is worthwhile.

References

1. Anderson, L.W., Krathwohl, D.R.: A taxonomy for learning, teaching, and assessing: a revision of Bloom's taxonomy of educational objectives. In: Theory Into Practice (2001). https://www.amazon.com/Taxonomy-Learning-Teaching-Assessing-Educational/dp/080131903X
2. Bullen, M.: A case study of participation and critical thinking in a university-level course delivered by computer conferencing. Ph.D. thesis, University of British Columbia (1997)
3. Chhabra, A., Iyengar, S.R.S., Saini, P., Bhat, R.S.: A framework for textbook enhancement and learning using crowd-sourced annotations. CoRR (2015)
4. Chickering, A.W., Gamson, Z.F.: Seven principles for good practice in undergraduate education. AAHE Bull. **3**, 7 (1987)
5. Chua, S.H., Monserrat, T.J.K., Yoon, D., Kim, J., Zhao, S.: Korero: facilitating complex referencing of visual materials in asynchronous discussion interface. Interface **1**, 6 (2017)
6. Feiden, G.: Pilot Study assessing student perception of the collaborative annotation platform open rev in a classroom environment. In: Uppsala Workshop on Pedagogical Research Projects (2015)
7. Glassman, E.L., Kim, J., Monroy-Hernández, A., Morris, M.R.: Mudslide: a spatially anchored census of student confusion for online lecture videos. In: Proceedings of the 33rd Annual ACM Conference on Human Factors in Computing Systems, CHI 2015, pp. 1555–1564. ACM, New York (2015)
8. Henri, F.: Computer conferencing and content analysis. In: Kaye, A.R. (ed.) Collaborative Learning Through Computer Conferencing: The Najaden Papers, pp. 117–136. Springer, Heidelberg (1992). https://doi.org/10.1007/978-3-642-77684-7_8
9. Lamia, L.M.: Video annotation for choreographers on the NB platform. Ph.D. thesis, Massachusetts Institute of Technology (2015)
10. Pandeliev, V.: Anchored discussion as a source of feedback for lecturers. Ph.D. thesis, University of Toronto (2016)
11. Yoon, D., et al.: RichReview++: deployment of a collaborative multi-modal annotation system for instructor feedback and peer discussion. In: Proceedings of the 19th ACM Conference on Computer-Supported Cooperative Work and Social Computing, pp. 195–205 (2016)

12. Zhang, A.X.: Systems for improving online discussion. In: Adjunct Publication of the 30th Annual ACM Symposium on User Interface Software and Technology, UIST 2017, pp. 111–114. ACM, New York (2017)
13. Zhu, J., Warner, J., Gordon, M., White, J., Zanelatto, R., Guo, P.J.: Toward a domain-specific visual discussion forum for learning computer programming: an empirical study of a popular MOOC forum. In: Proceedings of IEEE Symposium on Visual Languages and Human-Centric Computing, VL/HCC, pp. 101–109 (2015)
14. Zyto, S., Karger, D., Ackerman, M., Mahajan, S.: Successful classroom deployment of a social document annotation system. In: Proceedings of the SIGCHI Conference on Human Factors in Computing Systems, pp. 1883–1892 (2012)

Students Teach a Computer How to Play a Game

Sylvia da Rosa Zipitría(✉) and Andrés Aguirre Dorelo(✉)

Institute of Computing, Facultad de Ingeniería,
Universidad de la República, Montevideo, Uruguay
{darosa,aaguirre}@fing.edu.uy

Abstract. This paper describes a study into how secondary school students construct knowledge of programming. The study consists of three classroom sessions. In the first session the students play a simple video game called LumberJack. Then, they are asked to describe the rules of *they themselves* playing the game as an algorithm in natural language. In the second session, the students are asked to design *an automata* for a program that plays the game. In the third and final session, the students write *programs* that play the game and execute them in the programming language called TurtleBots.

The aim of the study is to help learners establish a correspondence between the algorithm and the elements relevant to the execution of the program. The results obtained in this study offers significant insights which contribute to the development of didactic guidelines for the introduction of programming to novice learners. These results are presented and analysed in Sect. 4.

Keywords: Learning to program · Novice learners · Piaget's theory

1 Introduction

Over the years we have investigated the construction of knowledge of algorithms and data structures by novice learners with the main purpose of developing of insights conducive to students learning how to write program texts [8–11]. However, if the key to education research in computer science is programming, then knowledge about the text is necessary, but insufficient for learning how to program. This is due to the dual nature of computer programs [14].

Therefore, the study described in this paper focuses on students' awareness of the relationship between knowledge of algorithms and data structures (the text) and knowledge of the program as an object executed by a physical device.

In this paper we make two claims. First, we claim that the process of gaining awareness of said relationship plays a fundamental role in learning to program. This claim builds on a specific perspective of the didactics of programming, grounded on a philosophical understanding of the notion of program, as a text (an algorithm and data structures) and as an object executed by a machine [12].

S. N. Pozdniakov and V. Dagienė (Eds.): ISSEP 2018, LNCS 11169, pp. 55–67, 2018.
https://doi.org/10.1007/978-3-030-02750-6_5

Our second claim is that for the development of didactic guidelines for the introduction of programming to novice learners, each step involved in the process of knowledge construction must be considered. We argue that the point of departure for teaching formal knowledge must always be at the level of knowledge that the student has already constructed. This claim is based on our theoretical framework, based on Piaget's theory of Genetic Epistemology, briefly described in Sect. 1.1. In Sect. 2 we formulate an instance of Piaget's general law of cognition [3].

Average school students between 13 and 15, of an ordinary public High School in Uruguay, participated in this study. They were asked to play a simple video game called Lumber Jack (https://tbot.xyz/lumber). We consider that playing this game is an easily understandable activity to be programmed by the students. The game is described below.

The game consists of helping the woodcutter, Jack, to cut a large tree, as shown in Fig. 1. As Jack hits the tree with the ax, the tree descends a fixed unit. Jack must prevent the branches of the tree from touching his head, if this happens, then the game ends.

The player can move Jack to the left or to the right by pressing two arrow buttons on the screen or the keyboard keys. Each time Jack moves he gives an ax blow on the side of the tree where he has been positioned himself. The player must choose where to position Jack to avoid being hit by the branches of the tree as it descends. It is always possible to dodge the branches that appear since the combination of having branches on the left and on the right is never given.

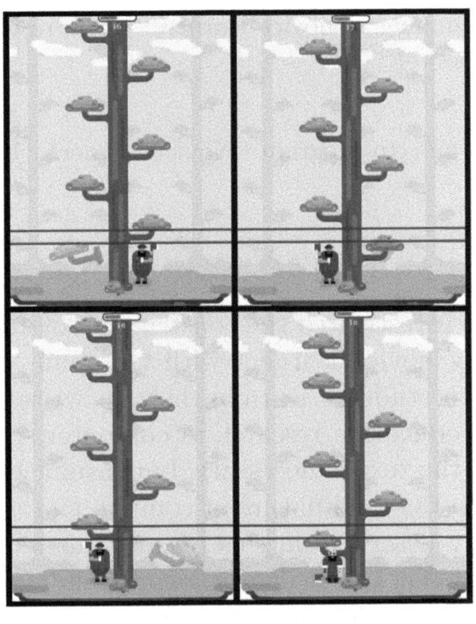

Fig. 1. Game playing sequence with row 2 highlighted

1.1 Main Theoretical Principles

We have adopted Piaget's theory -Genetic Epistemology- as our theoretical framework. This theory explains the construction of knowledge and offers a model that can be used in all domains and at all levels of development [4].

In Piaget's theory, human knowledge is considered essentially active, that is, knowing means acting on objects and reality, and constructing a system of transformations that can be carried out on or with them [4]. The more general problem of the whole epistemic development lies in determining the role of experience and operational structures of the individual in the development of knowledge, and in examining the instruments by which knowledge has been acquired **before** their formalisation. This problem was deeply studied by Piaget in his experiments about genetic psychology. From these he formulated a *general law of cognition* [3,6], governing the relationship between know-how and conceptualisation, generated in the interaction between the subject and the objects that he/she has to deal with to solve problems or perform tasks. It is a dialectic relationship, in which sometimes the action guides the thought, and sometimes the thought guides the actions.

Piaget represented the general law of cognition by the following diagram

$$\mathrm{C} \leftarrow \mathrm{P} \rightarrow \mathrm{C}'$$

where P represents the periphery, that is to say, the more immediate and exterior reaction of the subject confronting the objects to solve a problem or perform a task. This reaction is associated to pursuing a goal and achieving results, without awareness neither of actions nor of the reasons for success or failure. The arrows represent the internal mechanism of the thinking process, by which the subject becomes aware of the coordination of his/her actions (C in the diagram), the modifications that these impose to objects, as well as of their intrinsic properties (C' in the diagram). The process of the grasp of consciousness described by the general law of cognition constitutes a first step towards the construction of concepts.

Piaget also describes the cognitive instrument enabling these processes, which he calls *reflective abstraction* and *constructive generalisation* [3,5].

The problem about the construction of computer science concepts is an instance of the ones deeply studied by Piaget. The general law of cognition regulates the construction of knowledge about (basic) algorithms (C) and data structures (C') from problems that students are asked to solve (P) (for instance sorting, counting, searching elements) [7].

However, in the case that *the object on which knowledge is to be constructed is a program*, some challenges inherent to the relevance of the machine that executes it appear. These challenges took us to instantiate the law to the case of knowledge about programs, as described in the next section.

2 Instantiating the General Law of Cognition

The construction of knowledge about algorithms and data structures is a process regulated by the general law of cognition. Over the years we have investigated the construction of knowledge by novice learners of algorithms and data structures. Our research methodology is based on applying Piaget's general law of cognition to make students solve problems (for instance sorting, counting, searching elements [7–10]) and reflect about the method they employ and the reasons for their success (or failure), as a first step towards the conceptualisation of algorithms and data structures.

We developed an instance of Piaget's general law of cognition as we identified the need to describe cases where the subject must instruct an action to a computer. The thought processes and methods involved in such cases differ from those in which the subject instructs another subject, or performs the action themselves.

Our instance of Piaget's law was developed to take into account the specificities of the subject instructing a computer to solve the problem of playing a video game, in this case the Lumber Jack one. In such a case, the aim are for students; on the one hand, to express the rules of *they themselves* playing the game as an algorithm in natural language, on the other hand, to design *an automata* for a program that plays the game, and finally to write and execute *a program* that plays the game.

As Simon Papert says in [13] (p. 28) referring to the programming of a turtle automata, *Programming the turtle starts by making one reflect on how one does oneself what one would like the Turtle to do.* In this case, programming an automata that plays a game starts by making the student reflect on how he/she does herself what he/she would like the automata to do.

To programming an automata solving a problem, the learners have to establish a causal relationship between the algorithm (he/she acting on objects), and the elements relevant to the execution of the program (the computer acting on states). Not only they have to be able to write the algorithm (the text), but also they have to be able to understand the conditions that make *the computer* run the program.

The generalisation of Papert's words above can be described as: programming an automata starts by making one reflect on

$$\underbrace{how\ one\ does\ oneself}_{what\ one\ would\ like\ the\ automata\ to\ do}$$

The causal relationship between the first row and the second row is the key of the knowledge of *a machine executing a program.* It is indicated with the brace in above description.

By way of analogy with Piaget's law we describe this relationship in the following diagram

$$\underbrace{C \leftarrow P \rightarrow C'}_{newC \longleftarrow newP \longrightarrow newC'}$$

where *newP* is characterised by a periphery centred on the actions of the subject and the objects he/she acts on. The centres *newC* and *newC'* represent awareness of what happens inside the computer.

The diagram describes the situation in which the subject reflecting on his/her role as problem solver becomes aware of how to do to make the computer solve the problem. According to Piaget, we identify that the construction of knowledge of methods (algorithms) and objects (data structures) occurs in the interaction between C, P and C'. Likewise, we claim that the construction of knowledge of the execution of a program takes place in the internal mechanisms of the thinking process; marked by the arrows between newC, newP and newC'. In other words, the general law of cognition remains applicable to the thinking process represented by the arrows; in both lines of the diagram pictured above.

2.1 A Pilot Study

The application of our research methodology in the case of this study is based on getting the students to reflect about the method they employ to successfully play the game and the reasons for their success, as a first step towards the conceptualisation of the rules of the game as an algorithm. In order to achieve such a reflection, we conducted activities consisting in several questions and exercises. To designing those questions and exercises we conducted a pilot study to detect aspects that could eventually be improved. In the pilot study the players (not the students participating of the study) were asked to play the game for a while and then to describe how they play in natural language in their own words. They described actions and objects related to themselves; as exemplified by the quotes below:

1. *I try to play on the phone ... it is uncomfortable ... I use a notebook as support to improve my posture. I get frustrated when I do not succeed and I start again; paying attention to any mistakes in order to correct them. When I start I look up the tree to anticipate movement ... I change the position of my fingers; with index fingers it's better.*
2. *I go slowly when I see a branch and I go faster if there is no branch. I try to prevent. I go slower when it approaches.*
3. *Jack is cutting the trunk; moving to the right and left depending on where the branches appear. When the branch is on the right side Jack runs to the left and when the branch appears on the left side Jack moves to the right.*

The most notable observation at this stage is that the players did not notice that Jack's movement depends on the actions of the player (for instance, at the third quote the player describes Jack's movements as independent from his/her own actions of pressing the keys/buttons.) In other words, there is a lack of awareness of the causal relationship between what the player does and what Jack does.

Keeping in mind our task of inducing students' reflection on how he/she does herself what he/she would like the program to do, we set out to design questions aimed to direct students' attention away from newP (e.g. the position of their fingers or how they feel) to newC and newC' (Jack's positions, branches states at the row above Jack and what has to be done for not losing). By this we mean, to be aware of the causal relationship between their own actions (perceive the branches, press the keys/buttons) and the events in the computer (Jack's positions, the descending branches, the key/buttons events).

The result of the pilot study is the list of questions **Q1 - Q4** of Sect. 3.1.

3 Describing the Study

The main objective of the study is to help learners establish a correspondence between the algorithm and the elements relevant to the execution of the program. To achieve this main objective the following tasks are proposed to students:

1. play the game and learn how it works
2. reflect on the rules and express them as inference rules in natural language
3. represent the rules in the previous point as a state machine (an automata)
4. program the automata in TurtleBots and make the program play the game

The strategy described by tasks 1 to 4 and the results of the study are based and validated within our theoretical framework, as explained in Sect. 4.

These tasks were grouped into three classroom sessions conducted over several months. In order of recalling the main concepts, each session began by handing out students' previous work with feedback. We also used activities, not included here for space reasons, with the same purpose of recalling concepts.

Points 1 and 2 in the list above make the first session; the second session includes point 3. Finally, point 4 takes place during the third session of the study. We describe the three classroom sessions in the following sections. The activities listed above are included in the descriptions but not explicitly numbered as listed. The description of each classroom session also includes the motivation behind the chosen formalisms.

3.1 First Classroom Session

The first classroom session took place on March 23 of 2017. The class taking part consisted of 25 students and the session was divided into two sessions of 45 min each with a break of 5 min. As a first task, the students were asked to play the game for approximately 15 min. All 25 students were able to play the game successfully. Based on the results of the pilot study, our assumption is that the players would be unaware that their game playing caused the computer to follow certain instructions of the algorithm of the game. Therefore, the first objective of the session was for the students to become aware of this relationship and conceptualise the rules of the player's algorithm; successfully expressing them in natural language in the form of inferences like *if ... then ....*

In order to facilitate the process we described the game emphasising the critical moment before Jack changes side of the tree by displaying Fig. 1 on the whiteboard (see p. 2) and using a table similar to Table 1 to represent the critical situation of the game (as Jack may be hit) and the decisions of the player (pressing of buttons to avoid Jack's fall).

Table 1. Table used in question 3

Line	Jack	Branch	Button
1	Left	No	Left
2	Left	Yes	Right
3	Right	No	Left
4	Left	No	?
5	Left	Yes	Right
6	Right	Yes	Left
7	Left	No	Left
8	?	Yes	Right
9	Right	No	Right
10	Right	Yes	?
11	Hit	X	X

Having played the game the players were asked to individually write down the answers to the following questions:

Q1 Before starting to play, what are the possible positions that Jack can be in, in relation to the tree?
Q2 How do you decide which buttons to press?
Q3 Could you complete the cells that have the symbol '?' in the Table 1?
Q4 Could you explain in your own words when success and failure occur?

Examples of Students' Answers. In the analysis we organised the answers according to three levels; level 1, intermediate level and level 2. A description of each level is included after the examples.

- Student 20 (level 1): Q4: *You succeed when you press the correct buttons, for example: Jack is on the left side and the branch is almost on top of him. You have to go to the right so that the branch does not hit you and you die.* Q3: only line 1 has been filled in incorrectly.
- Student 14 (level 1): Q2: *We press right when there is a branch on the left and if one is on the right, we move to the left.* Q3: all the lines are correct. There is no inference in Q4 in this case. However, it is often the case that students omit an answer if they feel they have already answered the question elsewhere.
- Student 7 (intermediate level): Q2: *Depending on the position of the branches, the key we are going to press is: branch on the right, we press the arrow on the left so that Jack moves to the left.* Q3: No answer.
- Student 19 (intermediate level): Q2: *You can use left or right buttons; the one you use will depend on where Jack is.* Q4: *Success occurs when, for example, Jack is on the left, there is no branch and we press the left button, or when*

Jack is on the right, there is a branch and we press the left button. Q3: line 10 has been filled in incorrectly.
- Student 18 (intermediate level): Q4: *Success occurs when we press the right button: if Jack is on the left side and there is a branch, you press the other button.* Q3: line 10 has been filled in incorrectly.
- Student 4 (level 2): Q2: *I decide to press the keyboard which is easier.* Q3: all lines incorrectly filled.
- Student 3 (level 2): Q2: *I decide to go to the opposite side in order to cut the tree.* Q3: only line 4 is correct.

Analysis of Students' Responses and Their classification in Three Levels. For analysing students answers we use the following criteria: In the students' answers to questions 2 and 4 (Q2 and Q4) we were looking for explicit inferences similar to "if Jack was on such a side and there is a branch on that side, then the pressed button was such ... ". In the students' answers to question 3 (Q3) we were looking for implicit inferences, because the correct answer has to be deduced from the lines above and/or below of Table 1 (used in question 3, see p. 7). The students find that on lines 4 and 8, the correct answer can be deduced by looking only at the "Jack" and "Button" columns.

In contrast, line 10 of the table is a challenge because the correct answer has to be deduced from the failure in the line below. In general students answered correctly in lines 4 and 8 (in this case; success) and wrongly in line 10 (in this case; failure). As a result we classify the thinking of the students into three distinct levels:

- Level 1 is formed by the answers in which inferences appear in the students' answers to Q2 and/or Q4 and the student has managed to fill line 10 in the Table 1 correctly.
- The intermediate level is formed by two possible scenarios:
  - inferences appear in the students' answers to Q2 and/or Q4. However, in this case the students did not manage to fill in line 10 correctly. Or:
  - there are no inferences, but the Table 1 has been filled in correctly in its totality; which indicates an implicit inference.
- Level 2 is formed by cases where there are no inferences to Q2 and Q4, and the Table 1 has been filled in with the wrong answers, particularly in line 10.

Table 2 shows the distribution of the answers of the students according to these three levels. The students are referenced by numbers from 1 to 25 and NA means "no answer".

3.2 Second Classroom Session

We now turn to the second classroom session in which the students face the challenge of designing an automata like the one in the Fig. 2. This challenge refers to the third point in the list of activities (see Sect. 3, p. 6).

Table 2. Classification by level

Level	Student	Total
Level 1	14, 16, 20, 21	4
Intermediate	6, 7, 8, 13, 17, 18, 19, 22	8
Level 2	1, 2, 3, 4, 5, 9, 11, 12, 15, 23, 24	11
NA	10, 25	2

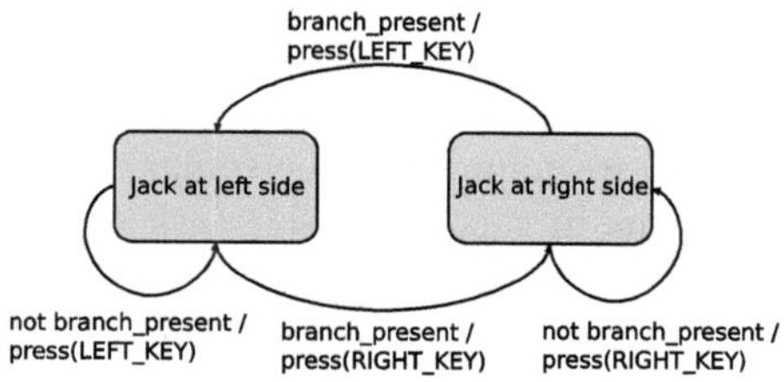

Fig. 2. Finite state machine that represents the winning behaviour of Jack as an automata. The input predicate, branch_present, represents the state of the row above Jack, is true when there is a branch and false otherwise. The function press() used as output in the machine, takes as parameter the constants LEFT_KEY and RIGHT_KEY, to simulate a left key event and a right key event respectively.

The second activity of the study was carried out on May 9 of 2017 with the same class of 25 students.

Following Piaget's general law of cognition, our premise is that: having participated in the first session, players now possess a higher level of knowledge of the program/game than that of a novice learner who simply plays the game. The qualitative difference resides in the experience of the novice learner who gains knowledge about the game by playing, and the players whose gaming experience has been followed by a process of reflection as a result of the activities in the first classroom session. This fact is, indeed, revealed by the answers that players provide during the first classroom session.

Therefore, the aim of activity three (see Sect. 3, p. 6) is to ground the knowledge constructed during the first session by expressing the rules of the game as a state machine. To do so, we begin the second classroom session by introducing the concepts of automata and of state machine as diagrams that provide a visual representation that encompasses all the elements of an automata. We use the example of programming instructions to help a blind person, connected to devices equipped with sensors, to cross the street where there is a traffic light. For space reasons this part is not included here.

For homework, the students were asked to design an automata for the Lumber Jack game, based on the work they had done in the first classroom session, and on the problem of the traffic light. A few days later, we received all of the students' homework: of the 18 returned answers only four contained mistakes, all of which were of minor significance. These mistakes were: three failed to indicate one of the transitions in the diagram, and one failed to indicate the direction of the transitions as the arrows were replaced by lines.

It is worth mentioning at this point that the state machine formalism is generally introduced in tertiary or university education, and is often considered complex by the students. By including the state machine formalism in the study we were able to determine whether this formalism in itself implies a level of difficulty that is inappropriate for students aged 13 to 15. In other words; whether novice learners would be able to convert an algorithm expressed in natural language, into a diagram with representations of elements of implementation (states, inputs, outputs) (see Fig. 2 p. 9).

Keeping this in mind, the students' work on the state machine diagram was kept fairly simple. Even so, we found it to be remarkable that out of all of the activities in the study, it was in this particular task of designing the automata using the state machine formalism that the students achieved the best results.

3.3 Third Classroom Session

The third and final session was held on August 10 of 2017. The purpose of this session was to complete activities of point 4 of Sect. 3, p. 6. The students were asked to implement the game Lumber Jack in TurtleBots. We chose the programming language TurtleBots [2] because students already have some experience with the Scratch language which is based on blocks like TurtleBots. In addition, TurtleBots contains a plugin called Xevents [1] that programmatically generates keyboard and mouse events, and gathers screen information. These features are necessary to implement the actuation and sensing components of the LumberJack game controller. They were given a central axis and a series of scattered blocks on which to work with, as shown in Figs. 3 and 4 in the Appendix. The task consisted in placing the blocks in the correct places in order to assemble the program and then execute it. Although every student completed the task, they generally did not handle the blocks with ease, and mistakes were made in the assembly of the blocks. In the following section, this and others results are analysed.

4 Conclusions

The study has provided us with new theoretical and practical insights which we will discuss here. Our premise is that the depth of the results of this study are not clearly visible until we locate them within our theoretical framework. We therefore use our theoretical principles in this section to explain, validate and verify our results. More specifically, our results can be explained from theoretical principles about the relationship between non-formal, conceptual and formal knowledge. By non-formal we mean the instrumental knowledge constructed at the level of actions [3]. This is the level in which novice learners can develop a skill simply by playing. Their knowledge of the game may allow them to play it successfully, but it remains at the level of action nonetheless.

The first step towards the conceptual construction consists in the students' reflection about the rules of the game in terms of inferences involving the elements of the program (Jack and branch positions, key/buttons). The reflection players experienced during the first session, implies the transit of the students' thought from a periphery (where it is focused on the goal of the player) towards the awareness of how to do for an automata to play. This awareness implies a conceptual construction and, therefore, a higher level of knowledge.

We argue that the point of departure for teaching formal knowledge (by this we mean conceptual knowledge expressed in some formalism different from natural language) must always be at the level of knowledge that the student has *already constructed.* In other words; any learning process is built stepwise and is governed by the general law of cognition. In the specific case of learning to program, the process is governed by the instance of the law of cognition as we have formulated it on p. 4.

Our theoretical argument is verified experimentally by students answers to questions Q1 to Q4 in Sect. 3, p. 7. Two main factors are central to the task of answering the questions: first, that the students have already internalised the rules of the game by playing the game for 15 min and, thus, have developed gaming skills in terms of their actions. Second, that the first question is formulated directing students' attention away from *they themselves* (newP) towards the elements in the *world model of the game* (newC and newC'). They were then able to express the causal relationship between their own actions and the events in the computer. This factor is a direct consequence of applying our framework of the instantiated law of cognition in designing the questions.

By explaining and theoretically locating the learning process that we have studied empirically, we reaffirm the significance and fundamental role of the learning process when developing teaching guidelines: the key is to respect the process when teaching a class; for the conceptual we start at the non-formal, and for the formal we begin at the conceptual. In accordance to this, we have verified that the activity of introducing the formalism of a state machine for designing the automata, which is usually considered complex, can be carried out without difficulties by novice learners aged 13 to 15.

The fact that the results of the first classroom session revealed greater difficulties also confirms the transition from actions to the construction of conceptual knowledge. The reflective process the students have to experience in order to successfully express themselves about the game in natural language, is a difficult one. For this reason we felt it necessary to dedicate this part of the process a section of analysis (see, p. 8).

In terms of the limitations we encountered we would highlight the unexpected difficulties of the students in the implementation of the proposed exercise with TurtleBots. In order to address this limitation we pose the following questions:

Given that the program in TurtleBots introduces repetition and variables to represent the states, is the level of prior knowledge of the students sufficient to model these concepts or is it necessary to work with them more carefully?

Are block languages an adequate tool to implement this type of problem with students aged between 13 and 15? Or would it be more convenient to use a textual programming language, like Python for example?

When considering future work we would direct our research towards answering the questions mentioned above.

Finally, we find necessary to point out that we have not included references to other authors in this paper because the aim of the study is contributing of designing a didactics for programming, based on our model of applying Piaget's theory. References to related work are included in our previous papers, already cited in this paper.

Acknowledgements. We would like to thank teacher Néstor Larroca and students of second year of Liceo 2, La Paz, Uruguay, where we developed the study; Bruno Michetti for supporting the activities; and Manuela Cabezas for correcting the English. The comments of the anonymous referees are gratefully acknowledged.

A Appendix

Figures of the third classroom session

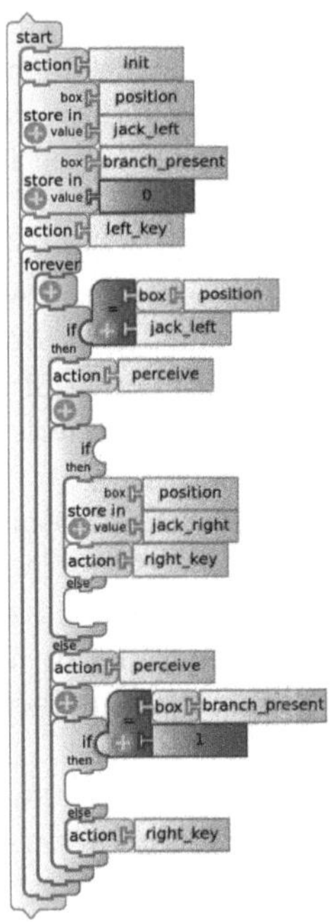

Fig. 3. TurtleBots program template for Jack's automata

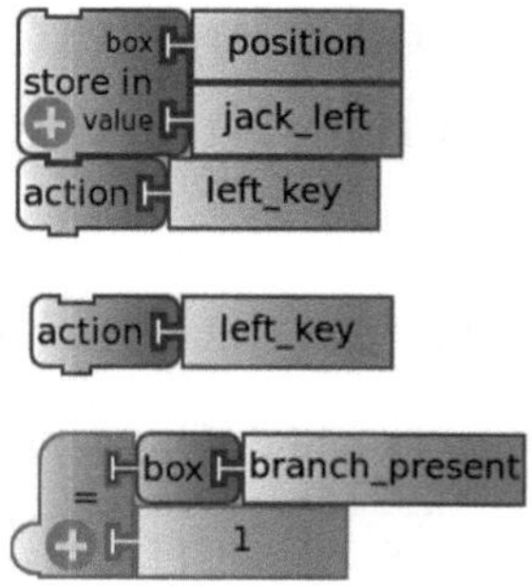

Fig. 4. TurtleBots blocks for Jack's automata

References

1. InCo (2015). https://www.fing.edu.uy/inco/proyectos/butia/mediawiki/index.php/Xevents. Accessed 17 Feb 2018
2. InCo, Sugarlabs: Turtlebots. https://www.fing.edu.uy/inco/proyectos/butia (2015). Accessed 19 Apr 2017
3. Piaget, J.: La Prise de Conscience. Presses Universitaires de France (1964)
4. Piaget, J.: Genetic Epistemology, a series of lectures delivered by Piaget at Columbia University. Columbia University Press (1977). Translated by Eleanor Duckworth
5. Piaget, J.: Recherches sur la Généralisation. Presses Universitaires de France (1978)
6. Piaget, J.: Success and Understanding. Harvard University Press, Cambridge (1978)
7. Rosa, S.: Designing algorithms in high school mathematics. In: Dean, C.N., Boute, R.T. (eds.) TFM 2004. LNCS, vol. 3294, pp. 17–31. Springer, Heidelberg (2004). https://doi.org/10.1007/978-3-540-30472-2_2
8. da Rosa, S.: The learning of recursive algorithms from a psychogenetic perspective. In: Proceedings of the 19th Annual Psychology of Programming Interest Group Workshop, Joensuu, Finland, pp. 201–215 (2007)
9. da Rosa, S.: The construction of the concept of binary search algorithm. In: Proceedings of the 22th Annual Psychology of Programming Interest Group Workshop, Madrid, Spain, pp. 100–111 (2010)
10. da Rosa, S.: The construction of knowledge of basic algorithms and data structures by novice learners. In: Proceedings of the 26th Annual Psychology of Programming Interest Group Workshop, Bournemouth, UK (2015)
11. da Rosa, S., Chmiel, A.: A study about students' knowledge of inductive structures. In: Proceedings of the 24th Annual Psychology of Programming Interest Group Workshop, London, UK (2012)
12. da Rosa, S., Chmiel, A., Gómez, F.: Philosophy of computer science and its effect on education - towards the construction of an interdisciplinary group. Special edition CLEI Electron. J. **19**(1), 5 (2016). http://www.clei.cl/cleiej/
13. Papert, S.: Mindstorms: Children, Computers, and Powerful Ideas. Basic Books (1980)
14. Tedre, M.: The Science of Computing: Shaping a Discipline. CRC Press (2014). ISBN 9781482217698

Teaching Programming and Algorithmic Complexity with Tangible Machines

Tobias Kohn[1] and Dennis Komm[2,3](✉)

[1] University of Cambridge, Cambridge, UK
tk534@cam.ac.uk
[2] Department of Computer Science, ETH Zurich, Zurich, Switzerland
dennis.komm@inf.ethz.ch
[3] PH Graubünden, Chur, Switzerland

Abstract. Understanding the notional machine that conceptually executes a program is a crucial step towards mastery of computer programming. In order to help students build a mental model of the notional machine, visible and tangible computing agents might be of great value, as they provide the student with a conceptual model of who or what is doing the actual work. In addition to programming, the concept of a notional machine is equally important when teaching algorithmic design, complexity theory, or computational thinking. We therefore propose to use a common computing agent as notional machine to not only introduce programming, but also discuss algorithms and their complexity.

Keywords: Python · Turtle graphics · Complexity · Efficiency
Notional machine

1 Introduction

Computer Science is in the process of becoming an accepted and integral part of general education. This is mostly in the form of an introduction to programming. However, the common goal of computer science programmes is "computational thinking" and a fostering of problem solving skills, not necessarily the mastery of a programming language. Hence, introductory programming is only a first step on a path that is supposed to lead to computational thinking.

Unfortunately, programming has turned out to be difficult to master, and few students advance to a level where they can start expressing and implementing algorithmic thinking and design. As a consequence, many courses on K-12 levels focus on just the programming. On the other hand, another approach is taken by the "Computer Science Unplugged" programme of Bell et al. [2–5] or Gallenbacher [8], which does away with the programming altogether, and introduces algorithms without the need for either programming or a computer at all. Eventually integrating both approaches into a curriculum is, of course, a good and fruitful idea. Yet, if programming courses cannot advance to a level where

S. N. Pozdniakov and V. Dagienė (Eds.): ISSEP 2018, LNCS 11169, pp. 68–83, 2018.
https://doi.org/10.1007/978-3-030-02750-6_6

algorithmic principles and computational thinking can be taught, what is the actual benefit of programming education?

Despite popular belief, we are convinced that the mastery of a programming language is not a necessary prerequisite to discuss and implement various algorithms. Rather, learning to program offers a great opportunity to connect to the concepts of algorithms, complexity theory, and eventually lead to the goal of computational thinking even without the need of having introduced the full range of programming structures. The key aspect of our approach is to shift attention from the syntax of the language to the concept of the computing agent or notional machine. In short, the crucial thing is not whether to use a "for"- or a "while"-loop, but rather how the machine can do repetition and iteration to solve a task or problem (cf. [10]).

The approach presented in this article has been used in outreach programmes, and several workshops with the explicit goal of introducing the audience to the basics of complexity theory within a very limited amount of time (cf. [13]). So far, we have not had the opportunity to employ the concepts in large scale teaching, and we therefore do not include any statistics on its actual usefulness but leave this to future research.

2 The Notional Machine

One of the greatest challenges a programming novice faces is to understand the *notional machine*. Originally, du Boulay named the notional machine as one of five difficulties in learning to program, alongside syntax, semantics and other issues [7].

The notional machine is a model of the machine that *conceptually executes the program code*. In principle, it answers the question: what does a machine need in order to understand, follow and execute the program code? As such it differs from the actual implementation on any level, and is therefore not bound to the physical computer, or a virtual machine. The notional machine is primarily determined through the programming language, libraries and frameworks used. An excellent treatment of the notional machine can be found in Sorva [23].

Getting a good understanding of the notional machine is crucial for programming. When we regard programming as communication between man and the machine, with the programmer being the sender of the message (the program code), then the notional machine is the receiver of the message. It determines the effect of a given program code, and answers accordingly to the programmer. Of course, successful communication can only take place with a working model and understanding of the second party involved, i.e., the notional machine.

2.1 The Notional Machine for Algorithms

The concept of the notional machine is not limited to programming, but is equally important for algorithms in a more general setting. In the discussion of algorithms, the notional machine is frequently not made explicit, but only assumed implicitly. When discussing searching in graph theory, for instance, we usually implicitly assume a notional machine that can visit one vertex or node of the graph at any given time, and travel along edges between the vertices. Hence, in our discussion of search algorithms, we imagine to be "the mouse trapped in the maze" rather than having a bird's-eye view of the entire maze as a whole. This also means that we cannot "look down an aisle" and determine that it is an impasse to be skipped in our search.

Occasionally, we do make the notional machine explicit. For instance, when we classify *quicksort* as a "comparison sort". Or when we pose a specific problem in the form "You only have a balance scale to compare items...". Note that, in an educational setting, we might be required to go to great lengths to force students to work with a specific notional machine, and keep them from "cheating" (they might, for instance, determine the relative weight of objects without requiring the scale at all).

Taking the view of complexity theory, we might argue that all algorithms are executed by a Turing machine. However, when effectively designing and working with algorithms, there is seldom the need to take such a drastically abstract approach. Instead, the notional machine executing the algorithm might already "know" how to add or subtract two numbers. Yet, based on our physically available machines, the numbers for addition could be limited in size, requiring special algorithms for large numbers. Thus, depending on the model of the machine, we might wish to factor in the size of the numbers when computing the runtime of such operations, say.

It is imperative that we make the notional machine explicit when teaching specific algorithms. For instance, most programming languages and computing systems offer a function to compute the square root of a number. It can then seem useless, even a waste of time for students to discuss Heron's algorithm for computing the square root – obviously, this is already there and available.

In the context of problem solving skills, the notional machine can be seen as the toolbox that is available to solve a given problem. In education, we then intentionally limit the toolbox, of course, to prompt and foster creativity, and to effectively help the students train their problem solving skills "in the small".

2.2 The Difficulty of the Notional Machine

The computer in its entirety is an incredibly inappropriate notional machine to start with. On the one hand, almost no part of a modern computer can be directly inspected. Unlike a steam engine, there are no moving parts that can be observed and understood. The computer is a black box. Various studies have found that, indeed, invisible parts in programming are one of the greatest source of difficulties and misconceptions (cf., e.g., Sorva [23]).

There are three possibilities to address the situation.

First, we can use metaphors like the famous box-metaphor used for variables, to help the student form a picture of the notional machine. Unfortunately, such static metaphors tend to tacitly introduce misconceptions as students derive inappropriate analogies from the metaphors. The box metaphor for variables, for instance, suggests to some students that a variable can store an arbitrary amount of values.

Second, we can use visualisations to provide a window into the black box. Debuggers allow to trace a program step by step, and display the current value of variables during program execution. However, while such visualisations show the machine's state between two steps, the actual working remains hidden. It is like taking pictures of a steam engine, and trying to understand its working without actually seeing the parts move.

Besides displaying the execution of a student's program code, visualisations are also popular when explaining algorithms. For instance, the sorting of an array of integers might be visualised by bars, where each bar represents a value inside the array through its height. Even though the bars might be moving around during the visualisation, it is important to understand that such a visualisation does not display the algorithm itself, but rather its effect on the data.

Hence, visualisations do not automatically foster a better understanding. Instead, students must be trained in using and understanding the visualisations themselves (cf., e.g., [14,17,24]).

Third, we can use a simpler machine to work with. Instead of programming the abstract "computer" with variables, memory, etc., we have the students program a simple, tangible, and understandable machine. This machine can either be physical or simulated. The crucial part is that no parts of it are hidden, and that the students can build a conceptual model of what it can do and how it works.

In reality, a simple machine might not be enough to truly act as the notional machine for the entire program. However, the simple machine could act as the *computing agent*. With "computing agent" we refer to a relatable and tangible entity that is the receiver of the commands in the program code, and acts upon them. In fact, the idea of a computing agent has been proposed in various forms for decades, and a plethora of different systems exist (cf, e.g., Kelleher and Pausch [11]). However, note that there is a danger in making the computing agent too "human", or too complex.

For our teaching, we use a *turtle*, as found in on-screen turtle graphics, as the computing agent. The turtle executes commands such as `forward(20)`. However, the program code occasionally contains elements that escape the strict turtle-as-agent metaphor. Examples for this might be `forward(100/5)` with a computation in the program code (the turtle metaphor does not explain how such a computation is performed), or control structures such as loops.

Even though the computing agent is not a full blown notional machine, it seems to be sufficient for educational purposes, as it helps the students to form a mental model of *how the machine works* and *what it can do*. It is, in fact, elucidating to realise that practically all successful education environments provide a computing agent (or several) as a core feature (cf., e.g., Logo [19], Greenfoot [12], Kara [9], Scratch [20], Alice [21]). We might even hypothesise that large parts of the success can be attributed to the computing agent rather than, say, what programming language is used (for instance, Lewis [15] found little difference between Logo and Scratch).

3 Turtle-Graphics

The turtle, seen as a machine, has a small set of clearly defined and understandable basic commands. Most importantly, the semantics of these commands is concrete: there is no need for variables, or hidden state to explain this machine (even though the implementation typically makes heavy use of such abstractions). Instead of abstract variables to capture state, we can use, for instance, the turtle's colour, or the colour of its pen.

3.1 The Turtle as Computing Machine

We regard the turtle as a machine with two data registers (its proper colour and the pen colour, respectively), and one address register (its location on the canvas). The canvas itself acts as storage or memory. The turtle's orientation has the role of a "direction bit" to control the direction of commands such as `forward()`.

According to our model, we provide basic commands to read a value (which is always a colour) from the storage (canvas) to a register, store a value in the storage, copy a value between the registers, or swap the values of the two registers or a register with the storage. If we denote the turtle's colour value by r_T (r for "register"), the colour value of its pen by r_P, and its position (address) by r_A, we can express the turtle commands in a more abstract manner as follows:

`set_pos(`v`)`	$r_A \leftarrow v$
`set_color(`v`)`	$r_T \leftarrow v$
`set_pen_color(`v`)`	$r_P \leftarrow v$
`dot()`	$r_P \rightarrow [r_A]$
`swap_color( )`	$r_T \leftrightarrow [r_A]$
`swap_turtle_colors()`	$r_T \leftrightarrow r_P$
`assume_pixel_color()`	$r_T \leftarrow [r_A]$

In principle, the canvas is a two-dimensional array of pixels. With modern devices, however, the pixels are far too small, so that, for most purposes, we use *dots* with a diameter similar to the size of the turtle.

Comparing Colours. There are various colour models and spaces, such as *RGB*, *CMYK*, *HSB*, etc. The prevalent colour model in programming is probably the *RGB*-model, and colours are usually accessed as 24-bit integer values.

Since our algorithms are based on comparing colour values, we need to impose an ordering on a usually three- or even four-dimensional space. We could, of course, just use the 24-bit *RGB*-values, along with the usual ordering of integers. However, we found the results to be aesthetically more pleasing when switching to an *HSB*-model, where the primary key for comparison and ordering is the *hue* of a colour value.

Further Extensions. In addition to the basic operations on the turtle's state, we have added two more concepts to our implementation: first, the turtle can determine not only the value of the pixel underneath the turtle, but also the value of the pixel directly in front of the turtle. Second, some dots are subject to "gravity" and will fall down to the bottom of the screen, unless they hit another dot (exposed through the command `drop_dot()`).

4 How to Measure Efficiency

For a theoretical computer scientist, the term "efficient algorithm" commonly refers to an algorithm with polynomial time complexity. In a broader sense, it depends on the context what is meant; "efficiency" may at times also correspond to memory usage, energy consumptions, code maintenance, or scalability. However, our current efforts address algorithms' time complexities, i.e., running time as depending on the length of a given input.

Without a formal introduction to computer science, what usually first comes to mind is to use some absolute measurements such as milliseconds. For the purpose of discussing algorithms, however, this is unsatisfactory, because the absolute time taken depends on many things that are independent of the algorithm used, such as the machine it is run on, or the programming language. What makes more sense is to count the number of elementary operations carried out by the machine. This, of course, depends on the notional machine, and its set of "elementary" operations. In fact, counting elementary operations is a prime example of requiring a notional machine.

Different Classes of Complexity. Measuring the runtime of an algorithm is in itself not an adequate measure for the quality of an algorithm. In the overall picture, a particularly good algorithm distinguishes itself not by handling a specific instance of the problem well, but by scaling well with the size of the problem instance.

In the context of single-number-based algorithms, we take the number of bits (or digits) of the input number as a measure for the "problem size". For a list of values, we take the number of values in the list to be the appropriate measure. We would then like to assess how much longer the algorithm needs if we add another bit to the number, or value to the list, respectively.

To give a hands-on example, consider the problem of assessing the divisibility of an integer N, represented by n decimal digits. We can then give three examples of different complexity:

- We can check if N is divisible by 2 by checking the last digit of N, irrespective of the size of N. Hence, assessing if a number is odd or even can be achieved in constant time.
- In order to check if N is divisible by 3, we can build the sum of all digits, and then check if the resulting sum is divisible by 3. This is commonly known by all students. Building the sum of all digits depends on the number of digits n. If we add one more digit, we have to add one more number. Hence, time complexity for this problem is linear in n.
- To check if an integer N has any non-trivial divisor at all, much more work is needed. As a first approximation, we can argue that we need to check more or less each integer between 2 and $N - 1$, to assess if it is a factor of N. Adding another digit usually multiplies the required work by a factor of 10. Time complexity is therefore exponential and can be expressed as 10^n.

Efficiency in Programming. The actual implementation of an algorithm may seem to differ significantly from a theoretical presentation of the same algorithm. Switching to an implementer's perspective bears the danger of focusing too much on the efficiency of implementation details, as opposed to the efficiency of the underlying algorithm as discussed above. This issue can be understood in part originating from a change of the underlying notional machine: the notional machine of any given programming language hardly ever coincides with the one used to discuss the algorithm in a theoretical framework.

To smoothen the transitions between a theoretical discussion of an algorithm, and its implementation, it is desirable to use a unified model. Turtle graphics as presented here offers an opportunity for such an unified model. The efficiency can then be described in turtle operations, which in turn, have direct correspondence in code, and on the screen during program execution.

5 Primality Testing

In this section, we describe two different approaches of how to sharpen the student's view on complexity theory using the example of primality testing.

5.1 Geometric Approach

Testing for primality can be seen as a geometric problem. Given a number of dots $N \geq 2$, we try to arrange the dots in the shape of a rectangle. If this succeeds only when all dots are in one column or one row, respectively, N is a prime number; for instance, 15 dots can form a rectangle with dimensions 3×5, whereas there is no rectangle with dimensions $k \times m$ for 17 dots with $1 < k, m < 17$.

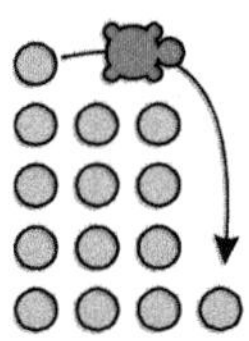

Fig. 1. Given a number of dots, the turtle takes dots from the top, and drops them into the column on the right, trying to balance all columns and thereby create a rectangle.

Starting a single column of N dots on the very left of the screen, the turtle tries to rearrange the dots so that they form a rectangle. To that end, the turtle picks up the top-most dot, and drops it into the column to the right. During this process, the turtle works its way from left to right, and jumps down to the next row if no dot remains on the top-layer. If the column to the right has been filled to the top, such that all columns have equal height, the number N is (literally) obviously divisible. Otherwise, the turtle starts to drop the dots into the next column, trying to balance all dots with one more column. By adding a new column to the right whenever needed, the turtle continues trying to balance the dots into the existing columns until it finds a solution (which always exists in the form of a row of height one).

Program 1 in Appendix A shows the implementation of a geometric primality testing algorithm, using the dot-based turtle graphics (see Fig. 1).

Given this geometric approach, it is indeed evident that each possible arrangement is actually tried twice. Divisibility by two, for instance, is once tried using two columns, and once using two rows (if the number is a prime). It can directly be reasoned that the algorithm can stop as soon as the number of columns exceeds the number of rows. In a more abstract way, the turtle has to test only factors up to $\lfloor\sqrt{N}\rfloor$, because once it is found out that there is no rectangle with dimensions $k \times l$ with $k \leq \lfloor\sqrt{N}\rfloor$, all possible k, l-combinations to follow have already been tested with k and l being switched.

5.2 Semi-Geometric Approach

The geometric approach presented above has various limitations, particularly with respect to possible optimisations. We therefore describe a semi-geometric variant, which allows us to introduce various optimisations.

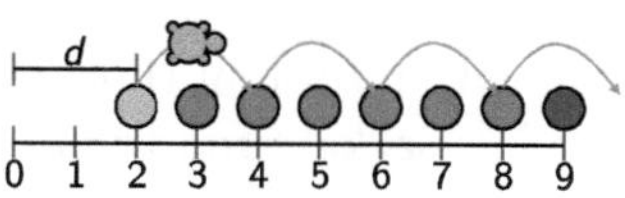

Fig. 2. For each possible factor d with $2 < d < N$, the turtle jumps d steps, trying to reach the Nth dot (coloured red in our implementation). The dot at position d is removed, and the turtle starts again at position $d + 1$. (Color figure online)

The basic algorithm is shown in Program 2 in Appendix A. Based on the idea of the sieve of Eratosthenes [18], we visualize a number N as a row of $N - 2$ blue, and one red dot (we have to omit the dot representing "1" since we do not want to test whether N is divisible by 1). The turtle is then set on a dot d and jumps forward in steps of d dots. If the turtle hits the red dot, d is a factor of N. Otherwise, the dot representing d is removed and the turtle checks the next possible factor. This is illustrated in Fig. 2.

In contrast to the true sieve of Eratosthenes, Program 2 does not cross out any multiples of a given number d. Hence, the turtle checks each integer up to N.

A first optimisation can be introduced by crossing out multiples of any tested factor d, implementing Eratosthenes' sieve properly. In our semi-geometric variant, this means that the turtle has to remove any dot it encounters. In our actual implementation, this could be done by colouring the dot in a darker blue (against a black background).

6 Sorting

As a second example to demonstrate the power of turtle graphics to illustrate the efficiency of certain algorithms, we use the standard problem of sorting. Due to space restrictions, we can only include a version of *Minsort* here.

As setup for our algorithms, the turtle starts by drawing a column of coloured dots in the middle of the screen. The colours are chosen at random, based on the HSB-model, where only hue varies. Before a sorting algorithm starts, the turtle is placed at the bottom of the column of coloured dots, heading up, and having no colour of its own.

The turtle picks up the first (bottom-most) dot it encounters, assuming its colour and removing the dot from the screen. Subsequently, the turtle moves through all remaining dots, swapping its colour with any dot, whose colour is to be found "less" than the current colour. Once the turtle reaches the top, it moves slightly to the right and drops the coloured dot into a new column, before returning to the initial position (called "origin" in Program 3 in Appendix A) at the bottom of the original column.

As before, the algorithm is simple enough so that no variables are needed, beyond the turtle's own colour. In other words, the entire algorithm is directly visible on screen with no hidden state.

In addition to Minsort, we have also implemented Bubblesort, Quicksort, and Mergesort in our turtle framework. However, the limited capabilities of the turtle adds additional issues, and complexities. Mergesort, for instance, lends itself very well to a framework with a total of three turtles cooperating. This, in turn, requires more programming background from the students.

For a manageable implementation of Quicksort (see Appendix B), we had to make use of a variable, thereby going beyond the initial framework of no hidden state. Instead of discussing the Python code, we have discussed the visualisation with the students, who were often quick to point out that the presented algorithm would not be optimal if the initial array was "already sorted in reverse".

7 Related Work

In order to make algorithms and complexity theory accessible to students in a K-12 context, CS unplugged programs, such as those by Bell et al. [3] or Gallenbacher [8], have been developed, and found widespread success. Moreover, Bell et al. [2] argue that understanding complexity theory, even on a rather intuitive level, gives high-school students a very good picture on what computer science is about, and makes them less likely to choose studying it for the wrong reasons.

Turtle graphics is often associated with the Logo programming language; see, e.g., Thornburg [26]. Today, however, most educational programming languages provide libraries for turtle graphics, including Python. Caspersen and Christensen [6], for instance, present an access to object-oriented programming based on turtle graphics. One of the most essential aspects of turtle graphics are its immediate visual feedback, and the support for a teaching style that goes from the concrete towards the abstract [6].

One of the most extensive treatises on turtle graphics is offered by Abelson and DiSessa [1]. In the early tradition of turtle graphics, their discussion, however, has a strong focus on geometry, mathematics, as well as simulations.

According to du Boulay, building a conceptual model of the notional machine is one of the five difficulties a novice programmer faces. In the light of his and subsequent research, as presented below, we would argue that a comprehension of the notional machine is, indeed, one of the crucial prerequisites to succeed in learning to program.

The notional machine is often implicit or hidden from the novice programmer. This invisibility of the machine's operation has been mentioned as a hurdle and source of misconceptions several times. Sorva [23], for instance, writes that "Many misconceptions, if not most of them, have to do with aspects that are not readily visible, but hidden within the execution-time world of the notional machine".

Sorva [23] reports that conceptual models, which might just be "a simple metaphor or analogy, or a more complex explanation of the system", are not only useful tools, but help improve the understanding and performance of the students (cf. also Schumacher and Czerwinski [22]). He advocates the use of visualisations and metaphors, in particular to "concretize the dynamic aspects of programs." In addition, Sorva points out that an active engagement by the students is, in fact, more important than the particular visualisation technique used.

We see this in accordance with our approach to use a concrete, and visually oriented notional machine to teach programming. The crucial part, however, is that we do not use a visualisation of an underlying machine, but rather a visually tangible computing agent, as this means that students actively engage with the "visualisation" instead of merely consuming it.

Finally, it is interesting to compare these findings with the neo-Piagetian theories as reported by Lister [16], or Lister and Teague [25]. Lister argues that novice programmers initially work on a preoperational stage (or even sensimotor stage), where "they can trace code accurately, but they struggle to reason about code." [25] In particular, his findings indicate that students use *concrete values* to trace and understand code, and that this is a necessary step in the development of higher abstraction and reasoning skills.

Hence, using concrete and directly visible values during program execution might address students better on the level of their respective stage in reasoning, and thereby help them progress in their learning. Further studies in this direction are certainly warranted.

8 Conclusion

Even though programming is an important part of Computer Science Education, it should not be limited to programming alone. Computational, or algorithmic thinking needs to be treated as an equally important part. Computer Science Unplugged programmes offer a great way to introduce computational thinking early on, without extensive programming prerequirements.

In this article, we have presented an approach with focus on the notional machine, and computing agent. Education in both programming, as well as algorithmics could benefit strongly from explicit incorporation of assumptions about the underlying computing agent. Instead of visualising just states of the machine, we can then visualise the actual work of the agent itself, and provide a firmer framework for learning metaphors. For beginning classes, we have used an enhanced turtle as the computational agent, with so far very positive experience.

Future research, as well as classroom experience will be needed to properly evaluate the applicability, and validity of our approach.

A Python Programs

Program 1. Starting with a single column of dots, the turtle tries to rearrange the dots to a true rectangle. If this succeeds, the number of dots is not prime.

```
def remove_dot():
    pickup_dot()        # remove a dot from the top
    head_right()        # and drop it to the right
    forward()           # of the current dots
    while not is_pixel_empty():
        forward()
    drop_dot()          # let dot fall down
    # check if the column to the right is full
    if not is_pixel_empty():
        head_left()
        if is_pixel_ahead_empty():
            pickup_dot()      # drop the dot into
            head_right()      # a new column to
            forward()         # the right
            drop_dot()

def find_next_dot():
    head_left()
    # check if the rectangle is complete, i. e.
    # the number of dots is not prime
    if is_pixel_ahead_empty():
        turn_left()
        forward()
        turn_right()
        if not is_pixel_empty():
            if current_y() <= 1:
                print "prime!"
            else:
                print "not␣prime!"
            exit()
    while not is_pixel_ahead_empty():
        forward()

while True:
    remove_dot()
    find_next_dot()
```

Program 2. An graphical implementation of a primality testing algorithm. In contrast to the sieve of Eratosthenes, multiples of prime factors are not "crossed out." Hence, the algorithm tests each number up to N.

```
def test_factor():
    set_pos("origin")
    while is_pixel_empty():
        forward()
    if is_pixel_of_color("red"):
        print "prime!"
        exit()
    drop_dot()
    d = current_x()
    while is_pixel_of_color("blue"):
        forward(d)
    if is_pixel_of_color("red"):
        print "not␣a␣prime!"
        exit()

while True:
    test_factor()
```

Program 3. This implementation of Minsort is straightforward: the turtle picks up the first colour in the list, and then swaps it whenever it finds a colour that is "smaller." The thus found minimal colour is dropped into the column on the right.

```
while True:
    # Find the first (lowest) dot
    set_pos("origin")
    head_up()
    while is_pixel_empty():
        forward()
    pickup_dot()
    # Search the dot with "smallest" colour
    while not is_pixel_ahead_empty():
        forward()
        if get_pixel_hue() < get_turtle_hue():
            swap_color()
    head_right()
    forward()
    drop_dot()
    # Is the second column completely filled?
    if not is_pixel_empty():
        break
```

B Quicksort

For Quicksort, the turtle assumes the colour of the first dot it encounters, and then compares the colours of all subsequent dots to its own colour (the pivot colour). Dots with a colour hue that is smaller (or equal) are placed to the left, those with larger colour hue are placed to the right (see Program 4 and Fig. 3). As long as more than one dot remains in any stack, the procedure is repeated recursively.

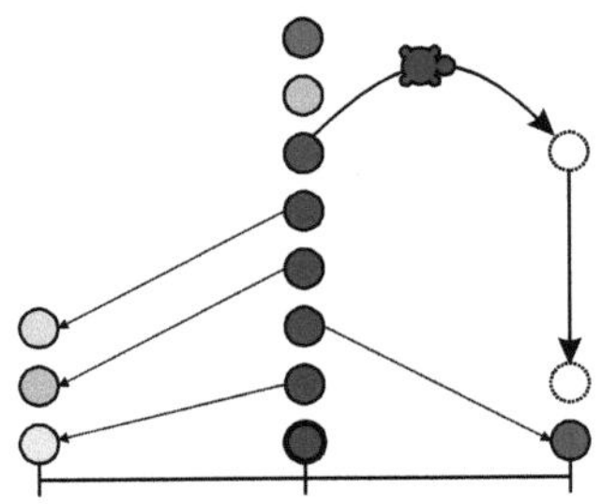

Fig. 3. In our implementation of Quicksort, the turtle takes the colour of the first dot at the bottom as the pivot. It then moves all dots either to the left or to the right, creating two new columns to be sorted afterwards. (Color figure online)

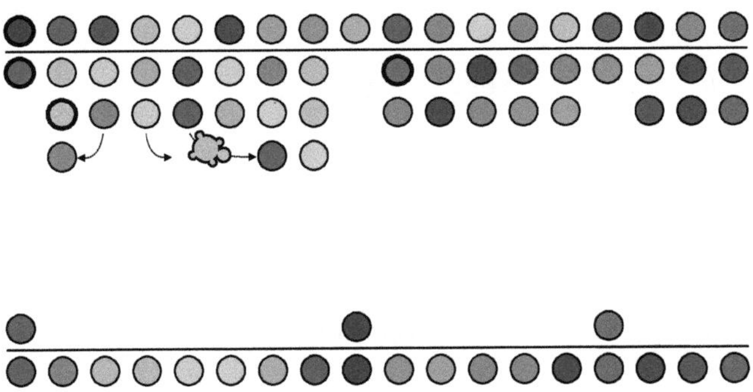

Fig. 4. An alternative implementation of Quicksort, where the dots are arranged horizontally. Each pivot colour is dropped to the bottom after the sorting step: due to the gap between the left and the right hand side, its position in the result is already known. At the very bottom, the final solution is shown. (Color figure online)

Instead of arranging the dots as vertical stacks as in Fig. 3, it is also possible to arrange the coloured dots as horizontal lines as in Fig. 4. Note that the line on the right side grows from right to left, leading to the order of the dots being reversed on each step. Since the pivot dot is neither added to the left, nor the right hand side, a gap forms in between the two sides. While an implementation without additional variables is, in principle, feasible, the search for the right spot to place the new dot might take a large amount of both program code, and execution time.

So far, we have never progressed in class enough to actually discuss Python code of Quicksort as shown in Program 4. The use of recursion makes a discussion on entry level difficult (it is possible to do it without recursion, but this does not necessarily lead to better understandable program code). However, we have presented the horizontal version several times as a basis for further discussion, with great results: students often realised, for instance, that the algorithm works best if the pivot colour divides the dots into two lines, or piles, of approximately equal size, and fails to be efficient for dots, "which are sorted in reverse" (it seems that the idea of sorting an already sorted line does not necessarily occur to high school students).

Program 4. An implementation of Quicksort using turtle graphics. Here we need an abstract variable "delta" to leave room for further columns, which appear due to recursion.

```
def sort(delta):
    set_pos("bottom")  # only change y-coordinate
    if delta < 1 or is_pixel_empty():
        return
    head_up()
    assume_pixel_color()
    while not is_pixel_ahead_empty():
        forward()
        swap_color()         # save pivot color
        if get_pixel_hue() > get_turtle_hue():
            jump_left(delta)
            drop_dot()
            jump_right(delta)
        else:
            jump_right(delta)
            drop_dot()
            jump_left(delta)
        assume_pixel_color() # assume pivot color
    head_left()            # sort columns on ...
    forward(delta)
    sort(delta // 2)       # ... the left ...
    head_right()
    forward(delta * 2)
    sort(delta // 2)       # ... the right ...
    head_left()
    forward(delta)         # back to middle pos
```

References

1. Abelson, H., DiSessa, A.: Turtle Geometry. MIT Press, Cambridge (1981)
2. Bell, T., Andreae, P., Lambert, L.: Computer science in New Zealand high schools. In: Proceedings of ACE 2010 (2010)
3. Bell, T., Witten, I., Fellows, M.: CS unplugged - computer science without a computer. http://csunplugged.org. Accessed 17 Sept 2017
4. Bell, T., Rosamond, F., Casey, N.: Computer science unplugged and related projects in math and computer science popularization. In: Bodlaender, H.L., Downey, R., Fomin, F.V., Marx, D. (eds.) The Multivariate Algorithmic Revolution and Beyond. LNCS, vol. 7370, pp. 398–456. Springer, Heidelberg (2012). https://doi.org/10.1007/978-3-642-30891-8_18
5. Bell, T., Alexander, J., Freeman, I., Grimley, M.: Computer science unplugged: school students doing real computing without computers. N. Z. J. Appl. Comput. Inf. Technol. **13**, 01 (2009)
6. Caspersen, M.E., Christensen, H.B.: Here, there and everywhere - on the recurring use of turtle graphics in CS1. In: Proceedings of ACSE 2000 (2000)
7. Du Boulay, B.: Some difficulties of learning to program. J. Educ. Comput. Res. **2**(1), 57–73 (1986)
8. Gallenbacher, J.: Abenteuer Informatik, 4th edn. Springer, Heidelberg (2017). https://doi.org/10.1007/978-3-662-53965-1
9. Hartmann, W., Nievergelt, J., Reichert, R.: Kara, finite state machines, and the case for programming as part of general education. In: Proceedings of the IEEE 2001 Symposia on Human Centric Computing Languages and Environments (HCC 2001), p. 135. IEEE Computer Society, Washington, DC (2001)
10. Hromkovič, J., Kohn, T., Komm, D., Serafini, G.: Combining the power of python with the simplicity of logo for a sustainable computer science education. In: Brodnik, A., Tort, F. (eds.) ISSEP 2016. LNCS, vol. 9973, pp. 155–166. Springer, Cham (2016). https://doi.org/10.1007/978-3-319-46747-4_13
11. Kelleher, C., Pausch, R.: Lowering the barriers to programming: a taxonomy of programming environments and languages for novice programmers. ACM Comput. Surv. **37**(2), 83–137 (2005)
12. Kölling, M.: The greenfoot programming environment. Trans. Comput. Educ. **10**(4), 14:1–14:21 (2010)
13. Komm, D., Kohn, T.: An introduction to running time analysis for an SOI workshop. Olymp. Inform. **11**, 77–86 (2017)
14. Lawrence, A.W., Badre, A.M., Stasko, J.T.: Empirically evaluating the use of animations to teach algorithms. In: Proceedings of 1994 IEEE Symposium on Visual Languages, pp. 48–54, October 1994
15. Lewis, C.M.: How programming environment shapes perception, learning and goals: Logo vs. Scratch. In: Proceedings of the 41st ACM Technical Symposium on Computer Science Education, SIGCSE 2010, pp. 346–350. ACM, New York (2010)
16. Lister, R.: Concrete and other neo-Piagetian forms of reasoning in the novice programmer. In: Proceedings of the Thirteenth Australasian Computing Education Conference, ACE 2011, vol. 114, pp. 9–18. Australian Computer Society Inc., Darlinghurst (2011)
17. Ma, L., Ferguson, J., Roper, M., Wood, M.: Investigating and improving the models of programming concepts held by novice programmers. Comput. Sci. Educ. **21**(1), 57–80 (2011)

18. O'Neill, M.E.: The genuine sieve of Eratosthenes. J. Funct. Program. **19**(1), 95–106 (2009)
19. Papert, S.: Mindstorms: Children, Computers, and Powerful Ideas. Harvester Press, Brighton (1980)
20. Resnick, M., et al.: Scratch: programming for all. Commun. ACM **52**(11), 60–67 (2009)
21. Rodger, S.H., et al.: Enhancing K-12 education with Alice programming adventures. In: Proceedings of the Fifteenth Annual Conference on Innovation and Technology in Computer Science Education, ITiCSE 2010, pp. 234–238. ACM, New York (2010)
22. Schumacher, R.M., Czerwinski, M.P.: Mental models and the acquisition of expert knowledge. In: Hoffman, R.R. (ed.) The Psychology of Expertise, pp. 61–79. Springer, New York, New York (1992). https://doi.org/10.1007/978-1-4613-9733-5_4
23. Sorva, J.: Notional machines and introductory programming education. Trans. Comput. Educ. **13**(2), 8:1–8:31 (2013)
24. Sorva, J., Lönnberg, J., Malmi, L.: Students' ways of experiencing visual program simulation. Comput. Sci. Educ. **23**(3), 207–238 (2013)
25. Teague, D., Lister, R.: Manifestations of preoperational reasoning on similar programming tasks. In: Proceedings of the Sixteenth Australasian Computing Education Conference, ACE 2014, vol. 148, pp. 65–74. Australian Computer Society Inc., Darlinghurst (2014)
26. D. D. Thornburg Friends of the Turtle: On Logo and Turtles. Compute! (1983)

A Diagnostic Tool for Assessing Students' Perceptions and Misconceptions Regards the Current Object "*this*"

Ragonis Noa[1,2(✉)] and Shmallo Ronit[3]

[1] Beit Berl College, Beit Berl, Kfar Saba, Israel
noarag@beitberl.ac.il
[2] Technion Israel Institute of Technology, Haifa, Israel
[3] Shamoon College of Engineering, Ashdod, Israel
ronitl@sce.ac.il

Abstract. Understanding of the object concept in Object Oriented Programming (OOP) is obviously the center of the paradigm. Many educators and researchers explored students' difficulties and developed teaching materials targeted at this central concept. The paper presents a diagnostic tool we developed that aims to reveal students' perception and understanding about the current object, referring to it by the *this* annotation. Proper conceptualization of *this* indicates an understanding of objects in general, and involves aspects of memory allocation and programming approaches. The tool contains five questions, each devoted to covering different aspects in various frameworks, such as: using *this* in constructors, using *this* as a visible parameter, using *this* in inheritance, or making necessary changes in transition from a non-static context that uses *this* to a static context. The questionnaire combines closed questions with a request to explain the answers and open questions. In the paper we present the purpose of each question, and address what it comes to examine. The diagnostic tool is based on known educational approaches: Bloom's taxonomy, assessment for, as, and of learning and learning from errors. The tool can be used by educators at high school or academic levels as a teaching tool, as a base for discussions, or as an evaluation tool. A short report on the use of the tool with different populations, including high school teachers, is presented. The paper uses Java as the programming language, but it easily can be translated to other OOP languages.

Keywords: Object oriented programming · The current object
The *this* annotation

1 Introduction

Objects are the core of Object Oriented Programming (OOP), and yet, they are the source of enormous types of difficulties for learners, which lead to different perceptions and misconceptions. Perceptions of different concepts regarding OOP have been extensively studied in the last two decades, including the understanding of the basic concept "Object" [e.g., 21, 27]. The *this* reference relates to the current object. It can be

S. N. Pozdniakov and V. Dagienė (Eds.): ISSEP 2018, LNCS 11169, pp. 84–100, 2018.
https://doi.org/10.1007/978-3-030-02750-6_7

used in any instance method including constructors, getters, and setters. The use of *this* is not mandatory, and it can be omitted from most of the codes. However, it is included by developers according to writing conventions or personal preferences. Understanding the meaning of the *this* reference involves varied aspects of abstraction regarding the object and its memory allocation. Previous studies pointed to different difficulties of understanding objects, but few of them mentioned the *this* reference [e.g., 6]. None of them was dedicated directly to the *this* reference and its varied interpretations.

To expand the understanding of students' conceptions and preferences regarding the use of *this*, we developed a diagnostic tool that can be used as an evaluation tool for the advancement of learning. Moreover, looking at students' errors allows in-depth discussions in the class. The tool contains five questions; each explores different aspects of using *this* in code, and hence sharpens students' perceptions and misconceptions. All questions reflect high order cognitive levels according to Bloom's taxonomy [2].

The tool can be used with any population that learns OOP, and can be easily translated to any OOP programming language. The tool was tested with 163 high school and college students, and 48 high school teachers. It was improved according to complications that occurred in its first version. Part of the findings from the research with high school students and teachers was published [23].

In what follows, we present: background on students' conceptions regarding "Object" and on the educational approaches that led to the development of the tool; the tool structure addresses the questions' targets, the goals of each of its clauses, interpretation of the question's cognitive level according to Bloom's taxonomy, and brief lessons we learned from using the tool. We will summarize by presenting some implications for teaching.

2 Literature Review

The literature review includes two sections that guided us in the construction of the diagnostic tool. The first discusses the essential understanding of the concept of "Object" in OOP and what was found by previous research, focusing on understanding the current object *this*. The second relates to educational approaches that reflect the origins for the development of the tool. Those are high order cognitive skills in the light of Bloom's taxonomy, along with considering the tool as an instrument to use in the framework of assessment and for learning integrated with the approach of learning from errors.

2.1 Understanding the Concept of "Object" in Learning OOP

An object is a capsule of attributes and their values, which is referred to by a single reference, and at the same time each of its attributes' values can be accessed separately. The reserved word *this* refers to the current object and is usually used to distinguish between parameters and their corresponding instance variables, when both share the same names. This common use of *this* is not mandatory and is manifested mainly in constructors and setters methods. Nevertheless, there are certain cases where the use of *this* is required, mainly in constructors in the context of inheritance when invoking overloaded constructors, or when passing an object as a parameter.

Studies that related to the comprehending of OOP fundamental concepts dealt with the understanding of the "object" and "class" concepts since they are essential for realizing the meaning of OOP. Many misconceptions and difficulties regarding the "object" concept arose: difficulties to distinguish between classes and their instances, the objects [e.g. 11, 13, 26]; difficulties in comprehending the static role of classes in comparison to the dynamic role of objects [e.g., 22, 25]; failure to distinguish between the "object itself" and the variable/modifier that refers to the object [e.g. 28, 29]; incorrect models of the way objects are stored in the memory [30]; and assume that all objects have the same size in the memory [14]. Some research related particularly to students' conceptions regard the role of "object" and "class" during program execution [9, 31, 32]. They addressed that students gain better understanding of the class concept than of the object concept; think of objects as pieces of code; and experience object as something that is active in the program.

The research accumulated knowledge about students' conceptions and misconceptions that has to affect the teaching and learning processes. The diagnostic tool offered in the paper is considered by us as an evaluation tool that can serve educators to identify their students' perceptions, conceptions, and misconceptions. The collection of students' answers generates a wide base for meaningful discussions in the light of "Assessment for, as and of Learning" and of "Learning from Errors".

2.2 Teaching Approaches that Served the Tool Development

The diagnostic tool was built on the reliance and integration of some recognized approaches in education: the development of high-order thinking skills, assessment for the advancement of learning, and learning from errors. In what follows we describe those approaches.

High-Order Cognitive Skills. The literature refers to high-order thinking skills in operational terms that express different ways of implementation [24, 34, 35]. High-order thinking skills involve skills such as problem-solving, asking questions, thinking critically, making decisions, and taking responsibility. The analysis of high-order thinking skills is based on Bloom's taxonomy [2], which is considered to be the most fundamental taxonomy. It consists of six levels involved in planning students' learning and evaluating their achievements: 1 - knowledge, 2 - comprehension, 3 - application, 4 - analysis, 5 - synthesis, and 6 - evaluation. Newman [17] suggested that high-order thinking skills relate to Bloom's taxonomy as complex and multifaceted thinking skills, challenging the learner to interpret and analyze information. Newman further defined the inclusive skill "thoughtfulness", which is based on four traits: the ability to reason, the tendency to reflect, the curiosity to explore new questions, and the flexibility to consider alternative and original solutions. A revision of Bloom's taxonomy was suggested by Anderson and Krathwohl [1], who regarded Bloom's levels 4, 5, and 6 as referring to non-hierarchical components but as expressing similar cognitive abilities, identified as metacognitive knowledge. This interpretation became accepted in the educational research community. Anderson and Krathwohl also suggested six verbs corresponding to Bloom's thinking levels: 1 - To remember, 2 - To understand, 3 - To apply, 4 - To analyze, 5 - To evaluate, 6 - To create. According to researchers investigating higher-order cognitive skills (HOCS), it is important to pose questions during the learning process while highlighting its different aspects. Paul and Elder [19] presented two complementary perspectives with respect to questions: (a) questions students are asked in teaching scenarios, and (b) questions students practice and experiment with themselves in problem-solving processes, i.e., questions that lead them to reflective, critical, and judgmental thinking.

Assessment for, as, and of Learning. Assessment is an essential component of the teaching and learning cycle, but should not be restricted in order to enable teachers to gather evidence and make judgments about student achievement. Assessment for learning and assessment as learning incorporate self-assessment or peer-assessment for students to actively check and evaluate their own knowledge and understanding. Assessment is probably the most important thing we can do to help our students learn [5]. Hence, we have to do our best to ensure that our assessment practices help rather than hinder learning.

Assessment as learning emphasizes using assessment as a process for developing and supporting students' metacognitions abilities [8]. The students critically connect between their assessment and their learning. They are active, and apply critical thinking to make sense of information and to relate it to their prior knowledge. This is a constructivist metacognitive process where students construct new knowledge. Students personally monitor what they are learning and use the feedback to make adjustments, adaptations, and major changes in what they understand. In terms of class practices, activities that evoke assessment as and for learning involve different pedagogical aspects such as student-teacher interaction, self-reflection, motivation, and planning of learning environments [10]. The support of teachers in those types of processes enables students to reach the next stage in their learning course. In this process students are responsible for their knowledge and do not lean only on the teacher's feedback. The approach of "learning from errors" can be interpreted and implemented as "assessment as and for learning".

Learning from Errors. Errors may trigger cognitive conflicts, which yield a process of reflection and critical thinking, and hence may be used for developing coherent knowledge [3]. Learning through errors supports the constructivist approach, as the utilization of errors is based on students' prior knowledge, which is vague or partly erroneous.

In the last two decades, researchers presented convincing results following the learning from errors approach in mathematics [e.g., 4, 16, 18] and physics [e.g., 20, 33]. Ginat and Shmallo [12] developed the approach of learning from errors in computer science, targeted on learning basic OOP concepts by college students. Their goal was to refine students' knowledge and skills by raising conflict or cognitive dissonance in using errors, based on the assumption raised by Confrey [7] that conflict causes review of one's knowledge and procedures. In their research, students indicated that learning from errors enabled them to realize their previous erroneous conceptions of which they were unaware and enabled them to deepen their understanding. It was further evident that students were able to specify terms and mechanisms more clearly and more accurately. The learning from errors approach in teaching contributed to students' understanding of OOP's fundamental concepts.

Based on previous studies including ours and our vast experience in teaching at academic levels, high schools, and training in-service and pre-service teachers, we developed the diagnostic tool that can serve educators in the teaching-learning-assessment processes they lead. Section 3 describes the tool in detail.

3 The Diagnostic Tool

The diagnostic tool is a questionnaire that contains five questions with different conceptual focus. Sections 3.1–3.5 present each question, display parts of the questions formulation, address the perceptions involved in the question regarding the current object, and analyze the question's contribution to assessing students' understanding. The full questionnaire appears in Appendix A.

3.1 Question 1: Where the Use of *this* is Needed

Question 1 presents a project that involves a simple class, a composed class, and a main class.

Clause (a) reflects basic usage of *this* in traditional methods: constructors, *toString*, and *equals*. The purpose of the question is to examine whether students can identify where *this* must be used, actually, only when parameters and attributes have the same identifiers. Otherwise, it is a matter of preference. Students were asked to mark where *this* is required and where it is superfluous. The codes relate to: (#1) traditional constructor that uses parameters with same identifiers as the attributes; (#2) copy constructor; (#3) *toString()* method; and (#4) *equals(...)* method. To demonstrate this question we present codes (#1) and (#2) in Table 1a.

Table 1a. Examples of question 1 codes.

Code #1	Code #2

public Date(int day, int month, int year) {
    this.day = day; // line #1
    this.month = month;
    this.year = year;
}
	public Date(Date other){
	    this.day = other.day; // line #2
	    this.month = other.month;
	    this.year = other.year;
	}

Clause (a) allows observing if students actually understand the meaning of using the *this* reference, or they just stick to their own/class/teacher habits.

Beyond the distinction whether *this* can or must be used, there are some commonly used syntaxes. It is important that students will understand when and why to use those common syntaxes. For example, in Code (#1) *this* must be used so that the method achieves its expected purpose, still syntactically it could be removed. Some students can state that without *this*, there will be a compilation error, or "the computer will not know what to do". With regard to Code (#2) students can raise the issue that the use of *this* is unnecessary, but state that it is clearer for them to see the referred relevant objects with similar syntax. Meaning: *this.day = other.day* is more readable than *day = other.day*.

Interpretation by Bloom's taxonomy: 5 - Evaluate. Students have to determine and to justify their decision based on their conceptualization.

The purpose of Question 1's clauses (b)–(d) is to examine several advanced issues of using and understanding the current object, in relation to calling a method that uses *this* and involves *static* aspects as well. The clauses are presented in Table 1b.

Table 1b. Description of question 1 clauses (b)–(d).

	Question code	Question wording

(b)	public boolean equals(Flight other) {
	if (this.flightDate.equals(other.flightDate)
	&& this.flightNum==other.flightNum)
	return true;
	return false;
	}
		Giving the method *equals* in class *Flight*, when excecuting the next instruction in the *main* method:
		if (flight001.equals(flight003))
		to what does the *this* appearing in the *equals* method refer?

(c)	Refers to the *equals* method in class *Date*	Develop a *static* method replacing the instance method *equals* in class *Date*.

(d)	public static void main(String[] args) {
	...
	}
		Can *this* be used in the code of the *main* method?

To answer clause (b) students should understand the meaning of executing an instance method that involves two objects. On the first one, the method is operated, and it appears implicitly in the call statement – flight001, but becomes explicit within the method using *this*. Particularly, it can be challenging in the case of composed class. To answer clause (c) students should understand the differences between instance methods to static methods. The needed changes are: (1) to include the reserved word *static* in the method signature; (2) to use two object parameters; (3) any use of *this* should be omitted; (4) using getters methods is expected. Answering clause (d) demands understanding that main methods do not relate to objects - they do not operate on objects.

Interpretation by Bloom's taxonomy: (b) 4 - Analyze. Students have to distinguish between the two objects; (c) 6 - Create. Students have to develop a new method taking into consideration a variety of aspects; (d) 5 - Evaluate. Students have to deduce that the *main* method is static, in opposition to the instance method, which is not static, and to support their answer.

3.2 Question 2: Personal Preferences

Question 2 includes four clauses, each displaying 2–3 different codes that execute the same task. All codes relate to class *Point*, which is represented by two attributes (x,y). Students are required to rank the versions in each clause according to their personal code preference and to state their criteria for making their choice. The questionnaire clearly states that all versions are correct.

The focus of the question clauses is: (a) the place where each *Point* object attributes are initialized to be (0,0); (b) the identifiers used as parameters; (c) the access to attributes in the copy constructor; (d) the access to attributes in *equals* method, where two of the three versions involve the use of *toString* method. To demonstrate this type of question we present clause (c) code versions in Table 2.

Table 2. Question 2 clause (c) codes.

Version1	Version2	Version3
public class Point {	public class Point {	public class Point {
private int x;	private int x;	private int x;
private int y;	private int y;	private int y;
public Point(Point p) {	public Point(Point p) {	public Point(Point p) {
this.x = p.getX();	this.x = p.x;	x = p.x;
this.y = p.getY();	this.y = p.y;	y = p.y;
}	}	}
}	}	}

The question enables exploring students' preferences, but actually enables discussion on the understanding of the current object. One issue that the question raises, seemingly to question 1, is where/whether/why *this* should be used. Another central issue that can be raised is where/whether/why getters methods should be used. Since it appears in the instance method it is not mandatory, but maybe it is a good practice to use it, and to not access the attributes of the parameter object directly – implementing the principle of information hiding.

Interpretation by Bloom's taxonomy: 5 - Evaluate. Students need to rank their code preferences, and to justify their criteria based on the concepts they acquire.

3.3 Question 3: Use of *this* as a Parameter

Question 3 relates to a project including a simple class *Circle* and a main class *Test.* The question focuses on the use of *this* as a formal parameter. Students are required to relate to the execution of the instruction *circle1.chooseWhatToDraw('X', circle2);* in the *main* method, and to answer what the *this* appearing in the method *choose-WhatToDraw(...)* in the instruction *drawFlower(this);* refers to. The method is displayed in Table 3.

This type of using *this* as a parameter is rarely taught in classes. But, students have the knowledge to understand the new context. It is expected that students who grasp the

Table 3. The method in focus of question 3.

Question code	Question wording

public void chooseWhatToDraw (char c, Circle circ) {
    if (c == 'F')
      drawFlower(this);
    if (c == 'X')
      drawX(circ);
}
	To what does the *this refer?*

"object" concept, and particularly understand the role of the object in instance methods, be able to apply it in the new context.

Interpretation by Bloom's taxonomy: combination of 3 - Apply, 4 - Analyze, and 5 - Evaluate. Students need to use and interpret previous knowledge in a new situation (Apply), to draw connections among ideas (Analyze), and to support their decision (Evaluate). We consider the cognitive skill needed here similar to the inclusive skill Newman [17] defined as "thoughtfulness" since it is based on the ability to reason, the tendency to reflect, and the curiosity to explore new questions.

3.4 Question 4: Inheritance

Question 4 relates to a project that involves inheritance and includes classes *AA*, *BB*, and *Program*. The question focuses on the use of *this* as the "name" of a method when calling for a self-different constructor method in the same class, which itself calls a *super* constructor. Students were asked to follow the execution of the *main* method by drawing a trace table, displaying the program output, and further to determine what does the *this* refer to in four different marked instructions when executing the particular object creation in the *main* method: *BB b = new BB();*. The constructors of class *BB* are presented in Table 4.

Table 4. The constructors of class *BB* in question 4.

Question code	Question wording

public class BB extends AA {
    public int y;
    public BB() {
        this(2); // line #3
    }
    public BB(int k) {
        super(k + 1);
        this.y = super.x + 1; // line #4
    }
}
	To what does the *this refer?*

Apart from using *this*, the question is considered as difficult since it is in the context of inheritance, a field that is known to be difficult to understand for learners [15].

Interpretation by Bloom's taxonomy: similar to question 3, answering the question requires a combination of high-order thinking skills: 3 - Apply, 4 - Analyze, and 5 - Evaluate. Students need to use and interpret previous knowledge in new and complicated situations (Apply), to draw connections among ideas (Analyze), and to support their decision (Evaluate). Here as well is a place to mention the inclusive skill "thoughtfulness" [17].

3.5 Question 5: Open Comprehension Question

Question 5 is an open comprehension question, where students need to give written answers that conceptualize their knowledge, conceptions, and perceptions. The question clauses appear in Table 5.

Table 5. Question 5.

Question wording
(a) When must *this* be used?
(b) When should *this* be used?
(c) When shouldn't *this* be used?
(d) What is *this*?

The question requires students to conceptualize their insights in writing and therefore to formalize their own understandings. Actually, the question is a summary of the understanding that was sharpened while answering the questionnaire. It enables the presentation of knowledge that became clear while answering the previous questions, especially on the basis of justifying their responses. The answers to clauses (a)–(c) can be formulated accurately and briefly. But clause (d) brings students to present their "pure" conception about the concept of "object" that is manifested in the *this* notation – that crucial central concept in OOP.

4 Summary

The paper presents a diagnostic tool for examining students' conceptions and perceptions regarding the current object *this*. The questionnaire is written in Java, but can easily translate to any OOP languages. The different questions in the questionnaire highlight wide and various aspects of the use of *this*, which actually reflects the understanding of the "Object" concept on which the OOP approach is based. Some questions related to basic aspects while other request to interact with new ideas and advanced aspects.

Regarding Bloom's taxonomy, all the questions reflect *High-Order Cognitive Skills*, most of them express 4 - analysis, 5 - synthesis, and 6 - evaluation. Students were asked to justify their decision, to distinguish between several options, to apply knowledge when developing new code, and more. Addressing complex and non-trivial questions, which do not usually appear in learning materials, allows accuracy and refinement of the understanding. Since the concept of "Object" is known to be abstract and difficult to grasp, as many previous researches showed, direct discussion about it in the teaching process is recommended. Students' success in completing the questionnaire indicates significant understanding of core OOP concepts.

We regard the tool as a learning tool and not as an assessment tool, even though it can serve to assess students' knowledge and conceptions. The questionnaire can be used as a tool for learning – *Assessment for and as Learning*. Students can answer it as an inquiry task, examine their understanding, check and run the codes on a computer, and reduce the gap between what they understand currently and better accurate knowledge. This approach corresponds to the second and significant type of questions Paul and Elder [19] defined, questions students practice and experiment with themselves in problem-solving processes that lead them to reflective, critical, and judgmental thinking. Educators can use it in the *Learning from Errors* approach. Students can interrupt their own mistakes, and educators can lead advanced discussion in the classroom on case studies of errors in order to promote significant and in-depth understanding. Discussions of errors have the potential to promote understanding as found particularly regarding OOP concepts in Ginat and Shmallo's [12] research. From an educational point of view, we believe that it is better to introduce students to contexts that compel them to validate their knowledge and attitudes with "reality". Such type of learning creates a conflict between prior knowledge and required knowledge, stimulates metacognitive thinking processes, and enables meaningful learning in accordance with the constructivism approach. In practice, enabling students to express the inclusive skill "thoughtfulness" defined by Newman [17], which is based on the ability to reason, the tendency to reflect, the curiosity to explore new questions, and the flexibility to consider alternative and original solutions.

The tool was applied with high school students and college students (N = 163) and also with high school teachers (N = 48), and was refined to the current version. The findings from the students' responses were surprising, meaning that significant aspects of misunderstanding were indeed revealed. Parts of the results were published in our previous paper [23]. Beyond the systematic analysis of students' answers, two aspects can be considered. First, students expressed satisfaction since they felt that they expanded their knowledge and sharpened their conceptions. Moreover, they felt that they learned during filling out the questionnaire. Second, students complained about the length of the questionnaire; hence, we recommend to split it and to not use all the questions in a row.

We believe that using this diagnostic tool can promote any teaching-learning process. In particular it advances students' understanding about the OOP core concept "Object", and emphasizes the different options of using the *this* reference or rather omit it. In general the type of the questionnaire can be used to diagnose other crucial concepts as well.

Appendix A: The Questionnaire

Question 1: Where *this* is needed

The following is a project that includes a simple class *Date*, a composed class *Flight* and a main class *Program*.

```
public class Date {

   private int day;
   private int month;
   private int year;

   public Date(int day, int month, int year) {
      this.day = day;                  // line #1
      this.month = month;
      this.year = year;
   }

   public Date(Date other) {
      this.day = other.day;            // line #2
      this.month = other.month;
      this.year = other.year;
   }

   public String toString() {
      return this.day + "/" + this.month + "/" + this.year;          // line #3
   }

   public boolean equals(Date other) {
      if (this.day == other.day && this.month == other.month
                          && this.year == other.year)          // line #4
         return true;
      return false;
   }
}
```

```
public class Flight {

   private int seats;
   private int booked;
   private Date flightDate;
   private String flightNum;

   public Flight(int seats, Date flightDate, String flightNum)  {
      this.seats = seats;
      this.booked = 0;
      this.flightDate = new Date(flightDate);
      this.flightNum = flightNum;
   }
```

```
    public Flight(Flight other) {
        this.seats = other.seats;
        this.booked = other.booked;
        this.flightDate = new Date(other.flightDate);
        this.flightNum = other.flightNum;
    }

    public String toString() {
        return ("Date : " + this.flightDate + "\nFlightNum  " :
                        + this. flightNum + "\nCapacity :"+ this.seats + "\nBooked   " :
                        + this.booked + "\n;)"
    }

    public boolean equals(Flight other) {
        if (this.flightDate.equals(other.flightDate)
                    && this. flightNum==other.flightNum)
            return true;
        return false;
    }
}
```

```
public class Program {
    public static void main(String[] args) {
        Date date1 = new Date(1, 3, 2013);
        Date date2 = new Date(3, 3, 2013);
        Flight flight001 = new Flight(100, date1, "F83838");
        Flight flight002 = new Flight(150, date2, "R38383");
        Flight flight003 = new Flight(flight001);
        System.out.println(flight003);

        if (flight001.equals(flight002))          // line #5
            System.out.println(flight001 + "," + flight002 + " are alternative flights");
        else
            System.out.println(flight001 + "," + flight002 + " are not alternative flights");
        if (flight001.equals(flight003))
            System.out.println(flight001 + "," + flight003 + " are alternative flights");
        else
            System.out.println(flight001 + "," + flight003 + " are not alternative flights");
    }
}
```

(a) In relation to the rows marked with numbers 1–4 (//line #n) determine where *this* is required to be used and where it is superfluous. Explain the reason for each of your choices.
(b) When executing instruction #5 in the *main* method, to what does the *this* in the *equals* method in class *Flight* refer?
(c) Develop a *static* method replacing the instance method *equals* in class *Date*.
(d) Can *this* be used in the code of the *main* method?

Question 2: Personal preferences on using *this* in code

Each of the following methods relate to class *Point* described by two coordinates (x,y). Some of the methods use *this* and some do not. The methods of each clause execute the same task, and they are all syntactically correct. Please rank in each line marked by (a)–(d) your personal preference codes by assigning numbers between 1 and 3, where 1 is your first priority. Explain your choices.

	Version1	Version2	Version3

(a)	public class Point {
	private int x = 0;
	private int y = 0;
	public Point() {
	}
	}
		public class Point {
		private int x;
		private int y;
		public Point() {
		this.x = 0;
		this.y = 0;
		}
		}
			public class Point {
			private int x;
			private int y;
			public Point() {
			x = 0;
			y = 0;
			}
			}

(b)	public class Point {
	private int x;
	private int y;
	public Point(int x1,
	int y1) {
	x = x1;
	y = y1;
	}
	}
		public class Point {
		private int x;
		private int y;
		public Point(int x,
		int y) {
		this.x = x;
		this.y = y;
		}
		}	

(c)	public class Point {
	private int x;
	private int y;
	public Point(Point p) {
	this.x = p.getX();
	this.y = p.getY();
	}
	}
		public class Point {
		private int x;
		private int y;
		public Point(Point p) {
		this.x = p.x;
		this.y = p.y;
		}
		}
			public class Point {
			private int x;
			private int y;
			public Point(Point p) {
			x = p.x;
			y = p.y;
			}
			}

(d)	public class Point {
	private int x;
	private int y;
	public boolean
	equals(Point p) {
	return
	this.x==p.getX()
	&&
	this.y==p.getY();
	}
	}
		public class Point {
		private int x;
		private int y;
		public boolean
		equals(Point p) {
		return
		this.toString().
		equals(p.toString());
		}
		}
			public class Point {
			private int x;
			private int y;
			public boolean
			equals(Point p) {
			return
			toString().equals
			(p.toString());
			}
			}

Question 3: Using *this* as a parameter

The following is a project that includes a simple class *Circle* and a main class *Test*. Some of the methods of class *Circle* include only the method signature without the method full body. The method *drawX(...)* accepts a circle as a parameter and draws it, the method *drawFlower(...)* accepts a circle as a parameter and draws a flower consisting of circles, and the method *chooseWhatToDraw(...)* accepts a circle and a character and determines what to draw.

```
public class Circle {

    private int diameter;
    private int xPosition;
    private int yPosition;
    private String color;

    public Circle(int diameter, int xPosition, int yPosition, String color) {
        this.diameter = diameter;
        this.xPosition = xPosition;
        this.yPosition = yPosition;
        this.color = color;
    }

    private void drawX(Circle c) {
        //
    }

    private void drawFlower(Circle c) {
        //
    }

    public void chooseWhatToDraw(char c, Circle circ) {
        if (c == 'F')
            drawFlower(this);
        if (c == 'X')
            drawX(circ);
    }
}
```

```
public class Tester {

    public static void main(String[] args) {
        Circle circle1 = new Circle(10, 100, 100, "yellow");
        Circle circle2 = new Circle(10, 100, 100, "magenta");
        circle1.chooseWhatToDraw('F', circle2);
    }
}
```

In relation to the *main* method, and the execution of the instruction:

$$circle1.chooseWhatToDraw('F', circle2);$$

to what does the *this* appearing in the method *chooseWhatToDraw(...)* in the instruction *drawFlower(this);* refer?

Question 4: Using *this* in inheritance

The following is a project that includes classes *AA*, *BB*, and *Program*. Review the classes and answer the questions that follow.

```
public class AA {
    public int x;
    public AA()              { this(1); }                    // line #1
    public AA(int k)         { this.x = k * 10; }            // line #2
    public String toString() { return "x = " + x; }
}
```

```
public class BB extends AA {
    public int y;
    public BB()              { this(2); }                                  // line #3
    public BB(int k)         { super(k + 1); this.y = super.x + 1; }       // line #4
    public String toString() { return "x = " + x + " y = " + y; }
}
```

```
public class Program {
    public static void main() {
        AA a = new AA();
        System.out.println(a);
        BB b = new BB();
        System.out.println(b);
    }
}
```

Follow the execution of the *main* method, and:

(a) Use a trace table to present all variables' values and all objects, including the objects' attributes values.
(b) Display the program output.
(c) In relation to the rows marked with numbers 1–4 (//line #n) determine to what does the *this* refer, when executing the next instruction:

$$BB\, b = new\, BB();$$

Question 5: Using *this* – an open comprehension question

Please answer the following questions briefly:

(a) When must *this* be used?
(b) When should *this* be used?
(c) When shouldn't *this* be used?
(d) What is *this*?

References

1. Anderson, L., Krathwohl, D.A.: Taxonomy for Learning, Teaching and Assessing: A Revision of Bloom's Taxonomy of Educational Objectives. Longman, New York (2001)
2. Bloom, B.S.: Taxonomy of Educational Objectives Handbook I - The Cognitive Domain. David McKay Co., Inc., New York (1956)
3. Borasi, R.: Reconceiving Mathematics Instruction: A Focus on Errors. Ablex Publishing, New York (1996)
4. Borasi, R.: Using errors as springboards for the learning of mathematics: an introduction. Focus Learn. Probl. Math. **7**(3), 1–14 (1985)
5. Brown, S: Assessment for learning. Learn. Teach. High. Educ. **1**, 81–89 (2005). ISSN 1742-240X
6. Chen, C., Cheng, S., Lin, J.M.: A study of misconceptions and missing conceptions of Novice Java programmers. In: Proceedings of the 2012 International Conference on Frontiers in Education, pp. 307–313. Computer Science & Computer Engineering (2012)
7. Confrey, J.: What constructivism implies for teaching. J. Res. Math. Educ. **4**, 107–122 (1990)
8. Earl, L.M.: Assessment as Learning: Using Classroom Assessment to Maximize Student Learning, 2nd edn. Corwin, Thousand Oaks (2012)
9. Eckerdal, A., Thun', M.: Novice Java programmers' conceptions of "object" and "class", and variation theory. SIGCSE Bull. **37**(3), 89–93 (2005)
10. Gardner, L., Sheridan, D., White, D.: A web-based learning and assessment system to support flexible education. J. Comput. Assist. Learn. **18**, 125–136 (2002)
11. Garner, S., Haden, P., Robins, A.: My program is correct but it doesn't run: a preliminary investigation of novice programmers' problems. In: Proceeding of ACE 2005 (Australasian Computing Education Conference), pp. 173–180 (2005)
12. Ginat, D., Shmallo, R.: Constructive use of errors in teaching CS1. In: SIGCSE 2013-Proceedings of 44th ACM Technical Symposium on Computer Science Education, pp. 353–358. ACM New York (2013)
13. Holland, S., Griffiths, R., Woodman, M.: Avoiding object misconceptions. SIGCSE Bull. **29**(1), 131–134 (1997)
14. Kaczmarczyk, L.C., Petrick, E.R., East, J.P., Herman, G.L.: Identifying student misconceptions of programming. In: Proceedings of the 41st ACM Technical Symposium on Computer Science Education (SIGCSE 2010), New York, pp. 107–111 (2010)
15. Liberman, N., Beeri, C., and Ben-David Kolikant, Y.: Difficulties in learning inheritance and polymorphism. ACM Trans. Comput. Educ. **11**(1), 23 (2011). Article 4
16. Melis, E., Sander, A., Tsovaltzi, D.: How to support meta-cognitive skills for finding and correcting errors. In: Proceedings of the AAAI Fall 2010 Symposium, pp. 64–68 (2010)
17. Newman, F.M.: Higher order thinking in teaching social studies: A rationale for the assessment of classroom thoughtfulness. J. Curric. Stud. **22**, 41–56 (1990)
18. Ohlsson, S.: Learning from performance errors. Psychol. Rev. **103**, 241–262 (1996)
19. Paul, R., Elder, L.: The Thinker's Guide to the Nature and Functions of Critical and Creative Thinking. Foundation for Critical Thinking Press (2008). http://www.criticalthinking.org/files/CCThink_6.12.08.pdf
20. Pinkerton, K.D.: Learning from errors. Phys. Teach. **43**(8), 510–513 (2005)
21. Ragonis, N., Ben-Ari, M.: A long-term investigation of the comprehension of OOP concepts by novices. Comput. Sci. Educ. **15**(3), 203–221 (2005)
22. Ragonis, N., Ben-Ari, M.: On understanding the statics and dynamics of object-oriented programs. SIGCSE Bull. **37**(1), 226–230 (2005)

23. Ragonis, N., Shmallo, R.: On the (Mis) Understanding of the "this" reference. In: Proceedings of the 2017 ACM SIGCSE Technical Symposium on Computer Science Education (SIGCSE 2017), pp. 489–494. ACM, New York (2017)
24. Resnick, L.: Education and Leaning to Think. National Academy Press, Washington D.C (1987)
25. Sajaniemi, J., Kuittinen, M., Tikansalo, T.: A study of the development of students' visualizations of program state during an elementary object-oriented programming course. In: Proceedings of the 3rd International Workshop on Computing Education Research (ICER 2007), pp. 1–16. ACM, New York (2007)
26. Sanders, K., Boustendt, J., Eckerdal, A., McCartney, R., Mostrɤm, J. E., Thomas, L., Zander, C.: Student understanding of Object-Oriented programming as expressed in concept maps. In: Proceedings of SIGCSE 2008, pp. 332–336 (2008)
27. Sanders, K., Thomas, L.: Checklists for grading object-oriented CS1 programs: concepts and misconceptions. SIGCSE Bull. **39**(3), 166–170 (2007)
28. Shmallo, R., Ragonis, N., Ginat, D.: Fuzzy OOP: expanded and reduced term interpretations. In: Proceedings of ITiCSE 2012, pp. 309–314. ACM Press, New York (2012)
29. Sorva, J.: The same but different – students' understandings of primitive and object variables. In: Proceedings of the 8th International Conference on Computing Education Research (Koli Calling 2008), New York, pp. 5–15 (2008)
30. Sorva, J.: Students' understandings of storing objects. In: Lister, R., Simon (eds.) Proceedings of the Seventh Baltic Sea Conference on Computing Education Research (Koli Calling 2007), Koli National Park, Finland, CRPIT, vol. 88, pp. 127–135. ACS (2007)
31. Teif, M., Hazzan, O.: Partonomy and taxonomy in object-oriented thinking: Junior high school students' perceptions of object-oriented basic concepts. In Working Group Reports on ITiCSE on Innovation and Technology in Computer Science Education (ITiCSE-WGR 2006), pp. 55–60. ACM, New York (2006)
32. Xinogalos, S: Object-oriented design and programming: an investigation of novices' conceptions on objects and classes. ACM Trans. Comput. Educ. **15**(3) (2015). Article 13
33. Yerushalmi, E., Polingher, C.: Guiding students to learn from mistakes. Phys. Educ. **41**, 532–538 (2006)
34. Zohar, A.: The nature and development of teachers' meta-strategic knowledge in the context of teaching higher order thinking. J. Learn. Sci. **15**, 331–377 (2006)
35. Zohar, A., Ben David, A.: Explicit teaching of meta-strategic knowledge in authentic classroom situations. Metacognition Learn. **3**(1), 59–82 (2008)

On Preferences of Novice Software Engineering Students: Temperament Style and Attitudes Towards Programming Activities

Tatjana Jevsikova(✉), Valentina Dagienė, and Vladimiras Dolgopolovas

Vilnius University Institute of Data Science and Digital Technologies, Akademijos 4, 04812 Vilnius, Lithuania
{tatjana.jevsikova,valentina.dagiene, vladimiras.dolgopolovas}@mii.vu.lt

Abstract. Educators' experience shows that learning programming is in many aspects problematic for novice software engineering students. On the other hand, software engineering processes and the view of programming has been changing during the recent years. In this paper, we address socio-cognitive aspects of computer science and software engineering in order to contribute to programming education enhancement: the research is focused on students' temperament style and favorite programming learning activities. The study of 158 first and second year students, studying programming specialties in five higher education institutions, has been presented. The "psychological portrait" of the surveyed students reflects the evolution of the temperament style in programming during last decades. The attitudes towards the programming activities, presented in this paper, may contribute to the development of enhancement of existing programming courses in higher education.

Keywords: Temperament style and programming
Personal characteristics and programming · Programming students
Novice programmers

1 Introduction

The topic we address in this article originally stems from the problem we face as educators: novice software engineering students have difficulties in learning programming. This often leads to students' dissatisfaction, failure and high drop-out rates. This problem has numerous roots. Most usually mentioned important factors for the successful completion of programming courses, besides one's abilities, are time consumption and motivation [1, 2]. Therefore, factors that motivate students to learn programming are important to know. An important reason is instruction type (in many cases has remained the same in upper secondary school since the beginning of the 1970s, which could be the rationales for the difficulties in learning and teaching computer programming) [3].

S. N. Pozdniakov and V. Dagienė (Eds.): ISSEP 2018, LNCS 11169, pp. 101–113, 2018.
https://doi.org/10.1007/978-3-030-02750-6_8

On the other hand, we observe changing trends in what students wish and how students learn programming: application-oriented programming, programming as combining and modifying pre-made components, and sharing programming projects [4].

With this research we wish to better understand socio-cognitive aspects of computer science in order to enhance learning and teaching programming, and to help students make carrier choices. In this study, we examine novice software engineering students' temperament style (in some publications addressed to as personality types or personality traits) and students' preferences towards programming activities in learning programming, and possible relations within them. The study presented here contributes to the knowledge on the topic in several aspects. First, it presents a "psychological portrait" of novice software engineering students and helps to observe the evolution of the temperament style in programming during last decades. Second, the study presents Lithuanian case of temperament style distribution among programming students and therefore reflects cultural differences. Third, we analyze the most attractive programming tasks for students in conjunction with temperament style.

The rest of the paper is organized as follows. In Sect. 2 we discuss the main research points done on temperament style in programming and software engineering. Then we present the study conducted among first and second year students, studying programming (software engineering) specialties in five higher education institutions. In the next following sections we present results, discuss them, state the limitations of our research, make conclusions and formulate directions for further research.

2 Background

2.1 Temperament Styles

Researchers show interest in studying programmers' personal characteristics since the start of the growth of demand in programmer's profession and since the instruments to study personality types have been developed, i.e. since 1970s. There are many instruments to describe and assess personal characteristics (temperament styles). As systematic literature review on personality type in programming shows [5], the most popular instrument to describe and measure temperament style is Myers-Briggs type indicator (MBTI), based on Jung's type theory [6]. According to this type indicator, personal preferences are classified according to four dimensions (dichotomies):

Extraversion (E) or Introversion (I). This dimension describes favorite world of the person. Extraverts prefer to focus on the outer world of people and things, while Introvert's attention is focused on the inner world of ideas, emotions and impressions.

Sensing (S) or Intuition (N). This dimension describes preferences of information processing. People who prefer sensing like to take in information that is real and tangible, observe what is happening around them, and they are especially attuned to practical realities. People who prefer intuition take in information by seeing the big picture, focusing on relations and connections between facts, and grasping patterns, and are especially attuned to new possibilities.

Thinking (T) or Feeling (F). This dimension shows how one prefers to make decisions. People who prefer thinking like to look at the logical consequences of the choice or action, and they draw conclusions or make judgments dispassionately and analytically. People who prefer feeling like to consider what is important to them and others involved, they weight human factors, and place themselves into the situation.

Judging (J) or Perceiving (P). This dimension reflects preferences to the structure. Judging means preference to live in a planned, orderly way, and seeking to regulate and manage his/her life. People who prefer perceiving like to live in flexible, spontaneous way, seeking to experience and understand life, rather than to control it.

MBTI person's style is described by the combination of these four preferences of the person, e.g. ENFJ and ISTP. In total, there are 16 type indicators. The authors of the instrument emphasize that the types (styles) cannot be accepted as labels since they are rather a person's preferences, as can be compared to the preference of writing using right or left hand.

According to Myers et al. [6], the combination of how the person prefers to process information (S or N) and make decision (T or F) influences career interests and choices. Analyzing descriptions, provided by the authors of MBTI, the combination of NT might be most suitable for a programmer (software engineer) specialty: focusing on possibilities, applying theoretical concepts and systems, being logical and analytical, finding the scope of their interests in theoretical and technical frameworks like physical sciences, research, management, computers, law, engineering, and technical work. Another described combination that maps with general software engineering tasks might be ST, which focuses on facts, applying objective analysis and experience, tending to be practical and analytical, and finding their scope of interest in technical skills in objects and facts, for example within applied sciences, business, administration, banking, law enforcement, production, and construction. The kind of work a person chooses within the field may relate to the Extraversion–Introversion preference. The way how people organize and complete the tasks of the particular job is influenced by the Judging–Perceiving preference.

2.2 Temperament Styles in Software Engineering

The influence of personality in the education of a software engineer is seen by some researchers as a key factor for successful learning [5]. Researchers are therefore seeking to understand how teaching practices and styles can be tailored to specific student temperament styles to improve learning process.

Previous studies, done in programmers' temperament style, have shown that the dominating dimensions among programmers are Introverts (I) over Extraverts (E), Thinking (T) over Feeling (F), and Judging (J) over Perceiving (P). The percentage of Sensing (S) and Intuitive (N) programmers are approximately equal [7]. A detailed summary of personality type distribution in research done on this topic during the last 40 years is given in [5].

However, there are contradictory results regarding the relation between students' temperament style and academic success. Some report that individual personality helps to predict academic performance in programming [8–10]. Others report that personality traits were not a significant factor in predicting academic success [11–13].

Even if there have been skeptical views on the ability of MBTI test to predict success in professional area, and additional factors such as passion, professional experience and financial rewards have been highlighted [14], personality type indicator is successfully used by many researchers and is a helpful tool to learn about professional preferences in order to predict in which area a person's motivation might be stronger [7].

Capretz and Ahmed suggest mapping of temperament styles with software engineering tasks [7]. In their research, the authors split the software engineering job into categories (system analyst, software designer, etc.), formulate job requirements for each category and skill required, and connect MBTI dimensions with every skill.

A broad range of personality types is beneficial to software engineering, especially during the visible changes we observe in programming and its education.

2.3 Observing Changes in Programming Education

The capacity to code has been conceived for many years as a trait that an individual is born with rather than as a craft that one can learn [15]. However, the diversity of software engineering tasks is increasing: the skills necessary to successfully work in this area 30 years ago might no longer apply. For instance, software design has become much more than manipulating formal notations—it now revolves around the interaction between designers and users [7].

During recent years, coding has been referenced to as a new literacy, alongside with reading and writing [16]. Educators recognize significant shifts in (a) what students are interested in programming, (b) the contexts in which they do it, and (c) how they do it [4]. Kafai and Burke [4] highlight three dimensions, and in their more recent publication [15] add a fourth dimension of social shift in programming education:

1. *A shift from code to actual applications.* Attention is focused on the application project being programmed and not on the programming language and its syntax.
2. *A shift from tools to communities.* A supportive and resourceful community is, in fact, a tool in and of itself, and learning is built around these communities.
3. *A shift from starting from scratch to remixing.* The goal is not to build an entirely new program but rather to leverage existing resources to improve and reimagine content.
4. *A shift from screens to tangibles.* The question is no longer what is on your screen but what is in your hands. Students learn programming a variety of devices.

Originally, these dimensions are addressing K-12 programming. In this paper, we base on the dimensions of social shift in order to learn which types of programming activities seem most attractive for university 1st–2nd year students, and whether programming preferences are connected with temperament style.

3 Research Methodology

In this study, we utilize quantitative statistical research methods, including multivariate methods (factor analysis) and non-parametric statistics. To detect students' temperament style we use the Student Styles Questionnaire (SSQ) test, officially approved in Lithuania. The study has been conducted by researchers in computer science, education and psychology areas. The following **Research Questions** are posed in our study.

RQ1: What is the distribution of temperament styles among novice software engineering students?
RQ2: What are the students' attitudes towards different programming tasks?
RQ3: How are programming student's temperament style and attitudes toward programming activities related?

3.1 Respondents

In total, 158 students studying in five higher education institutions took part in the study. These higher education institutions include three Universities and two Universities of Applied Sciences, located in four different cities of Lithuania.

The study was conducted in 2 stages. The first stage was carried out with 30 students (80% males and 20% females), studying programming-related specialties in one of the Universities of Applied Sciences. The participants were those students who expressed motivation to work as programmers in future and indicated their wish to take part in the study. Among them, 23 were first year students, 6 students studied their second year, and 1 student was a third year student. 90% of the respondents were 19–22 years old.

During the second stage, the study was continued with 128 students, studying first or second year in programming-related study programs. 119 of them were University students, 9 studied in the University of Applied Sciences. Male students made up 82.8% of the respondents and female students 17.2%. 94% of the respondents were 19–22 years old. The participation in the study was on a voluntary basis, and the main selection criteria of participants in this stage therefore was a student's expressed interest in the study, which was shortly presented to the students.

Students' average score in completed programming courses was 7.7 out of 10, with median = 8.

In this paper, we analyze general results of the 2 stages, i.e. of total 158 respondents, not detailing into differences between the groups of stage 1 and stage 2 due to the differences in the group size.

3.2 Instrument

In order to define student's temperament style and answer Research Question 1, we used SSQ (Student Styles Questionnaire), patterned after the original Jungian constructs that were popularized by Myers and Briggs [17]. The SSQ instrument is adopted in Lithuania by the psychologists, so the respondents filled in the questionnaire in their native language. The questionnaire consists of 90 questions and requiring to select one of the two suggested answers for each question. As MBTI instrument, the Student Styles Questionnaire measures preferences rather than actual behaviors.

SSQ uses 4 dimensions: Extraverted (E) or Introverted (I), Practical (P) or Imaginative (I), Thinking (T) or Feeling (F), and Organized (O) or Flexible (F). These dimensions correspond to the same concepts of the MBTI instrument, described in Sect. 2.1. For simplicity and compatibility reasons with other published research, further in this paper we "convert" SSQ labels into MBTI, i.e., we use MBTI dimension labels, corresponding to the same construct as SSQ labels.

In order to answer Research Question 2, we used a questionnaire developed collaboratively by the authors of this paper. The statements were developed taking into account the dimensions of social shift in programming, discussed in Sect. 2.3. The participants of the study had to evaluate each statement using the 5-item Likert scale ("totally disagree", "disagree", "neither agree, nor disagree", "agree", "totally agree"). The questionnaire was made out of 14 statements and was intended to learn about students' preferences toward the main programming tasks (activities). The students' had to think about the question "Programming assignment (programming project) tasks I like" and rate presented statements using the 5-point Likert scale. The questionnaire is presented below.

Programming Assignment Tasks (Activities) I Like
Please rate each statement from 1 (totally disagree) to 5 (totally agree):

Q1. To make a program's plan
Q2. To search for possible programming solutions on the Internet
Q3. To code (write program's text)
Q4. To learn programming language syntax and programming constructions
Q5. To look for errors in programs developed by other people
Q6. To debug each step of a program
Q7. To compose a program out of ready-made blocks
Q8. To develop a program's graphical user interface
Q9. To develop a program that one can apply (e.g. game, mobile app)
Q10. To develop a program in collaboration with group-mates (working in pair/group)
Q11. To lead a group and to delegate roles in a group working on a programming task
Q12. To discuss selected solution methods with my group-mates/professor
Q13. To discuss selected solution methods in social networks and/or forums
Q14. To share programs I develop (e.g. on social networks or other websites).

4 Results

4.1 Temperament Style Distribution Among Students

In the group of students who took part in the research (both stages, N = 158), Introvert, Visual style (Intuitive), Thinking and Organized (Judging) styles dominate (Table 1).

Table 1. Temperament style dimension distribution

Dimension	Number (%)	Dimension	Number (%)
Extraversion	58 (36.7%)	Introversion	100 (63.3%)
Practical (Sensing, MBTI)	75 (47.5%)	Visual style (Intuitive, MBTI)	83 (52.5%)
Thinking	126* (79.7%)	Feeling	56* (35.4%)
Organised (Judging, MBTI)	99 (62.7%)	Flexible (Perceiving, MBTI)	59 (37.3%)

*24 respondents have the same value for Thinking and Feeling dimension

The SSQ instrument allows to have T = F, which differs from the MBTI. Our results show that 24 students have got equal values for the T and F dimensions. Therefore, we included these types twice into the diagram.

The temperament style "portrait" of the students is presented in Fig. 1.

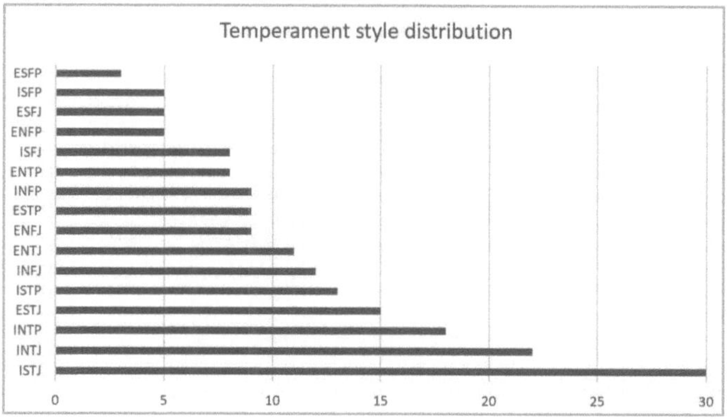

Fig. 1. Temperament style distribution among the students (N = 158 + 24 due to those 24 with T = F)

As we can see, the dominating types are ISTJ (16.5%), INTJ (12%), INTP (9.9%), ESTJ (8.2%), and ISTP (7.1%).

Most frequent temperaments (the pairs of dimensions) are presented in Table 2 below. The asterisk on the right of the number marks respondents who received equal value for T and F. We see that Introverts and Thinking as well as Thinking and Judging combinations are the most frequent.

Table 2. Dominant temperament among students, N = 158

Temperament	Quantity	%	Temperament	Quantity	%
SJ	50	31.6	TJ	78 = 65 + 13*	49.4
NT	59 = 48 + 11*	37.3	TP	48 = 37 + 11*	30.4
IJ	63	39.9	IN	53	33.5
ST	67 = 54 + 13*	42.4	IT	83 = 66 +17*	52.5
NJ	49	31.0			

*T = F

If we compare temperament style and average score in programming subjects (10-point system), we see that the highest score belongs to INTJ type students (mean = 8.4, std. deviation = 1.2, number of students = 22), INFJ (mean = 8.3, std. deviation = 0.8, number of students = 12), and ISTJ (mean = 8.2, std. deviation = 1.2, number of students = 30).

4.2 Attitudes Towards Programming Tasks

The results on rating statements on the favorite programming tasks (full questionnaire is presented in Sect. 3.2) are shown in Fig. 2.

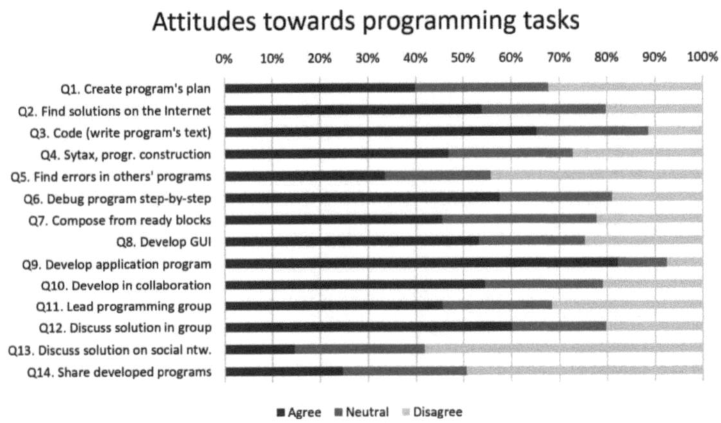

Fig. 2. Attitudes towards programming tasks in terms of whether the students agree to liking the task

The activity most liked by the students was *developing programs one can apply* (e.g. game, mobile app) (82.3% answered *totally agree* or *agree* to liking the task). A majority of the students (65.2%) positively evaluated *coding* (writing program's text) as a task they like. Another activity liked by the students *was discussing programming solution in group (with their group-mates, professor)* (liked by 60.1% of the students). 57.6% of respondents liked *debugging program step-by-step*. The majority of students (54.4%) positively evaluate *collaborative programming projects* in groups. 53.8% of respondents like *searching for programming solution on the Internet. Developing graphical user interface* is a task liked by 53.2% of the respondents.

4.3 Relations of Students' Temperament Style and Programming Activity Preferences

In order to examine dependencies between students' temperament style and preferences on programming activities (tasks), exploratory factor analysis has been performed. Factor analysis aims at identifying clusters of items for which responses for the questionnaire on preferable programming tasks (Sect. 3.2) had common patterns of variation. Each factor is denoted by a group of variables whose members correlate more highly among themselves than they do with variables not included in the factor. As a result, there were 3 factors identified for the attitudes towards programming tasks.

Table 3 shows the results of the factor analysis of the part of the study regarding students' attitudes towards programming tasks and the 3 factors identified: *Tasks requiring analysis* (decomposition into steps) (includes questions Q2, Q3, Q4, Q5, Q6); *Product creation tasks* (Q1, Q7, Q8, Q9, Q10), and *Tasks requiring social interaction* (Q11, Q12, Q13, Q14).

Table 3. The results of factor analysis on the attitudes towards programming tasks

Question	Factors		
	F1. Tasks requiring analysis (decomposition into steps)	F2. Product creation tasks	F3. Tasks requiring social interaction
Q1	0.283	0.216	**0.351**
Q2	**0.649**	0.202	0.118
Q3	**0.608**	0.233	0.054
Q4	**0.852**	0.058	0.111
Q5	**0.708**	0.138	0.038
Q6	**0.806**	0.046	0.197
Q7	0.394	−0.034	**0.640**
Q8	0.005	−0.052	**0.787**
Q9	0.098	0.337	**0.564**
Q10	0.031	0.480	**0.650**
Q11	0.076	**0.598**	0.422
Q12	0.255	**0.623**	0.295
Q13	0.207	**0.743**	−0.005
Q14	0.101	**0.675**	0.013

First, we looked at the ratings of each factor by each of the 16 different temperament styles. In the following analysis we have derived students' average ratings for each factor. Table 4 presents average ratings of each factor, and the highest ratings are written in bold font. The highest ratings correspond to students' ratings "Agree" or "Totally agree" (≥ 3.5).

Quite surprisingly, *tasks requiring analysis (decomposition)* were highly rated by quite diverse set of temperament styles: ENTJ, ENFJ, ENTP, ESTP, ISFP, ESTJ, INTJ, ISTJ. Several high ratings were given by students with Feeling (F) dimension, however this factor might be predicted as more preferable for Thinking (T) dimension. *Product creation task* was in general the most highly rated activity by any temperament style students. *Tasks, requiring social interaction*, not surprisingly, are more preferable for Extraverts: ESTJ, ESTP.

In order to find out if there were differences between the two "poles" of each personal style dimension (Introversion–Extraversion, Sensing–Intuitive, Thinking–Feeling, Judging–Perceiving), we have run Pearson's Chi squared and Fisher's Exact

Table 4. Average rating for factors by different temperament styles

Temp. Style	F1. Tasks, requiring analysis (decomposition into steps)	F2. Product creation tasks	F3. Tasks, requiring social interaction
ENFJ	**3.7**	**3.8**	3.3
ENFP	3.0	**3.6**	2.9
ENTJ	**3.9**	**4.0**	3.0
ENTP	**3.6**	**3.7**	3.1
ESFJ	2.6	**3.6**	2.8
ESFP	3.0	3.2	2.9
ESTJ	**3.5**	**3.8**	**3.6**
ESTP	**3.6**	3.4	**3.5**
INFJ	3.4	**3.9**	2.8
INFP	3.1	3.4	2.8
INTJ	**3.5**	**3.6**	2.9
INTP	3.1	3.2	2.6
ISFJ	3.1	**3.6**	2.6
ISFP	**3.6**	3.3	2.9
ISTJ	**3.5**	**3.6**	2.7
ISTP	3.1	3.1	2.6

tests for every factor. Null-hypothesis for each pair of groups was: *There are no significant difference between groups.* In order to count positive, negative or neutral answers, we counted average factor ratings falling into the appropriate interval (e.g. (3.5; 4.5] for "agree" and (4.5; 5] for "strongly agree"). The results of p-value counted for each dimension and each factor have shown that there was little significant difference between the answers of personality "opposite" dimension groups. Out of 12 results counted for 3 factor ratings by 4 dimension pairs, the null-hypothesis can be rejected only in two pairs of groups if we consider $p < 0.05$:

- There is significant difference between Judging and Perceiving groups' ratings of factor F2 (Product creation tasks). Pearson's Chi squared p-value = 0.0106, Fisher's Exact test p-value = 0.01124. Judging students tend to more positively evaluate product creation tasks.
- There is significant difference between Extravert and Introvert groups' ratings of factor F3 (Tasks, requiring social interaction). Pearson's Chi squared p-value = 0.0029, Fisher's Exact test p-value = 0.0038. Extraverts prefer more than Introverts tasks requiring a higher degree of social interaction.

The next step of our analysis was to see if there were significant differences between positive ratings of the 3 factors by groups of two "poles" of each personal dimension. However, no significant differences were found (p-value > 0.05). But if we use confidence level $\alpha < 0.1$, the difference is noticed between Extravert and Introvert positive ratings. Introverts tend to like tasks requiring analysis (F1) more than Extraverts, but Introverts tend to like tasks requiring social interaction (F3) less.

5 Discussion and Conclusion

The "psychological portrait" of novice software engineering students, surveyed in this study, is quite diverse. We see representatives of all 16 styles distinguished by the instrument we use. However, the dominating types among surveyed students are ISTJ, INTJ, INTP, ESTJ, and ISTP. This corresponds to the previous research in the area (the most frequent types reported among programmers are ISTJ, INTJ, and INTP), and confirms carrier preferences for software engineering described for perception and judgement dimension combinations NT and ST in [6]. The rarest types among surveyed students are ESFP, ISFP, ESFJ, and ENFP. The dominant dimension pairs among students are IT, TJ, ST, IJ, NT, IN, and SJ. The rarest temperaments are SF, EP, FP, EF, and SP. However, NF temperament, rarely present in other research results, was comparatively frequent in our case (22%). The diversity of types might appear for several reasons: (1) results reflect our exact case; (2) software engineering process and the view on programming have been changing, and this attracts students with various personal preferences to the programming specialty.

The two dimensions of social shift in programming education were confirmed by students' ratings of favorite programming tasks. The vast majority of students highly positively evaluated application-oriented programming tasks (82%), which confirms the first dimension of the social shift. 60% of students liked discussing programming solution in group (confirms the second dimension of the social shift). However, regarding discussions on programming tasks, students prefer face-to-face environment rather than discussing solutions on a social network, forum, etc. (positively rated only by 15% of the students). The majority of the students (65%) positively evaluated Coding (writing program's text) as a liked activity (which contradicted our expectations and the statement about the change that students like composing program out of ready-made blocks rather than to code from scratch (third dimension of social shift).

Tasks, requiring analysis (decompositions) were highly evaluated by different temperament styles (not only by those of Thinking preference). Therefore, we can make an assumption that the reason for such result might stem from the instruction methods dominating today in universities (with focus on coding, programming language and its syntax). Product creation task was in general the most highly rated activity by many temperament style students. However, judging (J) students tend to more positively evaluate product creation tasks than perceiving (P) students (possibly due to lack of planning for perceiving preference). Tasks, requiring social interaction, not surprisingly, are more preferable for Extraverts: ESTJ and ESTP.

Limitations of our study include the fact that only students who have shown interest in the study (the programming profession and/or personality of programmers) took part. Therefore, we see that the average score in programming-related subjects of the participants was relatively high (7.7 out of 10). The results might be different if we run this study among all students studying programming specialties.

The findings of little statistically significant differences between opposite pole groups of each personal preference dimension and programming task factor ratings let us formulate an assumption that regardless of personal preferences, students are affected by the social shift in programming education. This assumption makes us to rethink the ways we teach programming and develop appropriate programming course materials.

The future steps of the research include studying of factors that motivated students to select software engineering specialty, as well as relationships between motivational factors, academic performance, and programming task preferences. The data are under procession. The study, presented in this paper, should not be considered as research giving "universal" results that can be generalized, but more as a process that can be applied in other groups to shine light on socio-cognitive processes of the group and help to enhance programming education in order to help students with professional choices.

References

1. Kinnunen, P., Malmi, L.: Why students drop out CS1 course? In: Anderson, R., Fincher, S. A., Guzdial, M. (eds.) 2nd International Workshop on Computing Education Research. University of Kent, Canterbury, UK, 9–10 September 2006, pp. 97–108. ACM, New York (2006)
2. Konecki, M.: Problems in programming education and means of their improvement. In: DAAAM International Scientific Book 2014, Chap. 37, pp. 459–470 (2014)
3. Rolandsson, L.: Changing Computer programming education: the dinosaur that survived in school: an explorative study about educational issues based on teachers' beliefs and curriculum development in secondary school. In: LaTiCE 2013: Learning and Teaching in Computing and Engineering, Macau, China. IEEE (2013)
4. Kafai, Y.B., Burke, Q.: The Social turn in K-12 programming: moving from computational thinking to computational participation. In: SIGCSE 2013: Proceeding of the 44th ACM Technical Symposium on Computer Science Education, pp. 603–608 (2013)
5. Cruz, S., da Silva, F.Q.B., Capretz, L.F.: Forty years of research on personality in software engineering: a mapping study. Comput. Hum. Behav. **46**, 94–113 (2015)
6. Myers, I.B., McCaulley, M.H., Quenk, N.L., Hammer, A.L.: MBTI Manual. A Guide to the Development and Use of the Myers-Briggs Type Indicator. Consulting Psychologists Press, Palo Alto (1998)
7. Capretz, L.F., Ahmed, F.: Making sense of software development and personality types. IEEE IT Prof. **12**(1), 6–13 (2010)
8. Layman, L.: Changing students' perceptions: an analysis of the supplementary benefits of collaborative software development. In: CSEET 2006: Proceedings of the 19th Conference on Software Engineering Education and Training, pp. 159–166. IEEE (2006)
9. Alspaugh, C.: Identification of some components of computer programming aptitude. J. Res. Math. Educ. **3**, 89–98 (1972)
10. Pocius, K.E.: Personality factors in human–computer interaction: a review of the literature. Comput. Hum. Behav. **7**, 103–135 (1991)
11. Golding, P., Facey-Shaw, L., Tennant, V.: Effects of peer tutoring, attitude and personality on academic performance of first year introductory programming students. In: 36th Annual Frontiers in Education Conference, pp. 7–12. IEEE (2006)
12. Lutes, K., Alka, H., Purdum, J. Do introverts perform better in computer programming courses? In: Proceedings of the American Society for Engineering Education Conference, pp. 12255–12263 (2009)

13. Corman, L.: Cognitive style, personality type, and learning ability as factors in predicting the success of the beginning programming student. ACM SIGCSE Bull. **18**, 80–89 (1986)
14. Norman, L.K., Weinberg, J., Coplien, J.: Call for the rational use of personality indicators. Computer **31**, 146–147 (1998)
15. Burke, Q., O'Byrne, W.I., Kafai, Y.B.: Computational participation: understanding coding as an extension of literacy instruction. J. Adolesc. Adult Lit. **59**(4), 371–375 (2015)
16. Rushkoff, D.: Program or be Programmed: Ten Commands for a Digital Age. O/R, New York (2010)
17. Oakland, T., Glutting, J., Horton, C.: Student Styles Questionnaire (SSQ). Pearson (1996)

National Concepts of Teaching Informatics

Standards for Higher Secondary Education for Computer Science in Germany

Arno Pasternak[1](✉), Lutz Hellmig[2](✉), and Gerhard Röhner[3](✉)

[1] Fritz-Steinhoff-Schule Hagen, Technische Universität Dortmund, Dortmund, Germany
arno.pasternak@cs.tu-dortmund.de
[2] Universität Rostock, Rostock, Germany
lutz.hellmig@uni-rostock.de
[3] Lichtenberg-Schule Darmstadt, Studienseminar Darmstadt, Darmstadt, Germany
groehner@t-online.de

Abstract. In this paper we will report on the *Standards for Higher Secondary Education for Computer Science in Germany.* After the first results of the PISA-studies in Germany the administration in the central and the federal states switched standards and curricula from setting teaching aims and cognitive learning objectives to describing students' learning outcome with practices.

On the central level this work was only done for the major subjects like Mathematics, Mother Tongue, Foreign Language and Natural Science. This is a disadvantage for the other subjects in school.

Therefore the German CS society—*Gesellschaft für Informatik (GI)*—installed a working group to develop standards for higher secondary education in 2013. By the end of 2015 this group finished the task and in January 2016 the board of the GI published this academic work as the official standards in Germany for higher secondary CS education [2].

It is to be hoped that these standards will have a positive impact on the standardisation of computer science teaching in the various German federal states, just as the standards for lower secondary education had almost 10 years earlier.

Keywords: Higher secondary computer science education
Education standards · CS in Germany

1 Introduction

In the late 1990s OECD has started to monitor and compare the performance of students with the PISA studies [11–13]. Germany's students did not match the expectations. As a consequence, stakeholders in Germany's educational system decided to shift from setting teaching aims and cognitive learning objectives

S. N. Pozdniakov and V. Dagienė (Eds.): ISSEP 2018, LNCS 11169, pp. 117–128, 2018.
https://doi.org/10.1007/978-3-030-02750-6_9

to describing students' learning outcome with practices. In subsequent years, federal authorities developed standards for a set of important subjects—but not regarding CS education [1,7].

The German non-governmental professional organisation for CS—Gesellschaft für Informatik (GI)—took this task to empower CS education as a subject in schools. GI published national standards for lower secondary education in 2008 [1,15]. These standards left an evident impact on the development of curricula in the 16 federal states of Germany. However, there is no compulsory CS in the lower secondary education in many schools.

In 2013 the GI continued by appointing a working group to develop standards for the higher secondary education. This working group finished its work in the end of 2015, and in January 2016 the GI board adopted these standards as the official position of the GI [2].

In this paper we give an account of the key ideas of these standards.

2 Computer Science Education in Germany

2.1 German Educational System in a Nutshell

Due to the responsibility of the 16 federal states of Germany, the German educational system is a 'hexadecimal assortment' of different approaches to establish a general education in each federal state. Nevertheless, there are some key points in common for all federal states: Education starts at the age 6 with primary school from grade 1 to grade 4 or in some federal states to grade 6. In each federal state, three degrees of qualification can be achieved by students: SEK I after grade 9 or grade 10. The range from grade 7 to grade 9 or grade 10 is called the lower secondary level. The third degree of qualification is attainable in the 'Gymnasiale Oberstufe'. It includes the lower secondary level together with the higher secondary level in grades 11 and 12—in some federal states until grade 13—and implies the higher education entrance qualification. In the higher secondary level, students are taught in a few core subjects (i.e. German, Mathematics, English), furthermore they attend lectures of an individual selection of subjects in different scientific domains. Besides that, the students may choose which subject he or she attends on a basic level[1] or on an advanced level[2].

Efforts to ensure a common, standardized higher education entrance qualification in Germany are conducted by the *Permanent Conference of the Ministers of Education and Cultural Affairs of the States of the Federal Republic of Germany (KMK).*

2.2 Higher Secondary Education

The history of CS education in schools started in the 1960s. In some schools, voluntary courses took place in physical logic and programming with minicomputers. These were the precursor for CS in school. In the middle of the

[1] In German: Grundkurs or Grundfach.

[2] In German: Leistungskurs or Hauptfach.

1960s many people were involved in general discussions about the educational system in Germany [3,14]. The result of these discussions was a new constitution of the higher secondary education in Western Germany with a system with compulsory and elective courses in grade 11 to grade 13 [5]. CS as a full-credit-subject was one of the innovations. The problem in 1972 was the same as today: the lack of CS teachers. Consequently there were many schools without an offer in CS.

In the GDR, between 1949 and 1990 an independent state of Germany, the government enacted a comprehensive program for CS education from grade 9 in schools up to vocational training and university education in 1985. As a part of this, eleven special schools for STEM education started to teach CS in 1986. Furthermore, curricula for CS education in grades 9/10 and 11/12 at schools for general education were developed and implemented successively. These offers were accompanied by a program of computer science teacher education [9].

Meanwhile in most of the federal states of Germany there are educational programs for CS, but the quantity is too small. The curriculum of CS in schools is different in the federal states. For example databases were not always part of the curriculum in the past. The quantity of lessons with information about hardware is slight. The programming language changed from mostly preferred language Basic in the first years via Pascal to Java.

Students have to fulfill many conditions in other subjects like Mathematics, First Language etc., so they often are not interested in learning CS. It is not easy, to make CS a part of a special permanent education.

In other papers there are more details about CS education in some federal states of Germany [4,8].

2.3 Lower Secondary Education

CS as a topic in the lower secondary education in German schools followed CS in higher education a few years later. With a few exceptions only the situation in schools was worse than in higher education. There were and are not enough teachers for CS. Often teachers have to devise their own curriculum. Many teachers and administrators mistake CS for ICT. Mostly CS is offered as an elective course for the students. In the last few years there is a new discussion about CS in lower secondary education. In some federal states CS is established with a minimum of lessons and importance. Unfortunately a significant number of influential people struggle again and again with the idea of a compulsory subject in lower secondary education.

3 Standards for Computer Science for Higher Secondary Education

The lack of consideration for Computer Science Education by nationwide educational authorities was the reason for the German Society of Computer Science (GI) to develop recommendations for standards in computer science education, beginning with standards for lower secondary education in 2008. Since the standards for CS for higher secondary education are continuing the ideas in this paper, it is advised to describe the main ideas of lower secondary standards first in Sect. 3.1.

The situation for higher secondary education is similar to lower secondary education. There are some official standards for some subjects, but not for CS Education yet. Instead of that the *Unified Requirements for Examinations in Higher Secondary Education* [6] describe the demands for the final exams for the higher education entrance qualification. The authors of the higher secondary standards also had to keep in mind the compatibility of the unified requirements with the higher secondary standards.

3.1 Standards for Computer Science Education for Lower Secondary Education

History. From 2003 to 2008 researchers and teachers of CS developed national standards for CS in lower secondary education. After its finalisation they asked the German society for CS (GI) for a takeover of these standards as an official GI-paper [1]. At the beginning of 2008 the GI approved this request.

As a result, in Germany we have on the one hand 'official' standards for some key subjects developed by the inter-federal-state official organisation KMK, on the other hand 'semi-official' recommendations for standards, including the *Standards for Computer Science Education*, developed by the GI.

While there were no official nationwide curricula in CS and additionally in many federal states there were no experience and no paper either, administration in most federal states orientated towards these GI-standards in the following years. This was not the expectation at the beginning of the work and represents a great success of these standards.

Today CS in lower secondary education is effectively defined by these standards in Germany.

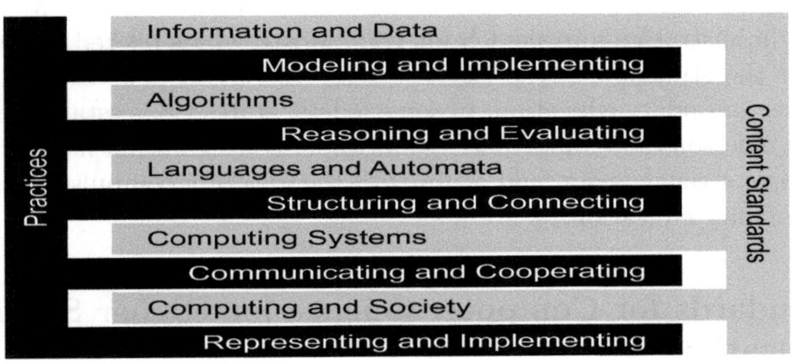

Fig. 1. Matrix of practices in lower secondary education, according to [15]

Structure. The structure of these guidelines is based on the *Principles and Standards for School Mathematics* [10]. The standards are divided in two parts: *principles* and *standards.* The principles are sub-divided in *equal opportunities, curriculum, teaching and learning, quality assurance and the multidisciplinarity of CS.* The standards are sub-divided in *contents and practices* respective Fig. 1. Afterwards these standards are first described and made concrete for grades 5 to 7 and secondly for grades 8 to 10.

3.2 Underlying Views on Computer Science

In Germany, CS in schools is generally referred to as the science of theoretical analysis, conception and the concrete implementation of complex IT systems. We consider an IT system as a specific assembly of hardware, software and components of networks to solve a problem. This assembly contains the non-technical aspects of embedding IT systems in social contexts. Therefore CS contains elements of Mathematics, Engineering, Social and Natural Science as well as Humanities.

The core products in CS are immaterial in contrast to the traditional engineering sciences. The impact of these products is very powerful. The development of an IT system is based on strategies that are not learnable from experiences from real life.

We need a new additional view for the information society inside the general education – the computational education. The basic science of this computational education is computer science.

CS makes aware of the regularity of information processing in society, nature and technology. Additionally CS and computational thinking completes the professional spread of other subjects. Computational development and problem solving is a creative process with covering theory, abstraction and design. Computational thinking and tools are involved in all parts of science, economy and technology. Everybody is concerned with CS at least as a user.

CS lessons give students many opportunities for the increase of competences, which are important for a self-determined life in a computational society. Students cannot extrapolate the comprehension of the modern computational society with everyday experiences. The qualification in knowledge, methodical, social and self competences happens in CS lessons in a mutual and a holistic way with situations of the students' everyday life. The use of and the interaction with concepts of modeling and structuring, software tools and programming languages is essential in a CS education. Learning and working in teams lead to a better qualification in study and profession.

3.3 Model of Competences for Higher Secondary Education

The model of competences for higher secondary education (respective Fig. 2) is based on the *Tyler matrix* of practices and contentual competences [16] and on the standards of computer science education for lower secondary education (see Fig. 1). The structure is the result of a longer discussion in the community of scientists, educators, and teachers in the field of computing.

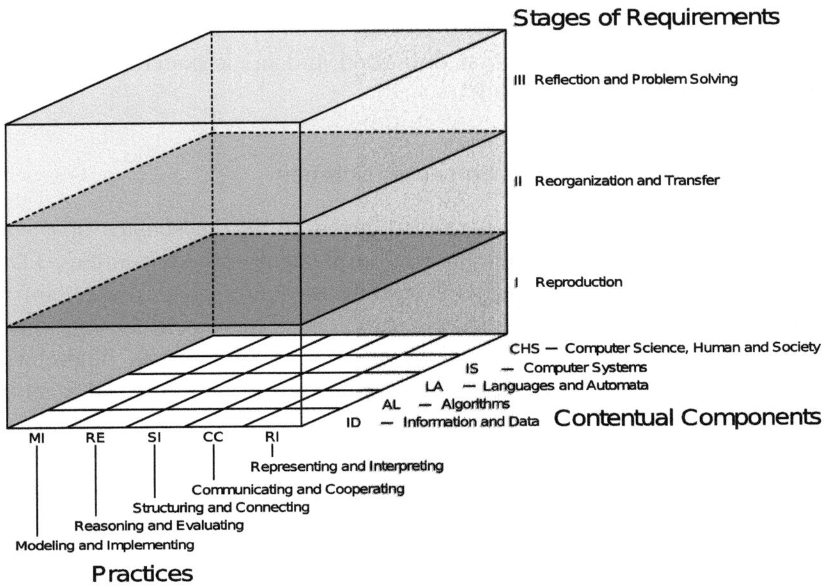

Fig. 2. Competence model of the standards for computer science in higher secondary education

Competences are the result of the amalgamation of contentual and practical components. Upholding this system is a key concept for the acceptance and the use of the standards by stakeholders. Regarding the framework conditions of higher secondary education in Germany, it was necessary to modify the system.

3.4 Practices

Practices describe the way in which students should deal with specific content. Thus the inherently cognitive abilities and skills, which are specific to the subject, are linked, but are not tied to special computer science contents. They can be used by students only in active involvement with the content and enable them to apply their acquired knowledge and skills for solving problems in new situations.

The following five different practices are used according to the educational standards for the lower secondary education:

Modeling and Implementing
These are the central parts of the modeling cycle: to analyze a problem, to design and implement a CS-model, test and evaluate the implementation on a computer system.

Reasoning and Evaluating
Reasoning is the idea of verification of a given statement or fact by rationally comprehensible arguments. The evaluation is to formulate a value judgement by considering the context and using transparent and appropriate criteria.
Structuring and Connecting
In structuring, facts are analyzed from a CS point of view. Objects and process as well as their interaction are systematically noted. In networking, existing contexts, effects and analogies in and outside of computer science are recognized and used.
Communicating and Cooperating
Communication in oral and written form uses the technical language as well as the use of methods for information dissemination from different sources.
Cooperation is necessary for teamwork in the field of computer science, especially for a project. Students use network based platforms for communication and cooperation and reflect their opportunities and risks.
Representing and Interpreting
Concepts and facts of computer science are presented in a variety of forms. Formal representations enable automatic information processing and serve for professional communication. Representations of the modeled reality are interpreted. Interpreting is a prerequisite for assessing facts. Data are obtained by interpretation of information.

3.5 Stages of Complexity in the Dimension of Practices

Since the *standards* are only recommendation up to now, the *Unified Requirements for Examinations in Higher Secondary Education* are obligatory in all federal states. They are based on a system of three stages with increasing complexity. Since the construct is in common for all subjects in every federal state of Germany, it has been included in the standards for higher secondary education for CS. The authors of the standards have labeled the stages.

They have been labeled in the standards for higher secondary education for CS.

1. **Reproduction** contains the display of known facts of a definite area in a trained context; the description and representation of procedures, methods, and principles of computer science as well as the use of skilled procedures in well-known situations.
2. **Reorganization and Transfer** connotes the self-reliant use of known facts for answering further questions in familiar contexts; the transfer of knowledge to slightly modified questions, situations, and methods; and the use of known techniques, methods and principles for solving new problems in familiar situations.
3. **Reflection and Problem Solving** is represented by a systematic approach to understand, represent and judge complex conditions and to draw conclusions. Furthermore, the students purposely choose and modify their acquired knowledge to solve new problems.

The levels of complexity relate to the competences of the students to be developed. Therefore, they were transferred into the section of practices. For each of the five components Modeling and Implementing, Reasoning and Evaluating, Structuring and Connecting, Communicating and Cooperating as well as Representing and Interpreting, three stages of complexity are defined separately and cumulatively.

We describe the levels of practices by the example of *Modeling and Implementing*. Modeling and Implementing are the key elements of the circle of modeling, including the analysis of a problem and the design of a computational model, which will be implemented, tested and evaluated.

At the lowest stage of *reproduction*, the students are able to display an already known model in a familiar representation; discover a given model or investigate a given implementation and test an implementation with given cases. The medium level—*reorganization and transfer*—has been achieved if the students prove the applicability of a given model for solving a problem, accomplish modeling and implementing—according to an analysis of a problem—with a familiar method of modeling. Furthermore, they use IDEs in an appropriate way for implementing a model and prove an implementation on functionality and correctness, including special cases, systematically. Reflection and Problem Solving takes place, if students—according to an analysis of a problem with a higher grade of complexity—model and implement with a method (not necessarily with a familiar one) of modeling. They revise their own work, considering aspects of efficiency, generality, and reusability. Students reflect their practice of problem solving and use their insights for further work.

3.6 Fundamental and Extended Level of Requirements in the Contentual Dimension

Each subject in higher secondary education can be offered on a basic level or on an advanced level with twice the time. For that reason, the standards have two stages for each contentual section. The first stage is mandatory for both levels, while the second stage describes advanced contents and concepts in addition to the first level.

There are five areas of contents: Computer Science and data, algorithms, languages and automata, Computer Science systems, Computer Science and society. Each content area is described with about five notes in each stage.

In the next paragraph we will extensively outline three examples of content areas and the other two briefly.

Selected Examples of Content

Information and Data. Information is the context-related sense of a statement, instruction or message. Computer science is characterized by the systematic representation and automatic processing of data as a carrier of information.

Data is a representation of information in a formalized way for communication, interpretation and processing, represented by strings that follow in a suitable syntax. Data become information again when interpreted in a concrete context.

Fundamental Level. The students ...

- distinguish between characters, data and information as well as between syntax and semantics,
- analyze data on their structure,
- form information as data with data types and data structures,
- use, model and implement operations on static and dynamic data structures,
- create a data model and implement a data model as a database,
- investigate and organize data while regarding redundancy, consistency and persistence,
- use a query language to display and manipulate data and interpret the data.

Advanced Level. The students ...

- use, model and implement operations on complex datastructures,
- develop a real part of the life with complex relationships in a database.

Algorithms. Algorithms are finite descriptions of processes for solving problems and result in a clearly defined sequence of actions during execution. An execution on a computer requires the formulation in a programming language. Complex problems can be solved, if—in addition to the algorithmic basic structures—design methods and data structures are developed. The implementation of an algorithm requires sufficient testing and, if necessary, revisions.

Fundamental Level. The students ...

- use algorithmic basic structures (sequence, alternative, repetition) and implement an application using a programming language,
- analyze given programs respectively the basic concepts including variables, references, nesting and functional decomposition,
- implement algorithms and describe them in adequate form,
- use modularization for structuring of algorithms and use them for their implementation,
- use software libraries or available modules to implement an algorithm,
- test and revise a program systematically.

Advanced Level. The students ...

- model and implement iterative and recursive algorithms and data structures,
- compare and assess algorithms for solving a problem, including efficiency,
- analyze examples of the complexity of algorithms
- assess the practical and theoretical boundaries of algorithmization.

Languages and Automata. Formal languages are the basis for communication with automata and are used in a variety of application scenarios in computer systems. In contrast to natural languages, formal languages have a definitive syntax defined by grammar, syntax diagrams, or language descriptions.

Automata are state-based systems that read and handle an input character after character. Automata types can be differentiated according to the design of their memory and thus according to their basic possibilities and limits.
(Following ditto the fundamental and the advanced level.)

IT Systems. A computer system is a specific combination of hardware, software and network components to solve an application problem. Also included are non-technical aspects that are relevant by e.g. embedding in a sociocultural system, inclusion of the potential users in the development process, the economic and environmental consequences. Competent use, design and evaluation of computer systems require a fundamental understanding of their structure and functioning. For the development of computer systems, machine-processable facts of the real world are identified and modeled. Typical fields of application of computer systems are data management, communication, graphics, simulation, robotics, process control and regulation or speech processing.
(Following ditto the fundamental and the advanced level.)

Computer Science and Society. Information systems shape our information society and interact with people and society. Based on socially relevant questions or own experiences in dealing with IT systems, interactions between IT systems and their social embedding are analysed. In confrontation with normative, legal, ethical and social aspects, an orientation framework and a sense of responsibility in dealing with modern information technology are developed. Freedom of choice in dealing with IT systems in accordance with social norms and standards and appropriate responses to risks when using computer systems are reflected.
(Following ditto the fundamental and the advanced level.)

3.7 Illustrating Tasks

Presenting tasks is an effective way to illustrate the generally formulated items and make them vivid. Depending on the situation, different kinds of tasks are needed to acquire new knowledge, to consolidate knowledge or examine the adopted competencies. Learning is a process which includes phases of performing as a subset. Performing can be a self-examination to reflect the improvement of the learning progress by the learner. If somebody else (e.g. a teacher) judges the result of the learning process by giving marks, we call it scoring. A model of the relationship between Learning, Performing and Scoring is given by Fig. 3.

Regarding the model, three types of tasks illustrate the standards: A collection of eight complex tasks from written exams of different federal states of Germany show an impression of different approaches to prove students' competences. Furthermore, the document includes four tasks for oral exams developed

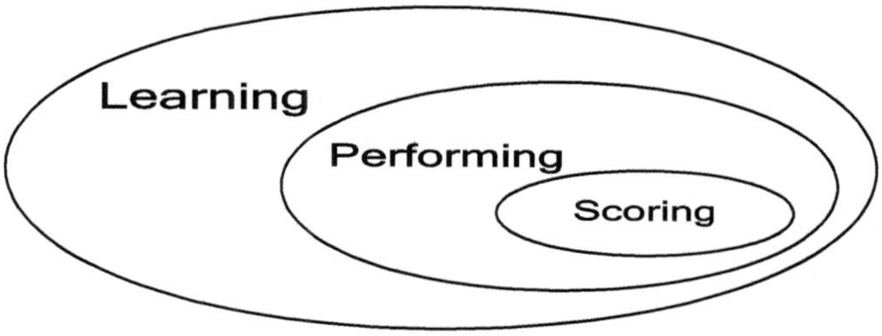

Fig. 3. Relationship between learning, performing and scoring

by experienced teachers. Last but not least, five tasks show examples how knowledge can be developed and trained according to the standards.

Every task is complemented with an anticipated typical solution and an assignment to the related contentual and processual sections, and to the stage of complexity.

Finally a list of suitable operators is part of the document to ensure a clear understanding of the required demands of the tasks.

4 Conclusion

CS in Germany today is not a substantial part of education in lower and higher secondary education. During the last 10 years the *Permanent Conference of the Ministers of Education and Cultural Affairs of the federal states in the Federal Republic of Germany* have developed standards in subjects like Mathematics, Languages and Natural Sciences. In the majority of the federal states of Germany curricula are introduced, the contents are more or less different. The German CS organization GI undertook the task and developed CS standards for higher secondary education in Germany. In January 2016 these standards were adopted by the board of the GI. These standards can be seen as an extension of the standards for lower secondary education, written in 2008.

Better than expected the standards for lower secondary education have been involved in the development of curricula in the federal states of Germany. We hope the standards for higher secondary education fulfill the same role.

Acknowledgments. In Germany standards were usually developed in working groups installed by administration organizations without a considerable discussion with teachers or other people. These standards for CS were developed without involving any administration structure. The goal was to involve many teachers in this process. Experts were invited by the working group to discuss part of these standards. In September 2015 these standards were reviewed on the German conference *INFOS* (Informatik und Schule). Additionally an online survey was conducted in November 2015. Thanks to all the people involved in this process.

References

1. Arbeitskreis 'Bildungsstandards' der GI: Grundsätze und Standards für die Informatik in der Schule. LOGIN-Verlag, Berlin (2008)
2. Arbeitskreis 'Bildungsstandards SII' der GI: Bildungsstandards Informatik für die Sekundarstufe II. LOGIN-Verlag, Berlin (2016). http://informatikstandards.de/docs/Bildungsstandards_SII.pdf. Accessed 09 June 2016
3. Dahrendorf, R.: Bildung ist Bürgerrecht. Plädoyer für eine aktive Bildungspolitik. Nannen-Verlag, Hamburg (1965)
4. Hubwieser, P.: Computer science education in secondary schools – the introduction of a new compulsory subject. Trans. Comput. Educ. **12**(4), 16:1–16:41 (2012)
5. KMK (Ständige Konferenz der Kultusminister der Länder der Bundesrepublik Deutschland): Vereinbarung zur Gestaltung der gymnasialen Oberstufe in der Sekundarstufe II (1972)
6. KMK (Ständige Konferenz der Kultusminister der Länder der Bundesrepublik Deutschland): Einheitliche Prüfungsanforderungen in der Abiturprüfung Informatik. Luchterhand, Neuwied (2004)
7. KMK (Ständige Konferenz der Kultusminister der Länder der Bundesrepublik Deutschland): Bildungsstandandards im Fach Physik für den mittleren Bildungsabschluss - Beschluss vom 16.12.2004. Wolters Kluwer Deutschland - Luchterhand, Neuwied (2005)
8. Knobelsdorf, M., et al.: Computer science education in North-Rhine Westphalia, Germany. A Case Study. Trans. Comput. Educ. **15**(2), 9:1–9:22 (2015)
9. Merkel, G.: Über Informatikkenntnisse des gebildeten Bürgers. In: Stetter, F., Brauer, W. (eds.) Informatik und Schule 1989: Zukunftsperspektiven der Informatik für Schule und Ausbildung, pp. 56–68. Springer, Heidelberg (1989). https://doi.org/10.1007/978-3-642-75163-9_5
10. NTCM: Principles and Standards for School Mathematics. National Council of Teachers of Mathematics, Reston (2000)
11. OECD: Measuring Student Knowledge and Skills A New Framework for Assessment: A New Framework for Assessment. Measuring Student Knowledge and Skills A New Framework for Assessment, OECD Publishing (1999)
12. OECD, Adams, R., Wu, M., Program for International Student Assessment, Organisation for Economic Co-operation Development: Pisa 2000 Technical report. OECD (2002)
13. OECD, Statistics, U.: PISA Literacy Skills for the World of Tomorrow Further Results from PISA 2000: Further Results from PISA 2000. OECD Publishing (2003)
14. Picht, G.: Die Deutsche Bildungskatastrophe. Deutscher Taschenbuch Verlag, München, 2 edn. (1965), 1. Auflage 1964, Walter-Verlag Olten
15. Puhlmann, H., Schulte, C., Brinda, T.: Bridging ICT and CS: educational standards for computer science in lower secondary education. Source ACM SIGCSE Bull. Arch. **41**(3), 288–292 (2009)
16. Tyler, R.W.: Basic Principles of Curriculum and Instruction. University of Chicago Press, Chicago (2010)

Computer Science Teachers Perspectives on Competencies - A Case Study in the Kingdom of Saudi Arabia

Fayiq Alghamdi[1,2](✉), Arnold Pears[3], and Aletta Nylén[1]

[1] Uppsala University, Uppsala, Sweden
{fayiq.alghamdi,aletta.nylen}@it.uu.se
[2] Al-Baha University, Al-Baha, Saudi Arabia
[3] KTH Royal Institute of Technology, Stockholm, Sweden
pears@kth.se

Abstract. The Kingdom of Saudi Arabia (KSA) has recently adopted the Saudi Teaching Competencies Standard (STCS). This paper tries to answer how these competencies are achieved, how they are maintained, and what support exists to support teaching CS competently in the KSA. This paper presents the results of an investigation of teacher awareness of, and attitudes to, the STCS in the Kingdom. Through the study reported here, we address an urgent need in the Kingdom to understand teacher preparedness in terms of CS teaching competencies. The study draws on interviews with ten CS teachers in five different cities in the KSA. A thematic coding analysis approach was used. This study explores the CS teaching competencies held by teachers in three areas of CS teaching, focusing on connection to society, professional practice and professional development. The results of the study highlight the CS teaching competencies that CS teachers feel they currently grasp well in the KSA. By enhancing awareness of what teachers currently do well we contribute to the adjustment and improvement of the STCS and help to build a program which addresses the current in-service training needs of CS teachers. The outcomes also help to raise awareness of the challenges of implementing the Computer Education curriculum in KSA schools.

Keywords: CS teachers · Computing education
Teaching competency · CS teaching competencies

1 Introduction

Computer Science (CS) is a fast-moving field. Paradoxically, it is often taken for granted that teachers who graduated from CS colleges are qualified to teach the technical content of the CS subject. Clearly a continuous learning process is required to become an excellent CS teacher, as the CS domain develops rapidly. While there are challenges faced by teachers who have graduated with CS degrees, there are also many teachers with mathematics, business or other

S. N. Pozdniakov and V. Dagienė (Eds.): ISSEP 2018, LNCS 11169, pp. 129–140, 2018.
https://doi.org/10.1007/978-3-030-02750-6_10

backgrounds who teach CS in schools for these teachers for the challenges are much more severe [9]. Excellent CS teachers are necessary if high-quality learning outcomes are to be achieved in the Kingdom's schools. As a result teachers need to improve their competencies in order to teach CS effectively.

Crick defines competencies as the *"complex combination of different knowledge, skills, understanding, values, attitudes, and desire which lead to effective, embodied human action in the world, in a particular domain"* [1]. Competencies are self-motivated and multidisciplinary, and teachers' competencies can be classified into five groups specialized by the European Council: cognition, collaboration, connection, creativity and communication [2]. Indeed, teaching competencies are related to all activities in the classroom, as Hagger claims *"focused on the role of the teacher in the classroom, directly linked with the 'craft' of teaching - with professional knowledge and skills mobilized for action"* [3].

The National Center for Assessment (NCA) has concluded in a recent assessment of teaching standards that CS teachers in KSA lack a number of key competencies. Approximately, half of the teachers have not passed the Computer Teacher Exam (CTE) annually that tests the teachers' competencies in CS in compliance with the Saudi Teachers Competencies Standards [4]. Alrshedi observes that CS teachers in the KSA tend to have low competency in teaching CS, and many teachers are in need of more in-service training in CS professional development [5]. In addition to this, Alrshedi notes that using a professional website in the CS subject created a positive trend in CS female teachers' self-efficacy [6].

Studies in other countries have also addressed the issue of teachers' competencies. Bender et al. investigated a new competency model for teaching CS in Germany and proposed a framework to support CS teachers based on results reached using content analysis of thirteen curricula [7]. Sentance et al. developed a program to support CS teachers in England using action research with twenty-two teachers. They focus on CS content knowledge and pedagogical expertise and resulted in teachers changing their practice [8].

Sue and Csizmadia described a program called the Certificate in Computer Science Teaching (CCST) that supports teachers who have made the transition to teaching CS. The participants were thirty-six teachers, and the method was a short survey with five open questions. The program is based on three parts: the reflection on the journey, programming skills, and focus on pedagogy. The CCST was adopted as the national certification standard for CS teachers, and it is an appropriate approach through which to support in-service teachers in other countries [15]. Finally, Hubwieser et al. compared the education system for CS Education in thirteen countries aiming a deductive qualitative text analysis. They arrived at a classification based on four competency groups which are; representing, understanding, creating, and testing [10].

The identification of new issues related to preparing CS teachers in schools and universities is the result of AlGhamdi [11]. In this study we argue that students were positively motivated to choose to study CS due to the influence their CS teachers had during their studies. In light of the previous discussion, the current study focuses on conceptions of KSA teachers in terms of what constitutes teaching competencies in CS. The outcomes contribute to insights into how these competencies are achieved, how they are maintained, and what support mechanisms currently exist to support CS teaching competence in the KSA.

2 The Saudi Teachers Competencies Standards

The Government in the KSA approved the Saudi Teachers Competencies Standard (STCS) in 2016 under authority of the governor of the Public Education Evaluation Commission [12]. The standard is based on educational research that emphasizes the influential role teachers who are active life-long learners [13]. These educators are those who are most likely to actively engage in seeking new knowledge and skills [14]. The Ministry of Education, through this initiative, expects to improve teachers' educational practices thus ensuring that the Kingdom maximizes the chances of students' accessing their full potential within the educational system. The STCS is structured into three major areas; values and responsibilities; knowledge and practice. See Fig. 1. The standard builds on the premise that the quality of learning depends on the quality of teaching, and that excellence in teaching requires high levels of specialized knowledge and skills, and a high degree of commitment, passion, and professionalism. Among the most important specifications on which the STCS are based are the following:

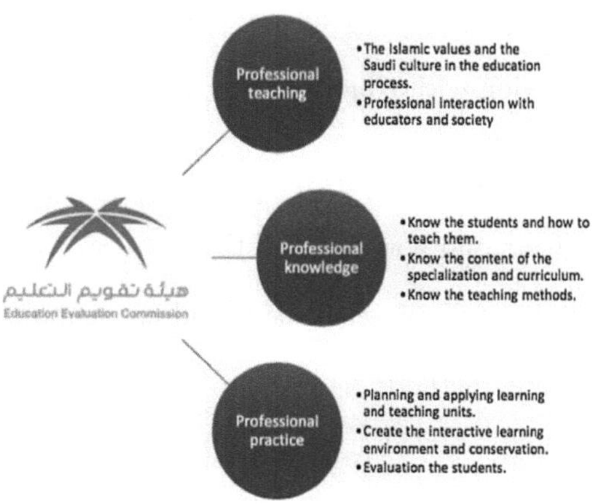

Fig. 1. The Saudi Teachers Competencies Standard, STCS.

- Student-oriented improvement: Focus on teachers' knowledge and practices that have a greater impact on outcomes.
- Focus on development: Supporting development for all teachers.
- High quality: Highly relevant and achievable standards.

- Inclusiveness: Standards cover all stages of the teachers' careers.
- Credibility: Standards accurately describe the work of teachers in the KSA.
- Focus on practice: Standards are built professionally.

The STCS is the core of all initiatives that are relevant to the teaching profession, including:

- Pre-service teacher qualification.
- Issuing professional licenses and associated incentives.
- Rewards for teachers.
- Assessment of the professional performance of teachers.
- Growth, development and professional learning.

The STCS consists of eight interrelated standards, grouped into three overlapping and interrelated areas and eight standards:

Professional Teaching

- The Islamic values and the Saudi culture in the education process.
- Professional interaction with educators and society.

Professional Knowledge

- Knowing the students and how to teach them.
- Knowing the content of the specialization and curriculum.
- Knowing the teaching methods.

Professional Practice

- Planning and applying learning and teaching units.
- Creating an interactive learning environment and sustainable practice.
- Evaluating students.

The STCS as a national standard occupies an interesting position in relation to the particular cultural context in which it is devised and the relationship of the standard to the broader international context regarding knowledge and skills in different educational domains [4].

3 Research Question

The aim of this paper is to explore the relationship between CS teaching competencies held by practicing teachers, and those required by the STCS in the KSA. This work is based on the CS teachers experiences in the Saudi context. The question is: What competencies in teaching CS do teachers experience as valuable and how are these practices related to the STCS?

4 Methodology

A case study approach was chosen as the basis for an initial empirical exploration of the phenomenon within its local context [16]. Semi-structured interview data collection was selected as a means to obtain in-depth data from the ten participants [17]. The interview questions are based on the major competencies identified in the STCS. The interview was structured to follow the standard, and consists of items addressing the three main parts, professional teaching, knowledge, and practice. The responses of teachers provide the researcher with a pool of data in which teachers reason about their skills in the areas covered by the standard. In order to perform a classification of competencies in teaching CS in the population represented by the study participants a detailed analysis of the pool of data was conducted by the first author.

The informants in this study are CS teachers who are working in KSA schools. Participants were contacted through the director of CS teachers in the Ministry of Education. The director forwarded the proposal of this study to the CS teachers mailing list. As a result, twelve male CS teachers and three female CS teachers indicated interest in participating in the study of whom ten completed the interview. The three female CS teachers were later excluded due to logistical difficulties associated with conducting the interviews. The KSA culture implements gender segregation in Education [18], and it is consequently difficult to interview female teachers face to face. The researcher also excluded two male teachers who were not available during the interview time frame. Finally, ten CS teachers representing five different major cities in the KSA were interviewed. The interviews were conducted in Arabic, and the data (questions and answers) were transcribed in Arabic then translated to English with effort taken to preserve the nuances of the original narration. In order to ensure the credibility of the translation the first author translated it, then, an English teacher who is also an Arabic speaker read and confirmed the translation.

Thematic coding analysis [19] was used to categorize the competencies of teaching CS that teachers hold in the KSA.

First the recording was listened to and then the researcher read the transcript of each interviewee, highlighted the statements associated with value, feeling and practicing in relation to the standard. Next, the first author began to generate codes, which resulted in forty-two initial themes. As the first author is familiar with the CS curriculum and context in the KSA, it was possible through further analysis to merge themes which were close to each other. This phase of analysis resulted in a reduction of the original thematic grouping to twelve intermediate themes. Further clustering and abstraction of themes resulted at six high level themes. In the last step, these were grouped into three main categories. These three categories are linked to society, professional practice, and professional development.

While the primary analysis is based on the translated data file, the Arabic version has been used in parallel throughout the analysis to provide additional assurance that the thematic interpretations were justified. The researcher chose to analyze the data in English to allow for an open discussion with fellow researchers. The outcome of the analysis is supported using citations from the responses of teachers.

5 Results

Based on our thematic analysis a tree of categories emerges, in which nuances of CS teachers experiences and practices have been thematically grouped At the highest level, the most commonly discussed aspects of CS teaching practice are described. The high level themes in each category are listed in Table 1 and described in detail later in the section.

The categories and high level themes discussed by the CS teachers correspond to the categories mentioned in STCS to a considerable extent. The main difference lies in the theme "professional development", where the teachers experience that self-directed learning plays a significant role in their practice and competence development. This is, however, a task that the standard does not consider.

Table 1. Categories of the CS teaching in the KSA

Category	Theme	Example
Connection to society	Culture	Arabic language
		Islamic values
	Context	Student
		Teachers
		Charity
Professional practicing	Need of technical infrastructure	Equipment
		Maintenance
	Teaching approaches	Active learning
		Students centric
		Focusing on practical
Professional development	Formal requirements	Teachers' license
	Self-directed learning	Students' need

5.1 Connection to Society

The first category deals with teacher's experiences of CS teaching in connection to society. In the interview, CS teachers were asked questions related to their CS teaching experiences in the classroom. This category illustrates how teachers talked about the connection between CS education and society. In this high level category two sub-themes emerge from more detailed analysis, one culture and the another to context. The two most frequently mentioned aspects of Saudi Arabian culture are language and religion. The participants refer to Arabic as a teaching language and also as a means to keep their culture visible. Most of the participants teach in Arabic, and they are using English for CS terminology. Thus, the teachers use two languages while they are teaching. This could explain the teachers' values when they are keeping Arabic language visible. for example CS teacher D said: *"Both are best without disturbing them. Arabic is important to us as a culture and English is important to keep up with the development"*.

The Islamic religion is mentioned as a fundamental moral ground which permeates the students' learning. Half of the participants declared that they apply the values and morals in their teaching that are mandatory in regards to the education policy document in the KSA [20] which describes what is required in order to conform to the legal requirement to implement Islamic values in the school system. The teachers referred to Islamic religion guidelines such as honesty and devotion. For example, CS teacher B said *"I want to instill Islamic values in my students. As well as I seek to develop students knowledge-abilities and skill. They should know that specialization is required in order to deliver their missions as they are entrusted to them according to the teaching of our religion and under the leadership of our kingdom"*.

The "context" theme is dominated by statements concerning aspects of CS education. Most commonly mentioned are students, teachers and content. Four CS teachers expressed the one aspect of the learning outcomes is to make students increase the use of technology at home. They specified that this goal is achievable when students have learned some applications and e-services in class, or when they have had a project related to family duty. CS teacher B mentioned *"I seek to make students benefit from what they have learned in a school and apply that in their daily life."*.

The CS teaching community provide both formal and informal support to practicing teachers. For instance, CS teacher E said *"There is certainly a special group on "Whats up" for CS teachers, and it benefits us through sharing experiences with colleagues regarding problems face us and how to solve them. In addition, we learn about the methods of teaching and explanations of some programs"*.

Three of the participants said CS teachers are always expected to help other teachers with technology or solve technological problems. Being regarded as experts in technology serves as a motivation for CS teacher to stay updated. CS teacher B said *"As CS teacher, teachers and students will look at you as their first reference in technology"*. The respondents talked about student projects as a way to connect what students learn to different ways of applying it to support the community. An example is that students work on digital learning materials for other subjects as projects. CS teacher C said *"Building educational lessons for other materials or teachers is a core object for student projects. Teachers, and students will look at you as their first reference in technology"*. Four participants stated that they encouraged students to work on projects aimed at charity. For instance, CS teacher B observed that *"Students collaborated with the social development committee of our neighborhood to design a program that fostered knowledge on alms each deserves and knowledge on revenues, expenses, and inventory"*.

5.2 Professional Practice

The second category, professional practice, describes issues related to the actual teaching activities of our interview participants. The main two themes are need of technical infrastructure and teaching approaches. Almost all CS teachers stated that technical infrastructure in the lab is an under-addressed issue. Some of them talked about obsolete devices without plays for replacement, some mention the broken computer networks. Also, they believed the new curriculum requires the Internet as a platform, but unfortunately the reliability of the Internet connection in most schools is weak. The participants see adequate equipment as necessary to teach CS effectively. For example, CS teacher D said *"There is not enough equipment in the laboratory, and the ministry does not care about that"*, and CS teacher H said *"Most labs have no Internet access; this brings difficulties upon teachers in teaching some lessons"*.

Half of the CS teachers mentioned poorly structured maintenance in connection with labs. In fact, many of them do the maintenance in addition to their teaching duties and are often viewed as technical support for teachers in other subjects. In their view, labs need to be maintained to fully support teaching and learning according to the new curriculum. For example, CS teacher F observed *"Labs in schools, infrastructure, and maintenance as well as licenses programs that we work on it are only for a year and then shut down and need to renew and follow-up ongoing"*, and CS teacher B said *"We are confronted with the lack maintenance of some of the devices"*. Two of the respondents do not speak about problems with labs (equipment and maintenance). These respondents teach in a new school, and in a school where the labs have been upgraded recently.

Regarding teaching approaches, the participants discussed student centered approaches to teaching and active learning strategies. We observe that , the amount of experience of teaching CS affects the particular practices used. Our study participants were in agreement that there is a gap between the way they had been taught during their own studies at the university and the way they are currently teaching CS. Six of the CS teachers identified that they learned in the past thought indoctrination or lecturing, they reflect that this is a weak and passive way to learn CS. Today the CS teachers are applying active learning strategies in their classrooms, a trend started by the new CS curriculum. For instance, CS teacher B said *"In the first year, I adopted a purely traditional teaching method which is synonymous with the style of indoctrination. Today,*

I use the active learning method which contains many strategies. Each strategy fits a specific lesson and fits a specific category. I always follow active learning methods in my preparation".

Most of the CS teachers are focusing more on practice than theory. They spent more of the teaching time on giving students chance to apply what they learned. Some CS teachers assessed students based on projects. For instance, CS teacher J mentioned *"My overall goal is to focus on the practical part so that students will need not to know the new terms, but how to use it in reality. I want my students to be creative and innovative in terms of new ideas. As we develop an application in CS curriculum today, teachers also need to professionally develop themselves to be able to transfer knowledge to students"*.

5.3 Professional Development

The third category identified is that of professional development. Participants utterances linked to this theme include, the CS teachers' Exam, teachers performance indicators, special course-training (Computer Teachers for the New Curriculum), and teacher's book guidelines. They referred to a kind of evaluation that teachers must pay attention to, and that performance is necessary in order to gain a pass in these evaluations. For example, CS teacher C said *"The exam measured the degree of achievement of the professional competency of the teacher and proved the reality of his success. Meanwhile, some teachers oppose the test, but it is an exam of honest measurement"*, and CS teacher E claimed *"I am a supporter of the exam because it aims to measure the extent of the advanced knowledge and skills required for teaching. This is because of its significant impact in the educational process"*.

It is clear that teachers appreciate the intent of the accreditation examination, and also the need for re-certification despite the stress involved. Most of the CS teachers obligate themselves to develop and keep updating CS knowledge and teaching approaches. Some of them are working to achieve the curriculum outputs only, however, some of them aim to achieve more than curriculum. These teachers talk about the need to engage in self-directed learning as an appropriate method to continue learning and develop their capabilities. For instance, CS teacher K said *"Keep updating with the technology and new information. This is the most important thing we suffer from. Self-development depends on the teacher himself"*. Moreover, CS teacher J said *"Today, the professional development is very fast, and CS teachers need hard work to bridge this gap. However, my self-efficacy has been evolving in front of my students"*.

6 Discussion

This study investigates the link between the Saudi teaching competencies standard (STCS) and, how a group of CS teachers perceive their practice. The main research question was: What competencies in teaching CS do teachers experience as valuable and how are these skills related to the STCS?

What teachers need is obvious from their reflections. They identify the need to provide a connection to society, develop professional practice and engage in professional development. The link between what they need and what the STCS emphasis is also discussed by many of our participants. The STCS focuses on the importance of the professional teaching contents, Saudi values, and communication with society. It is clear from our results how the participants express their connection to society, as you can see in Fig. 2. Moreover, the professional knowledge in STCS establishes that teachers should focus on knowing student, technical CS content and methods. That is explicit in our data when we consider how participants' responses emerge as grouped in teaching approaches under the branch of the professional practice.

Furthermore, the professional practice areas of the STCS emphasize planning lessons, managing the learning environment and evaluating students. However, in our results, planning and evaluating is one of the teaching approaches that grouped under the focus on practice. Finally, there is a branch regarding the support and maintenance of labs and other infrastructure, which is not covered by the STCS.

The standard refers to how to teach students, but the participants identify the need for functioning laboratories, computers, and Internet. Two of the categories found in the study, the connection to society and the professional practice, are almost identical to the STCS categories professional teaching and professional knowledge. Regarding more general teaching practice, these categories cover exactly the same themes, but they have been grouped differently. The STCS covers teaching all subjects, CS specific themes do not occur.

One new item not covered by the STCS has been identified in this study, the need of technical infrastructure. In this area the teachers mention both need of equipment and the requirement for timely and regular maintenance, a task that is now often delegated to these very same teachers with a negative impact on

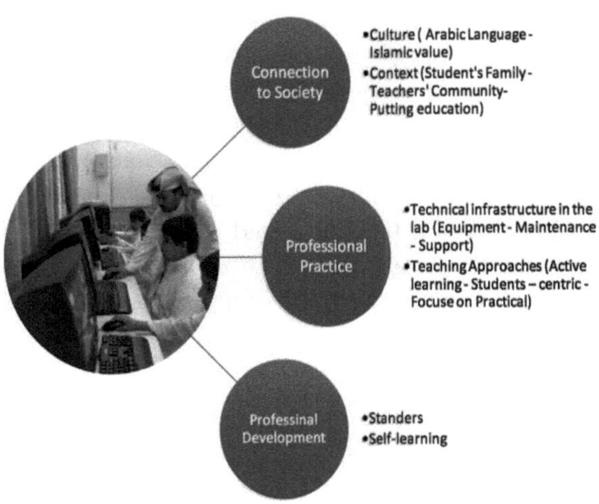

Fig. 2. The CS Teaching Competencies (Model), CSTC.

their workload. Indeed, the professional development category is unique when the teacher's point out what they needed and that was less important in the STCS. However, the self-directed learning is priority for CS teachers in this study.

7 Conclusion

The Ministry of Education in the KSA has commenced implementation of the SCTS to increase the quality of CS education. This study investigates what CS teachers' competencies carefully exist, and what further support for teachers might be needed. The procedures of becoming a CS teacher in the KSA ensues that all teachers should be well qualified, since all CS teachers had a college degree in CS and passed the CS teachers' exam. Our study identified a gap between what the CS teachers have learned and what they teach. The gap alerts us to the attitudes and approaches to professional development of CS teachers as they strive to keep pace with rapid development in CS in one side and in teaching CS in another. The Ministry of Education should now focus on enhancing CS teachers' competencies by improving CS teachers' professional development.

The STCS is the new standard in the KSA schooling, and it will take time to combine with the teachers performance indicators. The Ministry of Education should be aware of the need for professional development of teaching especially self-directed learning and encourage teachers to engage in this practice. In addition, the results of this study show that CS teaching competencies are strongly related to teachers' views on society, professional practice and professional development.

While the number of participants in this study was relatively few, each participant represents a different region in the KSA, and this makes the sample quite representative of the Kingdom as a whole. Teachers were selected from both new and older schools to gain an overview of the level of infrastructure in place in schools throughout the Kingdom. More investigation is needed, but this paper provides an important first step in analyzing the impact of the STCS. Indeed, the result contribute significantly to the understanding of the CS teaching competencies, and the model could be the basis of the new teachers competencies standard in the CS subject in the KSA.

This study recommends that the Ministry of Education needs to improve the CS curriculum in schools and colleges and reduce the gap between the CS college and the curriculum in schools. Also, CS teachers should pay attention to the teachers license as a mechanism for enhancing teaching competencies during the teaching career. The Ministry of Education should review approaches to introducing CS into primary schools and encourage transfer of some topics between school level. CS teachers should be more involved in developing their self-directed learning, and be ready to change the belief of teaching CS.

Acknowledgment. I would like to thank the Ministry of Education of the Kingdom of Saudi Arabia, and especially the director of CS teachers. I would also like to extend my sincere thanks to the CS teachers who participated in this study for many inspiring discussions, comments and their time.

References

1. Deakin Crick, R.: Pedagogy for citizenship. In: Getting Involved: Global Citizenship Development and Sources of Moral Values, pp. 31–55 (2008)
2. Hutmacher, W.: Key Competencies for Europe. Report of the Symposium, Berne, Switzerland, 27–30 March 1996. A Secondary Education for Europe Project (1997)
3. Hagger, H., McIntyre, D.: Learning Teaching from Teachers: Realizing the Potential of School-Based Teacher Education. McGraw-Hill Education, London (2006)
4. Public Education Evaluation Commission: Saudi Teachers Competence Standard. The Minstry of Education, Al-Riyadh, KSA (2016)
5. Alrshedi, H.: Methods of teaching CS, reality, and hope in KSA, knowledge, p. 4115 (2016)
6. Alrshedi, H.: Training program for CS female teachers parameter skills. Master thesis (2011)
7. Bender, E., et al.: Towards a competency model for teaching computer science. Peabody J. Educ. **90**(4), 519–532 (2015)
8. Sentance, S., Sinclair, J., Simmons, C., Csizmadia, A.: Teacher research projects in computing. In: Proceedings of the 11th Workshop in Primary and Secondary Computing Education, pp. 110–111. ACM (2016)
9. Sentance, S., Csizmadia, A.: Professional recognition matters: certification for in-service Computer Science Teachers. In: Proceedings of the 2017 ACM SIGCSE Technical Symposium on Computer Science Education, pp. 537–542. ACM (2017)
10. Hubwieser, P., et al.: A global snapshot of computer science education in k-12 schools. In: Proceedings of the 2015 ITiCSE on Working Group Reports, pp. 65–83. ACM (2015)
11. Alghamdi, F.: Why do female students choose to study CS in the Kingdom of Saudi Arabia? In: Fifth International Conference on Learning and Teaching in Computing and Engineering. IEEE Digital Library (2017)
12. Alsadaawi, A.S.: Raising the quality of education: developing professional standards for Saudi teachers (2018). https://iaea.info/documents/raising-the-quality-of-education-developing-professional-standards-for-saudi-teachers/
13. Alarfaj, M.M.: Science education in Saudi Arabia. In: Mansour, N., Al-Shamrani, S. (eds.) Science Education in the Arab Gulf States. CHPSE, pp. 155–168. SensePublishers, Rotterdam (2015). https://doi.org/10.1007/978-94-6300-049-9_8
14. CSTA K: Computer Science Standards, Computer Science Teachers Association
15. Quais: Teachers Standers Indecetrs (2017). http://www.qiyas.sa/Sites/English/Tests/VocationalTests/Pages/Teachers-Test.aspx
16. Yin, R.K.: Case Study Research: Design and Methods. Sage Publications, Thousand Oaks (2013)
17. Drever, E.: Using Semi-Structured Interviews in Small-Scale Research. A Teachers Guide. ERIC (1995)
18. El-Sanabary, N.: Female education in Saudi Arabia and the reproduction of gender division. Gend. Educ. **6**(2), 141–150 (1994)
19. Braun, V., Clarke, V.: Using thematic analysis in psychology. Qual. Res. Psychol. **3**(2), 77–101 (2006)
20. Oyaid, A.: Education Policy in Saudi Arabia and its Relation to Secondary School Teachers ICT Use, perceptions, and views of the future of ICT in education (2009)

A Core Informatics Curriculum for Italian Compulsory Education

Luca Forlizzi[1], Michael Lodi[2], Violetta Lonati[3], Claudio Mirolo[4], Mattia Monga[3](✉), Alberto Montresor[5], Anna Morpurgo[3], and Enrico Nardelli[6]

[1] Università degli Studi dell'Aquila, L'Aquila, Italy
luca.forlizzi@univaq.it
[2] Alma Mater Studiorum, Università di Bologna & INRIA Focus, Bologna, Italy
michael.lodi@unibo.it
[3] Università degli Studi di Milano, Milan, Italy
mattia.monga@unimi.it
http://aladdin.di.unimi.it
[4] Università degli Studi di Udine, Udine, Italy
claudio.mirolo@uniud.it
[5] Università degli Studi di Trento, Trento, Italy
alberto.montresor@unitn.it
[6] Università degli Studi di Roma "Tor Vergata", Rome, Italy
nardelli@mat.uniroma2.it

Abstract. In order to bring informatics, its ideas and ways of thinking of major educational value to all primary and secondary school students, the Italian Inter-universities Consortium for Informatics (CINI), in collaboration with the academic associations who gather together researchers in informatics (GRIN) and computer engineering (GII), has recently proposed a core informatics curriculum for all the levels of compulsory school. This paper summarizes the proposed curriculum, highlights the key underlying motivations, and outlines a possible strategy to ensure that its implementation in schools can be effective.

Keywords: Curriculum · Compulsory education
Non-vocational programs

1 Introduction

Informatics[1] is no longer a subject area cultivated only by professionals, but is relevant to every citizen and should be part of general education since the earliest stages in order to develop "students' computational and critical thinking skills" and show "them how to create, not simply use, new technologies." Informatics "provides a fundamental set of concepts and skills needed to prepare students for

[1] We adopt here the term "Informatics," more common in continental Europe, instead of "Computer Science" or "Computing".

S. N. Pozdniakov and V. Dagienė (Eds.): ISSEP 2018, LNCS 11169, pp. 141–153, 2018.
https://doi.org/10.1007/978-3-030-02750-6_11

the 21st century, regardless of their ultimate field of study or occupation."[2] As a matter of fact, the role of computing in school curricula is currently a topical issue of the education policies all over the world. In the US, for instance, the Computer Science Teachers Association (CSTA) in cooperation with the ACM have proposed comprehensive standards for K-12 education [19], and since 2015 the "Computer Science for All" initiative[3] puts school informatics on a par with other scientific and technological fields. In the UK, following the exhortations from the Royal Society Report "Shut Down or Restart" [22], Computing is a mandatory subject for all instruction levels starting from s.y. 2014–15—see in particular England's "Computing at School" curriculum [9]. Similar démarches are under way in several other countries, although there is not yet full consensus as to what should be taught in K-12, and the associations Informatics Europe and ACM Europe have jointly put forth to the European Commission the "Informatics for All" proposal,[4] whose aim is to establish informatics as an essential discipline for students in Europe at all levels throughout the educational system. A broad picture of the state of CS education worldwide can be found in [1,16].

In this paper we present a recent proposal on behalf of our academic informatics community, which is meant to contribute to the development of informatics education in the Italian primary and secondary school [7]. It is the outcome of a long process, which has also benefited from important contributions of pedagogists and experienced school teachers who took part in the discussion. We are nevertheless aware that it is just a step in a longer path to make all people in charge of school policies aware of what is at stake for the students' future. As stated in the preamble to our document, informatics is having, and will continue to have, a growing impact on the development of production, economy, health, science, culture, entertainment, communication and society in general. In order to cope with the ubiquity of information technology, all citizens must acquire the conceptual tools necessary to understand the science underlying the digital world in which they are immersed and on which the quality of their life will depend. Although we are experiencing a rapid evolution of digital devices and of their applications, its scientific foundations are firm and rest on a homogeneous range of concepts, methodologies and skills. Informatics should then be considered as an independent knowledge field with its peculiar ways of thinking, of interpreting the world, of approaching problems. As Duchâteau pointed out [11], informatics is a relentless endeavor to disclose meaning from form and to confine meaning within form. The conceptual understanding of the scope of its tools revealed, according to Mazoyer [15], the "miracles" that combining a large number of times a small set of elementary operations can achieve a huge potential; that this potential is not specific to some particular type of operations; that the limits to this potential can be expressed and explored formally.

---

2 "Why K-12 computer science?" http://code.org and http://computinginthecore.org.
3 http://cs4all.nyc.
4 http://www.informatics-europe.org/news/434-inf4all.html.

2 Context, Process and Background of the Proposal

In the following subsections we briefly outline the Italian context of primary and secondary education; then we summarize the overall process which has led to the current version of the proposal [7]; finally we review its relevant background.

2.1 The Italian School System

Starting from 2007, the Italian school system has undergone a broad reform process, aimed at renewing both the educational approach and the curricular organization. Compulsory education spans now over 10 years, usually corresponding to the age range 6–16, and is subdivided into three main stages: primary school (grades 1–5), lower secondary school (grades 6–8) and early upper secondary school (grades 9–10). In 2012 the Italian Ministry of Education, University and Research (MIUR) issued the curricular recommendations for the primary and lower secondary levels, that are common to all schools. As opposed to the previous instructional programmes, where the content of each subject area was mainly arranged in temporal sequence, the new framework aligns with the recent European trends in pre-tertiary education, focusing on skills and competences to be acquired in broad areas.[5] The upper secondary level, on the other hand, is characterized by a variety of strands, whose curricula are substantially differentiated from the outset, as appears from the list of specific documents. See [4] for a more comprehensive summary of the secondary school system in Italy. In the outlined picture, primary school teachers do not have subject-specific qualifications.

According to the current national curricular recommendations, computing-related topics and digital technologies should pertain to two rather broad areas:

- A cross-disciplinary key citizenship *digital competence* area:[6] proficiency and critical attitude in the use of ICTs for work, life, communication; use of computer to retrieve, assess, retain, produce, present, share information as well as to cooperate through the Internet.
- A general *technology* subject area (grades 1–8) or a specific informatics/IT-related subject (grades 9–10 for some types of schools, to be taught by qualified teachers), which partly overlaps with the above area, but *may* also include some computer and/or robot programming.

Moreover, with regard to the basic competences at the end of lower secondary education for the scientific-technological area, the national recommendations refer to some general awareness of the implications of using ICTs (for society, environment, health, etc.) and just add that "whenever possible, students can be introduced to simple and flexible programming languages in order to develop a taste for creation and for the accomplishment of projects [...] and in order to understand the relationships between source code and resulting behavior."[7]

[5] In particular, the Italian Ministry has adopted the "Recommendation of the European Parliament and of the Council" of 18 December 2006 on key competences for lifelong learning (2006/962/EC).

[6] *Digital competence* is one of the seven broad areas listed in 2006/962/EC.

[7] http://www.indicazioninazionali.it/ (in Italian).

However, the actual implementation of the curricular recommendations is to a large extent responsibility of each school, in accordance with the degree of autonomy introduced by the reform—autonomy that may occasionally be exploited by self-motivated teachers to propose valuable initiatives also in informatics education.

2.2 Writing and Revision Process

The proposal of a core informatics curriculum for all the levels of compulsory education is a recent initiative of the Italian Inter-universities Consortium for Informatics (CINI), promoted by its interest group for "Informatics and School", and carried out in cooperation with the academic associations who gather together researchers in informatics (GRIN) and computer engineering (GII). The process started in June 2017, when the assembly of the interest group charged an editorial board to write a first draft of the proposal. The draft was subjected to discussion and refinement during several distance meetings of the editorial board, held between June and early August. The document was then made available to all members of the CINI interest group for Informatics and School, who contributed some valuable feedback and were eventually able to reach an agreement on it in a meeting convened in September 2017. The next step was to publish the proposal in the form agreed upon by the interest group and to invite the whole informatics community (represented by CINI, GRIN and GII) to provide comments and suggestions. In the meanwhile, further contributions were collected through discussions with experienced teachers, pedagogists and other experts of school policies. By the end of October 2017 the editorial board examined the feedback from the informatics community and edited the current revision of the document. The revised proposal obtained an official status in November, after formal approval from the assemblies of CINI, GRIN, GII. Finally, in December 2017 it was presented within an initiative of the Italian Chamber of Deputies. For convenience, the proposal[8] has been organized in conformity with the competence-based model of MIUR documents reporting curricular recommendations. It attempts to introduce the general educational motivations as well as to explain as clearly as possible our community's cultural and scientific perspective. The discussion is currently continuing on practical issues, such as the need for instructional material and the involvement of in-service teachers. In March 2018 the document was also submitted to the chair of the MIUR Scientific Committee for the National Curricula for the primary school.

2.3 Background of the Proposal

Informatics has recently been introduced in the official curricula for compulsory school of several countries [12]. Regardless of the approach or tools used, as

[8] An English translation of the official proposal [7] is available at https://www.consorzio-cini.it/gdl-informatica-scuola.

pointed out by Hubwieser *et al.* [13], "there is a convergence towards computational thinking as a core idea of the K-12 curricula" and "programming in one form or another, seems to be absolutely necessary for a future oriented" informatics education. As far as the learning of programming is concerned, we should also note that its scope is now broader than it used to be. Indeed, practicing programming can be seen as a means of self-expression and social participation [14,18], as a component of a new form of literacy [6,24], as a way to widen experience and experiment with personal ideas [5], and maybe also as an instrument to foster children's metacognition [17].

However, to set the background of the present proposal, we can mention, in particular, three noteworthy curricular models:

1. The CSTA/ACM K-12 standards [19], which identify five major strands: *computational thinking*, *collaboration*, *computing practice and programming*, *computers and communication devices*, and *community, global and ethical impacts*.
2. The English implementation of the new computing subject [10], structured into three components emanating from the Royal Society report [22]: *computer science*, *information technology,* and *digital literacy.*
3. The report of the French Academy of Science [8], which distinguishes between three ways of learning informatics, each appropriate for a different instruction level: *discovery* (primary school), *acquisition and autonomy* (lower secondary), and *mastering concepts* (high school).

3 A Core Informatics Curriculum

Informatics at school is often misrepresented as mere use of digital technologies, but this is of course a distorted view. Its real educational value, both as an independent *scientific* discipline and as a cross-disciplinary field, lies in that it offers new and meaningful ways to interpret the world around us and to approach problems. The general term *Computational Thinking* (CT) [25,26] is commonly used to refer to such new ways of characterizing natural as well as artificial systems. However, students need an adequate informatics education to actually take a CT perspective as well as to fully participate in the digital society.

The proposed curriculum has been conceived in a two-dimensional framework. The former dimension, starting from grade 1 of primary school, is characterized by three main learning stages:

1. In the first stage (primary school) pupils are encouraged to *ask questions*, as well as to *discover* in their everyday life and to *explore* some basic ideas of informatics. They can be engaged either in *plugged*, i.e. implying the use of computing devices, or *unplugged* activities, i.e. without using digital technologies [2].
2. In the second stage (lower secondary school) students are expected to *grow in autonomy.* To achieve this educational objective, they have to learn more about the organization of data and the concept of algorithm. Moreover, they

should be offered opportunities to develop *abstract thinking* and to acquire new specific as well as *cross-disciplinary* skills. In particular, programming tasks can play a key role in this respect.
3. The first two stages lay the foundations for mastering the concepts and for enhancing the skills at the core of the third stage (upper secondary school), at the end of which students should be able to *model problems* and to *design algorithms*. Abstraction, organization and accuracy are essential traits of the problem solving approach in the informatics field, that foster the development of critical thinking and provide helpful keys to master complexity.

The latter dimension concerns the content, which is organized into five key areas: *algorithms*, *programming*, *data and information*, *digital creativity* and *digital awareness*. Each such area will be the subject of a separate subsection. Overall, as reported in the list of general learning goals, at the end of compulsory school each student should be able:

- to understand and to apply basic concepts and principles of informatics;
- to approach problems by exploiting tools and methods of the field;
- to solve problems by devising formal representations, by designing algorithms and by coding the algorithms in a programming language;
- to evaluate the potential benefits as well as the limits of applying a range of digital technologies to achieve a given task;
- to use digital technologies in a conscious, responsible, confident, purposeful and creative way.

3.1 Area of Algorithms

Algorithms are at the core of informatics. They predate programming, as several noteworthy algorithms have been designed well before the advent of computers. Pupils should meet the concept of algorithm since the early years of primary school, in an informal and playful way at first. Starting from the lower secondary school, the level of formality is progressively increased and the concept of algorithm is linked to other school subjects. By the end of the curriculum, pupils are expected to master the notion of algorithm and the related scientific concepts. To achieve these general goals, the curriculum tackles four main topics.

Algorithms as Procedures. Pupils first encounter algorithms in grades 1–3, as a way to describe the procedures representing the activities of everyday life; *e.g.*, brushing one's teeth, dressing, leaving the classroom in an emergency drill. The initial approach could be unplugged, to later evolve into plugged activities, for example to solve coding puzzles. In grades 6–8, the collection of processes that are studied algorithmically is extended to include examples taken from other disciplines, such as mathematics, science and technology. Towards the end of the curriculum, pupils should know a selection of simple algorithms that solve fundamental informatics problems such as search and sorting. Apart from studying existing ones, pupils should progressively grow in autonomy and start to design their own algorithms, a skill that should be accomplished by the end of the curriculum.

Interpretation and Disambiguation. The process of learning and designing algorithms should be accompanied by an increasing understanding that algorithms need to be described in a precise and unambiguous manner. In grades 1–5, this goal could be accomplished by having the pupils perform the role of the executor, in an unplugged way. In grades 6–8, the need of precision is reinforced, by making pupils reflect on the instructions performed by the automatic executor and how they are always completed in the same way. Pupils are thus expected to reflect on the ambiguities hidden in an algorithm described using natural language.

Decomposition. By grade 3, pupils should understand that difficult problems could be solved by breaking them down in smaller parts; by grade 5, such understanding should become operational, *i.e.*, pupils should be able to actually solve simple problems in such way. These concepts are later reinforced by the concept of modularity introduced in Sect. 3.2.

Reasoning About Algorithms. During the second and third stage of the curriculum (lower and upper secondary school), pupils are introduced to a larger spectrum of issues related to algorithmics. They should move away from the concept of algorithms solving specific instances of a problem, and understand that algorithms should solve problems in their generality. By grade 8, pupils should be able to reflect on the correctness of their solutions, in particular by detecting and describing the conditions under which these processes can terminate. By grade 10, pupils should also be able to evaluate, in simple terms, the efficiency of basic algorithms and use logical reasoning to evaluate different algorithms that solve the same problem. They should also be able to understand that not all problems can be solved by algorithms in an efficient way.

3.2 Area of Programming

Starting in the early grades pupils should get familiar with writing computer programs. In primary schools pupils write structurally simple programs, that possibly react to events, within a friendly—*e.g.*, visual—programming environment. By grade 8, pupils are expected to design, write and debug, using easy-to-use programming languages, programs that apply selection, loops, variables and elementary forms of input and output. By grade 10, pupils are expected to comply with syntax while writing simple programs in a textual programming language; moreover they should be able to define, implement and validate programs and systems that model or simulate simple physical systems or familiar processes, that occur in the real world or are studied in other disciplines. Overall, pupils should be able to operate on a program in order to understand its behaviour, modify it, identify and fix flaws. In primary schools, pupils first observe errors in programs and act spontaneously to correct them, then they start examining programs in order to detect and fix errors and should be able to use logical reasoning to understand why a simple program fails; by grade 8 they should intentionally experience small changes in a program to understand and modify its behaviour; by grade 10 they should recognize how the various parts of a program contribute to its functioning, and be able to predict the outcome of a program without running it. To achieve these general goals, the following specific skills should be progressively developed from grade 1 to 10.

Sequencing, Selection and Iteration. In early primary school pupils are expected to sort a sequence of instructions correctly, use one-way selection to make decisions within simple programs, and explore the use of two-way selection to implement mutually exclusive actions. The first use of loops in primary school is to concisely express that a certain action has to be repeated a given number of times; then loops can be used to repeat a certain action while an easy-to-test condition holds. By grade 8 pupils should be able to nest selection and loops as above, and start using variables in the conditions of selections and loops; by grade 10, they should be able to write conditions that use a logical operator, and use conditionals/selections within loops to describe the repetition of parametric actions.

Use of Variables. In primary school, variables are used to represent input and output data, or to represent data computed during the execution of a program; by grade 8, simply typed variables are used to represent the state of a program and track the progress of the computation; by grade 10, students should write programs with structured variables, and be able to use variables in loops to define exit conditions or parametric actions.

Modularity. By grade 5, pupils recognize that a sequence of instructions can be considered as a single action subject to repetition or selection; by grade 8 they should be able to re-arrange a program to improve it, by organizing it in modular components as functions and procedures; by grade 10 they should design and develop modular programs using procedures and functions.

3.3 Area of Data and Information

The possibility of representing information through symbols, which can be stored and manipulated by an automatic processing system, lies at the very foundations of computing and then must be part of any informatics curriculum. Representing information is inherently connected to an abstraction process. Therefore concepts and methods in this area are acquired throughout the whole span of the curriculum, following the progression of pupils' abstraction abilities. Starting at grade 5, the curriculum aims at developing awareness that computers deal merely with raw data, encoded as symbols, and that information pertains only to the sphere of meaning, intrinsic to the human mind, what necessarily implies some degree of subjectivity. The main goals of the curriculum in this area can be classified by theme as follows.

Data Representation. Starting from grade 1, pupils gradually explore potential representations of various kinds of data (*e.g.,* numbers, images, sounds), using different formats, possibly even some of their own conception. By the end of grade 3, they should be able to select and use suitable items to represent simple data they are familiar with (*e.g.,* colors, words). At the end of grade 8, pupils should realize whether two alternative representations of the same data are interchangeable for a given purpose. The conventional character of any data representation, relative to what it is meant to describe, should be fully understood in grades 9–10. As a consequence, pupils become aware that different ways of representing data may affect both the effectiveness and the efficiency of a computation on such data. This achievement is also a prerequisite for the subsequent development of the ability to identify and choose the data representations best suited to an intended purpose.

Structure and Organization of Data. At grades 4–5 pupils start to represent simple structured data (*e.g.,* bitmap images) as well as, through combinations of symbols, a little more complex data familiar to them (*e.g.,* secondary colors, sentences). From grade 6 to 8 they develop the ability to classify data according to their kind (*e.g.,* numerical, textual), that leads to the data type concept. At the same time, they should learn to perform simple manipulations of symbols that represent structured data (*e.g.,* binary numbers, bitmap images), and to use structured variables to represent collections of homogeneous data (*e.g.,* vectors, lists). At the end of grade 10, pupils should know the features of basic data structures (*e.g.,* lists, vectors, matrices, dictionaries) and learn how to select an appropriate structure to approach a given problem.

Roles of Data. The perception that data can be used in fundamentally dissimilar ways is to be developed in parallel with the programming skills, in particular those in connection with the use of variables. At the end of grade 8, pupils should be capable to distinguish the different roles played by the data within a program. Starting with the identification of input and output data, pupils should become familiar with the representation of the state of a computation carried out by a computer program. The idea of metadata should be introduced, in some specific context such as HTML or a simple data description language, in grades 9–10.

3.4 Area of Digital Creativity

Information Technologies (IT) are a very powerful means of self-expression and creativity. Starting from grade 1, pupils should become aware that they *can* use IT to express themselves, whereas too often they are just passive consumers of ready-to-use technological products and applications. As their ability to program improves, they are encouraged to engage with actively creating digital content and computer programs (in suitable environments), progressively using and combining different media, technologies and services. Moreover, they should start to reflect, to decide whether to use or not available technologies, and possibly to select appropriate technologies for different expressive purposes or to solve small problems they are personally interested in.

Use and Creation of Digital Content. Using digital content and computer applications is just a first step: in grades 1–5, pupils should learn how to create simple and multimedia digital content; in addition, they start to select appropriate content, as well as to modify and combine it in simple ways. In grades 6–8 pupils should experiment with different ways of processing digital content (*e.g.*, bitmaps versus vectorial images), while learning how to effectively present it.

Active Creation of Software Applications. From grade 3, pupils should start to create simple computer applications like stories, games, music, using environments designed for their age (*e.g.*, visual programming languages with blocks). In grades 6–8 they should be able to take advantage of their increasing experience with programming to create applications. In grades 8–10, pupils should use more advanced environments (*e.g.*, text-based programming languages) to create more elaborate content. Moreover, they should combine programming and on-line services to solve problems and to achieve tasks.

3.5 Area of Digital Awareness

Computer-based devices have pervaded everybody's life and it is important to develop awareness in pupils, since early years at school, with respect to their use and how they affect life and relations. This goal is pursued by our curriculum along two paths: a first one focusing on expanding pupils' knowledge of the information technology systems and devices, and a second one where students reflect, in increasing depth, on the personal and social impact of digital technologies.

Knowledge of Information Technology. In primary school pupils progress from recognizing the presence of IT devices all around them to being able to identify their main components and the main services they provide, while becoming aware of the importance of protecting personal data also in their various digital instantiations. In lower secondary school this knowledge is deepened with a comprehension of the main physical and functional principles at the core of computing systems and their communication networks, and through first experiences of interconnecting computer-based systems and input-output peripherals, and collecting and analyzing data. In the early upper secondary school pupils understand the importance of taking into account enduser requirements for the development of computer-based applications and deepen their experience with using computers to interact with and control external devices.

Social Impact. In primary school pupils are progressively sensitized to the importance of interacting respectfully with others, even when using digital platforms, and to identifying and reporting problems in social interactions mediated by information technology. In lower secondary school they grow in their understanding of the value of data, both from a personal viewpoint and from a general one, and of how the collection and processing of large quantities of data affects society. In the early upper secondary school pupils arrive at critically reflecting on the multifaceted relations between information technology and society, spanning any domain of interest, and on the importance of keeping human beings in control of critical steps whenever computer-based decisions affect people.

4 The Future of Our Proposal in the Schools

In order to have a real impact on schools we need to face several challenges and operational difficulties. A major challenge is to cope with the general shortage of teachers with sufficient familiarity with the basic concepts of informatics, an issue emerging also in other countries [21,23]. Even in vocational schools it is common to find teachers with a poor background in the field [3] and, given the current state of the recruitment process, we can hardly hope that the situation will improve in the next few years. Thus, the teachers at all levels, but especially at the earliest grades, need support to cope with the need to reshape their teaching practice. A national effort is then required to identify and validate suitable instructional methodologies and learning materials that can support effective learning by distilling and formalizing what in essence amounts to the so called *Pedagogical Content Knowledge—i.e.,* the "the knowledge of teachers to help others learn", including "the ways of representing and formulating the subject that makes it comprehensible to others" [20]. We believe this could be achieved by designing and carrying out small-scale action-research projects in cooperation between school teachers and researchers in computer science education, as well as by documenting the results, strengths and weaknesses of a variety of teaching approaches. However, the next crucial steps to be successful in introducing informatics in the Italian school are to design a systematic way to disseminate best practices and to make available appropriate textbooks.

The recommendations outlined here may still sound a little utopian to anyone who knows the current state of the Italian schools. In fact, our main goal was to raise awareness among stakeholders and, in particular, policy makers by offering a comprehensive view of how informatics could be introduced in schools as well as by pointing out the potential benefits for every citizen of the 21st century. Our proposal has gained the endorsement of the reference informatics communities and is based on a sensible pedagogical analysis of its major themes. Moreover, as we have tried to explain in this paper, the informatics curriculum has been conceived as a whole, built up of strongly interconnected parts: the learning goals of later grades would appear much more plausible in light of the achievements expected at earlier stages. Finally, we are well aware that the strategy we envisage presupposes a strong political commitment towards informatics education in schools with a focus, beyond the hype of digital competences, on the scientific principles underlying the development of a digital society.

References

1. Barendsen, E., et al.: Concepts in K-9 computer science education. In: Proceedings of the 2015 ITiCSE on Working Group Reports, pp. 85–116. ACM (2015)
2. Bell, T., Alexander, J., Freeman, I., Grimley, M.: Computer Science Unplugged: school students doing real computing without computers. N. Z. J. Appl. Comput. Inf. Technol. **13**(1), 20–29 (2009)
3. Bellettini, C., Lonati, V., Malchiodi, D., Monga, M., Morpurgo, A., Pedersini, F.: La formazione degli insegnanti della classe 42/A-informatica: l'esperienza

dell'università degli studi di milano. In: E questo tutti chiamano informatica: L'esperienza dei TFA nelle discipline informatiche, Collana Manuali, Chap. 4, vol. 14, pp. 53–76. Sapienza Univ. Ed. (2015). In Italian
4. Bellettini, C., et al.: Informatics education in Italian secondary schools. Trans. Comput. Educ. **14**(2), 15:1–15:6 (2014)
5. Boyatt, R., Beynon, M., Beynon, M.: Ghosts of programming past, present and yet to come. In: du Boulay, B., Good, J. (eds.) Proceedings of the 25th Annual Workshop of the Psychology of Programming Interest Group - PPIG 2014, pp. 171–182 (2014)
6. Burke, Q.: The markings of a new pencil: Introducing programming-as-writing in the middle school classroom. J. Media Lit. Educ. **4**(2), 121–135 (2012)
7. CINI: Proposta di indicazioni nazionali per l'insegnamento dell'informatica nella scuola, December 2017. https://www.consorzio-cini.it/index.php/it/component/attachments/download/745. In Italian
8. Committee on Science Education: Teaching computer science in France: tomorrow can't wait. Technical report, Institut de France - Académie des Sciences (2013). http://www.academie-sciences.fr/en/Advice-Notes-and-Reports/teaching-computer-science-in-france-tomorrow-can-t-wait.html
9. Computing at School: Computer science: a curriculum for schools (2012). http://www.computingatschool.org.uk/data/uploads/ComputingCurric.pdf
10. Department for Education: National curriculum for England: computing programme of study. Technical report, Department for Education (2013). https://www.gov.uk/government/publications/national-curriculum-in-england-computing-programmes-of-study/national-curriculum-in-england-computing-programmes-of-study
11. Duchâteau, C.: Peut-on définir une "culture informatique"? Journal de Réflexion sur l'Informatique (Institut d'Informatique, FUNDP, Namur) **23–24**, 34–39 (1992)
12. European Schoolnet: Computing our future: computer programming and coding: priorities, school curricula and initiatives across Europe - Update 2015 (2015)
13. Hubwieser, P., Armoni, M., Giannakos, M.N., Mittermeir, R.T.: Perspectives and visions of computer science education in primary and secondary (K-12) schools. Trans. Comput. Educ. **14**(2), 7:1–7:9 (2014)
14. Kafai, Y.B., Burke, Q.: The social turn in K-12 programming: moving from computational thinking to computational participation. In: Proceeding of the 44th ACM Technical Symposium on Computer Science Education, pp. 603–608. ACM (2013)
15. Mazoyer, J.: Universalité de la notion de calcul. L'enseignement de l'informatique de la maternelle à la terminale, Académie des sciences - workshop (2005)
16. McCartney, R., Tenenberg, J. (eds.) Special issue on computing education in K-12 schools. Trans. Comput. Educ. **14**(2) (2014). https://dl.acm.org/citation.cfm?id=2642651
17. Resnick, M., et al.: Scratch: programming for all. Commun. ACM **52**, 60–67 (2009)
18. Schulte, C.: Reflections on the role of programming in primary and secondary computing education. In: Proceedings of the 8th Workshop in Primary and Secondary Computing Education, WiPSE 2013, pp. 17–24. ACM, New York (2013)
19. Seehorn, D. (ed.) K-12 Computer Science Standards - Revised 2011: The CSTA Standards Task Force. ACM (2011). http://csta.acm.org/Curriculum/sub/K12Standards.html
20. Shulman, L.S.: Those who understand: knowledge growth in teaching. Educ. Res. **15**(2), 4–14 (1986)

21. The Committee on European Computing Education (CECE): Informatics education in Europe: are we all in the same boat? (2017). http://www.informatics-europe.org/component/phocadownload/category/10-reports.html?download=60:cece-report
22. The Royal Society: Shut down or restart? The way forward for computing in UK schools. The Royal Society, London (2012)
23. The Royal Society: After the reboot: computing education in UK schools. The Royal Society, London (2017)
24. Vee, A.: Understanding computer programming as a literacy. Lit. Compos. Stud. **1**(2), 42–64 (2013)
25. Wing, J.M.: Computational thinking. Commun. ACM **49**(3), 33–35 (2006)
26. Wing, J.M.: Computational thinking: what and why? The Link Magazine (2011)

Comparative Analysis of the Content of School Course of Informatics in Russia and Subjects of the International Competition Bebras

Liudmila Bosova(✉)

Moscow Pedagogical State University, Moscow, Russian Federation
abosova@gmail.com

Abstract. During of the first twenty-five years of its existence, the informatics course in Russian school was structured around following cross-cutting content lines: information and information processes; representation of information; computer; modeling and formalization; algorithmization and programming; Information Technology; computer telecommunications, social informatics. Recently thematic block Mathematical foundations of computer science has been more clearly formed in it. In addition traditional line of algorithmization and programming, which was transformed into the thematic block Algorithms and programming elements, which includes robotics and mathematical modeling, has developed significantly. In general content of the course of informatics is stable, its fundamental component is the basis of the state final certification of graduates of primary and senior schools. At the same time students, their parents as well as representatives of the higher education and IT industry express concern about content of the modern school informatics course, rightly believing that this discipline has much greater potential for mastering such key competences of the digital economy as basic programming, basics of working with data, communication in modern digital environments. Since 2012, Russian students successfully participate in the international distant competition Bebras, in the tasks of which priority is given to the issues of theoretical informatics as the basis of modern information technologies. The subject field of the competition is in many respects consonant with the content lines of Russian informatics course in school, the main differences lie in approaches to the representation of key concepts, ideas, methods and algorithms. Materials of the international competition Bebras can become a basis for the modernization of Russian informatics course in school by expanding its theoretical base as well as ensuring the unity of its theoretical and practical components.

Keywords: Content of school course of informatics in Russia
International course Bebras

The course of Informatics, which appeared in Russian school in 1985, always had mandatory status, although it occupied a different place in educational plans

S. N. Pozdniakov and V. Dagienė (Eds.): ISSEP 2018, LNCS 11169, pp. 154–164, 2018.
https://doi.org/10.1007/978-3-030-02750-6_12

of educational organizations. At present, Informatics is formally represented at all levels of Russian school education; final state attestation (certification) on Informatics (exam for choice) for graduates of secondary and high school.

In Federal State Educational Standards of primary general education the subject area "Mathematics and Informatics" has been singled out, but compulsory study of the independent subject"Informatics" is not provided: the fundamental concepts of Informatics are integrated into mathematics; the formation of elementary user skills is envisaged within the framework of the course "Technology (Handicraft, manual training)". In a number of schools the study of an independent subject"Informatics" in an elementary school (2–4 or 3–4 grades) is introduced in the part of the curriculum, formed at the choice of participants in educational relations. In recent years, modern interactive media for early learning algorithms and programming have become widespread in primary school: Piktomir, Scratch, Studio Code, and others.

Compulsory study of Informatics at the level of basic general education is provided only in grades 7–9 in meeting 1 h per week, only 105 h for three years of study; trying to resolve the apparent contradiction between the educational potential of the school course of Informatics and the insufficient amount of study time allocated for its implementation, many educational organizations independently design a continuous course of Informatics in the secondary school, adding for this from the variable part of the curriculum (the parts formed by the participants in educational relations) hours on the study of Informatics in grades 5–6.

In high school, the study of the course of Informatics is not mandatory, although depending on the profile of education, educational organizations can choose to study this subject at a basic or advanced level. The results of the basic level of Informatics (1 h per week, 70 h in total for 2 years) are focused on general functional literacy, obtaining competencies for daily life and general development; the results of the advanced level of studying Informatics (4 h a week, 280 h in total for 2 years of training) are aimed at obtaining competences for the subsequent professional activities both within the framework of this subject area and in related fields.

During the first twenty-five years of its existence, the Informatics course at Russian school was structured around the following cross-cutting content lines: information and information processes; presentation of information; a computer; modeling and formalization; algorithmization and programming; Information Technology; computer telecommunications; social Informatics. Recently, the thematic block "Mathematical foundations of Informatics" has been more clearly formed in it, including such questions as: texts and coding; sampling; number systems; elements of combinatorics, set theory and mathematical logic; lists, graphs, trees. In addition, the traditional line of algorithmization and programming, which was transformed into the thematic block"Algorithms and programming elements", which now includes a number of aspects of robotics and mathematical modeling, has developed significantly.

A general idea of the current content of the Russian course in Informatics is given by the current basic educational program of compulsory education) [2], in which the material to be studied is structured as follows:

Section 1. Introduction

1. Information and information processes
2. A computer is a universal data processing device

Section 2. Mathematical Foundations of Informatics

3. Texts and coding
4. Discretization
5. Number systems
6. Elements of combinatorics, set theory and mathematical logic
7. Lists, graphs, trees

Section 3. Algorithms and elements of programming

8. Performers and algorithms. Managing performers
9. Algorithmic constructions
10. Building Algorithms and Programs
11. Analysis of algorithms
12. Robotics
13. Mathematical modeling

Section 4. Using software systems and services

14. File system
15. Preparation of texts and demonstration materials
16. Electronic (dynamic) spread sheets
17. Databases. Search for information
18. Work in the Informational Space. Information and communication technologies.

In general, the content of the course of Informatics is stable, its fundamental component is the basis of the final state certification of graduates of primary and senior schools. The set of requirements for the planned results of the study of Informatics, the planned results and the content of Informatics in the school are fully consistent with the principle of the didactic spiral underlying the methodology of teaching Informatics: first, the general acquaintance of students with the subject of study is carried out, assuming that their experience is taken into account; then the subsequent development and enrichment of the subject of study, which creates the prerequisites for scientific generalization in the upper grades.

At the same time, students, their parents, as well as representatives of the higher school and IT industry express concern about the content of the modern school Informatics course, rightly believing that this discipline has a much greater potential for mastering such key competences of the digital economy as basic programming, the basics of working with data, communication in modern digital environments. Correlation of our achievements in the field of school Informatics with foreign experience can be useful for determining the vector of further development of this subject, including for more substantiated adoption of certain decisions on the modernization of its content.

Since 2012 Russian schoolchildren of grades 1–11 successfully participate in the international remote competition "Bebras" (the official site of the contest in Russia http://bebras.ru/), in the tasks of which priority is given to the issues of theoretical Informatics as the basis of modern information technologies. The"Bebras" contest is the only contest in Informatics recognized by the world community as one for all countries. The contest provides tasks for different age groups of students, who are asked to solve 12 to 16 tasks in 40–45 minutes. A fairly complete idea of the subject of the problems of the "Bebras" contest can be formed on the basis of the materials of the site http://bebras.ru/, where currently the conditions of all the tasks of the 2013–2016 contests are presented. The subject field of the competition (algorithms and programming, data and data structures, computer architecture and processes, communications and network interaction, systems and society) is in many respects consonant with the content lines of the Russian course of school Informatics, the main differences lie in approaches to the representation of key concepts, ideas, methods and algorithms. We show this using the example of the tasks of the"Bebras-2015" competition for pupils of grades 7–8, comparing their subjects with the contents of the Russian Informatics course for grades 7–9 of the main school, since it is at this stage that the study of the Informatics course in our country is mandatory (Table 1). At the same time we will rely on the content of the school Informatics course, presented in the approximate basic educational program of basic general education (BEP BGE), as well as the contents of the author's program [1]. See Table 1

Table 1. Content of the Informatics course for the basic school in the Russian Federation.

N	Tasks of the competition "Bebras"	Sample program	Author's program
1	Country: Japan. Task title: Animation. The idea of the task: Objects, object classes. Information modeling of objects of the real world by means of the list of signs and their values. Computer image processing to find the differences between them	Content in the BEP BGE is not provided. It is advisable to include it in Section 1 "Introduction", the topic "Information and Information Processes". Current content:information as data that can be processed by an automated system, and information as information intended for human perception	The theme is presented fully in the textbooks of Informatics of grades 5–6

(*continued*)

Table 1. (*continued*)

N	Tasks of the competition "Bebras"	Sample program	Author's program
2	Country: Germany. Task title: Lunch of the beaver. The idea of the problem: A tree as a model of a hierarchical structure	The content in the BEP BGE is presented: Section 2 "Mathematical Foundations of Informatics", the topic "Lists, graphs, trees". Current content:Tree. Root, leaf, top (node). Previous vertex, successive vertices. Under the tree. The height of the tree. Binary tree. Family tree	The theme is presented fully in the textbooks of Informatics of grades 7–9
3	Country: Bulgaria. Task name: String Pyramid. The idea of the task: Imitation of simple calculations on a computer's chip, when input information is processed in several steps to get the result	Content in the BEP BGE is not provided. It is advisable to include it in Section 1 "Introduction", the topic "Computer - a universal data processing device". Current content:Computer architecture: processor, RAM, external non-volatile memory, input-output devices; their quantitative characteristics	In the textbooks of the 7th and 8th grades, the talk about microcircuits is conducted, but theoretically, without reinforcement by the solution of any problems.
4	Country: Austria. Task title: Phonebook. The idea of the problem: Finding specific data in a large data set	The content in the BEP BGE is presented, but somewhat already - as a file search in the file system: Section 4 "Using software systems and services", the theme "File system". Current content: principles of building file systems. Catalog (directory). Basic operations when working with files: creating, editing, copying, moving, deleting. Types of files. File manager. Search in the file system	The theme is presented in the 7th class Informatics textbook - as a file in the file system

(*continued*)

Table 1. (*continued*)

N	Tasks of the competition "Bebras"	Sample program	Author's program
5	Country: Spain. Task title: Baskets with flowers. The idea of the problem: Sorting algorithms as the most popular algorithms for processing large amounts of data. Sort by bubble	The content in the BEP BGE is presented: Section 3 "Algorithms and programming elements", the topic "Building algorithms and programs". Current content: familiarity with the formulation of more complex data processing tasks and algorithms for their solution - sorting the array, performing element-wise operations with arrays	The topic is presented in the Informatics textbook of the 9th grade.
6	Country: Hungary. Task title: Acrobats. The idea of the problem: A recursive algorithm. The variation of the famous puzzle "Hanoi Tower"	Content in the BEP BGE is not provided	The theme is presented fully in the textbooks of Informatics of grades 5–6, 7–9.
7	Country: Czech Republic. Task title: Relations between passengers. The idea of the problem: The graph as a means of modeling. A complete graph.	The content in the BEP BGE is presented (see clause 2). Complete graphs are not considered, their properties are not studied; tasks of this kind are not proposed for consideration	The topic is presented in part in the textbooks of Informatics 5–6, 7–9 grades
8	Country: Taiwan. Task title: Dams. The idea of the problem: The task of finding the longest path in the graph. Algorithm for topological sorting of vertices in an oriented graph	The content in the BEP BGE is presented: Section 2 "Mathematical Foundations of Informatics", the topic "Lists, graphs, trees". Current content:Graph. A vertex, an edge, a path. Oriented and undirected graphs. The initial vertex (source) and the final vertex (sink) in the oriented graph. Length (weight) of the rib and path. The concept of a minimal path. Matrix of contiguity of graph (with lengths of edges).Formally, the topic is presented in the course of Informatics of the main school, although similar algorithms are not considered in it	The topic is presented in part in the textbooks of Informatics 5–6, 7–9 grades

(*continued*)

Table 1. (*continued*)

N	Tasks of the competition "Bebras"	Sample program	Author's program
9	Country: Switzerland. Task title: Cheese price. The idea of the problem: Recording the algorithm using flowcharts. execution of an algorithm written using a flowchart. Cyclic algorithm. A cycle with a postcondition. Algorithm for calculating the factorial	The content in the BEP BGE is presented: Section 3 "Algorithms and programming elements", the theme "Algorithmic constructions". Current content: The construction of "repetition": loops with a given number of repetitions, with a run condition, with a variable loop. Checking the condition for executing the loop before the loop body starts executing and after executing the loop body: the postcondition and the precondition of the loop	The theme is presented fully in the textbook of Informatics of the 8th grade
10	Country Russia. Task title: Chakhokhbili. The idea of the problem: Multiprocessing, parallel computing	The content in the BEP BGE is presented: Section 1 "Introduction", the topic "Computer - Universal Data Processing Device". Current content: parallel computing	The topic is presented in the 7th grade textbook in the most general terms
11	Country: Canada. Task title: Fireworks. The idea of the problem: Binary coding. Uniform and uneven coding. Prefix code	The content in BEP BGE is presented: section 2 "Mathematical foundations of Informatics", the theme "Texts and coding". Current content:Coding characters of one alphabet using code words in another alphabet; code table, decoding. Binary codes with a fixed code word length. Dependence of the number of code combinations on the code capacity. Distortion of information during transmission. Codes that correct errors. The possibility of unambiguous decoding for codes with different code words length	The theme is presented fully in the textbook of Informatics of the 7th grade

(*continued*)

Table 1. (*continued*)

N	Tasks of the competition "Bebras"	Sample program	Author's program
12	Country Russia. Task title: Leaping kangaroo.Executor. System of commands of the executor.The idea of the problem: The theory of graphs. The problem of finding the Hamiltonian path	The content in the BEP BGE is presented: Section 3 "Algorithms and programming elements", the topic "Executors and algorithms". Current content:Performers. The states, possible situations and the system of commands of the performer.The content in the BEP BGE is presented (see clause 2).Topics are considered in isolation; tasks of this kind are not proposed for consideration	The topic is presented in part in the textbooks of Informatics of grades 8–9
13	Country: Poland. Task title: Elegant graphs. The idea of the problem: Weighted graph. Acquaintance with the graceful marking of the graph's vertices	The content in the BEP BGE is presented (see clause 2).Problems of this kind are not proposed for consideration	The topic is presented in part in the textbook of Informatics 9 class
14	Country: Slovenia. Task title: Spyware. The idea of the problem: Data exchange. Network. Cryptography	Content in the BEP BGE is not provided. It is advisable to include it in Section 4 "Using software systems and services", the topic "Work in the Information Space". Current content: Computer networks. The Internet. Addressing in the Internet. Domain name system. Site. Network storage of data. Large data in nature and technology (genomic data, the results of physical experiments, Internet data, in particular, data from social networks). Technologies of their processing and storage	Individual elements are presented in the textbooks of Informatics of 10–11 classes (advanced level)

(*continued*)

Table 1. (*continued*)

N	Tasks of the competition "Bebras"	Sample program	Author's program
15	Country Ukraine. Task title: Drinks and containers. The idea of the problem: Logic. Statements and their analysis. Truth tables	The content in BEP BGE is presented: section 2 "Mathematical foundations of Informatics", the theme "Elements of combinatorics, set theory and mathematical logic". Current content:Statements. Simple and complex statements. Logical meanings of statements. Logical expressions. Logical operations: "and" (conjunction, logical multiplication), "or" (disjunction, logical addition), "not" (logical negation). Rules for writing logical expressions. Priorities of logical operations.Truth tables. Building truth tables for logical expressions	The theme is presented fully in the textbook of Informatics of the 8th grade

So, the themes of the tasks of the "Bebras" competition and the content of the Russian Informatics course for the main school are quite close. At the same time, even if there is a general content, the approaches to its implementation are different. We will show this on the example of the elements of graph theory, which are quite fully represented in the national Informatics course for the main school. As for practical work with graphs, it is limited to an extremely narrow range of typical problems. Thus, one of the most common problems is the problem presented in Fig. 1, which has been consistently included in the control and measuring materials of the basic state exam in Informatics for the last several years [3]. See Table 2

To solve this problem, students are asked to move from the tabular form of information to the graph; it is even better to construct a tree whose branches will represent all possible paths between the vertices A and E.

It should be noted that the tasks related to graphs in the "Bebras" contest are very common: each year their number varies from 4 to 6, while the total number of tasks does not exceed 16. The tasks have a different level of complexity and

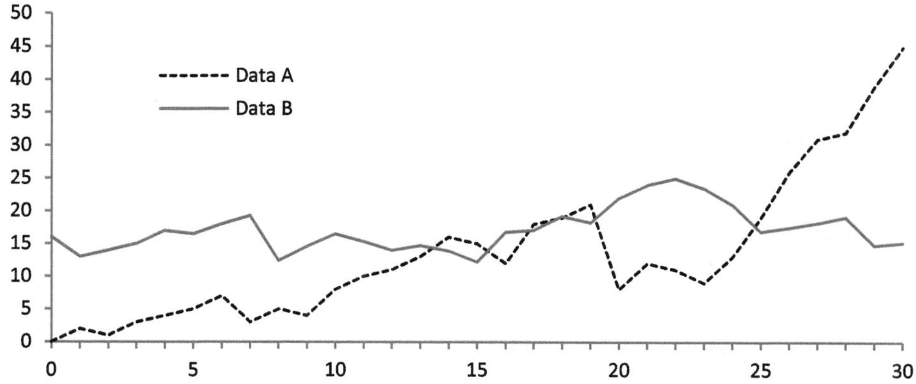

Fig. 1. Between the settlements A, B, C, D, E roads are constructed, the length of which (in kilometers) is given in the table. Determine the length of the shortest path between points A and E. You can move only on roads, the length of which is indicated in the table (1) 4; (2) 5; (3) 6; (4) 7;

Table 2. The problem of determining the shortest path in a graph.

	A	B	C	D	E
A		2	5	1	
B	2		1		
C	5	1		3	2
D	1		3		
E			2		

cover different issues from graph theory. It should be noted that the formulations of these tasks, the practice-oriented submission of material are fundamentally new for our schoolchildren. There is every reason to believe that schoolchildren will have difficulty in solving such problems: not everyone will be able to apply their knowledge of graph theory in a new situation or to come up with a way to solve the problem on their own. In addition, they are unlikely to be able to explain what kind of relationship such tasks have to do with Informatics. The inclusion in the Russian course of school Informatics of a wider range of questions from graph theory is one of the possible directions of its development.

Over the years of the contest existence there is a significant archive of assignments offered at previous competitions. Anyone can get access to them through the official website of the contest. These tasks develop logical thinking, they are interesting, not beaten, they practically do not repeat tasks from traditional problem books, although they are based on the same theoretical material.

Materials of the international competition "Bebras" can become a basis for the modernization of the Russian school Informatics course by expanding its theoretical base (for example, more complete representation of questions related to graphs), as well as ensuring the unity of its theoretical and practical components.

References

1. Bosova, L.L., Bosova, A.Y.: Informatics. The program for the main school: grades 5–6, 7–9 grades. - M.: BINOM. Knowledge lab (2014)
2. Approximate basic educational program of basic general education. Approved by the decision of the federal educational and methodological association for general education (protocol of April 8, 2015 No. 1/15) [Electronic resource]. http://fgosreestr.ru/wp-content/uploads/2017/03/primernaja-osnovnaja-obrazovatelnaja-programma-osnovogo-obshchego-obrazovanija.docx. (Date of circulation 19 May 2018)
3. Federal Institute of Pedagogical Measurements. Demos, specifications, codifiers OGE 2018. Informatics and ICT [Electronic resource]. http://www.fipi.ru/sites/default/files/document/1511540449/inf_oge_2018.zip. (Date of circulation: 19 May 2018)

Teacher Education in Informatics

Computational Thinking: Constructing the Perceptions of Pre-service Teachers from Various Disciplines

Ragonis Noa[1,2(✉)]

[1] Beit Berl College, Kfar Saba, Israel
noarag@beitberl.ac.il
[2] Technion Israel Institute of Technology, Haifa, Israel

Abstract. In the last two decades, educators have been following the terminology of Computational Thinking first posed by Wing. Different viewpoints and commentaries have been adopted, and accordingly course syllabi and learning materials were developed, particularly for K-12. The field has become a mandatory part of the curriculum in various countries, even for preschool age. The paper presents an academic course for pre-service teachers with the main aim to facilitate and instruct students in the process of building their understanding and interpretation of Computational Thinking, in the context of teaching their own discipline. The course pedagogical approach emphasizes the adoption of Computational Thinking while identifying significant, non-trivial, computational processes in different disciplines. The course model was implemented with three pre-service teacher populations studying for their teaching certificate in: (1) sciences for high school; (2) humanities and social sciences for high school; and (3) various disciplines for elementary school. The course allows future teachers to experience for themselves learning activities that are recommended for implementation with their future students. The course pedagogical approach and rationale are presented, followed by detailed course structure and learning assignments. The teaching, learning, and assessment approach yielded impressive achievements, although not without obstacles and difficulties. The details of the course presentation enable its implementation with different populations of pre-service and in-service teachers, and can also be implemented in schools.

Keywords: Computational Thinking (CT) · Teachers preparation
Active learning · Simulation of computational process

1 Introduction

The concept of computational thinking has many definitions, the common definition stated by Wing [21] is that "Computational thinking is the thought processes involved in formulating a problem and expressing its solution(s) in such a way that a computer—human or machine—can effectively carry out". The development of computational thinking skill of 21st-century students is accepted as central and important. To achieve this, consideration must be given to teacher training, which is always the most

S. N. Pozdniakov and V. Dagienė (Eds.): ISSEP 2018, LNCS 11169, pp. 167–179, 2018.
https://doi.org/10.1007/978-3-030-02750-6_13

significant link in the process. Although different definitions have been given to the concept there is a significant core acceptable to all. It is important to allow teachers to be exposed to the different approaches and to formulate their understanding and meaning. The paper describes our interpretation of connecting computational thinking with computational processes and algorithmic computational thinking. Emphasis is placed on the importance of imparting Computational Thinking (CT) to learners of different ages and in different school subjects as a thinking skill for life. The presented pedagogical approach enables the development of algorithmic CT that links to computerized systems, since understanding and control of those systems is also a necessary skill for graduates of today's education system. The course development maintained a constant link between the conceptual and the applied levels. The central pedagogical approach is that a school student can identify and define a computational process in a particular discipline, and develop a script (in *Scratch* for example, a well-established creative and community environment) that simulates the process. In so doing, the students use their CT skills in two related areas: first, in the discipline while identifying the process, and second, when developing the script. Students will deepen their understanding of the computational process in the discipline since it should be very precise in order to develop a computerized simulation. At the same time, students acquire skills in developing algorithms, and acquire knowledge, skills, and control of scripts environments.

To clarify the main pedagogical idea, we give an example of one of the teams' projects. The computational process identified and defined by the team was movement problems in mathematics. Most school students face obstacles when confronting a problem such as: "A car drove from town A to town B at a speed of V1, and a truck drove from town B to town A at a speed of V2. At what point did the vehicles pass each other?" To develop a visual simulation of that process, a student must understand precisely what factors have influence, how the relative movement of the vehicles looks, the impact of different speeds of the vehicles, and of different distances between the towns. It enables the student to move from an abstract technical question to a concrete process that allows better understanding of it. All while investigating and developing the algorithmic CT skill as well as a colorful and creative animation product.

In what follows we present a literature review and full details of the course structure and assignments, and also share some key impressions from running the course three times with three different populations.

2 Background

2.1 Computational Thinking

The concept of CT is recognized as first proposed by J. Wing in 2006 [19] and her successive publications [20, 21]. The definition of CT as: "the thought processes involved in formulating problems and their solutions so that the solutions are represented in a form that can be effectively carried out by an information-processing agent" has been adopted by many educators [7]. In the last two decades, various viewpoints and commentaries have been offered, many that connect CT to algorithms and computers

[1, 5, 8, 13, 17] and others that emphasize the need to disconnect it from technology and computers [12, 22]. With or without computers, some key skills and processes commonly mentioned regarding CT are: formulating problems, logically organizing and analyzing data, representing data through abstraction such as models and simulations, suggesting and evaluating several solutions, implementing a possible solution, and generalizing and transferring the solution to variety of problems [10, 12, 21]. Following that, many educators deal with the concept and its acquisition. The greater percentage of the interpretations linking CT to computerized systems is probably because the CSE community dealt with it in the beginning [12], but now there are highly diverse voices [22].

2.2 Implementation in Schools

Over time, the global teaching community has focused on the development of teaching and learning materials. The focus is particularly on developing suitable curricula for different ages, accompanied by developing extensive and varied learning materials [3, 4, 6, 9]. Less attention is paid to the teachers. There are teachers' guides, but a specially-guided training process is needed, particularly when addressing a broad audience of teachers. The computer science education research community falls short regarding assessment of the success of the programs. Most of the papers present descriptions of implementing the various curricula but offer less formal research to evaluate their implementation. A valuable approach for assessing CT dimensions, based on using *Scratch*, was presented by Brennan and Resnick [2], and results of competitions such *CodeMonkey* or *Bebras*, that are based on algorithms and use computerized systems, can serve as measures of success in developing students' CT skills.

2.3 Teachers Preparation

It is clear that the implementation of the different curricula is based on teachers' backgrounds, knowledge, mindsets, and attitudes. However, attention to planned, structured teachers preparation programs has appeared mostly in the last two years [11, 14, 22]. These programs were actually activated in parallel to the academic course for pre-service teachers presented in this paper. The course is an approach to change the state of mind of pre-service teachers in all teaching subjects. We wish them to leave the perception of CT as a mathematical or at least a scientific concept, for a broader concept, which actually has different facets even in the traditional scientific disciplines.

3 The Course

The course for pre-service teachers was developed based on our recognition of the importance to develop school students' CT skills, which should be led by teachers of all teaching subjects. A key aspect is that we are not aiming to develop a new discipline to be added to the school curricula, but rather relate to CT as a skill that students must acquire throughout their various learning processes, similar to the development of "critical thinking" in different contexts.

In this section, we present the prescribed course development, assumptions, rationale, aims, and learning outcomes. Subsequently we present the course structure and learning assignments.

3.1 Thoughts Towards Development

The implementation relies on three main pedagogical issues. First, we wish to develop teachers' Pedagogical Content Knowledge (PCK) as presented by Shulman [18], with its expansion to Technological Pedagogical Content Knowledge (TPACK) presented by Mishra and Koehler [15]. Second, we adopt the interpretation that CT can be implemented in any discipline, and hence assume that it is possible to define a computational process in any discipline. And third, we wish the computational process to be accurate and concrete, and being such, to be implemented in *Scratch* simulation.

The decision to concentrate on a computational process that has importance to be developed as a simulation, is significant. In relation to teachers this requires to lower their concerns and to disconnect the immediate and inaccurate association of CT with "computation" (or calculation). For teacher students who intend to teach Humanities, Social Sciences or Languages, there is need to decrease their concern about any aspects of math or technology. Teacher students who intend to teach Math or Sciences also need to change their accustomed conceptions. For example, computing the coordinates of a point on a graph in relation to a given function is an expression of a computational process. But, we wish to emphasize and expand to other approaches of computational processes, which go beyond obtaining a numerical value resulting from a direct calculation, as demonstrated in the introduction to traffic problems.

The development of simulation as a concrete product of a defined computational process is of great value. The development of a computerized script in a digital environment, requires a precise refined definition of the selected process and enables the development of algorithmic CT skills as well. *Scratch* was chosen as the environment because of its known advantages [16].

Regarding the learning process, students should be given space to build their own interpretation of computational thinking and computational process, since there are indeed multiple viewpoints, with no single, precise definition. Our entire teaching-learning approach is in light of constructivism, students must employ active learning, as reflected in both the course structure and the assignments.

3.2 Course Rationale, Aims, and LO

Rationale. The rationale of the course is to develop the students' CT, along with developing their understanding and confidence regarding its implementation in their teaching subject. Teachers should recognize the importance of the acquisition of CT by school students, to be able to teach it. They have to experience it in a supportive environment that encourages them to think about how to implement this "mindset" in schools. The course has two main interwoven foundations. The first is the definition of a computational process in the discipline – applying CT skills. The second is the development of a simulation (to some extent depending on the course population) by applying algorithmic CT skills.

Aims. The course's main aims are:

(a) expose students to the concept of CT and raise awareness of its various definitions;
(b) enable learners to build their own interpretation based on experience, literature reading, class discussions, and hands-on positive learning experiences;
(c) make learning concrete and relevant through assignments that relate to their future teaching and teaching subject;
(d) develop students' CT skills in two integrated aspects: (i) develop their ability to identify and define a Computational Process (CP) in their discipline; (ii) develop algorithmic CT skills by developing a project that simulates the process.

Learning Outcomes (LO). At the end of the course, we expect students to be able to:

(1) identify a relevant interpretation of their own view of the CT concept;
(2) define a clear and systematic CP in their discipline;
(3) develop a precise script using *Scratch* that simulates a CP in their discipline;
(4) analyze given scenarios, define which expresses a CP, and explain their choice;
(5) appreciate the importance of developing CT skills in students at any age, to equip them with essential skills in our era.

3.3 Course Structure

The course consists of 14 90-min meetings (28 academic hours), comprising five sections. Week 1: Explore the content and the environment; Weeks 2–3: Learning and working with *Scratch*; Weeks 4–5: Introduction to CT as a necessary 21st-century skill; Weeks 6–10: Project development; deepening the conceptual and the application levels; Weeks 11–14 Teaching CT. All content and activities were covered in each course launched; flexibility was essential to meet students' conceptual needs and progress. Table 1 presents the course schedule.

3.4 Learning Assignments

The course had seven assignments requiring different degrees of depth in thinking, in the time needed to accomplish them, and in type of performance – individual, in pair or team work. The project is an anchor task intended to support students' understanding and interpretation of the CT concept, and to scaffold their views and visions about how they might implement it in their future field work. Each assignment is presented below with a brief explanation of its intentions and goals.

Assignment #1: Preliminary Questions to Check Background and Pre-conceptions – Individually. Students are asked to complete a Google form questionnaire. Part A includes background: age, teaching disciplines, study track, previous experience with programming, and previous exposure to *Scratch*. Part B includes questions about

Table 1. Course schedule.

Week and assignments	Content
Week 1 Classwork: assignment #1 Homework: assignment #2	– Opening and completing a pre-questionnaire – Light exposure to *Scratch* – *Guidelines*: no definition of CT is presented; emphasis on the main course target - each participant will develop his/her own interpretation; we are learning together: they are the expert in their discipline and the lecturer will try to integrate his own knowledge with theirs
Weeks 2–3 Class and home work: assignment #3	– Demonstrating the *Scratch* environment and its main principles – Free personal or peer practice based on a suggested basic list of exercises or self-experience – Present solutions to some of the obstacles students faced – *Guidelines*: the main target is to let students enjoy and experience the environment mostly based on trial-and-error, thereby acquiring basic algorithmic CT without giving it a title. Reduce students' concerns and previous attitudes (against) technology/environments/computers
Week 4 Homework: assignment #4	– First discussion on the CT concept based on HW assignment #2 – Listen to students' comprehension and make some key remarks – Watch some of the videos students found for the task – *Guidelines*: Delineate students' current definitions; do not disqualify positions; lead students to see other aspects; enable different opinions
Week 5 Class and home work: assignment #5	– Continue discussion if needed – Present the main course project holistic perception – Students teams start to raise preliminary ideas for CPs in their discipline – *Guidelines*: Most teams will suggest inappropriate topics. Discuss the principles to evaluate the ideas
Weeks 6–10	– Main project development – *Guidelines*: The project development is challenging as described in assignment #5. Lecturer accompaniment and support is crucial to gain a positive learning process, while students construct their knowledge. Bring up leading questions and ideas, and suggest references
Week 11 Homework: assignment #6	– Present different curricula that implement CT ideas relevant to the course population. For example: *Code Monkey* activities and competition, *Beaver* activities and competition, *CS-unplugged* activities, the national schools curricula if they exist – *Guidelines*: The main aim is to expose students to existing worldwide varied approaches for implementation at schools
Weeks 12–13	– Project presentations and discussion – *Guidelines*: Teams present the CP they identified and characterized in their discipline and presents the process simulation on *Scratch*. The discussion enable reframing the central concepts and the main messages

(*continued*)

Table 1. *(continued)*

Week and assignments	Content
Week 14 Class and home work: assignment #7	– Demonstrating "fun" activities expressing CT in well-known problems – Course summary – Guidelines: The colorful activities enable ending the course with a good atmosphere, and at the same time exploring additional applications that facilitate further analysis and conceptualization. Examples: the *Hanoi Towers* problem or the *Konigsberg Bridges* problem addressed by Euler

concepts. It was emphasized that there are no incorrect answers; it is just to have the opportunity to stop and think about the concepts before studying them. The questions are: (1) Define briefly the concept "Computation"; (2) Define briefly the concept "Computational Process"; (3) Write the words you think are related to "Computational Process"; (4) Give an example of a Computational Process in your discipline; (5) Add any additional comments.

Intentions and Goals: Part A is for the lecturer, to be aware of students' backgrounds and options for building teams. Part B, students' pre-conceptions were considered and addressed in the first class discussion.

Assignment #2: Exploring Different Internet Resources - First Phase of Conceptualization – Individually. Students instructions: Locate a video on YouTube explaining what computational thinking is. Write a paragraph describing the video content and attach the video link.

Intentions and Goals: While choosing one video students usually explore more, and become aware of the extent and variety of existing implementations and interpretations. Students' outcomes are uploaded to a shared forum so they can learn from their peers.

Assignment #3: Basic Exercises Using Scratch – Individually or in Pairs. The course website offered students extensive web learning resources, among them guided learning with demonstrations and developing exercises. Students can choose, according to their preference and confidence, whether to practice using exercises that develop slowly and gradually, choose exercises from the different guides, or develop their own new idea script. The exercise guidelines relate to what knowledge students have to demonstrate in their scripts. For example: use at least three characters – that move and relate to each other or to the frame; include scheduled conversation or sounds.

Intentions and Goals: It is students' first targeted practice. Students can progress at a personal pace that suits them. The deliverables will be at different levels but the essence is on understanding the meaning of developing a script that "does something". This practice is the first step in coping with the concept and skill of algorithmic CT.

Assignment #4: Learning About Computational Thinking and Taking a Stand - Second Phase of Conceptualization – Individually. Students instructions: Read at least one mandatory paper and one elective, use some web sources and videos from assignment #2, and write a 1–2 page position paper referring to: (a) Your understanding of the CT concept; (b) Your personal attention to any difficulty/challenge the concept poses for you at this stage of learning; (c) Indicate what was interesting/surprising/confusing/raised objections/aroused your curiosity; (d) What do you think about developing CT skills among learners in your teaching subject? Explain your opinion. Any supportive or opposing position is relevant.

Intentions and Goals: After uncovering some different aspects of CT and CP throughout videos, discussions, and building scripts with *Scratch*, it is time to go deeper and read academic papers. Students are asked to conceptualize the knowledge, insights, and skills they have acquired, and reflect on their obstacles and impressions.

Assignment #5: Development of a Simulation Project - Concretizing Concepts – In Teams of 2–3 Students. Students instructions: After experiencing, reading, and learning about CT and experimenting with the *Scratch* environment, the goal of the task is to deepen the thinking about CT in the context of your teaching discipline. Based on the point of view that CT is a prerequisite thinking skill for citizens of the future, how do we develop and implement it in our discipline? The product will be a script in *Scratch*, which is a small simulation of a CP relevant to your discipline. Follow the next steps: (a) Find and define a CP in your discipline - consult with the lecturer about its suitability; (b) Consider a possible visual implementation of the process you introduced, i.e., develop a simulation that is a model for the behavior of the process in the real world; (c) Outline a script; (d) Create the simulation of the process. For the final submission, each student should address a personal reflective page relating to the change he/she experienced in relation to understanding the concepts of CT and CP.

Intentions and Goals: This assignment is at the heart of the course. It reflects the integration of the concepts and skills that the course wishes to impart. Students are active and develop a significant product that enables a deeper understanding of the concepts along with skills development. The project development consistently links abstract thinking around the computational process with refining the arising ideas with script-building skills and coping with the environment.

The main and unique pedagogical approach of the course is our desire for pre-service teachers to see the opportunity their own future school students can benefit from by doing the same assignment, as emphasized in the next text box.

> A school student who develops a script in the learned subject through the lens of CT, will deepen his understanding of the CP that takes place in the discipline, through the construction of a computerized simulation of the process. In doing so, he/she refines the understanding of the computational process in the discipline since it is translated into an appropriate and precise visual script; and at the same time develops the skills of algorithmic CT in relation to developing the script in the *Scratch* environment.

Assignment #6: Position Paper: Implementation in Teaching – In Pairs. Students instructions: Write a 2–3-page position paper that present your position on the integration of CT in school instruction. Your personal learning and thinking processes are valuable. There is room to express independent, supportive and/or critical, positions. The position paper should be based on the contents of the course, on the methods of learning in the course, and on at least three bibliography sources.

Intentions and Goals: After accomplishing the project development and being exposed to different school curricula used around the world, students should state their opinions in a reasoned and justified position paper, while looking at the application of CT in their future classes.

Assignment #7: Analysis of Projects, Clarification of Concepts, and Reflection - Third Phase of Conceptualization – Individually. Students are asked to complete a Google form questionnaire. Part A relates to the projects developed in teams. Some represented projects are selected by the lecturer and each student is required to evaluate his or her opinion in relation to the question: "To what extent do you believe the project reflects the principles of the computational process as you understand it?". The evaluation was ranked as insufficient application, limited application, reasonable application, good application, or excellent application. The goal is to enable students to apply their own conceptions and principles on peer projects. Part B includes three statements about concepts: (1) Today I understand that CT is: ___; (2) Today I understand that CP is: ___; (3) Rank your faith (on a 1–5 scale) that CT is a skill that can be applied in school and in your teaching subject, and explain your position.

Intentions and Goals: Bringing students to a high level of analysis while evaluating given application of CP in light of their own conceptual mental model, and explaining their judgments and conceptions.

4 Course Execution

The course was implemented similarly with three different populations. Changes and adjustments were made between each launch of the course following conclusions drawn from each previous course. The model shown here is the last approved one.

4.1 Populations

The course was conducted three times, each for different populations described in Table 2. All populations were studying for their teaching certificate.

4.2 Course Journeys: Difficulties, Successes, and What Lies in Between

In this section we elaborate on some key aspects that arose while running the courses. The course implementation was accompanied with research and the results will be published in the near future.

A Distant Starting Point. The vast majority of students stated the more obvious answers for "computation" and "computational process" and retained mathematical

Table 2. Description of the course populations.

Institution	Learning track	Teaching Subjects	Number of Students
A: Technion, Faculty of Education in Science and Technology. An obligatory course for the CS track, and elective for others.	Math, Sciences, and Technology for high school Year: 2015–2016	– CS (18) – Mathematics (11) – Chemistry (3) – Physics (5) – Electricity (1)	38
B: Beit Berl College, Faculty of Education. An obligatory course for the group of students.	Humanities and Social Sciences for high school Year: 2016–2017	– Social Sciences and Citizenship (28) – History (3) – English (1) – CS (2)	34
C: Beit Berl College, Faculty of Education. An elective course. Each student combines two disciplines in his/her track of learning.	Various disciplines for elementary school Year: 2017	– Literature – Language – Bible – History – Sciences – Mathematics	28

explanations. An exceptional and expected answer of CS students in course A related to computational theory, and in course B where students were adults with rich work experience. There, the frequent but not major answer related to building a model. However, looking farther to the following stages of the course, it was not easy to move most of the students from their starting position of "mathematical calculation".

Insecurity Since No Formal Declaration of CT Is Presented. Most of the students constantly felt insecure at the conceptual level. Since no clear definition of CT was presented by the lecturer, students felt confused. Emphasis on the varying interpretations and implementation of the concept and encouraging students to develop their own view, was a new and challenging teaching approach for all populations.

What Should Have Been Mentioned Again and Again? It was necessary in almost each course meeting to remind students that the focus of the course was on the interpretation that a computational process is not built on calculations (even thought it could include some). The process is composed of stages, which are developed to solve a problem or build a knowledge map. When developing their project, most students interpret their simulations as a tutoring tool for the school students. It was necessary to constantly emphasize the course's pedagogical approach that school students can develop the simulation by themselves, and thereby deepen their understanding of the CP occurring in a particular discipline.

When the Idea Becomes Understandable. As expected, difficulties arose in two significant stages of the project development process: one, in the selection and definition of the computational process, and the second, when programming the scripts, since students have no previous background in the environment. The first is in the area of CT, and the second is in the area of algorithmic CT (beyond the mastery of the environment). Coping and passing those two critical stages clarifies the pedagogical idea of the main assignment (#5) and makes it more understandable. In that stage of the course, when the animated simulations appeared on the screens, the tension fell away, leaving room for satisfaction, pride, and smiles. In relation to the main message we wished to deliver – there were no meaningful differences between the populations. Some of the topics of CP that students addressed in their projects, is presented in the Appendix. We present one quote taken from the position paper (assignment #6) of a student from course B, as an example of the success of the process:

> *"I would like to point out that there has been a profound change in my understanding and approach of 'There is nothing to do with computational thinking within the discipline of teaching citizenship', in a completely opposite direction, which indicates that this should be especially involved in the field of citizenship I specialize in. In addition, I understand that I have gone through a personal process with a clear disagreement about the ability to integrate the CT topic, while taking a stubborn stance of not accepting the subject in any way - for understanding the ability to integrate CT in humanities and verbal fields. Thanks for the opportunity given me to undergo an internal change and to be given the tools to implement such an important process, which I believe will contribute greatly to the youth in the education system"*

5 Reflective Summary

Following the process of designing and developing the course, the course achieved its aims and learning outcomes. The pre-service teachers expanded their Pedagogical Content Knowledge (PCK) and their Technological Pedagogical Content Knowledge (TPACK). They constructed their knowledge in many facets and were active in the entire learning process. They were able to define and elaborate on the main concepts: computational thinking, computational process, and algorithmic computational thinking. All in the relevant context and interpretation of their own teaching subjects.

The course was conceptually very challenging for the diverse student populations. As a lecturer, it took the skills of a magician and required great patience. The lecturer functions as a psychologist, a facilitator, a leader, a questions asker, and does not provide answers but only hints and reference to materials to follow. Although there was a need to cope with objections, the effort was fruitful. It was very satisfying to follow the students' thought processes, to see their final projects, and particularly read their reflections about the deep process that they went through and appreciated. Presenting the course content and outcomes in the national leading CS teachers seminar aroused interest and curiosity.

Acknowledgments. We wish to acknowledge all the students who participated in the three courses. They are groundbreakers in being the first to experience that academic course. Students overcame their obstacles since they trusted the route before them, despite the "bumps" along the way.

Appendix

Examples of Students' Projects

Following some of the topics of CP that students addressed in their projects, is presented, to enable partial expression from students' products.

- *Mathematics:* The movement of ducks with and against the river current.
- *Physics:* Throwing an object on a slope.
- *Chemistry:* Simulation of splitting particles moving inside a container and colliding with the walls and themselves.
- *Computer Science:* Simulation of the Dijkstra algorithm in Graph Theory.
- *Citizenship:* Presenting alternatives to building a coalition based on the political platforms of parties.
- *Social Sciences:* Making decisions about the location of a new school according to socio-economic, social, and infrastructure considerations.
- *Language:* Root word recognition.
- *Literature:* Identifying versification in songs.
- *Mathematics for Elementary School:* Identifying common and diagnostic properties of the square family.

References

1. Barr, D., Harrison, J., Conery, L.: Computational Thinking: a digital age skill for everyone. Learn. Lead. Technol. **3–4**(2011), 2–23 (2011)
2. Brennan, K., Resnick, M.: New frameworks for studying and assessing the development of computational thinking. Paper presentation at AERA 2012 (2012)
3. Csizmadia, A., et al.: Computational thinking: a guide for teachers. Comput. Sch. Community 1–18 (2015). https://community.computingatschool.org.uk/files/6695/original.pdf
4. Computing at schools web site. Material on Computational Thinking and related topics. http://community.computingatschool.org.uk/resources/252
5. Computer Science Teachers Association (CSTA): Operational definition of Computational Thinking for K–12 education – Flayer (2011). http://www.iste.org/docs/ct-documents/computational-thinking-operational-definition-flyer.pdf?sfvrsn=2
6. Computer Science Teachers Association (CSTA) and the International Society for Technology in Education (ISTE): Computational Thinking in K–12 education leadership toolkit (2011). https://c.ymcdn.com/sites/www.csteachers.org/resource/resmgr/471.11CT LeadershiptToolkit-S.pdf
7. Cuny, J., Snyder, L., Wing, J.M.: Demystifying computational thinking for noncomputer scientists. Unpublished manuscript (2010). http://www.cs.cmu.edu/~CompThink/resources/TheLinkWing.Pdf. Key: citeulike:13256108
8. Denning, P.J.: The profession of IT beyond computational thinking. Commun. ACM **52**(6), 28–30 (2009)
9. Duncan, C., Bell, T., Atlas, J.: What do the teachers think?: introducing computational thinking in the primary school curriculum. In: Proceedings of the Nineteenth Australasian Computing Education Conference (ACE 2017), pp. 65–74 (2017)

10. Google: Computational Thinking for Educators course. https://computationalthinkingcourse.withgoogle.com/course?use_last_location=true
11. Hodhod, R., Khan, S., Kurt-Peker, Y., Ray, L.: Training teachers to integrate Computational Thinking into K-12 teaching. In Proceedings of the 47th ACM Technical Symposium on Computing Science Education (SIGCSE 2016), pp. 156–157 (2016)
12. Hu, C.: Computational thinking: what it might mean and what we might do about it. In: Proceedings of the 16th Annual Joint Conference on Innovation and Technology in Computer Science Education (ITiCSE 2011), pp. 223–227 (2011)
13. Lye, S.Y., Ling Koh, J.H.: Review on teaching and learning of computational thinking through programming: what is next for K-12? Comput. Hum. Behav. **41**, 51–61 (2014)
14. Lodi, M.: Growth Mindset in Computational Thinking teaching and teacher training. In: Proceedings of the 2017 ACM Conference on International Computing Education Research (ICER 2017), pp. 281–282 (2017)
15. Mishra, P., Koehler, M.J.: Technological pedagogical content knowledge: a framework for teacher knowledge. Teach. Coll. Rec. **108**(6), 1017–1054 (2006)
16. MIT Media Lab: Scratch – a free visual programming language. https://scratch.mit.edu/about/
17. Sabitzer, B., Antonitsch, P.K., Pasterk, S.: Informatics concepts for primary education: Preparing children for computational thinking. In: Proceedings of the 9th Workshop in Primary and Secondary Computing Education (WiPSCE 2014), pp. 108–111 (2014)
18. Shulman, L.S.: Those who understand: Knowledge growth in teaching. Educ. Res. **15**(2), 4–14 (1986)
19. Wing, J.M.: Computational thinking. Commun. ACM **49**(3), 33–35 (2006)
20. Wing, J.M.: Computational Thinking: What and Why? The Magazine of Carnegie Mellon University's School of Computer Science (2011). https://www.cs.cmu.edu/link/research-notebook-computational-thinking-what-and-why
21. Wing, J.M.: Computational Thinking Benefits Society, Social Issues in Computing. Academic Press Blog, New York (2014). http://socialissues.cs.toronto.edu/index.html%3Fp=279.html
22. Yadav, A., Stephenson, C., Hong, H.: Computational thinking for teacher education. Commun. ACM **60**(4), 55–62 (2017)

Investigating the Pedagogical Content Knowledge of Teachers Attending a MOOC on Scratch Programming

Ebrahim Rahimi[1,2](✉), Ineke Henze[3], Felienne Hermans[3], and Erik Barendsen[1,2]

[1] Radboud University, Nijmegen, The Netherlands
{e.rahimi,e.barendsen}@cs.ru.nl
[2] Open University, Heerlen, The Netherlands
[3] Delft University of Technology, Delft, The Netherlands
{f.a.henze-rietveld,f.f.j.hermans}@tudelft.nl

Abstract. The goal of this study is to investigate changes in PCK (Pedagogical Content Knowledge) of Dutch primary and secondary computer science teachers participating in a MOOC about Scratch programming. We captured the teachers' PCK using identical pre- and post-questionnaires and conducted a qualitative deductive-inductive content analysis to identify changes in the PCK of the MOOC attendees. We relate the observed differences between PCK before and after the MOOC to Clarke and Hollingsworth's model of teacher professional growth and Van Driel and Henze's model of PCK development. Our analysis gives rise to four design principles meant to inform the pedagogical design of such MOOCs and improve their pedagogical affordances with regard to PCK development of their attendees.

Keywords: Pedagogical content knowledge
Computer science education · Secondary education · MOOC
Scratch programming

1 Introduction

An "effective CS teacher" needs to have a knowledge base consisting of both content knowledge (CK) and pedagogical content knowledge (PCK) [4,16]. PCK is needed by teachers to plan and deliver instruction and has been advocated as the unique sort of knowledge held by teachers that distinguishes them from experts and accounts more precisely for students' learning [11].

In an American context, it has been claimed that primary and secondary CS teachers generally have low PCK [22]. Solving this problem asks for proper professional development programs [22,33]. The Internet serves as a promising professional development platform for teachers. Teachers' participation in online professional development can enhance their self-efficacy and provide the possibility to connect with people sharing similar pedagogical and content problems

S. N. Pozdniakov and V. Dagienė (Eds.): ISSEP 2018, LNCS 11169, pp. 180–193, 2018.
https://doi.org/10.1007/978-3-030-02750-6_14

[10,22]. It has been suggested that online and face-to-face professional development programs may have similar learning outcomes for teachers [22].

Massive open online courses (MOOCs) represent a fairly new web-based education inititive seeking to extend and offer educational services in an unprecedented scale [10]. MOOCs have been proposed as a "cost and resource effective means" for addressing the professional development needs of teachers [7,10,20]. To do so, such MOOCs must provide teachers with "the features, tools, resources, and interactions that will enable the acquisition of the various elements of good teaching" (outlined by Burns in [4]) including PCK [10] (p. 3). Thus, given the prominent role of PCK in teacher professional development, an important and open question about such MOOCs concerns with their influence on the PCK development of their attendees.

This study aims to investigate occurred changes in PCK of Dutch primary and secondary CS teachers attending a MOOC about Scratch programming. Notably, this MOOC was not initially devoted to supporting PCK development of attendees. Instead, it was meant to help them learn the content knowledge about Scratch programming. As such content-directed MOOCs are attended frequently by teachers with the purpose of supporting classroom practices, it is justifiable to investigate their influence on the teachers' practical knowledge, in particular, their PCK.

One may question the idea of measuring PCK in the context of a course that is not meant for PCK development. Nevertheless, we support this idea for this MOOC based on two reasons: first, research has shown that there is a strong link between content knowledge (CK) and PCK in the context of mathematics and science education, so that teacher's CK is necessary for developing PCK, but is not sufficient on its own [6]. This connection makes it appealing to investigate what happens with the CS teachers' PCK when they participate in a content-focused course. Secondly, as the attendees are CS teachers, it is expected that they already have PCK of programming. Participation in this MOOC, as an external source according to [5,29], can contribute to changing their PCK of Scratch programming.

For the purposes of this study, two open-ended pre- and post-questionnaires, derived from the PCK model of Magnusson et al. [19] and a combination of CoRe instrument [18] and retrospective PCK-directed interviews [14], were administered among the MOOC attendees. Then, following a qualitative deductive-inductive research, the changes in the PCK of the attendees were identified. The results then were used to inform a set of pedagogical design guidelines for improving the effectiveness of such MOOCs concerning PCK development.

2 Background

The PCK concept has been introduced by Shulman as the "missing paradigm" in the research on teacher knowledge and refers to "the blending of content and pedagogy into an understanding of how particular topics, problems, or issues are organized, represented, and adapted to the diverse interests and abilities of learners, and presented for instruction" [27] (p. 8). Teachers' PCK is their "pedagogical know-how" knowledge that develops during the years of teaching experience and describes the processes that teachers follow and employ in response to the challenges of teaching a given topic to particular students in specific settings [3,27].

The most often cited model to describe teachers' PCK has been proposed by Magnusson et al. [19]. This model defines five elements for teacher PCK on a specific topic, of which we use four (hereafter referred to as M1, M2, M3, M4, respectively): teacher knowledge about the objectives of teaching that topic (M1), teacher knowledge about the students' understanding and learning difficulties with the topic (M2), teacher knowledge about effective instructional approaches to teach the topic (M3), and teacher knowledge about appropriate assessment strategies to assess the students' understanding (M4) [19]. The Content Representation (CoRe) instrument, [18], captures the collective key ideas (of a group of teachers) connected to a specific topic, and elicits the teachers' knowledge about each idea using 8 open questions. These questions cover the four elements of the PCK model of Magnusson et al. [19].

From a cognitive-constructivist perspective, the development of PCK goes through a non-linear, iterative and constructive process where new information is integrated with prior experiences, knowledge and beliefs captured from different domains, practices, and interactions. From a socio-cultural perspective, teacher PCK shapes and is developed through the transformation of subject-matter knowledge and communication process between teachers and students during classroom practices and interactions [13,15], while from a situative perspective PCK is situated in the everyday practices of teachers and not only residing in individuals but also is distributed in their surrounding environment including books, tools, and their communities [15]. Collegial cooperation and knowledge, experience, and relationship exchanges among teachers have been proven to be essential for the development of teachers PCK [30]. Such exchanges might occur during face-to-face interactions happening within "conferences, department meetings, casual hallway conversations" or remote interactions emerging in various online platforms including social networking sites, MOOCs, blogs, and mailing lists [10,12,30].

Clarke and Hollingsworth's empirical model for professional growth of teachers [5] and Van Driel and Henze's theoretical model of PCK construction [29] (see Fig. 1) seem promising models to explain the professional growth and PCK development of teachers. Clarke and Hollingsworth's model states that "external sources of information or stimulus" can make changes in the teacher's "personal domain" by triggering her reflection on personal knowledge, beliefs, and attitude. Furthermore, these external sources might change the teacher's "domain of practice" containing her professional experimentation by enacting new practices, for example, having experience with a new teaching strategy. According to Clarke and Hollingsworth's model, the professional growth of teachers results from enactment and reflection mechanisms among external domain, personal domain, the domain of practice, and domain of consequence.

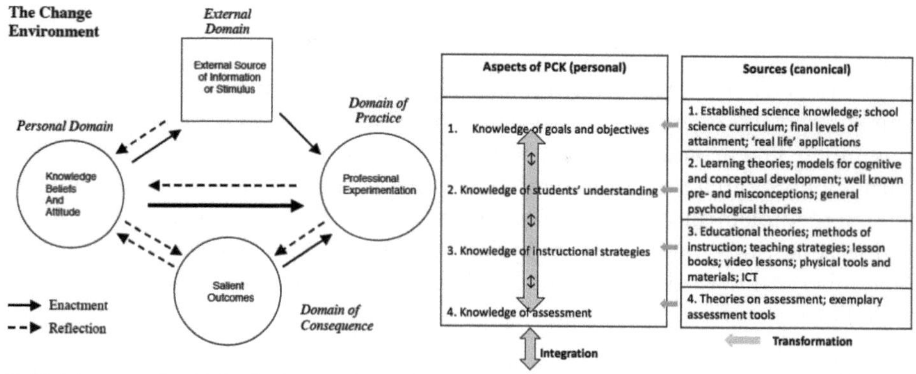

(a) The interconnected model of professional growth of teachers ([5]) (b) Pre-service teachers' initial PCK development ([29])

Fig. 1. Two models for explaining the PCK development process of teachers

As put by Van Driel and Henze, the development of PCK goes through two processes: a *knowledge transformation* process which (partly) draws upon external collective sources including learning theories, models for cognitive and conceptual development, well-known misconceptions, general psychological theories, methods of instruction, good practices, exemplary assessment tools, and so on, and a *knowledge connection and integration* process aiming at the internal coherence and relationship between the elements of PCK as a crucial factor to enable effective scaffolding of students' learning [21,29].

The PCK concept has been mainly investigated in connection with subjects such as physics, chemistry, and language [3,15]. CS teachers' PCK is a fairly new but promising research domain. As yet, there have been few attempts to elicit CS teachers' PCK [1,3,16,26,32]. While the majority of the research on investigating CS teachers' PCK has been conducted in connection with physical classrooms, we found only two studies examined the PCK development of CS teachers in online settings (i.e. [12,22]). In the first study, Go and Dorn investigated the PCK development of high school CS teachers participated in two online knowledge-sharing communities: one community provided the CS teachers with highly curated content devoted entirely to CS PCK, while another community was focused on unstructured content devoted to general CS education matters. The researchers discussed the strengths and weaknesses of both communities and speculated on how their benefits might inform an online community meant to facilitate CS teachers' PCK development [12]. Another research, conducted by Qian et al., presents the results of a 2-year study investigating how teachers teaching the CS principles course for the first time used online professional development (PD) materials. Their results show that novice teachers with a CS educational background needed and used PD materials for developing their PCK, while teachers with a Non-CS educational background needed and used PD materials for gaining content knowledge [22].

3 The Study Setting

As mentioned earlier, this study investigated the PCK change of a group of Dutch primary and secondary school teachers participated in a MOOC on Scratch programming. The primary aim of the MOOC in question was to help the attendees learn about Scratch programming (i.e. content knowledge) and become confident enough to implement it in their classrooms. The MOOC contained a set of videos, forums, questions, and course materials and was ran for 6 weeks starting from September 2017. Within the context of this MOOC, the study was directed by the following research question:

RQ: *How can the PCK and the changes in this PCK of the attendees of this MOOC be characterized?*

Data Collection: To answer the research question we constructed a questionnaire consisting of seven open-ended questions as presented in Table 1. The questions are based on the PCK model of Magnusson et al. [19] and a combination of the proposed questions by CoRe instrument [14, 18]. Two identical pre- and post-test online questionnaires as Table 1 were used as our data collection instruments in this study.

Table 1. The questions of pre- and post-test questionnaires

PCK elements ([19])	Questions about Scratch programming (adapted from [14, 18])
M1. Knowledge of goals and objectives	1. What do you intend students to learn about Scratch programming?
	2. Why is it important for the students to learn this?
M2. Knowledge of students' understanding and practices	3. What do you know about students' thinking (prior knowledge, learning difficulties) that influences your teaching of Scratch programming?
M3. Knowledge about instructional strategies	4. What do you think is a suitable method for teaching Scratch programming?
	5. What are your particular reasons for choosing this method?
M4. Knowledge about ways to assess students' understanding	6. What would be a suitable way of assessing students' understanding or confusion around Scratch programming?
	7. What are your reasons for choosing this particular way of assessment?

Participants: 375 people enrolled at the beginning of the MOOC. We selected the answers of those attendees who answered both pre- and post-test questionnaires (16 attendees) to do the analysis.

Data Analysis: A mixed deductive-inductive qualitative content analysis procedure [8] was followed. First, the answers in each phase were uploaded into Atlas.ti software collectively. Four elements (i.e. M1, M2, M3, M4) of Magnusson's PCK model [19] were used to group the answers in each phase. Within each group, the content of the PCK was analyzed inductively through identifying various codes, re-coding and merging into more general themes describing the variation among the teachers' PCK. Possible alternative interpretations of the identified codes were discussed within the research team until a consensus was reached.

4 Results

We present the results according to the PCK elements. Within each element, we describe the teachers' PCK organized by the themes emerging from the inductive analysis.

Knowledge About Goals and Objectives (M1)
We discerned three categories of objectives for teaching Scratch programming expressed by the participants in the pre- and post-test questionnaires:

i. *Knowledge-oriented objectives*: consisting of the following objectives: to learn about *the structure of a program and its concepts*, *to understand how computers think and work*, and *to be prepared for actual programming languages.*
ii. *Motivational objectives*: consisting of these objectives: *to make students interested in programming through making a game*, *to prepare them for a digital society*, *to motivate them by observing the influence of programming in their daily life*, *to provide them opportunity to experience more freely*, and *to make them prepared to work with Microbit.*
iii. *Personal development objectives*: consisting of the following objectives pertaining to improving soft and design competencies of students: *enhancing logical reasoning via drawing plan and decomposing a problem*, *building trust and self-confidence in own abilities through discovering and expressing own ideas*, and *collaboration.*

No significant difference between the patterns of appearing these objectives in the pre- and post-test questionnaires was identified.

Knowledge About Students' Understanding and Performance (M2)
The following items present the participants' knowledge on students' understanding and performance in Scratch programming:

i. *Students' general learning specifications*: reflected in statements such as *students can do more than what they show*, *students scare to try unknown subjects*, *students have difficulty with independent working*, *students' lack of thinking ahead and solution-oriented approach*, *students with more ICT knowledge and experience resist to follow the instruction*, and *primary students have problem with Micro: Bit.*

ii. *Students' reaction to Scratch*: including statements such as students find Scratch programming *childish*, *difficult*, or *interesting* and *students' knowledge about Scratch is more than me.*

iii. *Students cognitive development stages*: representing general understanding and concerns about the level of cognitive capabilities of pupils for programming highlighted by some of the teachers in the post-test questionnaire.

These responses were observed with an almost identical pattern in the pre- and post-test questionnaires. The only remarkable difference was about the last item in the above list (i.e. *Students cognitive development stages*) which was only observed in the post-test answers.

Knowledge About Instructional Strategies (M3)

The following items present the identified teachers' knowledge about instructional strategies associated with Scratch programming:

i. *The generation strategy for programming*: referring teachers' knowledge about the *generation* approach to Scratch programming that emphasizes the generation of new programs by students from beginning. This type of knowledge was demonstrated in the pretest more than the post-test phase.

ii. *The completion strategy for programming*: referring to teachers' knowledge about the *completion* approach to Scratch programming that emphasizes the modification and extension of existing programs by students. This type of knowledge was demonstrated in the post-test more than the pretest phase.

iii. *First giving concrete examples then teaching abstract concepts*: denoting teachers' knowledge about a specific instructional strategy that asks teachers to first provide and explain concrete examples about a topic in Scratch programming (e.g. using video clips) and then use these examples to unpack the abstract concepts related to that topic. It is noteworthy that the appearance of this type of knowledge in the post-test was remarkably more than the pretest phase.

iv. *First teaching abstract concepts then giving concrete examples*: implying teachers' knowledge about the traditional instructional strategy asking them to first explain the theory and abstract concepts about a topic in Scratch programming and then provide concrete examples to elaborate those concepts. This type of knowledge was observed in the pretest more than the post-test phase.

v. *Fun-driven learning*: referring to the teachers' knowledge about the ways of making students' learning more playful via creating fun projects and connecting Scratch programming to students-favorited contexts such as Lego Mindstorms. Patterns of this type of knowledge were observed more in the post-test than the pretest phase.

vi. *Unplugged activities*: denoting teachers' knowledge about unplugged activities and their benefits for teaching Scratch programming. We observed this type of knowledge mainly in the post-test phase.
vii. *Group-based learning*: implying teachers' knowledge about the group-based learning strategies and their advantages. We saw no remarkable difference between the patterns of this type of knowledge in the pretest and post-test phases.

Knowledge About Ways to Assess Students' Learning and Performance (M4)
The following items describe teachers' knowledge about ways to assess students' understanding and performance in Scratch programming:

i. *Generation-based assessment*: denoting teachers' knowledge about an assessment strategy that emphasizes the generation of a new program by students as a means for measuring their understanding and performance in Scratch programming. This type of knowledge was demonstrated in the pretest more than the post-test phase.
ii. *Completion-based assessment*: denoting teachers' knowledge about an assessment strategy emphasizing the completion, debugging, explaining and predicting the results of an existing program by students as means for measuring their understanding and performance in Scratch programming. This type of knowledge was demonstrated in the post-test more than the pretest phase.
iii. *Unstructured, observation-based assessment*: referring to teachers' knowledge about an open and observation-based assessment strategy that emphasizes allowing students' group working with Scratch and listening to their conversations to capture their possible understanding and misconceptions of Scratch topics. This type of knowledge was mainly observed in the pretest phase.

5 Discussion

The discerned teachers' knowledge about the objectives of Scratch programming (M1 element of PCK) in both pre-test and post-test phases depicts a continuum ranging from more theoretical and knowledge-oriented objectives to more practical objectives with no significant difference in pre- and posttest phases. These findings concur with the results reported by [1,23] pertaining CS teachers' knowledge about the objectives of programming.

The captured teachers' knowledge on students' understanding and performance in Scratch programming is limited to general learning specifications of students including knowledge about students general learning problems, their reactions to Scratch and their cognitive development stages. The latter item was only observed in the post-test phase which likely resulted from the explicit emphasis of the MOOC instructor on neo-Piagetian perspectives of cognitive development of novice programmers (see [17]). No specific knowledge about students' needs, motivations, misunderstanding and problems with Scratch was observed. Teachers' insufficient understanding of their students decreases their teaching quality [19,24]. As put by Berglund and Lister, "we know very little about our students' world and our students' motivations... We tend to base our teaching on our own needs, or our assumptions about the students' needs." [2] (p. 42).

Figure 2 presents the participants' evaluation of the MOOC elements. As shown, the forums were perceived as least useful element of the MOOC.

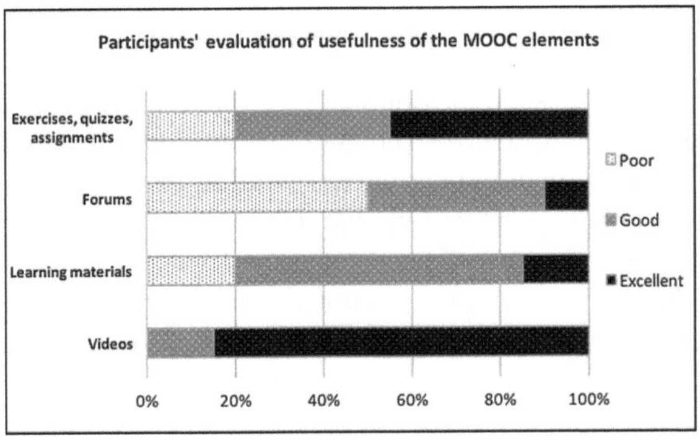

Fig. 2. The evaluation of the participants about the usefulness of the MOOC elements

There are two interesting observations related to the development of the participants' knowledge about instructional strategies (M3): a shift from the *generation* to *completion* instruction for programming (for more information about these instructional strategies see [31]) and, a shift from *First teaching abstract concepts then giving concrete examples* to *First giving concrete examples then teaching abstract concepts* strategy. Arguably, these developments can be attributed to the participants' exposure to the MOOC and its underpinning instructional strategy focused on the completion strategy as well as explaining concrete examples before teaching abstract concepts.

Clarke and Hollingsworth's model of teacher professional growth [5] along with Van Driel and Henze's model of PCK construction [29] (depicted in Fig. 1) can be used to explain the mentioned PCK developments. Through the lens of these models the external sources including the participants' exposure to the MOOC and its promoted instructional strategies as well as provided videos and content appeared to have served to initiate a *knowledge transformation* process or trigger the participants' reflection on their *personal domain* of knowledge, beliefs, and attitudes. The following quote by one of the participants is one of the few examples explaining the ways that some of the discussed concepts in the MOOC such as the Neo-Piagetian perspective of programming served to trigger the teacher's reflection on her personal knowledge domain (the *knowledge transformation* process) and connect and integrate her PCK elements (M2 and M3) (the *knowledge connection and integration* process):

I found the discussion about the Neo-Piagetian perspective of programming very interesting. There are teachers with high knowledge and experience in Scratch. If they want to teach pupils to program in Scratch, their teaching might be inappropriate to improve the thinking of a pupil who needs to learn something totally new [M2] ... I think recognizing the difference between teachers' and pupils' cognitive level [M2] is very important to teach programming and this difference asks for a step by step instructional approach [M3].

As suggested by the results, the observed changes in the participants' knowledge of instructional strategy seem to be influential in the changes happened to teachers' knowledge about assessment (M4 elements). This observation suggests a *knowledge connection and integration* process between M2 and M3 elements of teachers' PCK.

Although the presented analysis is based on the collective demonstration of the participants' PCK in the pre- and post-test phases, the outcomes can be traced back to the individual level. Table 2 in appendix A presents the developments in the demonstrated instructional knowledge of the participants. The developments of the instructional knowledge explained earlier can be seen at the individual level for several participants including teachers 2, 4, 14, 16.

Informed by the above findings and discussions, we formulated the following design principles to improve the pedagogical affordances of such MOOCs for enhancing CS teachers' PCK.

Explaining Well-Known Students' Misconceptions Related to a Specific Topic: The results indicated low developments in the participants' knowledge about students' understanding and performance in Scratch. Teachers' knowledge of students' understanding of a specific topic forms the core part of their PCK on that topic. According to [29], teachers' knowledge of strategies to teach a certain topic is related to their knowledge of how students learn that topic including their misconceptions [29] (p. 1). Thus, explaining the common misconceptions students experience in learning a topic and exploring their reasons and solutions can contribute to enhancing teachers' PCK on that topic.

Encouraging and Facilitating Social Interactions Around the Content: As depicted by Fig. 2, the quality of social aspects and interactions between the attendees in this MOOC was low. PCK is to some extent a collective and sharable knowledge [30]. Collegial cooperation and exchanging knowledge, experience (e.g. over students' misconceptions and difficulties), values and relationships among teachers is essential for the development of their PCK [30]. As asserted by [9], stimulated reflection, attending PCK courses, and contact with other teachers are typically part of effective interventions to promote PCK development in initial teacher education. CS teachers, in particular, may suffer more from this undermined social interaction given that they are most often the only people in their schools teaching CS subjects and may lack formal training in CS content [12,33].

Recognizing the Diversity of CS Teachers' Background and Experience: Diversity in the knowledge, background, and expertise of attendees is common in MOOCs [25]. As shown by [22], the teaching experience and computing background of CS teachers have a significant impact on their need for and use of online professional development materials including MOOC-based education. It has been observed that novice CS teachers needed and used online professional development materials for developing their PCK, while Non-CS teachers needed and used these materials to gain content knowledge. Addressing this diversity asks for matching professional development to teachers' background [22].

Facilitating the Interaction Between the PCK Gained from MOOCs and Teachers' Educational Practices: As shown, the participants' exposure to this MOOC appeared to have served to enhance their knowledge about instructional and assessment strategies. From the perspective of Clark and Hollingsworth's model [5] to promote professional growth of teachers this knowledge should inform their "domain of practice" through professional experimentation. On the other hand, through the lens of Van Driel and Henze's model of PCK construction [29], teachers' experimentation in their"domain of practice" can connect and strengthen their PCK elements through *knowledge integration* and *knowledge transformation* processes. Along similar lines, Van Driel [28] emphasized the importance of providing opportunities for teachers to experiment in their own practice as a key factor to develop their knowledge including their PCK. Explicating the pedagogical premises and strategies underpinning such MOOCs seems useful to ease transferring the gained PCK by participants to their domain of practice and facilitate the interaction between building PCK and experimenting in practice.

6 Conclusions

This paper investigates changes in the PCK of the attendees at a Scratch MOOC. Some remarkable PCK changes were observed mainly in the attendees' knowledge about instructional strategies and assessment. These changes likely stem from the attendees' exposure to the instructional strategies followed in this MOOC. Four design principles were formulated to inform the pedagogical design of such MOOCs and improve their effectiveness with respect to the PCK development of their attendees. The formulated design principles emphasize explaining well-known students' misconceptions about MOOC topics, facilitating social interactions within the MOOC, recognizing and capitalizing the diversity in background and experience of MOOC attendees, and encouraging attendees to apply their gained PCK in practice. The method and questionnaires used for capturing participants' PCK seem promising for supporting other studies about the PCK development in MOOCs. We propose a follow-up study to embed the suggested design principles in a similar MOOC and investigate the changes in the PCK of its attendees.

Appendix A

Table 2. The demonstrated instructional knowledge of the participants in the pre- and posttest phases

Teacher	Pretest	Posttest
1	-	First giving concrete examples then teaching abstract concepts
2	First teaching abstract concepts then giving concrete examples	First giving concrete examples then teaching abstract concepts education, Differentiated learning, Completion-based instruction
3	First teaching abstract concepts then giving concrete examples, the generation strategy	-
4	First teaching abstract concepts then giving concrete examples, the generation strategy	First giving concrete examples then teaching abstract concepts, group working, the completion strategy, unplugged activities, fun-driven learning
5	-	-
6	Fun-driven learning, First teaching abstract concepts then giving concrete examples	Group working
7	Group working	-
8	-	First giving concrete examples then teaching abstract concepts, the completion strategy
9	Conducting short assignments	First giving concrete examples then teaching abstract concepts, the completion strategy, fun-driven learning
10	Differentiated learning, First teaching abstract concepts then giving concrete examples	-
11	Accomplishing focused assignments	First teaching abstract concepts then giving concrete examples, Fun-driven learning
12	Fun-driven learning, group working, the generation strategy, contextualized learning, video-based teaching	-
13	the generation strategy, first teaching abstract concepts then giving concrete examples, fun-driven learning	-
14	The generation strategy, first teaching abstract concepts then giving concrete examples	First giving concrete examples then teaching abstract concepts, the completion strategy
15	The completion strategy	Group working
16	First teaching abstract concepts then giving concrete examples	Fun-driven learning, differentiated learning, group working

References

1. Barendsen, E., Dagienė, V., Saeli, M., Schulte, C.: Eliciting computer science teachers' PCK using the Content Representation format: experiences and future directions. In: Gülbahar, Y., Karataş, E., Adnan, M. (eds.) Proceedings of the 7th International Conference on Informatics in Schools: Situation, Evolution and Perspectives (ISSEP 2014), Selected Papers, pp. 71–82 (2014)
2. Berglund, A., Lister, R.: Introductory programming and the didactic triangle. In: Proceedings of the Twelfth Australasian Conference on Computing Education, vol. 103, pp. 35–44. Australian Computer Society, Inc. (2010)
3. Buchholz, M., Saeli, M., Schulte, C.: PCK and reflection in computer science teacher education. In: Proceedings of the 8th Workshop in Primary and Secondary Computing Education, pp. 8–16. ACM (2013)
4. Burns, M.: Distance Education for Teacher Training: Modes, Models and Methods. Education Development Center Inc., Washington (2011)
5. Clarke, D., Hollingsworth, H.: Elaborating a model of teacher professional growth. Teach. Teach. Educ. **18**(8), 947–967 (2002)
6. Daehler, K.R., Heller, J.I., Wong, N.: Supporting growth of pedagogical content knowledge in science. In: Re-examining Pedagogical Content Knowledge in Science Education, pp. 55–69. Routledge (2015)
7. Dikke, D., Faltin, N.: Go-Lab MOOC-an online course for teacher professional development in the field of inquiry-based science education. In: 7th International Conference on Education and New Learning Technologies (2015)
8. Elo, S., Kyngäs, H.: The qualitative content analysis process. J. Adv. Nurs. **62**(1), 107–115 (2008)
9. Evens, M., Elen, J., Depaepe, F.: Developing Pedagogical Content Knowledge: Lessons Learned from Intervention Studies. Education Research International 2015 (2015)
10. Fyle, C.O.: Teacher education MOOCs for developing world contexts: issues and design considerations. In: Proceedings of the Sixth Conference of MIT's Learning International Networks Consortium (LINC) (2013)
11. Gess-Newsome, J.: A model of teacher professional knowledge and skill including PCK. In: Berry, A., Friedrichsen, P., Loughran, J. (eds.) Re-examining Pedagogical Content Knowledge in Science Education, pp. 28–42. Routledge (2015)
12. Go, S., Dorn, B.: Thanks for sharing: CS pedagogical content knowledge sharing in online environments. In: Proceedings of the 11th Workshop in Primary and Secondary Computing Education, pp. 27–36. ACM (2016)
13. Greeno, J.G., Collins, A.M., Resnick, L.B.: Cognition and learning. In: Berliner, D.C., Calfree, R.C. (eds.) Handbook of Educational Psychology, pp. 15–46. Macmillan, New York (1996)
14. Grossman, P.L.: The Making of a Teacher: Teacher Knowledge and Teacher Education. Teachers College Press, New York (1990)
15. Henze, I., Van Driel, J.H.: Toward a more comprehensive way to capture PCK in its complexity. In: Berry, A., Friedrichsen, P., Loughran, J. (eds.) Re-examining Pedagogical Content Knowledge in Science Education, pp. 120–134. Routledge (2015)
16. Hubwieser, P., Magenheim, J., Mühling, A., Ruf, A.: Towards a conceptualization of pedagogical content knowledge for computer science. In: Proceedings of the Ninth Annual International ACM Conference on International Computing Education Research, pp. 1–8. ACM (2013)

17. Lister, R.: Concrete and other neo-piagetian forms of reasoning in the novice programmer. In: Proceedings of the Thirteenth Australasian Computing Education Conference, vol. 114, pp. 9–18. Australian Computer Society, Inc. (2011)
18. Loughran, J., Mulhall, P., Berry, A.: In search of pedagogical content knowledge in science: developing ways of articulating and documenting professional practice. J. Res. Sci. Teach. **41**(4), 370–391 (2004)
19. Magnusson, S., Krajcik, J., Borko, H.: Nature, sources, and development of pedagogical content knowledge for science teaching. In: Gess-Newsome, J., Lederman, N.G. (eds.) Examining Pedagogical Content Knowledge, pp. 95–132. Kluwer, Dordrecht (1999)
20. Misra, P.K.: MOOCs for teacher professional development: reflections and suggested actions. Open Praxis **10**(1), 67–77 (2018)
21. Park, S., Chen, Y.C.: Mapping out the integration of the components of pedagogical content knowledge (PCK): examples from high school biology classrooms. J. Res. Sci. Teach. **49**(7), 922–941 (2012)
22. Qian, Y., Hambrusch, S., Yadav, A., Gretter, S.: Who needs what: recommendations for designing effective online professional development for computer science teachers. J. Res. Sci. Teach., 1–18 (2018)
23. Rahimi, E., Barendsen, E., Henze, I.: Typifying Informatics teachers' PCK of designing digital artefacts in dutch upper secondary education. In: Brodnik, A., Tort, F. (eds.) ISSEP 2016. LNCS, vol. 9973, pp. 65–77. Springer, Cham (2016). https://doi.org/10.1007/978-3-319-46747-4_6
24. Rahimi, E., Barendsen, E., Henze, I.: Identifying students' misconceptions on basic algorithmic concepts through flowchart analysis. In: Dagiene, V., Hellas, A. (eds.) ISSEP 2017. LNCS, vol. 10696, pp. 155–168. Springer, Cham (2017). https://doi.org/10.1007/978-3-319-71483-7_13
25. Ross, J., Sinclair, C., Knox, J., Macleod, H.: Teacher experiences and academic identity: the missing components of MOOC pedagogy. J. Online Learn. Teach. **10**(1), 57 (2014)
26. Saeli, M.: Teaching Programming for Secondary School: a Pedagogical Content Knowledge Based Approach. Ph.D. thesis, Eindhoven University of Technology, The Netherlands (2012)
27. Shulman, L.: Knowledge and teaching: foundations of the new reform. Harv. Educ. Rev. **57**(1), 1–23 (1987)
28. Van Driel, J.: Model-based development of science teachers' pedagogical content knowledge. In: International Seminar, Professional Reflections, National Science Learning Centre, York (2010)
29. Van Driel, J.H., Henze, I.: Extended paper for PCK summit, Colorado (2012). http://pcksummit.bscs.org
30. Van Driel, J.H., Verloop, N., de Vos, W.: Developing science teachers' pedagogical content knowledge. J. Res. Sci. Teach. **35**(6), 673–695 (1998)
31. Van Merriënboer, J.J.: Strategies for programming instruction in high school: program completion vs. program generation. J. Educ. Comput. Res. **6**(3), 265–285 (1990)
32. Yadav, A., Berges, M., Sands, P., Good, J.: Measuring computer science pedagogical content knowledge: An exploratory analysis of teaching vignettes to measure teacher knowledge. In: Proceedings of the 11th Workshop in Primary and Secondary Computing Education, pp. 92–95. ACM (2016)
33. Yadav, A., Gretter, S., Hambrusch, S.: Challenges of a computer science classroom: initial perspectives from teachers. In: Proceedings of the Workshop in Primary and Secondary Computing Education, pp. 136–137. ACM (2015)

Informatics and Computational Thinking: A Teacher Professional Development Proposal Based on Social-Constructivism

Carlo Bellettini, Violetta Lonati, Dario Malchiodi, Mattia Monga(✉), and Anna Morpurgo

Università degli Studi di Milano, Milan, Italy
mattia.monga@unimi.it
http://aladdin.di.unimi.it

Abstract. Teaching informatics with a socio-constructivist approach is the theme of the Professional Development (PD) proposal for teachers we present in this paper. This proposal is built upon the expertise we developed in the last few years by designing and delivering enrichment activities to school students, where constructivist strategies are used to let students discover informatics as a scientific discipline, and to promote computational thinking skills and problem solving competences. Starting from the analysis of teachers' training needs, we structured the proposal into different units. We highlight their goals and contents, and illustrate some of the proposed activities. We held some training sessions to test our proposal; we report our findings and the feedback from the participants who amount to a total of ninety-five in-service and prospective teachers.

Keywords: Computer science/Informatics education
Teachers professional development · Costructivism
Computational thinking

1 Introduction

Informatics is intrinsecally reflection on what one does and how one does it. As Papert once said, "in teaching the computer how to think, children embark on an exploration about how they themselves think. The experience can be heady: Thinking about thinking turns every child into an epistemologist, an experience not even shared by most adults", and informatics has exactly this potential. However, to release this power, we definitely need to avoid sterile attempts to simply *transfer* informatic topics, or, even worse, to train people in using informatic applications. We need instead to empower people with an informatic understanding of the reality and everyone should feel in charge of improving her/his own creative ability of inventing new approaches and devising solutions to the problems — which we expect to be increasingly related to information processing — they face daily.

This work was partially supported by CS[4]HS by Google [13].

S. N. Pozdniakov and V. Dagienė (Eds.): ISSEP 2018, LNCS 11169, pp. 194–205, 2018.
https://doi.org/10.1007/978-3-030-02750-6_15

An awarded best practice with this purpose is the series of *ALaDDIn algomotricity workshops* we designed for primary and secondary schools [3,4,6,19,20]. *Algomotricity*, a portmanteau combining *algorithm* and *motoric*, is a teaching methodology that applies constructivist strategies to informatics topics and focuses on the central role of the learners as the active subjects of the process. In algomotricity, learners are engaged in information processing problems, initially through a mix of tangible and abstract object manipulations, and they have the responsibility of finding their solutions; in a second phase they are helped in building their mental models of the topic under investigation; finally they are proposed computer-based activities designed to connect their own perceptions, solutions, and models, with the ones used in the real world of pre-existing applications.

The *algomotricity workshops* were indeed quite popular, with around 3,000 participants in the 2010–2016 time span, and both teachers and pupils seem to appreciate the proposed approach; several school teachers decided to bring new classes to repeat the experience or to bring the same class to participate in algomotricity workshops on different topics.

In order to let this initiative scale up and not remain confined within the organizational power and time constraints of our research group, we held some presentations (lasting around 3 h) of the workshops to teachers; they first experienced one algomotricity workshop, then a sort of debriefing was carried out together with them, in order to highlight the purpose of the workshop, the underlying informatics content and related skills, the methodological approach.

Teachers attending these sessions did appreciate the constructivist approach applied to informatics topics. However, they generally expressed some difficulties in proposing these activites in their classes, claiming that: the constructivist approach is fascinating but somehow unpredictable and risky, they are not accustomed to manage problem-based active learning settings, their background in informatics is in general too limited.

From the mentioned experience, we inferred these main training needs:

(i) knowing the principles of informatics as a scientific discipline, its cultural contribution referred to as "computational thinking", and its connections with the other school subjects, especially for the majority of teachers who have no formal education in informatics [5];
(ii) acquiring competences and confidence in using constructivist strategies (group work, problem-based learning, open settings, authentic tasks, metacognitive reflection, ...);
(iii) learning how to apply the constructivist approach to informatics topics, clearly defining learning goals and steps.

We hence designed a PD proposal for in-service and prospective teachers aimed at addressing these training needs. We structured the proposal into separate units that can be activated according to the background of the attendees. The proposal obtained a CS[4]HS grant from Google [13] which allowed us to set up materials and a testing phase. The paper presents the proposal and is organized as follows. Section 2 presents the Italian context as far as informatics education is concerned, Sect. 3 summarizes the constructivist learning theory with some specific reference to learning informatics. Section 4 presents the format, methods and setting of the training proposal. The proposed units are therein described by highlighting their learning goals and contents, and illustrating some of the proposed activities and materials. Section 5 describes how the training activities have been tested with different groups of attendees and reports the positive feedbacks received. Some concluding remarks in Sect. 6 end the paper.

2 Informatics in Italian Compulsory Schools

The discussion about why and how informatics should be taught in schools is rich of interesting contributions. For instance [26] brings strong educational arguments in favour of teaching informatics in school, notwithstanding the difficulty in recruiting prepared teachers or training new ones, as studying informatics provides a fruitfull way of thinking; [14] is a guide for informatics teachers proposing an activity-based approach; [9] illustrates the use of Bebras tasks in school to develop computational thinking skills; [16] discusses the need to change our approach to teaching in order to prepare children for such a rapidly changing world and presents a spiral curriculum to teach informatics. We believe that the main reason to teach informatics is neither a desirable increasing of the consciousness in the use of technology by youngsters, nor the training of crowds of future computer scientists. Instead, informatics can bring an important contribution to the achievement of more general competences, also recalled in the "key competences for long life learning" recommended by the European Parliament [11]".

In particular, learning informatics, as the science that studies the *automatic processing of information*, promotes the acquisition of *computational thinking* skills, *i.e.,* those cross-disciplinary competences that computer scientists use in their typical problem-solving work, and that can be fruitfully applied in many school, work and everyday contexts: formulating problems in a way that enables us to use a computer and other tools to help solve them; logically organizing and analyzing data; representing data through abstractions such as models and simulations; automating solutions through algorithmic thinking (a series of ordered steps); identifying, analyzing, and implementing possible solutions with the goal of achieving the most efficient and effective combination of steps and resources; generalizing and transferring this problem-solving process to a wide variety of problems."[1]

Informatics is not a specific subject in primary and lower secondary Italian schools, however introducing informatics in schools would be widely consistent with the national recommendations for school curriculum. On the one hand, such recommendations only state goals and learning outcomes organized into

[1] Operational definition of computational thinking for K-12 education, by ISTE and CSTA http://www.iste.org/docs/ct-documents/computational-thinking-operational-definition-flyer.pdf. See also [25].

disciplinary fields, but do not prescribe precise topics to be presented, while the implementation of the curriculum is delegated to the schools, which can act in wide autonomy with this respect. On the other hand, even though the national recommendations mention informatics mainly with reference to ICT fluency and use of electronic devices and applications, they contain several goals that could be easily connected to informatics, in that learning informatics would help achieving those goals, too.

For instance, for Mathematics one reads: "gradually, thanks to teacher directions and peer discussion, pupils will learn to face problematic situations with confidence and determination. They will learn to represent them in different ways, to conduct proper explorations, to spend the right time in identifying what is known and what one has to find, to conjecture solutions and results, to characterize potential solving strategies. [...] They recognizes recurring patterns, establish analogies with known models, choose the actions needed, and effectively chain them together to solve the problem at hand. Special attention will be devoted to develop the ability of presenting and discussing solution strategies and methods with peers."

Other goals having this informatics flavour also occur in other fields that are usually considered distant from informatics, *e.g.,* "decode and interpret the notation" (Music, 8th grade); "use timeline to organize information, knowledge, spans, detecting sequences, contemporaneity, durations, intervals" (History, 5th grade); "follow written instructions to create objects or products, govern behaviors, accomplish a task, carry out a procedure" (Italian Language, 5th grade).

3 Social-Constructivism and Informatics

According to constructivist epistemology — that has its roots, among others, in the work of Piaget — knowledge is *built* (constructed) through experiences and reflection on these experiences themselves. Thus learners create their own knowledge, and they create it relying, to a large extent, on what they already know and understand: new concepts/facts should either fit on mental schemes and conceptions, or the latter should be modified in order to deal with them [21]. In particular *radical constructivism* [12] even denies the existence of an *ontological* truth, because knowledge derives from the learner's experience which is unique by definition. As a consequence, it is impossible to find a representation of an independent reality which is ready to be *transferred* to students. Of course something is needed in order to distinguish between what is knowledge and what is not: the adopted criterion, borrowed from evolution theory, is to check how knowledge fits with experiences (that is, its *viability*). Social-constructivism includes also Vygotskij's principle, according to which the construction of knowledge is guided and influenced by the social context, and thus by the interactions with others and in particular by their use of language [29].

With these premises, teachers cannot prepare 'prepackaged' representations of reality and transfer them to pupils. Rather, their role is to support the construction of knowledge through setting up contexts and scaffolding material favouring the activation of the learning process, in which the ultimate actor is the learner itself.

Teachers should facilitate learners in their discoveries by promoting metacognitive reflections about how their understanding is developing. This usually means encouraging students to use active techniques (experiments, real-world problem solving) to create more knowledge and then to reflect on and talk about what they are doing and how their understanding is changing. The teacher must make sure he/she understands a student's preexisting conceptions and misconceptions, guiding the activity to address them and then build on them.

Among the main aspects constructivist teachers should consider, we mention the following ones.

- Working in groups (cooperative learning [17]) has the power to foster cognitive development and thus to empower learning.
- Pupils may have different learning styles and strategies [10] that have to be taken into account when designing and proposing activities.
- Active listening [23] is a powerful tool to grasp pupil's point of view and cognitive models/processes, and help them reflect and elaborate new models and strategies.
- The way we naturally learn from experience is by taking into account the information we can gather on the effects of what we are doing with respect to a goal to reach; individualized feedback [28] from teachers can play the same role.
- Instead of a knowledge trasmitter, the teacher becomes the facilitator [22] of the learning process.
- Reflecting on their teaching practice [24] teachers can improve their professional work; in a continuous process of self-observation and self-evaluation, they are able to keep tools and strategies updated, in a research-action setting.

Competences in problem solving are usually difficult to acquire just by means of explanations and examples; indeed, learning starts happening precisely when the already known solving procedures are insufficient for a new problem [15,18].

The constructivist approach is especially fruitful to develop competences in problem solving in informatics and provides a new and powerful set of concepts to guide reasonings on CSE [7]. The author emphasizes the usefulness of a constructivist approach in that it is able to soften the harshness of the interaction with the computer and to facilitate the social dynamics by means of exploitation of group assignments and closed labs supported by teachers and lab assistants trained to encourage reflection. Moreover he suggests that considering the opportunity of explicitly teaching an initial model of the computer can be used, for example, also as an argument for the choice of the programming paradigm for novice programmers.

Algomotricity is a methodology that applies constructivist strategies to informatics topics. Algomotricity exploits kinesthetic learning activities to informally expose participants to a specific informatics topic, followed by an abstract learning phase devoted to let students build their mental models of the topic under investigation. Finally, a computer-based phase closes the loop with previous acquaintance with applications. Activities start "unplugged" [1,27], but they always end with work in which students are confronted with specially conceived pieces of software in order to make clear the link (but also the intellectual hierarchy) with the computing technology.

As an example, Fig. 1 shows an algomotorial workshop ("Wikipasta" [4,6]), designed to foster reflection on information and meta-information representation in formatted texts.

In the first activity, pupils in pairs are asked to freely play with pieces of pasta and other small objects in order to estabilish a representation of the formatting information of a simple formatted text. In the second phase, through the introduction of costs associated to the objects and a competition to reach the cheapest representation, pupils gradually switch from an evocative use of the objects (e.g., spaghetti are very naturally used to express underlined style) to an abstract/symbolic one (e.g., a cheaper object used to indicate the start and the end of an arbitrarily long underlined portion). With this game they arrive to discover mark-up languages' concepts. In the final activity they start using a computer and are introduced to a lightweight "wiki" syntax by means of the software tool shown in Fig. 1.

4 A PD Constructivist Proposal

Our PD proposal is for in-service or prospective teachers of any subject, who are interested in introducing informatics in their classes, especially in primary and lower secondary schools (grades 1–10). It takes into account Italian curricular recommendations, school context, and teachers' preparation [2]. It can be organized differently according to the participants' motivation and background, and is made up of the following units.

A. Informatics and computational thinking basics.
B. Teaching informatics with a constructivist approach.
C. Designing and planning constructivist informatics learning units.

In all units, starting from unit A, constructivist methods are used. Therefore we propose discussion groups and problem solving activities, interleaved with recaps and brief thought explanations. For each unit, an explicit statement of the methodological premises, the learning goals and the assessment criteria is made available to participants before or at the beginning of the session. Metacognitive sheets are used for self-assessment.

The constructivist methods applied to computing education become one of the main content in units B and C, where simulations and authentic tasks are used to let participants experience the role of the constructivist teacher as a facilitator. Here rubrics and metacognitive sheets are presented as operational tools for everyday teaching practice.

We now present purpose and learning outcomes of each unit and exemplify their content with brief descriptions of some of the proposed activities.

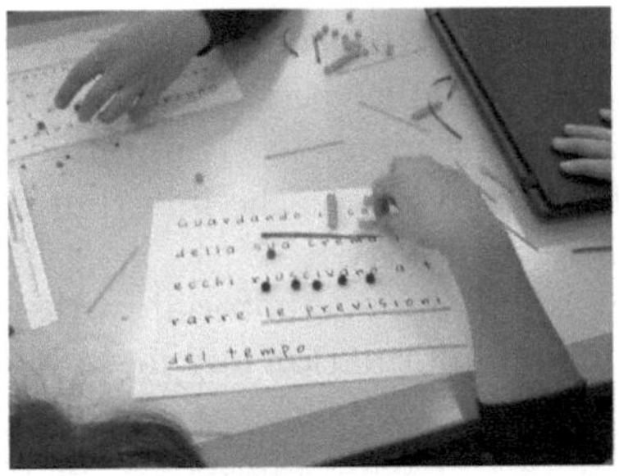

(a) Wikipasta

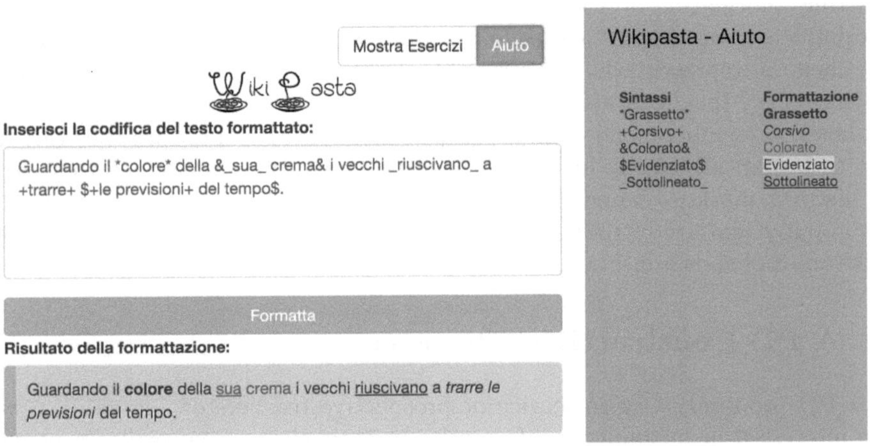

(b) The *ad-hoc* application developed to conclude the workshop

Fig. 1. An algomotorial activity designed to reflect on information and meta-information

A. Informatics and Computational Thinking Basics

Purpose. This unit aims at presenting informatics as a scientific discipline to teachers without a formal education in the field, and proposing the teaching of informatics as a discipline that fosters the development of important cross competencies, highlighting in particular the possible links with the other school subjects.

Learning outcomes. Participants will know:

- basics in informatics as a scientific discipline that deals with automatic processing of information (algorithmic thinking, information representation, introduction to programming or coding);
- the vocabulary and skills of computational thinking, viewed as a cultural product of the informatics discipline, and a cross-disciplinary competence.

Activities. Through algomotorial activities, attendees have the possibility to explore some fundamental informatics topics and to put into practice the skills that are typical of computational thinking, and at the same time experience directly, in the role of learners, constructivist tools and strategies. The proposed activities are mainly taken and adapted from our workshops or inspired by tasks taken from Bebras [8], a popular international initiative that "disguise" informatics problems in fun friendly setting, so that they are understandable by young pupils.

B. Teaching Informatics with a Constructivist Approach

Purpose. This unit's aim is to let attendees know and experience, now from a teacher's point of view, constructivist theory, strategies, methods, and tools, besides showing in particular, through a rich collection of both unplugged and plugged activities, how they can be applied to fundamental informatics topics. The focus is both on didactic aspects of the activities' informatics contents and on methodological aspects of the role of the teacher as a facilitator.

Learning outcomes. Participants will be able to:

- use active learning tools and methods applied to informatics topics,
- conduct algomotricity activities on informatics topics,
- reflect metacognitively about the role of a teacher in a constructivist learning environment.

Activities. Attendees participate in simulations of problem-solving sessions in small groups, playing the role of teachers, learners, or observers, so that they can experience and reflect upon how to manage group work and timing, facilitate work in an authentic task setting, give instructions and feedback. They are given some real products of pupils who participated in our algomotricity workshops, and have to analyze them in order to practice the ability to build a synthesis giving value to pupils' individual contributions. Finally, they examine different instructional material on the same informatics topic, based on taught lessons (slides and a book chapter) in one case, and on constructivist activities in another case, in order to contrast the two approaches with respect to the teacher's and the learner's roles.

C. Designing and Planning Constructivist Informatics Learning Units

Purpose. This module is focused around designing, planning, and assessing constructivist informatics learning units aimed at developing computational thinking skills.

Learning outcomes. Attendees will be able to:

- phrase specific goals for a unit,
- plan a sequence of both unplugged and computer-based activities useful to achieve the set goals,
- set up assessment criteria and tools (*e.g.*, rubrics) to evaluate the learning process and its outcomes,
- organize materials, assignments, and instructions.

Activities. Participants examine pre-existing constructivist learning activities (chosen also by considering those encountered within the two previous units) in order to phrase the learning goals in terms of knowledge, skills, and competences, identify and describe their main phases, highlight the connections between activities and goals. Then they are asked to design and plan a new learning unit starting from a Bebras task or setting, working in groups and with the help of trainers. To facilitate their work, a series of chained assignments is proposed: first they have to identify a learning goal that could be promoted by means of that task or setting; they identify intermediate steps and activities to achieve the goal; they prepare instructions and material; they set up rubrics or other assessment tools related to the goal.

5 Pilot Training Project and Preliminary Findings

In order to test the proposal described in Sect. 4, in 2017–18 we offered some PD opportunities with different formats.

- We held unit A in autumn 2017 (as a series of three-hour long sessions) and in spring 2018 (as a one-day long session) with a total of 57 in-service teachers. We asked to fill out an anonymous customer satisfaction questionnaire posing some questions with Likert 5-scale answers and space for free comments; 42 participants completed the form.
- We then scheduled a further one-day long session for unit B in spring 2018, after a request by a group of 16 participants to unit A. An anonymous customer satisfaction questionnaire for unit B was filled out by 14 of them.
- Since 2017 we have included units B and C as part of a master course on "Computing education" attended by students graduated in informatics interested in teaching; each unit takes 16 h divided into 4 sessions; the remaining 16 h of the course are devoted to programming teaching; 14 students attended in 2017, and 24 are attending in 2018. After the end of unit B during the first edition (in 2017) we asked attendees to fill out an anonymous online questionnaire, and 12 over 14 students completed the form. For unit C, we evaluated the assignments given during and at the end of the master course.

In all sessions, attendees showed interests and active participation. For unit A and B, question "Did the PD opportunity meet your expectations?" received generally positive answers (except a little number of neutral answers), and question "Are you satisfied about the unit" received only positive answers (in each edition more than half of the participants claimed to be totally satisfied).

In particular, in the free space for comments for unit A teachers wrote that the opportunity was clarifying, stimulating, interesting, satisfying, enriching, fun, intriguing, convincing (20 answers), but also, in some cases, confusing or tiring (2 answers). Some teachers, especially those who participated in unit B (that was indeed scheduled in response to their request), announced they plan to carry out some activities in their classes; moreover they suggested unexpected school contexts for the application of the proposed activities and methods. Many of them also expressed their interest in having further PD opportunities in next school year.

Master students were asked to evaluate the topics, teaching methods, materials and trainers' competency, and they gave positive feedback (except one partially critical answer). A couple of open questions asked for positive and critical aspects of the unit. Students appreciated the combination of theory and experimentation, the effect of practical exercises for experiencing the methodology directly, the discussion/sharing sessions at the end of the activities, the novelty of the topics w.r.t. the typical informatics lessons, the useful reflections about informatics topics usually taken for granted (*e.g.,* concept of algorithm). Criticisms were expressed mostly about the need for more time to complete the group activities and the mass of topics addressed in too little a time; the difficulties in the simulation activities without the real presence of students, some repetitive moments when groups presented their products. Assignments during the course were accomplished positively and students reacted well to individuated feedback, so that the quality of their products increased constantly. The final results and marks were in general satisfying. Moreover, after the course some of the students asked to be involved as tutors in workshops we hold in schools.

All in all, the activities and material proposed proved to be adequate with respect to the defined purpose and learning goals of the proposal.

6 Conclusions

Informatics has a preeminent role in the human enterprise of knowledge accumulation and dissemination. This creates an interesting and peculiar relationship between informatics and education, and it makes it crucial that all people (not just computer scientists) develop skills and competences in imagining new ways of processing information. We believe that general education would benefit a lot from introducing informatics in schools as the scientific discipline that studies the automatic processing of information, but informatics is not (yet) a compulsory subject in Italian schools.

And yet, even today, several goals stated in the national recommendations for the current Italian school curriculum, do actually have a computing flavour, even though they do not refer explicitly to informatics, mentioning it only as far as ICT literacy is concerned. Also, informatics is naturally well suited to be proposed using active learning approaches, like problem-based or cooperative learning and, more generally, approaches based on the constructivist cognitive theory: approaches that are often advocated by the current recommendations.

However, to introduce informatics successfully, with a real impact on pupils, we need teachers who know the basics of informatics, are aware of the potential of teaching informatics to pupils, and are able to manage the constructivist methods so well suited to learn it.

Thus, we designed a professional development proposal, aiming at giving teachers of different subjects and background — especially to the majority of them, who have no formal education in informatics — the knowledge and tools to introduce informatics and computational thinking in their teaching practice. We structured the proposal into three units, to be activated depending on the background of the participants, and we tested them in some different groups for a total of 95 in-service and prospective teachers. We collected feedback from the attendees and evaluated the process and product of their work, which proved that the activities and materials we proposed are adequate with respect to the defined purpose and learning goals of the PD proposal.

During the next school year we will implement a PD plan based on this proposal; we will schedule a series of periodical training sessions in order to involve a growing number of teachers in a research-action setting, and we will support the development of a community of teachers practicing the introduction of informatics in their classes.

References

1. Bell, T., Alexander, J., Freeman, I., Grimley, M.: Computer science unplugged: school students doing real computing without computers. New Zealand J. Appl. Comput. Inf. Technol. **13**(1), 20–29 (2009)
2. Bellettini, C., Lonati, V., Malchiodi, D., Monga, M., Morpurgo, A., Pedersini, F.: E questo tutti chiamano informatica. L'esperienza dei TFA nelle discipline informatiche, Collana Manuali, vol. 14, chap. La formazione degli insegnanti della classe 42/A – Informatica: l'esperienza dell'Università degli Studi di Milano, pp. 53–76. Sapienza Università Editrice (2015), http://www.editricesapienza.it/sites/default/files/5281_QuestoTuttiChiamanoInformatica.pdf
3. Bellettini, C., et al.: Extracurricular activities for improving the perception of informatics in secondary schools. In: Gülbahar, Y., Karataş, E. (eds.) ISSEP 2014. LNCS, vol. 8730, pp. 161–172. Springer, Cham (2014). https://doi.org/10.1007/978-3-319-09958-3_15
4. Bellettini, C., Lonati, V., Malchiodi, D., Monga, M., Morpurgo, A., Torelli, M.: What you see is what you have in mind: constructing mental models for formatted text processing. In: Proceedings of ISSEP 2013, pp. 139–147 (2013)
5. Bellettini, C., et al.: Informatics education in Italian secondary school. ACM Trans. Comput. Educ. **14**(2), 15:1–15:6 (2014). https://doi.org/10.1145/2602490
6. Bellettini, C., Monga, M., Lonati, V., Morpurgo, A., Malchiodi, D., Torelli, M.: Exploring the processing of formatted texts by a kynesthetic approach. In: Proceedings of WiPSCE 2012, pp. 143–144. ACM (2012). https://doi.org/10.1145/2481449.2481484
7. Ben-Ari, M.: Constructivism in computer science education. ACM SIGCSE Bull., vol. 8 (1998)
8. Calcagni, A., Lonati, V., Malchiodi, D., Monga, M., Morpurgo, A.: Promoting computational thinking skills: would you use this bebras task? In: Dagiene, V., Hellas, A. (eds.) ISSEP 2017. LNCS, vol. 10696, pp. 102–113. Springer, Cham (2017). https://doi.org/10.1007/978-3-319-71483-7_9
9. Dagienė, V., Sentance, S.: It's computational thinking! bebras tasks in the curriculum. In: Brodnik, A., Tort, F. (eds.) ISSEP 2016. LNCS, vol. 9973, pp. 28–39. Springer, Cham (2016). https://doi.org/10.1007/978-3-319-46747-4_3
10. Dunn, R.S., Dunn, K.J.: Teaching students through their individual learning styles: a practical approach. Reston Pub. Co., Reston (1978)

11. European Parliament, Council of the European Union: Recommendation of the European Parliament and of the Council of 18 December 2006 on key competences for lifelong learning, December 2006. http://data.europa.eu/eli/reco/2006/962/oj
12. Glasersfeld, E.V.: The radical constructivist view of science. Found. Sci. **6**, 31–43 (2001)
13. Google Inc.: CS[4]HS (2017). https://www.cs4hs.com
14. Hazzan, O., Lapidot, T., Ragonis, N.: Guide to Teaching Computer Science: An Activity-Based Approach. Springer, London (2011). https://doi.org/10.1007/978-1-4471-6630-6
15. Hmelo-Silver, C.E.: Problem-based learning: what and how do students learn? Educ. Psychol. Rev. **16**(3), 235–266 (2004)
16. Hromkovič, J., Lacher, R.: The computer science way of thinking in human history and consequences for the design of computer science curricula. In: Dagiene, V., Hellas, A. (eds.) ISSEP 2017. LNCS, vol. 10696, pp. 3–11. Springer, Cham (2017). https://doi.org/10.1007/978-3-319-71483-7_1
17. Johnson, D.W., Johnson, R.T.: Learning together and alone: cooperative, competitive, and individualistic learning. Prentice-Hall, Inc. (1987)
18. Kolb, D.A., Boyatzis, R.E., Mainemelis, C.: Experiential learning theory: previous research and new directions. Perspect. Think. Learn. Cognit. Styles **1**, 227–247 (2001)
19. Lonati, V., Malchiodi, D., Monga, M., Morpurgo, A.: Is coding the way to go? In: Brodnik, A., Vahrenhold, J. (eds.) ISSEP 2015. LNCS, vol. 9378, pp. 165–174. Springer, Cham (2015). https://doi.org/10.1007/978-3-319-25396-1_15
20. Lonati, V., Malchiodi, D., Monga, M., Morpurgo, A.: Nothing to fear but fear itself: introducing recursion in lower secondary schools. In: Proceedings of LATICE 2017, pp. 91–98 (2017)
21. Piaget, J., Inhelder, B.: The Psychology of the Child. Basic Books (1969)
22. Rogers, C.: Freedom to Learn. Merrill (1969)
23. Rogers, C., Farson, R.E.: Active listening. Organ. Psyc., pp. 168–180 (1979)
24. Schön, D.A.: Educating the reflective practitioner: toward a new design for teaching and learning in the professions. Jossey-Bass (1987)
25. Selby, C.C.: Relationships: Computational thinking, pedagogy of programming, and bloom's taxonomy. In: Proceedings of the Workshop in Primary and Secondary Computing Education, WiPSCE 2015, pp. 80–87. ACM, New York (2015). https://doi.org/10.1145/2818314.2818315
26. The Royal Society: Shut down or restart? The way forward for computing in UK schools, January 2012
27. Thies, R., Vahrenhold, J.: Back to school: computer science unplugged in the wild. In: Proceedings of ITiCSE 2016, pp. 118–123. ACM (2016). https://doi.org/10.1145/2899415.2899442
28. Thurlings, M., Vermeulen, M., Bastiaens, T., Stijnen, S.: Understanding feedback: a learning theory perspective. Educ. Res. Rev. **9**, 1–15 (2013)
29. Vygotsky, L.: Mind in Society: Development of Higher Psychological Processes. Harvard University Press, Cambridge (1978)

Real Time Classroom Systems in Teachers Training

Viktória H. Bakonyi(✉) and Zoltán Illés

Eötvös Loránd University, Budapest, Hungary
{hbv,illes}@inf.elte.hu
http://www.inf.elte.hu

Abstract. Nowadays students are surrounded by plenty of information resources and they use these multimedia streams parallel. This multitask working environment appears during lessons as well. This *hyper attention* symptom blocks students in the effective participating of the common work. Therefore more and more ICT tools appear and are used in schools from elementary schools to higher education. One of these possibilities is CRS (Classroom Response System) of which benefits are undoubted. Their usage makes lessons more diversified, more motivating for students who are used to and prefer to use applications and smart devices, more interactive. However we must not forget about the disadvantages either so in this paper we should like to give a look around this topic, present our own newly developed CRS system and speak about how we can use it in teachers training.

Keywords: Real-time · CRS · Higher education · Teachers training

1 Introduction

We may call the 21st century the age of information technology. Almost everybody has got at least one smart device to help in the daily life to find information, to give some entertain or to communicate with others. Therefore it would be wrong not to use ICT tools in teaching as well! The advantage of using applications, personal devices and smart boards is that they make lessons more engaging and more interactive. But be careful: *"Students are digital natives and teachers may lose the prestige if they do not use modern technology or if they use it awkwardly"* (anonymous author, from the internet) Though we do not have an up-to-date statistics about how many children owns a smart phone or a tablet, we can state that most of them are familiar with their usage in very early age. According to the paper [1] even in Hungary (which is not among the richest countries https://bit.ly/1MAMA8L these devices and their dragging functionality can be used for some experiments already in the age of 5 or 6!

Supported by organization EFOP-3.6.3-VEKOP-16-2017-00001: Talent Management in Autonomous Vehicle Control Technologies The Project is supported by the Hungarian Government and co-financed by the European Social Fund.

S. N. Pozdniakov and V. Dagienė (Eds.): ISSEP 2018, LNCS 11169, pp. 206–215, 2018.
https://doi.org/10.1007/978-3-030-02750-6_16

That is one of the reasons why it is highly important to teach future teachers of any specialities to be familiar with this world too. In schools the spectrum of the useable teaching applications are rather wide e.g. we may mention language teaching interactive applications like Duolingo (https://bit.ly/1ctJqfI), GeoGebra (https://bit.ly/1NGZwED) as a tool for teaching and learning geometry, or Edison application (https://bit.ly/2Ks4prl) to teach physics.

There are general applications with which teachers are able to manage the teaching process itself like LMS (Learning Management System), CMS (Content Management System) or CRS (Classroom Response System). In this paper we would like to focus on CRS systems and their possibilities. There are a lot of free or not free CRS systems, some of them based on hardware and software components, but the latest ones do not need additional hardware elements, they can run on any network connected device. The functionality of these CRS systems are generally available directly (without any installation) from the internet.

2 CRS - Classroom Response Systems

Using a CRS a teacher usually may send questions to the students, the system shows the answers immediately and sometimes the students may send feedbacks or questions to the teachers as well. Nowadays these systems are used from elementary schools to universities. There are several ready-made CRS used in education like Kahoot (https://bit.ly/2tcH72X), Sli.do (https://bit.ly/1lraGjY), Poll Everywhere (https://bit.ly/1A0QWPz) and much more. We may find some ready-made comparisons e.g. at [2] which may help us to choose from them. Just one data about the popularity of Kahoot: it reached 70 million users / month in 2018. More than 50% of students in the USA work with it [3]. Though our first question should be why they are so popular in modern schools at all. What kind of advantages do we have using them?

2.1 Advantages and Disadvantages of Using CRS

Advantages:

- Students are digital natives, they adore and always use their mobile devices (even during the lessons) therefore their usage should motivate them. It can bridge the gap between the learning methods at home and in the school [4].
- Students, even shy ones are brave enough to involve them into the common work if the system gives anonymous possibilities [5].
- It may inspire collaboration among students which is very important nowadays and engages students in learning [4].
- Doing and discussing something is much more effective than simply to read or listen to it [6].
- Nobody is able to pay attention too long, so some changes in activity may help to avoid mind wandering [7].

- *Real-time feed-backs* can be executed quickly and we all know its benefits from teachers and students viewpoints as well. One important viewpoint is to using a formative evaluation is to give feedback timely [8].
- CRS helps in *self-assessment* it makes comparing our own knowledge to the others possible.
- A modern CRS gives the possibility to make some data analyzes later to enhance the effectivity of teaching methods.

Disadvantages:

- It is a fact that using a CRS (interaction, communication) the teacher always loses time contrary to a frontal teaching method, therefore the whole content must be rethought. (Anyway in the age of internet where every data can be accessed within a click we should transform it to concentrate on contexts.) Though this loss in time results a more interactive and engaging learning process.
- Technology used in classrooms may distract students (but today we are not able to avoid it) they are chatting, playing etc. during the lesson with their devices [9]. Even worse case is that students may use feed-backs to disturb the lesson as we experienced sometimes.
- First, if a student accustomed to use always CRS in classroom it may make more difficult to pay attention in classical situations [10].
- If somebody is communicating always through a device may lose the skill of natural human communication [3,9].
- Technical problems may occur during the lesson and teacher may lose time using it [5].
- According to the answers teacher has to refine the methodology or even the content in fly [5].

2.2 CRS and Hungarian Teachers

What is the situation in Hungary? Do Hungarian teachers know CRS systems? Do they use them? We made a small survey which is available at (https://bit.ly/2I2KmSt).

The survey

- was filled by 102 teachers or students of teacher training
- anonymous, on Google
- participants are divided into three groups (20–35 year olds (39 person), 36–50 year olds (31 person), above 50 (32 person))

From the OECD database we can see that the participants of our survey is over represented in the case of the youngest group - the exact age groups used by OECD is not the same as ours. Though we can state that the age-tree of teachers are reversed from a point of view the youngest group counts the less active teachers. (see Fig. 1).

Dataset: Distribution of teachers by age and gender

Level of education	Primary to upper secondary		
Indicator	Share of teachers by age range		
Sex	Total		
Year	2015		
Unit	Percentage		
Age	Less than 30	50 and over	30 to 49 years
Country			
Hungary	6	37	57

Data extracted on 10 Apr 2018 14:53 UTC (GMT) from OECD.Stat

Fig. 1. Active Hungarian teachers' age groups.

- The first thing we were interested in was that how many of them used CRS in school. The possible answers were never, rarely and often. (some of the persons skipped the question only 92 answers arrived.) (see Fig. 2, Fig. 3) Not surprisingly, the younger the age group is the higher the percentage of the usage of CRS is, either as a student or as a teacher.

Age	Numb	Never	%	Rarely	%	Often	%
20-35	39	19	48,7	10	25,6	4	10,3
36-50	31	18	58,1	12	38,7	1	3,2
50-	32	20	62,5	6	18,8	4	12,5
Together	92	57	61,3	28	30,1	9	9,7

Fig. 2. Frequency of using CRS.

Background Information: We asked some Hungarian specialists about the facts. These researchers are working for the largest university in Hungary (ELTE) in which there are teacher trainings.

1. Lower elementary teacher training (1–4) During the university education (4 years long in ELTE) students learn about several CRS attending Digital Pedagogy in Practice curse. (The previously mentioned course is compulsory from this year for everybody.) Based on the knowledge students are able to choose the adequate system for a given purpose.
2. Higher elementary teacher training (5–8) Secondary school teacher training (6–12) During the university education (10–12 semesters in ELTE) students attend compulsory course: The Foundations of teaching and learning with ICT Innovative Teaching Practices. (The standard syllabus contains several

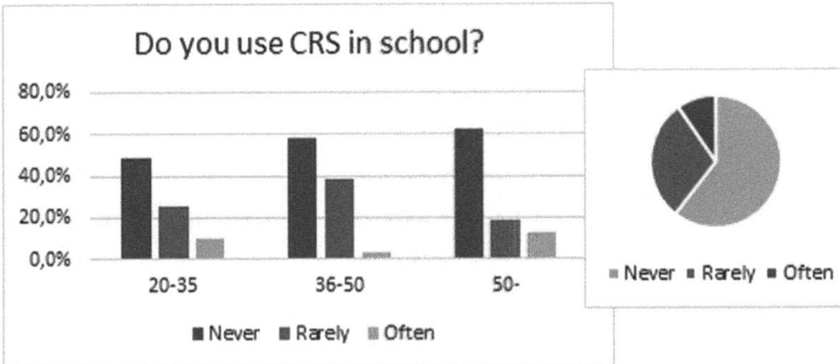

Fig. 3. CRS usage based on age groups and all together.

topics among them is CRS system.) Students have to try such systems in practice as well (mainly Kahoot, Socrative), but the content of the course slightly depend on the interests of the actual group and the research area of the teacher. Their usage in formative evaluations is highlighted. The topic got higher importance only in the last 2–3 years when free of charge systems appeared.

- Our second question was: Do you think CRS is useful in school? (see Fig. 4).

Age	Usefulnes
20-35	46,2%
36-50	35,5%
50-	40,6%
Together	41,2%

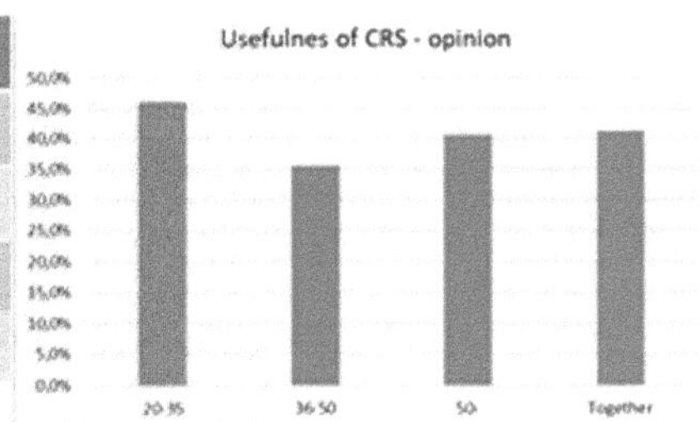

Fig. 4. Opinions about the usefulness of CRS.

The result shows that practiced teachers (over 35) are open to use new technologies.

- 3. Our third main question was whether they learned about CRS systems in university and if not are they interested in learning its usage? (see Fig. 5).

This results are very interesting, practiced middle-aged teachers (who never learned about it) are more interested to learn CRS than the youngest group. (Participants who filled the survey have to be engaged teachers or students therefore a standard groups result would be weaker.) In the future our next

Age	Learned	Interested
20-35	51,28%	20,51%
36-50	29,03%	58,06%
50-	25,00%	40,63%
Together	36,27%	38,24%

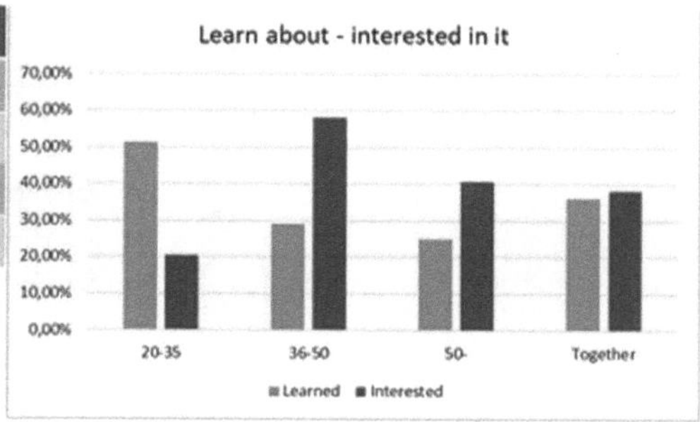

Fig. 5. Who learned about CRS & who are interested in learning it?

question should be why the youngest specialists are not motivated enough to learn new tools to improve the efficiency of teaching.

In the last decade professors all over the world experienced that classical university lectures are not effective any long. Students are always surrounded by smart devices and their learning methods have changed as well. To increase general student activity during lessons we also thought to use a CRS system. (Furthermore if they use their phones for getting information about the topic and to communicate with the teacher they will have less time for playing on them.) We must choose a cost effective solution with real authentication, with own collected data for further examination, so we had to throw away to buy any ready-made CRS with clickers.

3 E-Lection System

Therefore we decided to modernize our practice to involve students better into the teaching process, to engage them in learning. The one way to do it seemed to use a BYOD (Bring your Own Device) system

We made a survey (in 2015 and 2016) about smart device owners among our university students. The results showed [11] that more than 95% of students have got some smart mobile device. In the survey we asked: *Would you consider it benefiting if you could use your own mobile device (phone, laptop, etc.) during lectures?* (The aim of this question is to ask about their opinion using a BYOD).

We compared the collected data by a t-test and it shows that there is no difference between the need of mobile devices in 1st and in 5th semester students. Almost everybody wants to use them during lessons as well! (see Fig. 6).

Therefore we can state that we are ready to use a BYOD CRS for educational purposes. The next question was to find the adequate system to use, but we came up to against a lot of problems. One of the biggest problem was that, most of the CRS was not free of charge totally. From other hand these free systems are using anonymous or e-mail logins but in our future plans we wanted to do some data-mining to be able to give personal help to our students. Some of these systems are only able to handle one-way communication from teachers towards

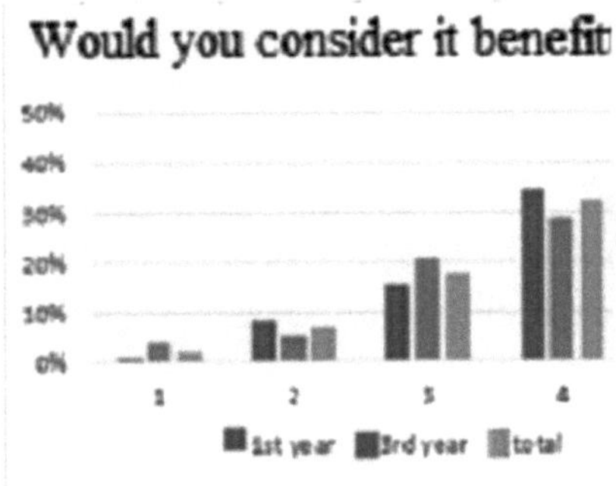

t-Test: Two-Sample Assuming Unequal Variances

	1st semester
Mean	4,683333333
Variance	0,352661064
Observations	120
Hypothesized Mean Difference	0
df	114
t Stat	1,04851103
P(T<=t) one-tail	0,148310529
t Critical one-tail	1,658329969
P(T<=t) two-tail	0,296621057
t Critical two-tail	1,980992298

Fig. 6. Need of using smart devices during lessons.

the students, but we wanted the ability of backward communication as well. Furthermore our university wants to stream the lectures only for authenticated users adding an interactive functionality to the system. After all, we did not find a CRS suiting to all our needs, therefore we decided to implement an own BYOD system, called e-Lection. We designed this as a web-based system avoiding to implement an application for different smart devices. This web application is a bidirectional lecture management system with which students also may send do not understand signals or proper questions to professors besides teachers questioning. (see Fig. 7) The system uses university LDAP to authenticate the participant and save all the collected data which can be asked any time later. (Naturally it can be used as an attendance list as well. The application is able to filter the university IP addresses.) [12,13].

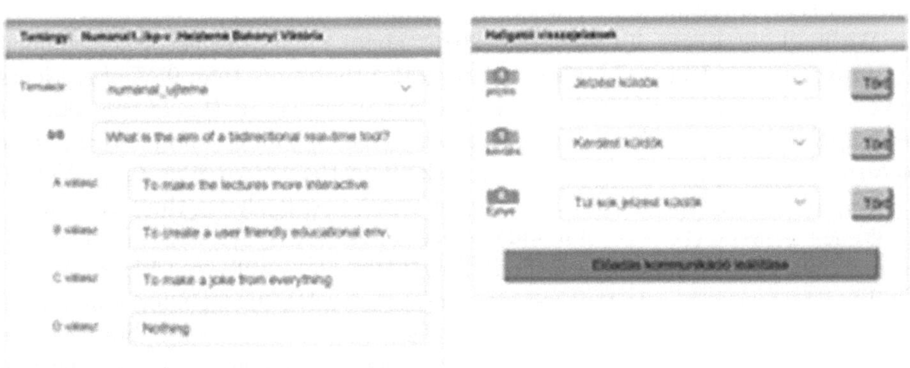

Fig. 7. Teachers user interface with questions and signals.

E-Lection is now available in ELTE Hungary at https://election.inf.elte.hu and a test version at university UKF Slovakia at https://election.fss.ukf.sk. We showed the functionality of the application to our students attending teacher-training and asked them to evaluate it, to evaluate the differences with the well-known Kahoot and Socrative. Generally they liked it but a great deal of them were against authentication. We are committed to use the system in teacher training program as well to give them as many personal experience in several CRS as it is possible. To use E-Lection is very easy, first the teacher must start his virtual lesson (with generating a lesson ID, see Fig. 8.) and after it students can join to this virtual course.

At the end of 2017 the stream functionality is built in our program (see Fig. 8) and the first trial of it was tested under real life circumstances. With this possibility we are able to build a mixed real and virtual classroom. Students may join to the lecture and interact with teachers through it. It would be a very good test possibility for future teachers. Though today we are still waiting for some more tests and a new streaming device for the final put in operation.

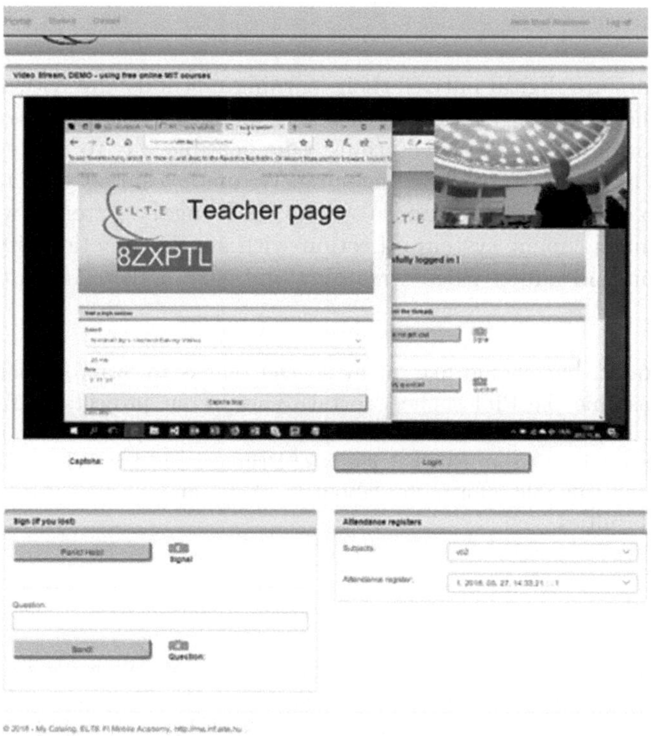

Fig. 8. 2 E-Lection in action (Open day program 30th November 2017).

We have further plans to give new question types to the system or to switch on/off mechanism of the authentication (sometimes anonymous usage has got additional benefits). We should like to create a question bank to help students in learning for the exams and a fine-tune of lecture content according to the students questions. We are thinking about the method how it can be used in personalized grading as well. Now we have all data related to lessons (e.g. questions, student activities, students answers, IP based connection places etc.) and this gives us possibilities to analyze them to improve our future work.

As a conclusion, after the intensive test period we experienced that students activity increased significantly with using e-Lection - though as we mentioned previously in the meantime we lost some time. Their attention also increased they used their devices not only for chatting and playing but mainly for interacting with the professor. Furthermore we got feedbacks that they know about the usage of such systems abroad (some of them experienced them during their foreign studies) and they feel that using e-Lection we made a step forward into the good direction.

4 Summary

Today students are digital natives their learning methods and attitudes are different from the previous generations therefore we have to modernize our teaching methods according to their expectations. One possible way to use technology to make lessons more interactive and engaging. We made a survey to map the teachers affinity to use classroom response systems in Hungary. After all we presented our lecture management system e-Lection with special functionality like strict authentication and added video streaming and gave a sketch about our future plans.

Acknowlegment. We should like to say special thanks to Szabó, Tibor (from University of Constanie the Philosopher) to take part in our project; to Misley, Helga; Raush, Attila; Rapos, Nóra (from ELTE Faculty of Education and Psychology) and to Temesi-Ferenczi, Kinga (from ELTE Faculty of Primary and Pre-School Education) to help us by giving valuable information about teacher training specialities according to CRS at their faculties.

References

1. Rausch, A. Pasztor, A.: Exploring the possibilities of online assessment of early numeracy in kindergarten. In: Proceedings of the 41st Conference of the International Group for the Psychology of Mathematics Education, vol. 4. PME (2017)
2. SocialCompare. https://bit.ly/2rK0hM8. Accessed 29 May 2018
3. 70 million unique users on the Kahoot! platform we are stoked! https://bit.ly/2k1yAdn. Accessed 29 May 2018
4. 6 Ways BYOD Technology in the Classroom Affects Students. https://bit.ly/2wO5uHE. Accessed 29 May 2018

5. Vanderbilt University, Center for Teaching, Classroom Response Systems (Clickers). https://bit.ly/2vxtWeJ. Accessed 29 May 2018
6. Kos, B.: The most effective way to learn new things. https://agileleanlife.com/the-most-effective-way-to-learn-new-things/J. Accessed 29 May 2018
7. Bunce, D., Flens, E.A., Neiles, K.Y.: How Long can students pay attention in class? A study of student attention decline using clickers. J. Chem. Educ. **87**(12), 1438–01443 (2010)
8. Grant Wiggins: Seven Keys to Effective Feedback September 2012, Feedback for Learning, vol. 70, no. 1, pp. 10–16. https://bit.ly/1bcgHKS. Accessed 29 May 2018
9. The Pros And Cons Of Technology In The Classroom. https://bit.ly/2IvQLXw. Accessed 29 May 2018
10. Ortiz, M. The effects of student response systems students achievement and engagement, thesis (2014). https://bit.ly/2KtE8K32A5Jhlq. Accessed 29 May 2018
11. Zitny, R., et al.: Education using mobile technologies. In: ICETA 24–25 November 2016, pp. 115–120. Stary Smokovec IEEE (2016). ISBN 9781509046997
12. Illés, Z., Bakonyi, V.H., Illés Jr., Z.: Supporting dynamic, bi-directional presentation management in real-time. In: CEUR Workshop Proceedings 2016, pp. 113–118 (2016). Proceedings of the 11th Joint Conference on Mathematics and Computer Science (MaCS 2016). Eger, Magyarország: 20–22 May 2016
13. Bakonyi, V.H., Illés, Z.: Real-time tool integration for lectures. In: 15th IEEE International Conference on Emerging eLearning Technologies and Applications: ICETA 2017. Star Smokovec, Slovakia, 26–27 October 2017, pp. 31–36. IEEE Computer Society Press, Denver (2017). ISBN 978-1-5386-3294-9

Case Study on the Process of Teachers Transitioning to Teaching Programming in Python

Eva Klimeková(✉) and Monika Tomcsányiová

Department of Informatics Education, Comenius University in Bratislava, Bratislava, Slovakia
{klimekova,tomcsanyiova}@fmph.uniba.sk

Abstract. The aim of our research was to investigate the process of teachers transitioning to teaching programming in Python, with respect to the challenges they face and support they require. Through the methods of qualitative research, we analysed a number of cases where computer science teachers transitioned from teaching in Pascal to Python. Based on the analysis of these cases, we propose a categorization for the transformation process. We identified influencing factors and present recommendations to support teachers transitioning to teaching a new language. We believe our research will contribute to improved support for teachers transitioning to teaching programming basics in new programming languages.

Keywords: Teachers' transition to a new programming language
Upper secondary education · Programming basics

1 Introduction

Trends in software development evolve quite dynamically. The popularity of programming languages is no exception to this and it would be beneficial to adapt computer science education to these trends. Therefore, the programming language used in education, including the upper secondary level, is of significant importance. Python is one of those languages with an ever increasing popularity and ranks among the most used languages nowadays [1]. Since it is already gaining ground in education [2–4], the continuation of this trend is anticipated at the expense of the Pascal language, widely used at universities and upper secondary schools. Beside pupils, this trend will also significantly affect teachers. How are they going to deal with the change of the programming language used for teaching programming basics.

Our goal was to understand the aspects of the transition to a different programming language, and simultaneously examine the factors affecting the process of this transformation. Another goal emerged during our research, to find ways to help teachers in the transition to the Python programming language. While

S. N. Pozdniakov and V. Dagienė (Eds.): ISSEP 2018, LNCS 11169, pp. 216–227, 2018.
https://doi.org/10.1007/978-3-030-02750-6_17

in our country there was no official textbook for teaching programming basics in Python, we decided to create a methodical material. The design process helped us better understand the process of transitioning to Python that indeed helped us to experience the nature of this process [5].

2 Methodology

The primary aim of our research was to examine the process of transition. A multiple case study was chosen as the main strategy and we used qualitative methods of data collection and data analysis, such as one-on-one interviews, asynchronous email interviews, questionnaires, observation (transcriptions and field notes) and audiovisual materials (their work by recorded video) [6,7].

We formulated our goals to the research question:

Q: How does the process of teachers' transition from teaching programming in Pascal to Python look like?
- What factors affect teachers' transition to a new programming language?
- How to help teachers with the transition to teaching in Python?

We used purposeful sampling, during our research (2014–2018) we were in contact with 20 teachers since the beginning of the first phase and observed diversity among them from the early stages of transition. We gradually gained understanding about the progress of their transition to the new programming language and the problems they face through personal and e-mail communication. By implementing a questionnaire, which was filled out by 103 teachers, we wanted to confirm and extend our knowledge about this process. In the last phase we focused on the in-depth analysis of five cases chosen by maximal variation sampling, conducted independently and in parallel. Subsequently we did a mutual comparison of these cases that resulted in a research report containing our findings.

3 Events Associated with the Transition

At the beginning of our research in 2014 a wave of transition to the Python language among teachers just emerged in Slovakia. Python textbooks already existing at that time often concentrated mainly at the syntax of the language, respectively highlighted differences between the commands of Python and other languages [8]. Though most teachers need materials for their teaching activities that teach pupils the language while using it to solve problems. Therefore a lot of teachers created their own materials [9,10], but their materials were often tailored for a small circle of students, adapted to the needs of their school and the characteristics along with the didactic principles of their teaching. At the time our research began Python training for teachers or methodical materials for teaching using this programming language did not exist. Python talks were very rare at conferences for teachers. As time passed this started gradually changing with meetings for teachers, materials, textbooks and training for teachers appearing. In 2016 training organized by teachers by their own initiative appeared to support other teachers in their transition to Python. These meetings were still not covered with a state institution and attendance was voluntary. In 2017 (and later in 2018) to support teachers we organized a section for education on the PyCon SK conference, on which we introduced them the Python language along with its advantages, disadvantages and the possibilities to use it in education.

4 Case Studies of Teachers Transition

Throughout our research we were systematically looking for teachers with recently awaken interest in the Python language and its feasibility as the language for introductory programming courses on upper secondary schools. We established e-mail communication with twenty teachers from such schools and repetitively contacted them to monitor their transition to Python. By analysing this communication, we created a categorization of steps that can be used by teachers in case of transitioning to a different programming language.

Contacted teachers were from a variety of schools in cities of different sizes. Three of them were from grammar schools and the rest from specialized secondary schools.

We focused on familiarization with Python, motives leading them to the transition and the materials they use for teaching. To establish a categorization of the transition to a new language we analysed cases, looking for both similarities and differences and identified three steps that may be essential in the transition:

1. Motives leading to the transition
2. Learning the language
3. Preparation and implementation of teaching activities with the new language

These steps can be further divided by other criteria, forming different forms of transitions.

4.1 Transition Motives

Transitions to a new programming language begin with motives that lead teachers to the decision whether to conduct the transition or not. We were interested in teachers who decided to undergo this transition. Our research sample included teachers looking for a more suitable programming language for a longer period, because the language (e.g. Pascal) or programming environment (e.g. Lazarus) they used didn't fulfil their expectations for various reasons. Some teachers were closely watching computer science education trends and got familiar with Python as a language suitable for teaching programming basics. Others were encouraged in the transition by their pupils or colleagues. Some of them were motivated by suitable and affordable Python training or books offered to them. We identified three significant motives:

- *internal* – following current trends
- *environmental* – recommendation of students, colleagues
- *external* – training, course, book offers

4.2 Learning the Language

The transition continues by learning and getting hands-on experience with the chosen language. This phase of the transition can be of significantly different course and duration. Based on the responses we identified these courses:

- *self-study only* – books, online courses, various materials from the internet
- *self-study and subsequent training*
- *training and subsequent self-study*
- *training only*

We investigated the reasoning behind choosing self-study over training or the other way around. Teachers who preferred training alleged reasons as lack of time and "To absorb something on a training is more comfortable than self-study". Teachers favouring self-study underpinned their choice by the need to complement their knowledge after a training or their unique style of teaching. One respondent used self-study for her previous languages, but decided for a Python training and started to use it immediately with the materials acquired on the training (i.e. didn't create any customized materials).

4.3 Preparation and Implementation of Teaching Activities

In this third step we focused on fundamental aspects of preparation and execution, the period of preparation and the materials used during the execution. By the period of preparation, we can partition teachers into two categories:

- *in advance*
- *continuously*

Some teachers prepare their materials *in advance* for a whole semester/year before starting to use the new programming language (e.g. summer holiday, etc.). Respondents who use already existing materials acquired on a training may be also included in this group. We were also in contact with teachers who *continuously* prepared their own materials or tailored materials from a training to their needs. These teachers reported to prepare for two-three lessons in advance.

A diversity showed up in the used materials as well. Teachers either created or customized their own materials or used an already available material without modifications. Some of them prepared their materials during the summer holiday, while at the beginning of our research there was no official textbook for teaching programming fundamentals using Python in Slovakia. There were various materials available on the internet as well as materials from teachers [9,11]. By the materials used we identified the following categories:

- *textbooks and course materials*
- *textbook supplemented with own tasks*
- *own, pre-existing materials adapted to the new language*
- *combination of various acquired materials*
- *specific materials from the internet*

Our analysis of these cases revealed that the identified three steps of teachers' transition to a different programming language and their further classification to categories define a number of different forms of transition. These forms are complemented by various aspects and factors that affect this process and create new, unique forms of transitions.

4.4 Questionnaire

To further strengthen the categories introduced in the previous section we decided to send out a questionnaire that was filled out by 103 teachers teaching at grammar schools, specialized secondary schools and elementary schools. 51% of teachers had less than 10 years of experience in teaching programming, while 32% of them had it between 10 and 20 years, 13% between 20 and 30 years and 4% over 30 years, with 36 being the maximum. The questionnaire was not only supposed to confirm our categorization, but perhaps even enhance it and depict different forms of transitions. We asked teachers about the difficulties they faced during the transition and also about the tools that helped them or they need for a fluent transition. Questions were based on our analysis of the e-mail communication with teachers we discussed at the beginning of this section.

For the question *What motivated you to transition to a different programming language?* we offered the following answers with the possibility of selecting multiple:

- *following current trends* (89.3%)
- *demand of students or parents* (14.6%)
- *training, course, book offers* (22.3%),

where the percentage of respondents picking the particular answer is indicated in brackets. There was a fourth option named *other*, where they could introduce other motives. We received answers such as *"the need to develop"*, *"graphics, objects"* or *"connection with real life and what is used in programming nowadays"*. It follows that most of the respondents were motivated by current trends and influences of their close environment. This result is of great importance as it demonstrates their effort to improve or at least preserve the quality of teaching programming despite it increases the time to prepare their teaching activities.

We also asked them the question: *How did you learn the new language?*

- *self-study only* – books, online courses, various materials from the internet
- *self-study and subsequent training*
- *training and subsequent self-study*
- *training only*

From the answers it follows that the dominant strategy of learning is self-study without any organized training (49% of respondents) that could have been caused by lack of available training. Slightly less, 42% of respondents preferred self-study in combination with training. Only a small number of them indicated to absolve training not complemented with self-study. Teachers who picked the

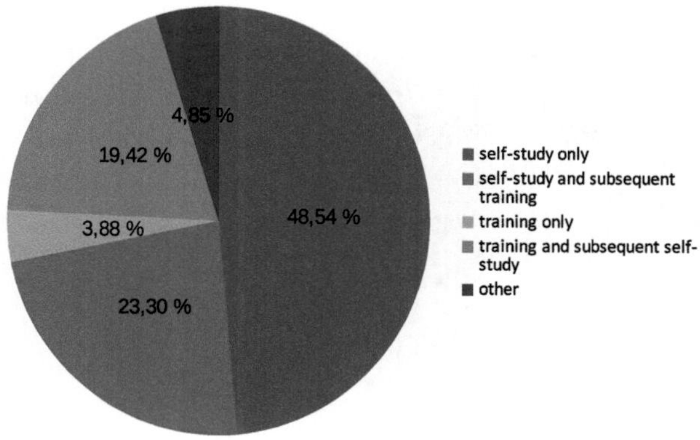

Fig. 1. Results for the question *How did you learn the new language?*

option *other* reported about books of the language or several transitions with different strategies used to learn the language. Our conclusion is that teachers do not choose the learning strategy based only on their personal preferences, but also considering the currently available options (Fig. 1).

We also asked a question regarding the preparation of educational materials. To the question *How does your preparation for teaching using a new programming language look like?*, 61% of teachers reported to prepare continuously (i.e. only a few lessons in advance) and prepare their own materials. The rest replied to be prepared in advance for the whole semester or year. Just like for other questions we also offered the *other* answer to which some them responded to use the combination of the prior answers. They prepared the materials in advance, but kept changing them continuously during the semester.

Our next question *According to what materials do you proceed during the transition to a new language?* offered the following answers:

- *textbooks and course materials*
- *textbooks supplemented with own tasks*
- *combination of various acquired materials*
- *own, pre-existing materials adapted to the new language*

Almost half of the respondents reported to use a combination of various acquired materials, from each only parts that fits them. The rest of the answers ended up with a lower percentage with one respondent choosing the answer *other*, describing his approach to be a combination of materials in the past, but currently using an unofficial textbook, in both cases supplemented with own tasks (Fig. 2).

Using the questionnaire we also wanted to seek out the problems that teachers face during the transition process. We asked them the question: *What were your greatest problems while transiting to the new programming language?*, offering the following answers:

- *lack of materials, textbooks and tests in Slovak language* (54.6%)
- *lack of training, courses for teachers* (39.2%)

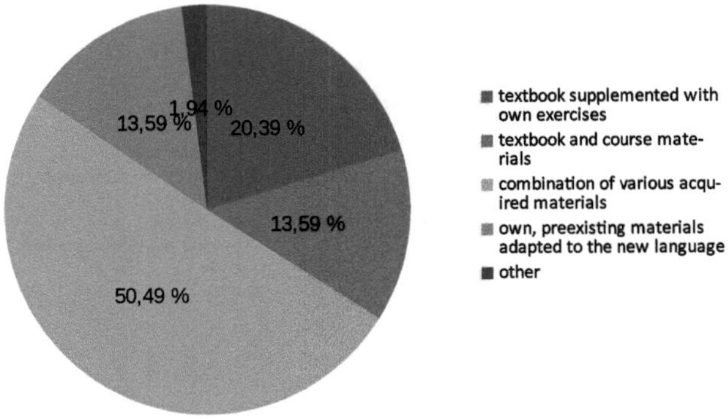

Fig. 2. Results for the question *According to what materials do you proceed during the transition to a new language?*

- *lack of time to learn a new language* (37.1%)
- *lack of support from colleagues* (15.5%)

By means of the answer *other* we wanted to uncover problems we did not encounter during the analysis of the e-mail communication. The question was accompanied by another, open question that asked them to describe what difficulties did they face during the transition to the new language. As the two questions are closely related, we examine answers to both together. Teachers elaborated on their lack of time and the time consuming nature to prepare materials. Some had problems that follow from the characteristics of the new language and gave answers like *Complexity of the programming language, missed some of the integrated functions of Pascal/Delphi in C++* or *Error notifications I did not understand and syntax errors.* Respondents also mentioned bad habits that evolved while using the previous development environment to cause them troubles. Another difficulty was the lack of cooperation with colleagues or as one of them described it *be left to oneself, having no possibility to consult my proceeding with colleagues.* Complications with mastering the language within the frame of a training or course were described as *When there were training sessions, they often emerged too late, Detailed training sessions are missing – the existing are short, shallow and we remain beginners after absolving them despite we are quite proficient in another language. It is hard then to catch-up with self-study.* and *Running into a problem while solving a more demanding task is followed by long lasting search for the solution on forums.*

By asking questions about the difficulties and necessary tools for teachers pursued two objectives, the first being the ability to find an approach to help teachers in their transition to a different programming language. The second was to identify ways to help them to transition specifically to the Python language. We also wanted to identify categories of the transition phases we did not encounter during the analysis of the first group of teachers, but the questionnaire having a larger group of respondents as the first group showed us that the already identified categories cover the stories of the second group and therefore there is no need to extend the set of categories. The results of this phase of the research acknowledged our opinion regarding the needs of teachers during the transition to a different programming language.

4.5 Transition Stories

In Sect. 4.1 we analysed information gathered from a group of teachers about their transition to a new programming language. We split up the transition process to three steps that we refined to different types and ended up with our final categorization of possible transition forms. We further strengthened our categorization by realizing a questionnaire with a larger group of teachers with being able to cover their transitions with our initial categories. Individual types of transitions are in fact descriptions of teachers' transitions to a new programming language from the motives until the execution of teaching activities. To get more insight into this process we decided to explore the transitions of selected teachers in greater detail.

The set of respondents selected for the following case studies was determined using the strategy of purposeful, maximal variation sampling. Our goal was to gather information from individuals selected using individual criteria so that we can cover various types of transitions. We selected five teachers representing different ways of familiarization with Python in combination with different materials used, and applied the method of one-on-one interview. We were in contact with three of them during the last three years of our research, visiting them at their workplace, thus knowing their stories personally. We also conducted interviews with them in their close environment. We expanded this sample by another two teachers about who we knew they went through a transition process different from the initial sample and likewise from each other. With these teachers we conducted interviews using voice calls that we later analysed and rewrote into the form of a story. We sent these stories back to them for completion and potential error correction.

By means of the collected stories of their transitions we wanted to complete our knowledge about the transition process and the needs they have during it. The conducted interviews provided us a complete overview of transition types as well as their approaches to the transition.

4.6 Conclusions from Case Studies of Teachers' Transition and Designing a Set of Recommendations

The result of analysing the case studies of teachers transition has confirmed the lessons we have learned from the analysis of the transition of a larger group of teachers. It has also brought some new insights that are beneficial to our research. We consider these observations as important findings that have emerged from our multiple case study. We used these findings to formulate a set of recommendations and a support proposal for teachers transition to a new programming language.

Based on the interviews we have conducted, we present the following common features that appeared in most of the teachers cases:

- They proceeded on the basis of their well-established approach to programming (Pascal), and the changes that they made were based primarily on the properties of the new language.
- After the first year of Python learning, they changed the details in their lessons based on deeper Python knowledge, such as the sequence of the topics, used didactic approaches or adding more tasks.
- Despite they learned Python by self-study, they later attended a training to enhance their knowledge, make some programming techniques clear or to prepare for discussion with colleagues. In case they attended a training first, they deepened their knowledge by self-study.
- The preparation time for lessons got higher for all teachers, because they either had to newly prepare whole lessons or in case of an acquired material had to go through the whole material and solve the tasks before they present them on the lesson.

The need for an inner motivation turned out to be a fundamental trigger of the transformation to the new language in case of every analysed teacher. The current acceptance of Python in world-leading companies also contributed to their decision. Teachers have met colleagues on conferences who were already teaching programming basics using Python, experts who recommend it and also learned about support materials for teaching. Consequent upon teachers' stories and our questionnaire is that the climate in their school and the response of their neighborhood that the transition is necessary contributes to their inner motivation. Consequently, this transformation did not yet reach teachers who do not have enough inner motivation to undergo the process of transition to a new language. Focusing on this group of teachers could be a subject for another research.

Based on our conclusions from teachers' cases and categorization of the transition process we assembled a set of recommendations that may help teachers during the transition to a different programming language:

- Ensure a convenient climate for the transition at schools and motivate teachers in various ways. Offer information about the suitability of the new programming language and show them possible paths of the transition.
- Perform training of the new language close to the place of their activity. Training should be extensive enough to not only introduce the new language, but give them also a deeper insight into useful didactic techniques applicable during the transition of the teaching process.
- Create and make available broad and detailed materials for teachers that should cover grades from the first up to the school leaving examination. These materials should not only contain the didactic principles on lessons, but should also contain examples, tasks along with their solutions and recommendations that support teachers even if they are new to the language or do not have much experience with it.

- Prepare them advice that emerges from the characteristics of the new language (e.g. Python) and includes warnings for differences from the language used previously (e.g. Pascal). For example, notes that help teachers find errors that pupils often do or clear warnings for constructs of the language that work differently.
- Create and contribute to discussion groups on social networks to support teachers who do not have other teachers in the same situation in their environment.
- Facilitate adoption of the new language on programming contests so that students learning programming using the new language can also participate.

To enable this support to reach teachers they themselves also have to perform some steps:

- Actively seek discussion groups on social networks, conferences and teacher's clubs.
- Realize that the transition can make their preparation time for the lesson significantly longer.
- Understand that in case of not having the chance to prepare sufficiently for the new language, their lessons can be more demanding and could not always be able to help pupils solving their problems with the elements and syntax of the new language.

5 Discussion

The process of teachers transition to Python programming language in Slovakia is not finished. Extensive long-term exploration of the transition process could bring new insights into this area. Due to our observations, after a certain amount of time, we expect the change of the situation in the area of support for teachers to transition to the new programming language: there will be probably less training of Python for teachers, but an increasing number of the available materials and textbooks for teachers. So the question arises as to how the process will be progress of these teachers who decide to transit to Python a few years later, when most of the teachers are already teaching in Python.

Contribution to this area could also be a comparison of our results with similar foreign studies dealing with teachers' transition to a new programming language. During our research, we have been searching intensively for publications in various available libraries, e.g. ACM, IEEE Xplore2, Scholar.Google, Springer catalog, ERIC, LearnTechLib, IATED. Researches on programming languages in education are mostly focused on pupils, such as [12–14], in which authors examined the transition between block- and textual programming languages focusing on pupils' perception of it, or compared pupils' results at the introductory programming courses [3,4]. However, we did not find studies that describe the process of transition between two programming languages in programming basic courses which would be focused directly at the teachers. Some common features can be found in researches that are concerned with changing curriculum or educational standards. Sentance and Czizmadia [15] focused on pedagogical strategies of teachers in introducing the content of computer thinking. They asked teachers what difficulties they encountered in teaching the non-programming part of the subject. Teachers mostly responded the lack of materials or technical problems. Also, researchers Thompson et al. [16] in their paper describe the process of implementing a new curriculum for Computer Science in New Zealand in years 2010 to 2013. Following the publication of the new curriculum they implemented a three-day symposium for teachers with workshops and seminars, but not all teachers have been able to attend this event. They also organized regional workshops and established mailing lists and a supporting website for material sharing. A year after the introduction of the new curriculum researchers implemented a questionnaire filled in by teachers from the mailing list, who were interested in implementing a new curriculum. Their results also show that teachers need training sessions available in the vicinity of their work.

Although in these researches transition of different aim and object were examined, the comparison of these processes points to a significant difference in the process of transformation. Researchers from the United Kingdom and New Zealand describe processes of transition *led by an institution*, providing teachers with materials and training. In Slovakia, the process of teachers' transition to Python took place *naturally, at the initiative of teachers themselves.* The process was not governed by any institution, teachers could decide to change the programming language. From the beginning of this process, they did not have any training, support mailing list or materials. Nevertheless, we can find common features in the investigated processes in Slovakia, the United Kingdom and New Zealand as they encounter similar problems and difficulties as our teachers.

6 Conclusion

In our research, we focused on using the Python programming language as part of teaching programming in the subject of Computer Science. The aim of our research was to investigate the process of teachers transitioning to teaching programming in Python, with respect to the challenges they face and support they require. Through the methods of qualitative research, we analysed a number of cases where computer science teachers transitioned from teaching in Pascal to Python. Based on the analysis of these cases, we propose a categorization for the transformation process. We identified influencing factors and present recommendations to support teachers transitioning to teaching a new language. We believe our research will contribute to improved support for teachers transitioning to teaching programming basics in new programming languages.

References

1. TIOBE Software: The coding standards company, January 2016. http://www.tiobe.com/index.php/content/paperinfo/tpci/Python.html
2. Zelle, J.M.: Python as a first language, February 2015. http://mcsp.wartburg.edu/zelle/python/python-first.htm
3. Ateeq, M., Habib, H., Umer, A., Rehman, M.u.: C++ or python? which one to begin with: a learner's perspective. In: Proceedings - 2014 International Conference on Teaching and Learning in Computing and Engineering, LATICE 2014, pp. 64–69. IEEE, April 2014. ISBN 978-1-4799-3592-5/14
4. Grandell, L., Peltomäki, M., Back, R.J., Salakoski, T.: Why complicate things? Introducing programming in high school using python. In: Proceedings of the 8th Australasian Computing Education Conference (ACE 2006), vol. 52, pp. 71–80. Australian Computer Society, Inc., Hobart, January 2006
5. Klimeková, E.: Curriculum intervention for learning programming in python with turtle geometry. In: Constructionism 2018 - Constructionism, Computational Thinking and Educational Innovation: Conference Proceedings, pp. 316–325 (2018), ISBN 978-609-95760-1-5
6. Yin, R.: Case Study Research: Design and Methods, 2nd edn. SAGE Publications, Thousand Oaks (1994)
7. Creswell, J.W.: Educational Research: Planning, Conducting, and Evaluating Quantitative and Qualitative Research, 4th edn. Pearson Education Inc., Upper Saddle River (2012). ISBN 978-81-203-4373-3
8. Summerfield, M.: Python 3, Výukový kurz. Computer Press a.s., Brno, CZK (2010). ISBN 970-80-251-2737-7
9. Belan, A.: Python, učebnica pre septimu osemročného alebo 3. ročník štvorročného gymnázia. Druska Books, Bratislava, SVK (2013). ISBN 978-80-89646-35-7
10. Kučera, P.: Programujeme v Pythone. Peter Kučera, Bratislava, SVK (2016). ISBN 978-80-972320-4-7
11. Mészárosová, E.: Python a korytnačia grafika: Metodický materiál pre vyučovanie základov programovania pre gymánziá. SVK, 1st edn. Knižničné a edičné centrum FMFI UK, Bratislava (2017). ISBN 978-80-8147-079-0
12. Kölling, M., Brown, N.C.C., Altadmri, A.: Frame-based editing: Easing the transition from blocks to text-based programming. In: Proceedings of the Workshop in Primary and Secondary Computing Education (WiPSCE 2015), pp. 29–38. ACM, New York (2015)
13. Dorling, M., White, D.: Scratch: a way to logo and python. In: Proceedings of the 46th ACM Technical Symposium on Computer Science Education, pp. 191–196. ACM (2015)
14. Robinson, W.: From scratch to patch: easing the blocks-text transition. In: Proceedings of the Workshop in Primary and Secondary Computing Education (WiPSCE 2016). ACM, Münster, GER (2016). ISBN 978-1-4503-4223-0/16/10
15. Sentance, S., Czizmadia, A.: Teachers perspectives on successful strategies for teaching computing in school. In: IFIP TCS 2015, June 2015
16. Thompson, D., Bell, T., Andreae, P., Robins, A.: The role of teachers in implementing curriculum changes. In: Proceeding of the 44th ACM Technical Symposium on Computer Science Education (2013)

An Investigation of Italian Primary School Teachers' View on Coding and Programming

Isabella Corradini[1], Michael Lodi[2], and Enrico Nardelli[3(✉)]

[1] Themis Research Centre, Rome, Italy
isabellacorradini@themiscrime.com
[2] University Bologna and INRIA Focus, Bologna, Italy
michael.lodi@unibo.it
[3] University Roma "Tor Vergata", Rome, Italy
nardelli@mat.uniroma2.it

Abstract. This paper reports the results of an investigation involving almost a thousand primary school teachers in Italy, to explore their views on the terms "coding" and "programming", and how they are related to their ideas on "computational thinking".

When directly asked "if coding is different from writing programs", roughly 2 out of 3 teachers answered "no". Among the teachers who answered "yes", almost 160 tried to motivate the difference: a few of them gave admissible explanations, while the others showed various misunderstandings, which we classify and discuss.

By contrast, when asked about their idea of "what coding is", only 4 out of 10 of the teachers explicitly linked coding to programming, but an additional 2 out of 10 cited an information processing agent executing instructions. The remaining part of the sample did not provide explicit or implicit links between coding and programming.

Our investigation shows that untrained teachers hold misconceptions regarding CS and its related terms. Given the general public and media attention on "coding" in schools, currently taught by existing teachers - mostly not appropriately trained, professional development actions focusing on CS scientific principles and methods are therefore a top priority for the effectiveness of CS education in schools.

Keywords: Coding and programming · Primary school teachers
Informatics education

1 Introduction

1.1 Context

The word "coding" is becoming more and more a buzzword in Computer Science Education (CSEd), especially in K-12 education. There are a lot of initiatives, like Code.org, CoderDojo, Code Clubs and so on, aiming to teach students to

S. N. Pozdniakov and V. Dagienė (Eds.): ISSEP 2018, LNCS 11169, pp. 228–243, 2018.
https://doi.org/10.1007/978-3-030-02750-6_18

"code". These initiatives are spreading and, since many governments are introducing *computational thinking* (CT) or *computer science* (CS) in school curricula, the term is used in many schools as well, especially referring to introductory programming activities.

Unlike the expression "computational thinking", that may sound abstract and pretentious, and "programming" that seems to recall a boring professional activity [4], the expression "coding" can capture the interest of students, and "*also provides an element of mystery (there are hints of a secret code), and achievement (cracking the code)*" [10]. There is a tendency in the media to use the term "coding" extensively, as noted - among others - by [1,14], when talking for example about "coding education". Some media observers have noted that "coding" is often used to denote a "*more playful and non-intimidating description of programming for beginners*" [13].

In popular culture, the term has also come to be used on the one hand as a synonym for the entire software development process, and on the other as a means to speak about what needs to be taught in school. This overlooks both the fact that coding/programming is only a part of the software development process, and that software development is only one of the important areas of computer science [3].

We think that, while in the scientific community it is clear that "coding" and "programming" have a strict relation, and that they are only tools to teach what matters (i.e., CS - or CT, used to denote CS core aspects), the confusion induced by this "coding mania" in the media can be very harmful. In fact, in our culture CS has been plagued almost since its teenage years by a lot of misconceptions [9] and it took decades to eradicate the limiting idea that CS is only programming [1,16].

The expression "coding" is currently invested with excessive importance [3], and this may lead to the wrong idea that its value is greater than the CS scientific concepts themselves. This is particularly relevant since, in this initial phase of introduction of CS in schools, many teachers self-train themselves and look for ideas and materials in the media, given training materials and professional developments initiatives are scarcely available.

Anecdotally, we spotted these tendencies in Italy too. Moreover, in Italian the term "programming" (translated as *programmazione*) has a very broad meaning (e.g. it is used for "schedules" like "movie show-times") and, in the context of schools, it is used to indicate "didactic planning"[1]. Furthermore, in Italy, there is a trend to incorporate "as they are" foreign terms indicating new concepts, rather than finding a corresponding Italian word. In facts, the term "coding" was explicitly used (untranslated) in a major plan launched in 2015 by the Italian government and aiming at rendering Italian schools more digital (Italian National Plan for Digital Education - *Piano Nazionale Scuola Digitale* [11]), and widely reported in communication actions related to it.

[1] For example in primary schools teachers meet weekly to do an "hour of programming", namely to agree on the content of lessons of the week.

In view of the above, we decided to investigate the theme of relation between *coding* and *programming* among Italian teachers.

1.2 Literature Overview

A few studies analyzed conceptions and misconceptions about computational thinking in school teachers (see [6]), however none of them specifically investigated their ideas about the relationship between *coding* and *programming*.

A research in the ACM Digital Library, restricted to the SIGCSE publications, returns 1,186 hits for the search term "coding" compared to the 8,674 hits for "programming". However, the former shows an exponential growth from 1970s, while the latter just a linear growth (Appendix, Fig. 1).

There is no agreement in the CSEd community about the relationship between coding and programming. In fact, some authors use the two terms interchangeably as synonyms or state both (e.g., they write "programming/coding"). On the other side, a few authors do not consider them as equivalent and analyzed their difference. They agree the term "coding" is more and more used in tech business world as a jargon synonym word for programming, understood by other professionals [1] (e.g. asking for "coders" instead of "programmers" in job offers). They also observe that on one hand the term "coding" has a broader meaning in CS (e.g. in cryptography or in information theory), and on the other hand it is often used to indicate the stage of software development when programs are actually written [1,2,10]. In other words, "coding" is considered as a narrower concept excluding important phases like analysis, design, testing, debugging [3].

1.3 A Related Study on CT Definition

We analyzed in [6] a large sample of 972 Italian teachers of primary school (students aged from 6 to 10) to investigate their knowledge level of CT. That analysis was based on the descriptions of CT that teachers in the sample provided by answering to the open-ended question "In my view computational thinking is...". Some of these answers did not provide a definition or were completely out of scope (e.g.: they answered "interesting" or "useful"). We assigned each of the remaining 779 *admissible* answers to one or more of 17 categories whose identification was grounded on the descriptions themselves.

Subsequently, we evaluated the level of teachers' understanding of CT with the following model. First, we rated each category with an integer weight in [-1, +2] to denote its relevance for CT definition, on the basis of the existing literature. Then, we computed the level of an answer as the sum of weights of categories it is assigned to. We used a value of at least 8 as the threshold to identify a "good" admissible definition (again on the basis of the literature) and a level of at least 6 to identify "acceptable" admissible definitions (since to reach a level of 6 an answer had to be classified with at least one category with weight +2 and at least some additional categories with positive weights).

We found the following results: 1% (8) provided a good admissible definition of CT, 10% (76) provided an acceptable (but not good) admissible definition, and the vast majority (89%, 695) of the 779 admissible answers did not provide an acceptable definition.

1.4 Purpose of the Study

This research has investigated how Italian primary school teachers define *coding* and which relations they see between it and *programming*. More specifically we addressed the following research questions:

RQ1 *how do they define coding?*
RQ1 *how do they perceive the relation between coding and writing programs?*

2 Methods

2.1 Context

The Italian project "Programma il Futuro" disseminates in Italian schools, since school year 2014–15, a better awareness of CS as the scientific basis of digital technologies [7] and carries out periodical surveys among teachers. The questionnaire sent in December 2016 received 3,593 answers from school teachers of all levels, from kindergarten to upper secondary. In [6] we analyzed the 972 answers of primary schools teachers, who participated to the project for the first time in school-year 2016–17, to questions regarding their viewpoint on CT. For the same set of teachers we analyze here their answers to a different set of questions.

2.2 Tools

We focused on teachers' answers to the following questions (in square brackets the actual Italian wording: *coding* is untranslated, as usual for this term in Italy).

The first one asked them to provide their definition of coding by completing:

Q1. *In your view coding is...* [Secondo te fare coding è...]

The second one asked teachers to answer:

Q2. *In your view is there any difference between coding and writing programs?* [Secondo te c'è differenza tra "fare coding" e "scrivere programmi"?]

and to those answering positively it was asked:

Q3. *If you wish, explain why* [Se vuoi, spiega perché:]

2.3 Sample Description

In the current study we considered the same sample of 972 teachers analyzed in [6]. The sample is made up for 93.7% (911) by women, hence 6.3% (61) are men, which is almost the double of the national value (3.6%) for Italian primary school teachers. This points in the direction of confirming the stereotype seeing men more attracted to computing than women.

This is the age distribution in the sample: up to 30: 8 (0.8%), 31 to 40: 133 (13.7%), 41 to 50: 415 (42.7%), 51 to 60: 374 (38.5%), 61 and more: 42 (4.3%).

Teaching seniority in the sample is the following: up to 2: 18 (1.9%), 3 to 5: 16 (1.6%), 6 to 10: 104 (10.7%), more than 10: 835 (85.8%).

Both distributions show the sample is made, to a very large extent (>80%), by mature and experienced teachers. This provides a reliable base of subjects for the research, but it is also a sign that they do not have a formal or structured CS training.

In fact, to become a pre-school and/or a primary school teacher in Italy, one currently has to get a 5-year (Combined Bachelor and Master) Degree in *Primary Teacher Education.* The course prepares students to become generalist teachers, by giving theoretical, methodological and practical training to teach all subjects included in primary school (Italian, Math, History, Geography, English, Science, Technology, Sports, Music, to name the most important ones). Most of the teachers teach more than one subject in a class, sometimes both literary subjects and scientific/technical ones.

Informatics is not part of the primary school national curriculum (but can be introduced as a local project of a specific school), even though it was associated with the subject "Technology" for a brief period of time some years ago: unfortunately, it was (and still is) mostly taught as learning how to use ICT tools (e.g. using drawing programs or word processors).

Because of the lack of Informatics in the national curriculum, its contents and teaching methods are not part of the Primary Teacher Education degree.

Much worse, that degree is mandatory to teach in primary schools in Italy only since 2002. Before that year, you could become a primary school teacher just with a High School Diploma specializing on Primary Teaching (again, preparing students to teach all the subjects), without even the need of a degree. All teachers that got the Diploma before 2002 (more or less all teachers older than 40) are primary school teachers without a Primary Teacher Education degree. Due to the seniority and age of teachers in our sample, the vast majority of them belongs to this category.

In both cases, apart from isolated professional development courses, all teachers most probably did not receive any formal training in CS and CS teaching methods.

2.4 Procedures

We used a mixed methods approach, including both quantitative and qualitative analysis.

Quantitative analysis. We used standard descriptive statistical methods to analyze the frequencies of both actual and relevant answers to our three questions. Moreover, we used the data and the model on CT definition of [6] to analyze how the values provided by that model are distributed when restricted to answers to our questions Q1, Q2 and Q3.

Qualitative analysis. We filtered out answers to Q1 that did not provide a definition (e.g. "innovative") and answers to Q3 that did not explained the difference (e.g. "coding is a discovery").

We then proceeded for each of the remaining *relevant* answers to identify, by reading and discussing, the conceptual categories to be used for their classification.

In a first phase each of us independently analyzed the definitions and proposed, for each question, a set of conceptual categories to classify them. We used a mixed approach: some categories were defined "a priori", on the basis of literature overview and related work described in Sect. 1.2, others were grounded on the definitions themselves.

Secondly, we jointly examined, for each question, the proposed sets of categories and through discussion we agreed to a preliminary set.

Subsequently, we manually assigned each answer to one or more categories, if the statement either declared the same nature as the category or stated being relative to or useful for the category. For this process the set of answers for each question was split between us, and we assigned answers in our own subset to one or more categories. During this process proposals for modifications to categories emerged.

Lastly, we jointly examined, for each question, both these proposed modifications and assignments. Through discussion, we came to agree on the final set of categories for each question (described in Subsects. 4.1 for Q1 and 4.2 for Q3) and the final assignment of each definition to one or more categories.

3 Quantitative Results

3.1 Q1 - Coding Is...

A definition was present in 88% (854) of all 972 answers. Among the 118 ones which did not provide it, 50.8% (60) did not answer to Q2 either, 24.6% (29) answered negatively with respect to (wrt, from now on) the difference between *coding* and *writing programs* while a same (by chance) 24.6% (29) answered positively (but only 2 answers contained an explanation). Among the 854 provided definitions, 7% (56) of them were not relevant (e.g., "coding is innovative"). The qualitative analysis of the remaining 798 (=854 − 56) ones is in Subsect. 4.1.

3.2 Q2 - Is Coding Different from Writing Programs?

An answer was provided to Q2 by 78% (758) of the 972 teachers in the sample and 60% (456) of them answered "no" and 40% (302) answered "yes". Among the 214 ones which did not provide an answer, 28% (60) did not answer to Q1 either.

Relationship with CT definition. We used the CT definition evaluation model and the related set of data in [6] to analyze the distributions of values provided by such model when restricted to the two significant subsets of possible answers to our question Q2 (namely, "yes" or "no").

The sample of 972 answers in [6] contained 779 answers with admissible CT definitions. We analyzed the admissible ones and found 396 "no" and 246 "yes" answers to Q2, while 137 did not answer at all. The percentage of *acceptable* CT definitions[2] is slightly higher for the admissible CT answers who also answered "no" to Q2 (12%, 46/396) than for those who answered "yes" (10%, 25/246).

This shows that teachers having correctly identified that there is no difference between *coding* and *writing programs* have performed slightly better, for what regards the definition of CT, than those who think there is a difference. This is confirmed also by comparing the average value for acceptable CT definitions in the two subsets of teacher having answered "no" (avg = 6.33) and "yes" (6.12).

3.3 Q3 - the Difference Between Coding and Writing Programs Is...

Among the 302 answers to Q2 incorrectly stating *coding* and *writing programs* are different, only 53% (159) explained why by answering Q3: 25 of these were not relevant, while the qualitative analysis of the remaining 134 ones is in Subsect. 4.2.

Relationship with CT definition. Among the 779 admissible CT definitions of [6] there were 123 who also answered to Q3, and none of these definitions has a value greater than 6 according to their model. Also, the percentage of those receiving a value at least 6 (acceptable definition) is lower in this subset of teachers (7%, 9/123) than in the overall set (11%, 84/779) and the percentage of unacceptable (<6) definitions in this subset (93%, 114/123) is higher than in the overall set (89%, 697/779).

The fact that teachers having tried to characterize a difference between *coding* and *writing programs* were not able to provide an acceptable CT definition shows an agreement between this research and the evaluation provided by the model in [6].

4 Qualitative Results

4.1 Q1 - Coding Is...

Categories. The analysis of the 798 relevant answers to Q1 using the procedure described in Sect. 2.4 resulted in 10 categories. We grouped them in two classes, according to whether they were somewhat related to *writing programs* or not.

[2] In [6] a value of at least 6 characterizes an "acceptable" CT definition.

- **Related**: All categories here somehow "speak" about writing programs, either in a full (PROG) or simplified (SIMP) way, or are concerned with writing algorithms (or lists of instructions) making reference to some information processing agent able to execute them mechanically (PROC).
  - PROC *Specifying processes*: devising an algorithm to solve a problem; providing a list of instructions to solve a problem; making an information processing agent execute a sequence of elementary steps
  - PROG *Writing programs*: using programming languages
  - SIMP *Simplified programming*: programming with simplified environments/ languages (e.g.: visually, blockly); learning the basics of programming
- **Unrelated**: Categories in this class are not directly concerned to writing programs in some form.
  - ACTI *Being active towards information technology*: creating computational artifacts instead of simply using them; being able to find creative or original solutions to problems
  - COLE *Cognition and learning*: reflecting about thinking or learning; program to learn; learning to learn; develop/ improve cognitive abilities; a method/ approach to teaching/learning
  - DECT *Developing computational thinking*: a way to teach/ develop/ apply CT
  - ENGA *Engagement*: doing playful/ funny/ attractive/ interesting/ inspiring activities
  - LOCR *Logical/critical thinking*: logical or reasoning or analytical skills; applying/developing critical thinking
  - PROB *Solving problems*: plan(s), design(s), action(s) or process(es) leading to solve a problem, to reach a goal, to face a complex situation (including splitting a complex problem in simpler subproblems to solve it more easily)
  - TRAN *Transversal competence*: e.g. fourth skill, transversal skill, life skill, useful in other fields, of general use

Analysis of Category distribution. The distribution of categories for the 798 relevant answers to this question is shown in Fig. 2 (see Appendix).

Category PROG, which directly relates *coding* to *programming*, is understandably the most frequent one, but appears in only 4 out of 10 relevant answers (323/798). If only the 456 teachers answering also "no" to Q2 are analyzed, this percentage slightly increases to 43% (194/456), a slightly positive sign that those teachers correctly relating "coding" and "writing programs" (i.e., the "no" answers to Q2) were also better able to describe coding in terms of programming.

On the other side, by aggregating the answers in the *related* class (i.e., PROG, PROC, and SIMP - remember each answer can receive more than one label) we obtain that 59% (469) of answers relevant for Q1 use an expression somewhat related to *programming*. In the light of the characteristics of our sample (see 2.3), the fact that 6 out of 10 teachers were somewhat able to identify a correct relation between *coding* (which for large part of their professional career most probably they never heard about) and *programming* is certainly positive.

Also note that, given each relevant answer was assigned to one or more categories, there is a 29% (232) of answers falling both in the *related* and *unrelated* classes. On the other side, there was a 30% (237) of answers belonging to at least one of the *related* categories and none of the *unrelated* ones and a 41% (329) of answers belonging to one of the *unrelated* ones and none of the *related* ones.

The third most frequent category is `PROB`, that with a 24% (190) is very close to the 25% (197) of the second one, `PROC`, confirming the trend emerged in [6] for CT, that in Italian schools CS education is often considered as a general instrument for problem solving. The strict relation between CT and programming is confirmed by the 17% (138) seeing coding as a way to teach/ develop CT (`DECT`).

It is interesting to note that 17% (138) of teachers highlights the *engagement* value of coding (`ENGA`) and 15% (117) sees it as an aid for teaching or developing cognitive abilities (`COLE`). We think these are important elements to ensure a diffusion of computing education in schools, although one has to pay attention they do not overshadow its core elements. The same reasoning applies to `LOCR` (11%, 87) and `TRAN` (4%, 31).

Only a 7% (54) of teachers has remarked the importance of coding to become active towards Information Technologies (`ACTI`), which is anyway positive given the question was not investigating the role/ purpose of *coding.*

Relationship with CT Definition. Among the 798 relevant answers to Q1 there were 743 who also provided an admissible CT definition.

We show in Table 1 (see Appendix) how these 743 definitions are distributed according to two subsets: one made up by all 458 answers to Q1 using terms somewhat *related* to "writing programs" and the other one made up by the 285 remaining answers. The average value of the CT definition evaluation model for all *related* teachers is 3.37, while for all the remaining ones is 2.62, showing a positive correlation between understanding CT and being able to properly define "coding".

4.2 Q3 - the Difference Between Coding and Writing Programs Is...

Categories. The analysis of the 134 relevant answers to Q3 using the procedure described in 2.4 resulted in the 11 categories described below. We grouped them in three classes according to how they described the difference between "coding" (C, in the following description) and "writing programs" (P). Some descriptions are tolerable while others are unacceptable. A few are completely out-of-scope.

- **Tolerable:** in this class we have categories expressing admissible relations, given the wide variety of ways in which the two terms are used in both literature and profession.
  `COMP` - C is a part of P
  `EASY` - C is a simplified P
  `PROP` - C is preparatory to P

- **Unacceptable:** categories in this class refer to wrong ways of describing relations between C and P.
  `CONC` - C is the conceptual part of P
  `GENA` - C is more general/ abstract than P
  `LUPR` - C is for playing/ learning, P is for working
- **Out of scope:** here we have categories which do not really address the difference but simply refer to characteristics of C.
  `DEVC` - C is a means to develop computational thinking
  `GECO` - C is a general competence
  `LOTH` - C is a means to learn other subjects
  `SOCI` - C has a social value
  `SOLV` - C is problem solving

Analysis of Category Distribution. The distribution of categories is shown in Fig. 3 (see Appendix).

In 43% (58) of relevant answers there were elements characterizing *coding* as simpler than (`EASY`, occurring in 35 answers, 26%) or preparatory to (`PROP`, 23, 17%) or part of (`COMP`, 5, 4%) *programming*: we collectively denote these answers as *tolerable*. In 54% (72) of cases there were elements expressing (at least one) actual (and *unacceptable*) misunderstanding of the relation between *coding* and *programming*. There were 17 answers with both *tolerable* terms and *unacceptable* ones.

We classified these misunderstandings in three *unacceptable* categories: both `CONC` (characterizing 13 relevant answers, 10%) and `GENA` (25, 19%) reverse the position, expressed in the literature (see 1.1), that considers *coding* as a narrower concept than *programming* in the software production process. The former by assigning it a conceptual role CT is concerned with, the latter by ascribing to *coding* a scope wider than the mere act of writing programs.

Answers classified as `LUPR` (28%, 38) have elements characterizing *coding* as just a "toy" activity distinct from "the real thing", that is programming in a professional context. Clearly, this misunderstanding goes in the opposite direction as the two previous ones, and none of the 134 relevant answers was self-contradictory by expressing both `LUPR` and (`CONC` or `GENA`).

Reconsidering the relation between *coding* and *writing programs*. Fig. 4 (see Appendix) shows the Venn diagram of the classification of answers to Q3 according to the 3 classes grouping the 11 categories. A minority of the 58 relevant answers classified in the *tolerable* class were also classified in the *unacceptable* one, but there were 41 whose classification did not have *unacceptable* categories.

These are therefore teachers considering *coding* as distinct from *writing programs*, but whose answers can be aggregated with the 456 negative answers to Q2 and removed from the positive ones. We thus obtain a 66% (497) of the 758 teachers who answered Q2 having an acceptably correct view of the relation between *coding* and *writing programs*.

Finally, we have also analyzed the subset of teachers whose answers to Q1 featured both a classification as (PROG or SIMP) and as PROC: there are 71 of them. In this subset of *strongly related* answers (9% of the 798 relevant answers for Q1) there are 51 (72% of the subset) who were able to correctly relate *coding* to *programming* (in the enlarged sense described in Sect. 4.2) while only 1 of them described an *unacceptable* difference between *coding* and *writing programs*.

Relationship with CT Definition. Let us now define as *tolerable-only* answers the 41 ones classified with at least one *tolerable* category and none *unacceptable*, and as *unacceptable-only* the 55 ones with at least one *unacceptable* and none *tolerable* (see again Fig. 4).

Table 2 (see Appendix) shows the values of CT definitions provided from the model in [6] for these two subsets. Remember that no teacher who answered Q3 received a value greater than 6 in the CT definition evaluation. Note that there are fewer answers in *tolerable-only* subset than in *unacceptable-only* (39 vs 48), and teachers in the *tolerable-only* subset have a slightly higher average value (3.49 vs 3.38) for the CT definition evaluation model.

4.3 Joint Distribution of Q1 and Q3

All the 134 teachers answering Q3 answered also to Q1. We present in Table 3 (see Appendix) the joint distribution of all answers to Q1 and those answers to Q3 classified as *tolerable-only* or *unacceptable-only*.

In Tables 4 and 5 we present the two respective marginal distributions.

Table 4 (see Appendix) shows that both a majority (68%) of relevant answers classified as *tolerable-only* wrt Q3 belong to *related* wrt Q1 and a majority (60%) of relevant answers classified as *unacceptable-only* wrt Q3 belong to *remaining*[3] answers in Q1. This indicates a positive correlation between the capability of describing what coding is (Q1) and the capability of providing a description of the difference between coding and programming (Q3).

This is confirmed also by Table 5 (see Appendix), showing that both a majority (56%) of relevant answers classified as *related* wrt Q1 belong to *tolerable-only* wrt Q3 and that a majority (72%) of the *remaining* relevant answers to Q1 belong to *unacceptable-only* wrt Q3.

5 Conclusions and Further Work

We analyzed Italian primary school teachers' ideas about coding and its relationship with programming.

[3] This is the subset of Q1 answers that has not been classified in any of the *related* categories.

Regarding RQ1, we found that only 4 answers out of 10 directly mentioned *programming* when defining *coding*. On the other hand, if we consider also answers mentioning simplified programming environments/languages or the act of designing algorithms or giving instructions to an executing agent in the definition of *coding*, the number of good answers grows to a more comforting 6 out of 10. Answers highlighted also side aspects of coding, often overlapping with elements more rightly belonging to CT.

For what concerns RQ2, when directly asked if there is a difference between *coding* and *write programs*, 60.2% of them answered *no*. Another 5.4%, even if answered *yes*, gave a completely tolerable explanation in the light of the variety of ways the term *coding* is used in different contexts, resulting in an overall 2 out of 3 teachers expressing an acceptably correct relation between coding and programming. The others giving an explanation (half of those answering *yes*) listed some characteristics of *coding* without really explaining the difference or used wrong (and conflicting) motivations: coding is the conceptual part of programming, or more general and abstract than programming, or just a toy while programming only for professionals.

We also compared our findings with ideas our sample had about CT [6]. We found that teachers having acceptable ideas about it performed slightly better in: (i) describing coding with programming-related terms, (ii) correctly identifying *coding* with *writing programs*.

Finally, when comparing *coding* definitions and explanations of differences between *coding* and *writing programs*, we found that 68% of those who provided a programming-related definition managed to provide also a completely tolerable explanation of the difference. Dually, the vast majority of those who failed to relate coding to programming activities in its definition also provided unacceptable motivations for the difference.

Despite being limited to Italy, our study - showing that teachers have not a clear picture of the relations between coding and programming - can be representative of similar situations in K-12 education of many developed countries. It would be interesting to learn more about the situation in other countries from the local replication of a similar investigation.

The most probable cause for the misconceptions revealed by this study is the fact that teachers have not been appropriately trained in CS and its teaching methods. The importance of teacher training has already been identified in other reports (e.g. [5,15]) as a key factor for a successful uptake of CS education in schools.

These results support worries about the fact that focusing only on a specific activity/ tool of CS (i.e., on programming) can be harmful, especially if referring to it with a "buzzword" like *coding*, which takes on conflicting meanings. In fact, our results show that such misconceptions have a high correlation with the presence of reductive or wrong ideas about CS. On the other hand, having an appropriate understanding of what coding and programming are is an important requirement for teachers to be able to provide good CS education in schools.

This research has shed some light on the fact that lack of proper training joined with confusion in terminology spread by media originated dangerous misconceptions, which may harm effectiveness of CS education actions.

We therefore recommend, when speaking about CS education, to stress the importance of CS scientific principles and methods. It has to be clearly stated that CS (and not CT or coding) is the scientific discipline to be taught at all school levels [12], both because it is the science underpinning the development of the current digital society and because it provides conceptual methods contributing to a better understanding of other disciplines [8]. This has to be done at a communication level when presenting and discussing CS school education initiatives, at the organizational level of CS school curricula specification and in the context of teacher training in CS.

We plan to extend our analysis to teachers of other school levels and to compare these results with those of teachers with more experience in CS teaching. It would also be interesting to carry out surveys in other countries to obtain a wider picture of the relations between misconceptions regarding CS related terms and teacher training.

Acknowledgements. We greatly thank teachers and students involved in Programma il Futuro project (coordinated by EN) and Code.org for their cooperation.

We acknowledge the financial support of Engineering, TIM; CA Technologies, De Agostini Scuola, SeeWeb. Other companies have financially supported the project for two school-years only: Samsung Italia; Microsoft Italia; Cisco, Hewlett-Packard, Oracle, Facebook.

Rai Cultura, the culture department of Italian national public broadcasting company, is a media partner of the project since February 2017.

Appendix

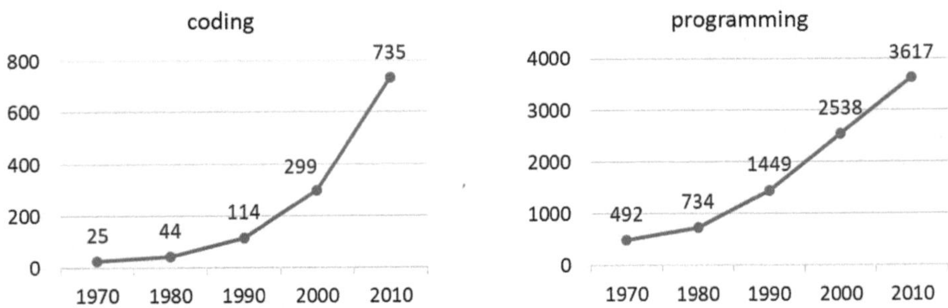

Fig. 1. Growth of search hits for terms *coding* and *programming* in ACM SIGCSE publications. Source: ACM Digital Library search results (Aug. 7th, 2018).

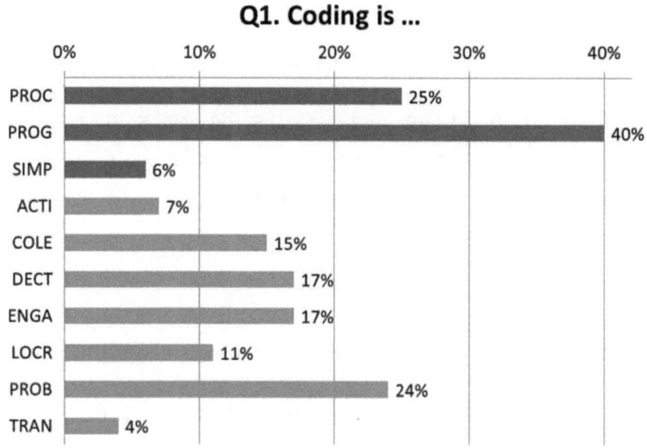

Fig. 2. Frequency of each category in Q1

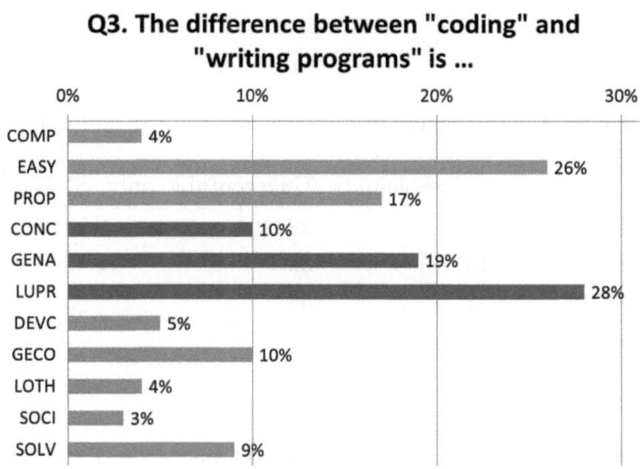

Fig. 3. Frequency of each category in Q3

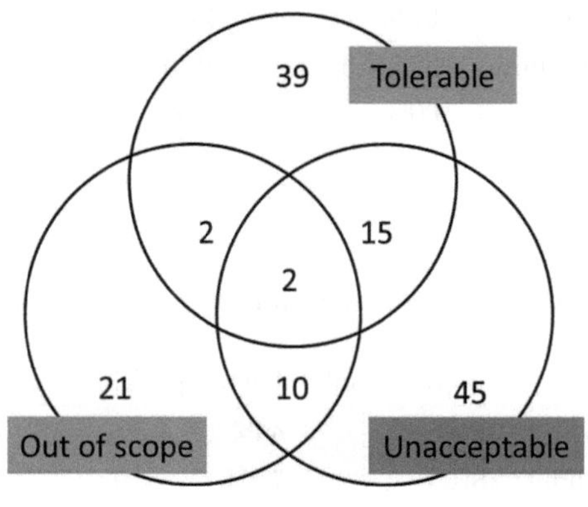

Fig. 4. Distribution of Q3 answers among classes.

Table 1. Distribution of CT values of relevant Q1 answers.

Value	−1	0	1	2	3	4	5	6	7	8	9	10	11	12
Related	1	16	40	105	57	149	32	47	6	3	1	0	1	0
Remaining	5	27	65	58	28	60	16	21	2	2	0	0	0	1

Table 2. Distribution of CT values for a subset of Q3 answers.

Value	−1	0	1	2	3	4	5	6
Tolerable-only	0	1	2	8	7	12	5	4
Unacceptable-only	0	3	5	7	4	18	7	4

Table 3. Joint distribution of answers to Q1 and Q3.

	Tolerable-only	Unacceptable-only	SUM
Related	28	22	50
Remaining	13	33	46
SUM	41	55	96

Table 4. Marginal distribution of Q3 answers wrt to Q1.

	Tolerable-only	Unacceptable-only
Related	**68%**	40%
Remaining	32%	**60%**
SUM	100%	100%

Table 5. Marginal distribution of Q1 answers wrt to Q3.

	Tolerable-only	Unacceptable-only	SUM
Related	**56%**	44%	100%
Remaining	28%	**72%**	100%

References

1. Armoni, M.: Computing in schools: computer science, computational thinking, programming, coding: the anomalies of transitivity in k-12 computer science education. ACM Inroads **7**(4), 24–27 (2016)
2. Barendsen, E., et al.: Concepts in k-9 computer science education. In: ITICSE-WGR 2015, pp. 85–116. ACM (2015)
3. Bell, T.: What's all the fuss about coding? In: ACER Research Conference 2016. Australian Council for Educational Research, Melbourne, Australia (2016)
4. Ben-Ari, M.: In defense of programming. In: ITiCSE 2015. ACM (2015)
5. Caspersen, M.E., Gal-Ezer, J., Nardelli, E., Vahrenhold, J., Westermeier, M.: The CECE report: creating a map of informatics in European schools. In: SIGCSE 2018 (2018)
6. Corradini, I., Lodi, M., Nardelli, E.: Conceptions and misconceptions about computational thinking among Italian primary school teachers. In: ICER 2017 (2017)
7. Corradini, I., Lodi, M., Nardelli, E.: Computational thinking in Italian schools: quantitative data and teachers' sentiment analysis after two years of "Programma il Futuro" Project. In: ITiCSE 2017. ACM, New York (2017)
8. Denning, P.J., Rosenbloom, P.S.: The profession of IT: computing: the fourth great domain of science. Commun. ACM **52**(9), 27–29 (2009)
9. Denning, P.J., Tedre, M., Yongpradit, P.: Misconceptions about computer science. Commun. ACM **60**(3), 31–33 (2017)
10. Duncan, C., Bell, T., Tanimoto, S.: Should your 8-year-old learn coding? In: Proceedings WiPSCE 2014, pp. 60–69. ACM (2014)
11. Italian Ministry of Education, University and Research: National Plan for Digital Education (2016)
12. Nardelli, E.: Do we really need computational thinking? Commun. ACM (2018, to be published)
13. Prottsman, K.: Coding vs. programming - battle of the terms! (2015). http://www.huffingtonpost.com/kiki-prottsman/coding-vs-programming-bat_b_7042816.html
14. Sentance, S.: Why teach computer science in school. In: Sentance, S., Barendsen, E., Schulte, C. (eds.) Computer Science Education. Perspectives on Teaching and Learning in School, chap. 1, pp. 3–4. Bloomsbury Academic, London (2018)
15. The Royal Society: After the Reboot: Computing Education in UK Schools. The Royal Society, London (2017)
16. Wing, J.M.: Computational thinking. Commun. ACM **49**(3), 33–35 (2006)

The Quality of Teaching - Is There Any Difference Between University Teachers and School Teachers?

Elisa Reçi and Andreas Bollin(✉)

Alpen-Adria-Universität Klagenfurt, Universitätstr. 65-67, Klagenfurt, Austria
{elisa.reci,andreas.bollin}@aau.at
https://www.aau.at/en/informatics-didactics/

Abstract. An important aspect of the profession of an educator is the assessment and the improvement of the quality of the underlying teaching process, but does this hold for all types of teachers? By collecting best practices of computer science teachers in school we created a teaching maturity model (called TeaM) and recently demonstrated its benefit. The paper now takes this maturity model as a basis and investigates the question about the differences in teaching at Universities and secondary schools. To do so, we randomly selected computer science lectures at our university, assessed them based on the Team Model and looked at the practices in more detail. In our setting it turned out that not all practices are covered at both types of institutions, and especially practices needing documentation and methodologies are lacking at university teaching.

Keywords: CMMI · Teaching maturity model · School teachers University teachers

1 Introduction

Even though university and school teachers (in informatics) deal with different types of students and contents, they all have, among many others, a common goal: assuring the quality of their lectures. There are different ways (and processes) in dealing with the situation of measuring and leveling up the quality of lectures. Existing standards, however, only consider specific factors (like teacher education, course layout, environment, etc.) [19, p. 2], and a recent study emphasizes the fact that a better quality of teaching is achieved when considering the teaching process as a whole (so all the teaching factors) [2,3]. The work of Chen et al. is based on the Capability Maturity Model Integration (CMMI) from the Software Engineering Institute (SEI) of Carnegie Mellon University [7]. The model of Chen et al. has several limitations. First, its content is not suitable for schools teachers (as it only focuses on university teachers). Secondly, they conducted only an exploratory study, and finally, no empirical investigation is done (so far) for a continual development of the model. Spurred by the work of

S. N. Pozdniakov and V. Dagienė (Eds.): ISSEP 2018, LNCS 11169, pp. 244–255, 2018.
https://doi.org/10.1007/978-3-030-02750-6_19

Chen et al., we thus created a Teaching Maturity Model (TeaM) [19] that tries to overcome the above limitations and expands the focus from university to also cover the teaching at schools.

The objective of this paper is now to investigate if, considering the TeaM process model, informatics university teachers can learn from informatics school teachers, and vice versa. To do so, a study was conducted with lectures at the Alpen-Adria-Universität Klagenfurt, looking at their maturity level in detail and comparing it with the official rating of their classes. It turns out that there are still a lot of differences between teaching at universities and at schools, but lessons can be learned from both settings.

The rest of the paper is organized as follows: Sect. 2 describes the background work and briefly mentions how the TeaM model works. A detail description of the study and the results is presented in Sect. 3. In Sect. 4 the results and the threats to validity are discussed. Section 5 concludes with a summary and future work.

2 Background

This section gives a short description of the Teaching Maturity Model's structure and the related models. It demonstrates how they are used to address the quality of teaching.

2.1 Related Work

The traditional form for addressing the quality of teaching by giving personal feedback is seen as quite subjective. This has opened a path for research in assessment models which rely on standards. Here, a lot of authors address the quality of teaching by mainly focusing either on teachers (preparation, communication, engagement), pupils/students, course content, or the environment. Taking a closer look at the existing work, we can divide these models into several groups.

There are models that, for addressing the quality of teaching, focus only on school teachers, and their results reveal the lesson learned by the teachers. Some of the well-known models are: The AQRT model which addresses the quality of teaching by assessing the teachers' teaching practices [4]. There, the authors applied the model in thirty physical education lessons with nine elementary teachers in physics. The results emphasize the applicability of the model. The competence based model is another model that assesses the teaching quality through teacher-licensure tests [12]. Mehrens study is more an investigation and analysis of licensure and teachers competency tests. A similar model is the "Competence based model for teachers" defining how to teach [20], and the assessment is based on these definitions.

Furthermore, there is the TALIS model which assesses the quality based on working condition of teachers and the learning environment [16]. The OECD article is a technical report where they applied the model in a pilot test with five volunteering countries: Brazil, Malaysia, Norway, Portugal and Slovenia. According to the article, the test was successful and helpful for teachers.

There are other approaches that consider the pupils/students and the teachers' interactions for addressing the quality. However, these models fail in demonstrating any practical effect. The CEM model is one of them. It assesses teacher quality based on students' outcomes [1]. Azam and Kingdon applied their model to compare the students' results of the exams from the tenth-grade to the twelfth-grade. Based on the results (that might have improved or not) the teacher's contribution was estimated. Another one is a standard-based learning and assessment system of the National Education Association to show how student learning standards can be connected with teacher education and assessment [14]. Although there is no concrete implementation in practice, they suggest to use the system to measure the quality of teaching. The assessment of teacher competencies and students learning and feelings is another model presented by Snook et al. [21]. In their article, they investigate the school system in New Zealand. The"Angebots-Nutzungs Modell" is a model used to address teaching quality based on teacher-student interaction (results, feelings, and environment) [8]. TEQAS is another model where quality is addressed by assessing the education of teachers [5]. Dilshad showed the applicability of the model by covering five quality variables through interviews (questionnaire) with 350 students and M.Ed. programmes.

Beyond the traditional forms and the assessment methods mentioned above, some maturity models based on principles of CMMI were created. These models do not considered teachers in particular so it is not possible to find out if teachers learned from the model. Researchers in the field of computer science education created maturity models to assess and to improve the curricula or the institution itself [6,9,10]. The validation of these models is referred to a later stage and so far no results are published yet. Ling et al. applied their model in a case study in a private institution of Higher Learning (IHL) in Malaysia and mention that a larger participation of IHLs will be used in future for a better validation of the model [9]. The adaption of CMMI in the educational domain has also be done for courses design either in a classroom environment [17] or online [11,15]. The model of Petri is not validated yet. Neuhauser did the validation of the model in relation to usability, and the answers from the questionnaires revealed that 88 percent of the responders agree with the suggested process areas [15]. Similarly, Marshall and Mitchell validated the processes and the model in the analysis of an e-learning module at New Zealand University [11].

Likewise, in primary and secondary schools, some CMMI-like implementation models with the focus on the institutional level or on the syllabus [13,22,23] were created as well. Montgomery applied her model in six schools for defining the level of using computers and technologies in schools. The models provides goals and practices for making improvements [13]. Solar et al. conducted a pilot study to test the validity of the model and its associated web-support tool [22]. They tested the applicability of the model in different schools and obtained positive feedback from them.

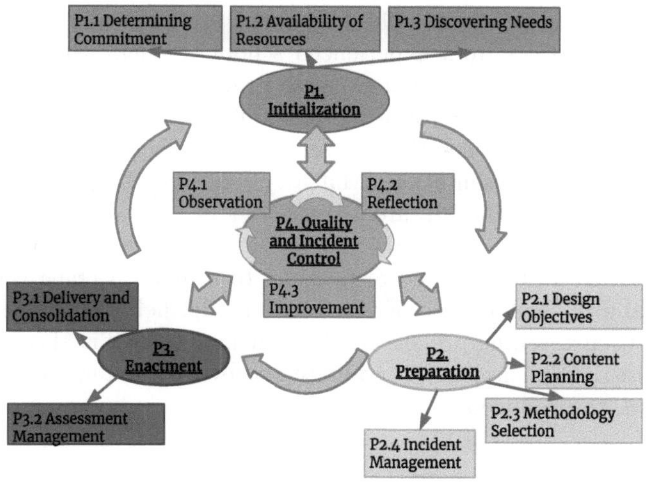

Fig. 1. Graphical representation of the teaching process as defined in the TeaM Model.

Only Chen et al. established a maturity model for observing the teaching process with the focus on university teachers [3]. Although not explicitly stated, teachers should learn from the model. In their paper, Chen et al. address the implementation of their model for primary and secondary schools, but to the best of our knowledge, such a model has not been implemented and/or published yet.

We believe that the quality of teaching is a process that includes all the relevant factors of teaching. So, unlike the aforementioned models, but like Chen et al., we address the quality by looking at the teaching process as a whole. In contrast to Chen et al. we consider not only university teachers but primary and secondary teachers as well.

2.2 The TeaM Model Context

This section contains a brief explanation of the TeaM model's structure and the way how it works. The TeaM model arose from the lack of standards to address the quality of the teaching process with the focus on informatics university and school teachers. Within the TeaM model, the teaching process is composed of four main phases (see Fig. 1):

- *Initialization* – where administrative issues are managed;
- *Preparation* – where the course is planned and prepared by teachers;
- *Enactment* – where the implementation of the teaching unit takes place;
- *Quality and Incident Control* – where possible incidents and the teaching process itself are observed, analyzed and refined.

For each of these phases, factors related to the quality of teaching are defined, and in the TeaM model they constitute the basic component named as Process Areas (PAs). The TeaM model has in total 12 PAs, and each consists of some goals and the related practices [19]. The set of practices was built by the collection of best practices from experienced school teachers (and one university teacher) [19]. The implementation of these practices and the associated goals is done by two representation forms: as continued representation (as Capability Levels - CL), where only one PA is assessed and further managed for improvement, and as stage representation (Maturity Levels - MLs), where a group of PAs associated to a specific ML are assessed.

Following the idea of the TeaM model, a teaching process is mature to a certain level when all the PAs corresponding to that level reach the maximum level of Capability. Making use of the TeaM model helps teachers to evaluate and improve their teaching process by their own, or (which is also possible), the educational institution uses it to evaluate the overall quality of teaching, and when required, to produce a ranking, too.

3 Learning from the TeaM Model

The TeaM model has a twofold aim: first, assessing the maturity of the teaching process and, secondly, learning from the practices of the more mature levels in order to improve the quality of teaching. The practices of the model were collected from informatics school teachers. Making the model more holistic means also testing the practices with university teachers.

3.1 Research Objectives

The focus of the TeaM model is on informatics university and school teachers, although the practices of the model stem from educational sciences and were mainly defined by informatics school teachers so far. The question now is, if the TeaM model is appropriate for all types of teachers, and thus, which practices are useful, useless, and eventually also new. The objective of the study presented in this paper is to deal with this question and to see which practices and goals of the model are shared and which, eventually, could be shared in order to improve the way of teaching. So, within the scope of this paper the following question is raised:

- To what extent do the informatics university and schools teachers differ in their way of teaching (and what could they learn from each other)?

For answering this question, the TeaM model was used by informatics lecturers at Alpen-Adria-Universität Klagenfurt and the results are presented hereinafter.

3.2 Settings

For conducting the study, we selected 19 informatics courses from the Bachelor and Master program at the Alpen-Adria-Universität Klagenfurt. A questionnaire covering the practices and goals of the TeaM model was distributed to the lecturers of these courses. The questions were answered by the teachers in the presence of members of the department of informatics-didactics, and it is worth to mention that we clearly stated at the beginning of each interview that the aim of the questionnaire was not to assess the quality of teaching but to check if and what teachers can learn from the model. The questions required “Yes/No” answers, but free-text answers were allowed and, for later analysis, recorded.

As mentioned before, the model has 12 Process Areas (PAs), and each PA contains one or more goals to be fulfilled during the teaching process. The goals itself contain practices. And, every practice was associated with one question. Thus, in total there were 76 questions. The questions were provided in an electronic format using Google forms. This makes the questionnaire public and accessible by those who are interested to use such a model[1]. The participation is anonymous as no personal data is collected. The questionnaire itself was divided in two parts. First, the 19 interviewees answered the corresponding “Yes/No” questions according to the practices. Secondly, they were invited to provide their opinion or suggestions concerning the practices, goals or the way of how they are assigned to Maturity Levels. All the answers from the interviewees were also collected in an electronic form.

3.3 Results

In the TeaM model framework, a Process Area is satisfied when the related goals are achieved. On the other side, the goals are achieved when the related practices are fulfilled. Due to the size of the TeaM's practices (76 practices), we generalized them with the corresponding goals and present the results of the study by focusing only on the 31 TeaM goals (running from SG1.1 up to SG4.3, see Fig. 2 for an overview). For a clear understanding of how goals and practices are introduced in the TeaM model, Appendix A in the article from Reci and Bollin [19] provides further information.

Feedback from Teachers. During the **initialization phase** of the teaching process, stakeholders think about their commitments (like defining their duties, checking the related curricula, etc.). Two goals are associated to it: *G1.1.1: Define Agreements on Duties* and *G1.1.2: Agree upon Embedding into Curricula.* Almost all the 19 interviewees (except 2) were aware and agreed about implementing the related practices. Another set of questions tangles the resources needed during the teaching process. More concretely, the goals are *SG1.2.1 Manage the Classroom Settings* and *SG1.2.2 Manage the Technical Infrastructure.* Half of the interviewees do not think about arranging the classroom settings based on the methodology they used, as methodology is stable to them. On the other side they take care to provide an adequate atmosphere in the classroom and to use technical infrastructure. *SG1.3.1 Specify the Requirements* is another goal that deals with the predefinition of the knowledge students should

[1] Interested readers can join and give their personal experience in form of practices by visiting the web-site of the TeaM project [18].

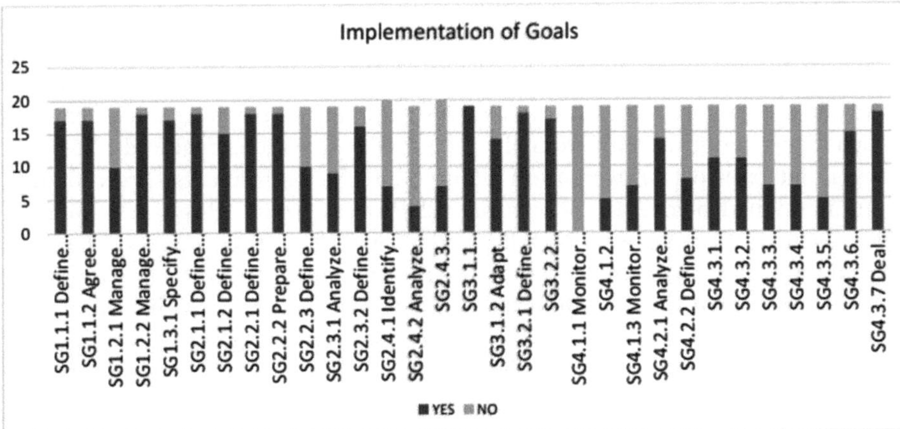

Fig. 2. The number of interviewees who did or did not implement the TeaM model's goals. In total, 19 university teachers interviewed.

have before starting a course, with the requirements that might come from other stakeholders and with their documentation. Almost all of the university lecturers do not implement only the documentation practice, while the other practices are fully fulfilled.

In the second phase of the teaching process (**preparation phase**), important goals of the lecture are related with the design of the course objectives (like course aim, course plan, measurable objectives, etc.). The two goals *SG2.1.1 Define the Course Aims and the Course Plan* and *SG2.1.2 Define the Quantitative and Qualitative Objectives for the Course* are known and implemented by the lecturers. Planning the content of the course is another process required during the second phase. The goals are: *SG2.2.1 Define the Learning Content*, *SG2.2.2 Prepare and Integrate the Materials* and *SG2.2.3 Define the Unit Schedule.* This includes all the steps like defining the course materials, topics and sub-topics, external material, a plan of the unit phases, etc. These goals include also the documentation of the practices. What is noticeable here is the fact that almost all the lectures are aware of such practices, implement most of them, but still do not consider those practices that require a documentation. One such example is "Assign time to each unit phase and document the schedule". Only four out of 19 lectures do it that way. Methodology selection deals with two goals: *SG2.3.1 Analyze Methodologies to be Used* and *SG2.3.2 Define the Methodologies to be Used.* This implies searching for available (suitable) methodologies, their advantages and disadvantages, their effects on the learning outcomes, etc. Ten from the lecturers do not deal with methodologies and consider them in their teaching process. They stick to the one they have been using for a while. However, they try to implement the rest of the practices. The good news is that nine lecturers look for methods of teaching and, when suitable, do implement them. Management of the risk is the last sub-process considered in the *preparation phase. SG2.4.1 Identify Possible Problems*, *SG2.4.2 Analyze Possible Problems* and *SG2.4.3 Establish Corrective Plan for Problems* are the goals related to this sub-process. The practices here consider problems in the classroom, with infrastructure, during unit delivery, and also their analysis, corrective plan and related documentation. Also, here is noticeable that the major part of the lecturers (13 of them) do not think about and document possible problems that might occur.

The third phase of the teaching process (**enactment**), comprises only two Process Areas. In the first PA the delivery and consolidation of the unit based on the schedule, plan, requirements, etc is established. It has two goals: *SG3.1.1 Conduct Lessons According To Agreements/Plan* and *SG3.1.2 Adapt the Lesson based on Requirements.* The results from the questionnaire shows that all the lecturers implements at least one practices, and four of them do not consider to adapt the lecture according to a corrective plan. As they do not consider possible requirement changes during their preparation phase they do not think about a following a plan. In the second PA the assessment is managed. The two goals *SG3.2.1 Define the Knowledge Test Criteria for the Delivered Units* and *SG3.2.2 Implement the Knowledge Test* deal mainly with practices like the definition of criteria for an assessment, type and form of an assessment, the implementation of the assessment, collection and analysis of results, etc. The lecturers interviewed are familiar with these practices and implement all of them during their teaching.

The last phase of the teaching process is **quality and incident control**. One necessary process is the observation of the teaching process. The related goals are: *SG4.1.1 Monitor Teaching (from Initialization and Preparation phase)*, *SG4.1.2 Aggregate the Monitoring Results* and *SG4.1.3 Monitor Incidents.* As their names reveal, the practices deal with the time plan of courses, objectives, methodologies, documentation from the observation and the problems during teaching, etc. The results from the interview show that only two practices are fully implemented by the lecturers. The documentation practices are again not considered at all from almost all the interviewees. As a results, this PA is basically unknown to university teachers. After the observation process, a reflection is necessary. All this is done in order to learn from the sub-processes, reflect on them and to improve teaching at the end. *SG4.2.1 Analyze the results* and *SG4.2.2 Define corrective action* are the two goals of the sub-process. The practices suggest to do periodically analysis of the experiences during observation, to reflect about with colleagues, document the results, think about corrective plans for incidents, etc. The results show that only two practices are implemented. The practices related to the documentation and corrective plan for incidents are not implemented by a considerable part of the lecturers. They explained this with the arguments that bad experiences are directly solved and no further analysis and documentation is needed. The improvement of the teaching process is the last area considered in the TeaM model. It contains seven goals: *SG4.3.1 Improve the Agreements and the Curricula*, *SG4.3.2 Improve the Classroom Settings and the Technical Infrastructure*, *SG4.3.3 Improve the Course Aims and the Plans*, *SG4.3.4 Improve the Learning Content*, *SG4.3.5 Improve the Teaching Methodology*, *SG4.3.6 Improve the Teachers Skills*, and *SG4.3.7 Deal with Incidents.* So basically, the practices point at the improvement of curricula, classroom settings, infrastructure, course aim and plan, the learning content of the course, methodology, personal training, documentation of all these practices, etc. Some of the practices are implemented by the lecturers, but when it comes to documentation again, nearly none of them does do it. It is also interesting to mention the fact that four lecturers do not do further personal training during their career (*SG4.3.6 Improve the Teachers Skills*).

Interviewees Suggestions and Comments. At the end of the questionnaire the interviewees had the change to provide feedback and suggestions for the model. Different interviewees gave different suggestions that were collected and assigned to answer categories. Looking at the results, a considerable part of the practices are known and implemented by the teachers. But, the documentation practices are seen as more problematic and not favorable by the lecturers.

Documentation seems to be an issue. One interviewee suggested to rethink the practices in these areas, as based on her/his opinion, not all the improvement activities should be documented. Other lecturers said that no documentation is done because there is no policy that required that, and he or she is not aware if this documentation will be used or shared with the others for further benefits. Another argument against documentation was that lecturers do not have time to do a documentation. Documentation should be considered only in shared laboratory courses as then it can be shared with the colleagues.

Apart from looking closer at the process areas, there has been a set of suggestions to improve the set of practices. In some sense, we see this as practices, that school teachers can now learn from university teachers.

- One interviewee suggested to include student feedback (as it is collected twice a semester in Klagenfurt) as a practice in the TeaM model. The feedback should then be analyzed and taken into consideration during the lecture.
- A lecturer suggested to add a practice where teachers use an anonymous forum to collect questions.
- On a goal level, it was suggested to add a subprocess for motivating and activating inactive students.

According to the questions dealing with practices and goals, we also got some useful comments: First, the TeaM model should consider the different types of lectures (seminar, lecture, lab, etc.) as some of the goals might then be obsolete or more important. Secondly, there should not just be "Yes/No" answers. Next, it was suggested to avoid longer questions (so breaking sentences apart). Finally, we were advised to not just stick to Google-Forms interviews, but also making use of an instructor (assessor) leading through the evaluation.

In all, acceptability was satisfying. The lecturers implemented quite some of the practices, but they were never thinking about some relation between them and that all of them are important for the teaching process as a whole. Have a TeaM model assessment now already had a positive impact on them as they started to think more about the quality of teaching and the use of standards to help them managing that quality.

4 Discussion and Threats to Validity

For answering the question about the (number of) differences in teaching practices between university and school teachers, we looked at all the different part of the teaching process step-by-step. The suggestions and comments received during the questionnaire now allows us to tell more about the commonalities and differences. The practices related to *documentation* aspects were the largest problem for university lecturers and they tried to argue why such practices were not to be implemented. From the perspective of school teachers, we still see documentation as something important and necessary. On the other side, university teachers are quite open-minded according to being evaluated, something that we find harder in the school setting.

Another difference between school and university teachers is to be found in SG2.4. There, *incident management* is not seen as something important by university teachers. Identification and resolution of incidents is only dealt with when required. This is, due to a different setting, handled different in the case of school teachers, where teachers, members of the rectorate and/or in the best case also psychotherapists work together to prevent or resolve incidents in classes.

Another difference can be found in SG4.1, where the *observation of the teaching process* is seen as not so significant by university teachers. Quite often the only feedback they get is by looking closer to the students' results and the students' feedback at the end of the semester. This is contrary to schools teachers, where the continuous observation is related to class improvements and also pupils motivations. A partial difference is also shown in SG4.2, where the absence of the *reflection over the teaching process* is observed. From the perspective of schools teachers, this is a practice that always needs special consideration and university teachers could learn a lot from it.

Finally, a small difference is to be found in SG2.3, *methodology selection*, and in its *improvement* in SG4.3. Choosing suitable methodologies is important for schools teachers, but the same holds for university teachers.

To summarize, only 12 out of 31 goals are nearly completely met by university teachers. 9 goals are at least partially fulfilled. The teachers are weak in the aspects of documentation, incident management, teaching process observation and reflection. But they are strong in the areas of commitments, dealing with resources, discovering needs, designing course objectives and in content planning.

To conclude, there might also be some threats to the validity of the study. For its implementation, we tried to avoid any bias by selecting different informatics lectures at our university, choosing lectures from different fields of study, and also of different characteristics. However, the results are restricted to our university and might not be generalizable to other universities.

The same interviewees were present until the end of the study. The questionnaire remained the same until the last lecturer was interviewed. The study duration was no more than three weeks, and the participant did not have the possibility to evolve their ways of teaching in-between. However, we can not guarantee that some of them had the chance to speak to each other, influencing the results. The participation in the questionnaire was voluntary, and we assume that the answers were correct. But, we can not guarantee that the interviewees were honest in their answers, even though that we belief so, as their answers had no influence on their reputation.

5 Summary and Future Work

It was clear from the beginning that there are differences between university and school teachers (in informatics). However, this work systematically focuses on all different areas related to teaching and analyzes the situation. This study shows that there are in total 4 main differences: Documentation, methodology, teaching process observation and reflection are not considered by university teachers. On the model level, we can say that university and schools teachers differ in 9 out of 12 PAs in our TeaM model. Apart from differences, we also have additional practices suggested by the university teachers that might be relevant and considered by the schools teachers. Basically two practices are suggested: the repetitive and standardized evaluation of the course and using different (and anonymous) ways in communicating with the pupils. The comments from the interviewees show that they like the idea behind the TeaM model and looking at the teaching process as a whole. They were somehow surprised about the compact representation of the practices in our framework. The TeaM model made them think about some practices they ignored before. Looking at the feedback results, we answered our research question and can also state that, eventually with some minor extensions, it is appropriate for university teachers, too.

For future work, we plan to look closer at the quantitative results that we collected and relate them to the quantitative feedback that students provide end of the semester. The objective is to see if there is a correlation that helps us identifying more influential factors in our model.

References

1. Azam, M., Kingdon, G.: assessing the teaching quality in India. In: Azam, M., Kingdon, G.G. (eds.) Assessing Teacher Quality in India, 21 October 2014. SSRN (2014). https://ssrn.com/abstract=2512933. https://doi.org/10.2139/ssrn.2512933
2. Bollin, A., Reçi, E., Szabó, C., Szabóová, V., Siebenhofer, R.: Applying a maturity model during a software engineering course - experiences and recommendations. In: 2017 IEEE 30th Conference on Software Engineering Education and Training (CSEE&T), pp. 9–18 (2017)
3. Chen, C.Y., Chen, P.C., Chen, P.Y.: Teaching quality in higher education: an introductory review on a process-oriented teaching-quality model. Total Qual. Manage. Bus. Excellence **25**(1–2), 36–56 (2014)
4. Chen, W., Mason, S., Staniszewski, C., Upton, A., Valley, M.: Assessing the quality of teachers' teaching practices. Educ. Assess. Eval. Accountability **24**(1), 25–41 (2012)
5. Dilshad, R.M.: Assessing Quality of Teacher Education: a student perspective. Pakistan J. Soc. Sci. **30**(1), 85–97 (2010)

6. Duarte, D., Martins, P.: A maturity model for higher education institution. In: Proceedings of the 23rd International Conference on Advanced Information Systems Engineering Doctoral Consortium (CAISE), pp. 25–45 (2011)
7. Forrester, E.C., Buteau, B.L., Shrum, S.: CMMI for Services: Guidelines for Superior Service. Pearson Education (2011)
8. Helmke, A., et al.: Studienbrief Unterrichtsdiagnostik. Projekt EMU (Evidenzbasierte Methoden der Unterrichtsdiagnostik) der Kultusministerkonferenz. Universität Koblenz-Landau, Landau (2010)
9. Ling, T.C., Jusoh, Y.Y., Abdullah, R., Alwi, N.H.: A review study: applying capability maturity model in curriculum design process for higher education. J. Adv. Sci. Arts **3**(1), 46–55 (2012)
10. Lutteroth, C., Luxton-Reilly, A., Dobbie, G., Hamer, J.: A maturity model for computing education. In: Proceedings of the 9th Australasian Conference on Computing Education, vol. 66, pp. 107–114. Australian Computer Society, Inc. (2007)
11. Marshall, S., Mitchell, G.: Applying SPICE to e-learning: an e-learning maturity model? In: Proceedings of the Sixth Australasian Conference on Computing Education, vol, 30, pp. 185–191. Australian Computer Society, Inc. (2004)
12. Mehrens, W.A.: Assessment of Teaching: Purposes, Practices, and Implications for the Profession, chap. Assessing the Quality of Teacher Assessment Tests, pp. 77–136. Digital Commons University of Nebraska - Lincoln (1990)
13. Montgomery, B.: Developing a Technology Integration Capability Maturity Model for K-12 Schools. Ph.D. thesis, Concordia University (2003)
14. National Education Association: The National Education Association's Framework for Transforming Education Systems to Support Effective Teaching and Improve Student Learning. http://www.nea.org/home/41858.htm. Accessed 06 Aug 2018
15. Neuhauser, C.: A maturity model: does it provide a path for online course design. J. Interact. Online Learn. **3**(1), 1–17 (2004)
16. OECD: TALIS Techn. Rep. Teaching and Learning International Survey. http://www.oecd.org/education/talis. Accessed 06 Aug 2018
17. Petrie, M.: A model for assessment and incremental improvement of engineering and technology education in the americas. In: Proceedings of Second LACCEI International Latin American and Caribbean Conference for Engineering and Technology (LACCEI2004) (2004)
18. Reçi, E., Bollin, A.: Department of Informatics-Didactics, Universität Klagenfurt. http://iid.aau.at/bin/view/Main/Projects. Accessed 01 June 2018
19. Reçi, E., Bollin, A.: Managing the quality of teaching in computer science education. In: Proceedings of the 6th Computer Science Education Research Conference, CSERC 2017, pp. 38–47 (2017)
20. Sekretariat der Ständigen Konferenz der Kultusminister der Länder in der Bundesrepublik Deutschland: Standards für die Lehrerbildung: Bildungswissenschaften. Beschluss der Kultusministerkonferenz (2004) (in German)
21. Snook, I., O'Neill, J., Birks, K.S., Church, J., Rawlins, P.: The Assessment of Teacher Quality: An Investigation into Current Issues in Evaluating and Rewarding Teachers. Education Policy Response Group, Institute of Education, Massey University (2013). SSRN: https://ssrn.com/abstract=2326315
22. Solar, M., Sabattin, J., Parada, V.: A maturity model for assessing the use of ICT in school education. J. Ed. Tech. & Soc. **16**(1), 206 (2013)
23. White, B.A., Longenecker, H.E., Leidig, P.M., Yarbrough, D.: Applicability of CMMI to the IS curriculum: a panel discussion. In: Information Systems Education Conference (ISECON 2003), pp. 1–5 (2003)

Contests and Competitions in Informatics

Piaget's Cognitive Development in Bebras Tasks - A Descriptive Analysis by Age Groups

Christine Lutz(✉), Marc Berges, Jonas Hafemann, and Christoph Sticha

School of Education, Technical University of Munich,
Arcisstr. 21, 80333 Munich, Germany
{christine.lutz,berges,jonas.hafemann,christoph.sticha}@tum.de

Abstract. The Bebras contest started as a small computer-science competition in Eastern Europe and is now well-established all around the world. In the meantime, the challenge also addresses primary school students; in Germany since 2015. In the light of the ongoing discussion on introducing computer science in primary education, the question of whether the tasks differ between the age groups moved to the focus. So, we analyzed how Bebras tasks look like, especially comparing the different age of the participants. Here, only characteristics of the task descriptions are examined, showing that both, text and pictures differ through the age groups. Their complexity increases and also, addressed objects and subjects manifest a clear separation of Piaget's stage of cognitive development between primary school and secondary school students. All the findings enable to concisely characterize Bebras tasks for their use in regular computer-science classes or for further research on the cognitive processes involved in solving those tasks.

Keywords: Bebras contest · Primary education
Computer science education

1 Introduction

Integrating computer science into primary school curricula is one of the urgent topics in computer science education at the moment. Most of these efforts concentrate on computational thinking as a synonym for computer science. Currently, numerous projects are trying to figure out which computer science or computational thinking topics can be integrated into existing curricula [1–4].

The Bebras Challenge focusing on computational thinking [5] started as a small contest in Eastern Europe and is now one of the biggest challenges around the world [6]. In 2011, the Bebras community introduced a challenge addressing primary school students [7]. The range of age groups covered by the tasks makes the Bebras Challenge a valuable source of investigations how to address computational thinking in primary education.

S. N. Pozdniakov and V. Dagienė (Eds.): ISSEP 2018, LNCS 11169, pp. 259–270, 2018.
https://doi.org/10.1007/978-3-030-02750-6_20

In design and evaluation of secondary education programming courses neo-Piagetian approaches have been followed [8–10]. Having in mind Piaget's stages of cognitive development [11] proofed to be of value for task creation when aiming at certain age groups.

So, in addition to the efforts conducted on the integration into curricula this article provides a closer look at how tasks are presented for different age groups and how these differences can be categorized. Therefore pictures and texts describing tasks are analyzed in a qualitative approach, focusing on the question whether tasks descriptions differ between primary school age levels and secondary school. For that reason, after introducing the theoretical background and related work, the methodology is briefly introduced, and the results are presented. Finally, the results are discussed and implications on the teaching practice or task development, respectively, is given.

2 Theoretical Background

2.1 Piaget's Theory of Cognitive Development

In his theory Piaget proposes four stages of cognitive development: sensorimotor (ages 0–2), pre-operational (2–7), concrete operational (7–11) and formal operational (11–16) [11]. According to his theory when entering the concrete operational stage children can engage in logical problem-solving processes that are linked to concrete objects and tasks. The latter restriction ceases to exist when they enter the formal operational stage. In this stage, children are capable of solving hypothetical problems and abstract tasks.

Neo-Piagetian approaches share the idea of stages in children's cognitive development but unlike Piaget they do not define the stages based on logical operations that children are capable of. Rather, the increasing ability of processing information is considered crucial. This leads to a variety of theories, some of which introduce substages and an ongoing development up to adultery [12]. These approaches are able to overcome shortcomings of classical Piagetian theory some of which have been observed in the field of novice programming. In particular, neo-Piagetian theory distinguishes several independent domains of a persons' development [8–10].

2.2 The Bebras Challenge

In 2004 Dagiene founded a contest named Bebras aiming to motivate children to learn and engage in computer science [13]. From its first year when 3,500 Lithuanian students took part in the annual Bebras online contest has grown continuously and in 2017 had over 2,000,000 participants from 36 countries.

Dagiene names interest in computer science and development of computational thinking abilities as main goals of Bebras [5]. For this purpose she provides 15 criteria for good tasks like "can be solved in 3 min", "are adequate for the age of contestants", "have easy understandable problem statements" as well as "should have pictures" [14].

Following these criteria, tasks of the German Bebras contest, for instance, are assigned to one or more of five age groups: grades 3–4 (introduced in 2015), grades 5–6, grades 7–8, grades 9–10, and grades 11–13 [6].

3 Related Work

As stated above, Dagiene and Futschek [14] demanded a good Bebras task should have a picture. "It should not be a mere illustration. Pictures are supporting visual thinking." Tomcsanyiova and Kabatova [15] have analyzed more than 300 contest tasks from the Slovak national Bebras database, regarding the "importance and meaning of pictures in a process of learning" especially with contest tasks. In short words, they considered every visual component as a picture that "cannot be handled as a plain sequence of ASCII characters", which for example also includes tables. According to this definition, 76.8% of tasks contained pictures. They aimed to find a categorization of task-pictures in matters of their use, content, and type to improve their understanding of "meaning and nature of the pictures". They concentrated on images directly linked to computer science concepts, such as algorithms or data structure.

Carney and Levin [16] offer a classification of pictures in textbooks according to their function: *decorational pictures* (without important connections to the task content), *representational pictures* (only reflecting all or a part of the task's content), *organizational pictures* (providing a structure for the content), *interpretational pictures* (clarifying the difficulties), *transformational pictures* (designed to improve recalling of a text's information). In [15] Tomcsanyiova and Kabatova found the necessity for an additional category *substitutional pictures* for pictures that are the task itself without a text, carrying the same information. For grouping pictures according to their content, they "proposed three categories (problem setup pictures, pictures depicting a computer science concept, and pictures showing a user application interface) covering majority of task pictures."

Also, Hubwieser et al. [17] found a connection between the appearance of the tasks' pictures and the performance of girls in these tasks. They analyzed the results of 217,604 participants in the 2014 Bebras challenge. First, they found out that boys performed significantly better compared to girls in every age group. However, the difference increased from the youngest to the oldest participants. The boys outperformed the girls in all 18 tasks of the two uppermost age groups, but the girls were better in certain tasks in the lower age groups. They could find three criteria based on Keller's ARCS model of motivation [18] that these type of questions share: "the tasks have to look nice to attract the attention of the girls, they have to represent a situation relevant for real life, and they have to be comparably easy to solve." [17]

A detailed analysis of the structure of task descriptions was provided by Ruf et al. in [19,20]. They classified programming tasks regarding the required knowledge and skills. With the help of qualitative content analysis, they categorized the knowledge elements represented in the given problem description as well as in the anticipated solutions. The cognitive processes underlying the used skills for transferring the problem to the solution was coded as well. In contrast to this work, the present research focuses on how the given problems are presented to the participants of the Bebras challenge.

4 Methodology

4.1 Data Gathering

All German Bebras tasks from 2007 to 2017 including example solutions are publicly accessible and can be downloaded[1]. To compare tasks for primary education to those tasks designed for secondary education, we survey all 125 tasks from 2015 to 2017. For the analysis, we picked the tasks without having a look at the solutions. All five age groups (grades 3–4, 5–6, 7–8, 9–10, and 11–13) were analyzed separately. Tasks that address more than one age group are put into the analysis of each presented age group which leads to some overlaps in the assignment of a code to the corresponding group. For a better identification for each task, an identifier built of the year of appearance and an ongoing number representing their position in the task booklet was added to the title.

4.2 Data Analysis

The data analysis we conducted on the tasks was twofold. Pictures, as well as task descriptions, were analyzed based on Mayring's qualitative content analysis (QCA). In [21] Mayring describes QCA as an approach to combine qualitative and quantitative methods, such as "working through many text passages" as qualitative and "analysis of frequencies of categories" as quantitative steps. His methods are designed to gain a high level of objectivity, reliability, and validity of analyzing texts [22]. The precise approach is described in [21]; the investigated text is cleaned up, generalized, and summed up to fit categories that are either found in the text or derived from literature. Generally, a category consists of its name, a definition, and a sample text illustrating the coding rules.

Similar to Tomcsanyiova and Kabatova [15] we consider every visual component as a picture, which provides more than only verbal information, which also includes components such as tables. For the analysis, we decided to write a brief description of the picture representing its content. An example is shown in Fig. 1. Several of those descriptions were validated by redrawing scatches (Fig. 1c). In the end, the resulting texts were coded according to the methodology described above.

To analyze the texts, we gather the information, who or what is actively taking action as a main grammatical subject in a task, who or what is passively taking part as an object in a task and what is the whole setting of a task. We develop categories inductively. Whenever there is only a name in a task's text, we consider it to belong to a human as they always act like humans.

[1] https://www.bwinf.de/biber/downloads/.

(a) Original picture

Three beavers in sporty outfits are standing in front of a mountain with stones on it. On the left, there is a checkered flag. Sun is shining.

(b) Description

(c) Sketch

Fig. 1. Sample of the recoding process (task: 2015.10)

To measure intercoder agreement quantitative measures are applied to a set of codes. For maintenance reasons, only a representative subset of codes is recoded (≈20%). Von Eye presents a set of coefficients that can be applied to calculate the ratio between agreements and the complete sample adjusted by the ratio of an agreement by chance. To be able to apply the coefficients, the rated objects have to be independent, the coders have to act independently, and the used categories have to be independent, mutually exclusive, and exhaustive [23]. The last assumption is difficult to hit in a setting of rating complex texts like the tasks that are the content of the provided research. For this reason, to improve intercoder-agreement, both coders analyzed a bunch of tasks together (about 22% of all tasks). Additionally, another 20% of the codings were reviewed between the two coders. Any disagreements are marked regarding the classification. The disagreements are discussed until the conflicts can be resolved. Moreover, during the complete coding process, the coders stayed in contact to discuss ambiguities immediately.

5 Results

5.1 Category System

The first result is the derived category system. On the top level, three main categories ultimately result from the methodology: picture objects (P), addressed subjects (S), and addressed objects (O). The picture objects can be separated into three basic categories regarding the level of abstraction. On the one hand, there are abstract objects including text-like objects (e.g., numbers, tables, graphs, or arrows) (P1), and geometric objects (e.g., triangles, rectangles, circles) (P2). In contrast, the pictures contain real things that are either lifeless (e.g., banners, furniture) (P3), or living (e.g., trees, flowers, beavers, bees, faces, hands). The living objects are distinguished between plants (P4), animals (P5), and humans (P6). Table 1 shows the categories, with samples of the description, the abstraction, and the category assignment. The sample for category P5 exemplifies that the assignment of the categories is not distinct and, therefore, the categories are not mutually exclusive.

The descriptions of the tasks address subjects acting on objects. While coding, basically the question "who or what is doing something with whom or what" was in focus, which leads to a categorization of the tasks focusing on subjects on the one hand and objects on the other hand. Table 2 shows the resulting categories for the subjects. Finally, a task can contain no acting subject (e.g., a set of pictures is meant to be rearranged to fit a specific order) (S0), an acting animal

Table 1. Categories of objects in the presented pictures

	Code	Name	Description	Abstraction	Categorization
Abstract	(P1)	Texturing objects	Tree diagram with fictitious animal names in its nodes. (task: 2016.02)	Tree diagram	P1
	(P2)	Geometric objects	Stars, squares, circles, triangles in different colors arranged on a string. (task: 2015.02)	Stars, squares, circles, triangles, string	P2
Real lifeless	(P3)	Lifeless objects	Smoking pizza oven made of stone with an open door. There is a pizza and a loaf of bread inside. (task: 2017.28)	Smoke, oven, pizza, bread	P3
Real living	(P4)	Plants	Ten flowers in different colors which are either opened or closed. (task: 2016.06)	Flowers	P4
	(P5)	Animals	Three beavers in sporty outfits are standing in front of a mountain with stones on it. On the left, there is a checkered flag. Sun is shining. (task: 2015.10)	Beaver, mountain, stones, flag, sun	P3, P5
	(P6)	Humans	Six children with different hairstyles and outfits. (task: 2016.39)	Children	P6

Table 2. Categories of subjects in the presented texts

Code	Name	Description	Step 1
(S0)	No acting subject	Six beaver pictures are meant to create an animation. Therefore the pictures have to be arranged in a way that only one characteristic changes in comparison to the following picture: whisker, mouth nose, ears, and teeth. The last picture is already set. (task: 2015.06)	-
(S1)	Animals	Beaver Ben collected five trunks on a plank. (task: 2017.22)	Beaver Ben
(S2)	Humans	Tina and Ben help to prepare a special exhibition at the Computer Science Museum. (task: 2016.33)	Tina, Ben

(e.g., Beaver Ben) (S1), or acting humans (e.g., Tina and Ben) (S2). Besides the category, sample task descriptions, and the abstraction are displayed.

The corresponding categories describing the objects of a task description are similar to the other categories. First, there are tasks with no object (O0). Furthermore, categories are describing real objects like the categories for the pictures. Here, they are grouped in things and plants (O1), animals (O2), and humans (O3). Finally, the non-physical objects build the last category (O5). As we could not find any humans acting as an object in the tasks, there is no sample in the following Table 3. Besides the code and the name the table

Table 3. Categories of subjects in the presented texts

Code	Name	Description	Abstraction	Categorization
(O0)	No objects	Three determined beavers compete in a race. [...] In the picture you can see the running course goes uphill first, followed by boulders. Afterward, the course goes downhill again, followed by boulders again. [...] What will be the finishing order? (task: 2015.10)	-	O0
(O1)	Things and plants	Tim wishes for a birdhouse as a birthday present. [...] (task: 2017.36)	Birdhouse	O1
(O2)	Animals	The magician can transform things. [...] How many shamrocks does he need to create a kitten. (task: 2015.15)	Shamrocks, kitten	O1, O2
(O3)	Humans	-	-	-
(O4)	Non-physical objects	Karaoke is big fun. [...] In which picture is the music app configured the loudest? (task: 2016.26)	Music app	O4

presents a sample from different tasks accompanied by the abstraction step and the corresponding categories. Again, like in Table 1 the sample in category O2 shows that more than one category can be assigned to a specific task.

5.2 Categorization

Figure 2 illustrates the occurrence of the six picture object categories throughout the tasks of all age-groups. Compared to other age groups tasks for grades 3–4 quite often show *real lifeless* (P3) or *living* (P4, P5, P6) objects but rarely any *texturing objects* (P1). For the successive age-groups, the shape of the frequency diagrams continuously changes as the frequency of *texturing objects* rises while the occurrence of real objects, in particular, those of categories P3 and P4 gets rare.

In our analysis of acting subjects, we found three categories. Some tasks have *no acting subjects* (S0) at all while in most tasks there were *animals* (S1) or *humans* (S2) acting as a subject. Only in one task humans and personified animals are acting together.

Figure 3a shows how the observed frequency of the categories changes over the tasks' age-groups: while the occurrence of acting subjects (S1, S2) decreases

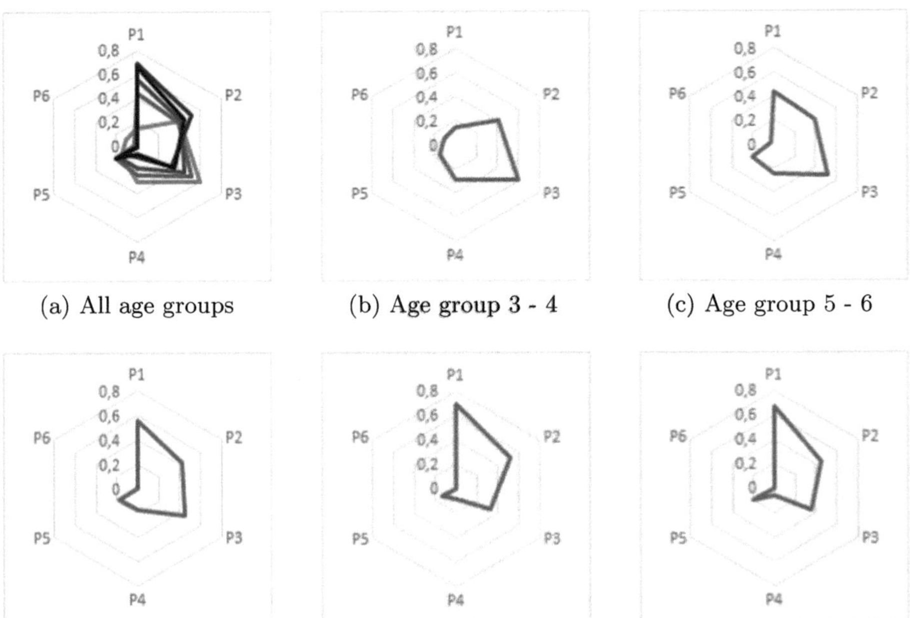

(a) All age groups (b) Age group 3 - 4 (c) Age group 5 - 6

(d) Age group 7 - 8 (e) Age group 9 - 10 (f) Age group 11 - 13

Fig. 2. Relative frequency of tasks' pictures that were assigned to the six picture object categories by age group. Categories are texturing objects (P1), geometric objects (P2), lifeless objects (P3), plants (P4), animals (P5), and humans (P6).

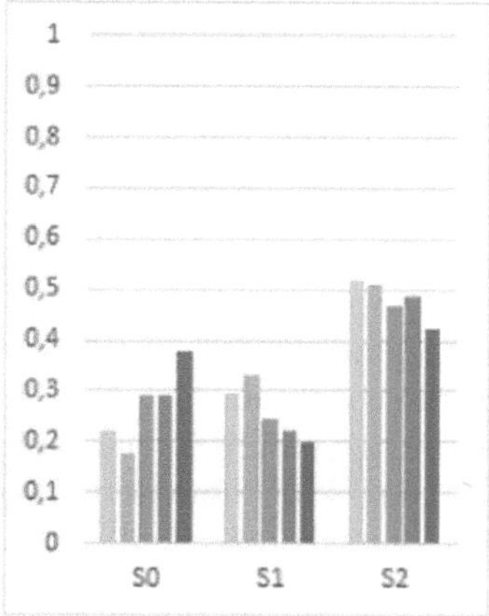

(a) Acting subjects assigned to category S0 (no acting subject), S1 (animals) and S2 (humans).

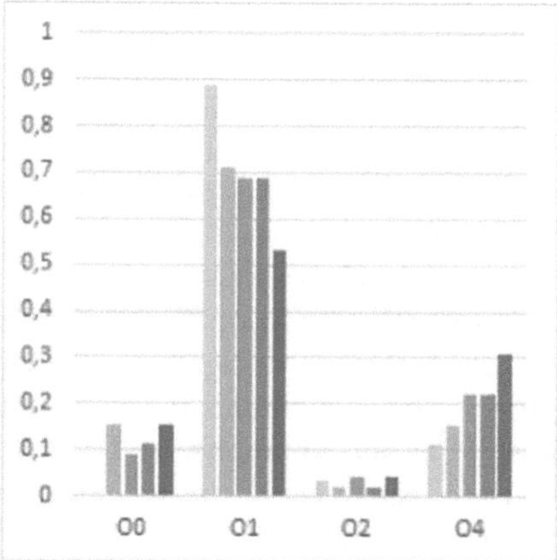

(b) Objects assigned to category O0 (no objects), O1 (things and plants), O2 (animals), and O4 (non-physical objects).

Fig. 3. Relative frequency of tasks regarding the occurrence of subjects and objects. Within each category, bars from left to right depict occurrence among the tasks for age groups 3–4, 5–6, 7–8, 9–10, and 11–13.

in the tasks for older pupils, tasks with no acting subjects at all become more common.

Regarding the passive objects we expand the subject-categories to five object-categories: *no objects* (O0), *things and plants* (O1), *animals* (O2), *humans* (O3), and *non-physical objects* (O4) like a chat-program, a music-app or the internet. As depicted in Fig. 3b O1 is very common in the grade 3–4 tasks and becomes less frequent in the tasks for older pupils. In opposite to O1, texts with *non-physical objects* (O4) appear with increasing frequency among the tasks for pupils in higher grades.

6 Discussion

According to Piaget at the age of 11 children's cognitive stage develops from concrete to abstract operational. In terms of German beaver age-groups, this development can be expected when changing from 3–4 (age 7–11) to 5–6 (age 11–16). As Fig. 2 shows, there is a well established difference in the pictures of the tasks for the age groups 3–4 (Fig. 2b) and 5–6 (Fig. 2c). The main difference can be seen in the increase of texture objects (P1, which is following the step from concrete operational to formal operational). A more detailed view of the Figs. 2b–f shows an ongoing smooth development of the categories from concrete to abstract. So, there is not only an increase of texture objects (P1) along with the age groups but also a decrease in the occurrence of pictures containing lifeless or living objects.

In addition to the analysis of the pictures, the tasks' descriptions were analyzed regarding acting subjects and objects. As Figs. 3a and b show, the step that can be seen in the pictures' analysis is either not present or only weak represented. However, the development mentioned above from concrete to abstract can be observed. Following neo-Piagetian theories, children undergo a cognitive development from concrete to formal operational independently for different specific domains. As Bebras tasks cover a variety of topics this may explain why there is a smooth transition between Piaget's age groups. Here, there is a high potential for further investigations described in the conclusion.

Figure 3a shows a similar development over the age groups in the categories "animals" (S1) and "humans" (S2). In this case, a special characteristic of the Bebras' tasks can have a strong influence. Most animals described in the text show human behavior. The description of task 2015.10 at the top of Table 3 gives an example. So we had a look at the data when combining S1 and S2, resulting in the same tendencies regarding the development over the age groups. Finally, however, we decided to keep the categories separated as in contexts other than Bebras categories S1 and S2 might have diverging characteristics.

Again, Fig. 3b supports the trend of presenting tasks more concrete for lower age groups and more abstract for higher age groups for O1 and O4. The category O3, which was introduced to cover the categories of the acting subjects, is missing in the figure because no codings were found. O0 and O2 have only a tiny number of codings. So no tendency is observable.

7 Conclusion and Future Work

According to Mayring [22], we qualitatively analyzed the Bebras tasks. Generally, there is a strong tendency from concrete to abstract addressing increasing age. This tendency is found in the presented pictures as well as in the describing text of the tasks. The presented methodology can be generalized for all tasks addressing different age levels. Especially, with the discussion whether computer science is to be introduced to primary education, the adaption of tasks from upper to lower age groups gets more important. Foremost, the "translation" of the pictures to descriptive texts and the following analysis enabled insights into the complexity as well as the degree of abstraction. The importance of illustrating pictures and the corresponding problems are discussed in the theory of instructional design [24] and cognitive load [25,26]. All in all, we were able to show that the design of the tasks for the different age levels of the Bebras contest follows the cognitive development described in the neo-Piagetian theory [12].

Nevertheless, we have to indicate some limitations: although our sample comprises the Bebras tasks of three years in one country, there might be differences when regarding several countries or even elder tasks. However, one of our goals was to compare tasks' descriptions for different age levels. Here, the Bebras tasks are unique as different age groups are addressed with one task. Another limitation is that we only analyzed the tasks descriptions. For future research, the cognitive processes implied by the tasks are of great interest. Here, another qualitative analysis is crucial that could be accompanied by quantitative research on the contest results using methods from item-response theory. So, next research can investigate, how the design of a task affects the result and the performance of students in this task.

Finally, we can conclude that we have shown a tendency in the level of abstraction following the steps of cognitive development introduced by Piaget. The specific methodology enabled us to get a deeper insight into illustrating pictures. Altogether, the presented methodology and the results can enhance planning of task by increasing the sense of age-specific addressing in tasks.

References

1. Sabitzer, B., Antonitsch, P.K., Pasterk, S.: Informatics concepts for primary education: preparing children for computational thinking. In: Proceedings of the 9th Workshop in Primary and Secondary Computing Education, pp. 108–111. ACM, New York (2014)
2. Falloon, G.: Building computational thinking through programming in K-6 education: a New Zealand experience. In: Gómez Chova, L., López Martínez, A., Candel Torres, I. (eds.) EduLearn15 Proceedings, pp. 882–892. IATED Academy, Valencia (2015)
3. Yadav, A., Hong, H., Stephenson, C.: Computational thinking for all: pedagogical approaches to embedding 21st century problem solving in K-12 classrooms. TechTrends **60**(6), 565–568 (2016)
4. Bell, T., Duncan, C., Atlas, J.: Teacher feedback on delivering computational thinking in primary school (2016)
5. Dagien, V., Stupurien, G., Vinikien, L.: Promoting inclusive informatics education through the Bebras challenge to all K-12 students. In: Rachev, B., Smrikarov, A. (eds.) Proceedings of the 17th International Conference on Computer Systems and Technologies 2016, CompSysTech 2016, pp. 407–414. ACM Press, New York (2016)
6. Dagiene, V., Stupuriene, G.: Bebras - a sustainable community building model for the concept based learning of informatics and computational thinking. Inform. Educ. **15**(1), 25–44 (2016)
7. Tomcsányiová, M., Tomcsányi, P.: Little beaver – a new bebras contest category for children aged 8–9. In: Kalaš, I., Mittermeir, R.T. (eds.) ISSEP 2011. LNCS, vol. 7013, pp. 201–212. Springer, Heidelberg (2011). https://doi.org/10.1007/978-3-642-24722-4_18
8. Lister, R.: Concrete and other neo-piagetian forms of reasoning in the novice programmer. In: Proceedings of the Thirteenth Australasian Computing Education Conference - Volume 114, ACE 2011, pp. 9–18. Australian Computer Society, Inc., Darlinghurst (2011)
9. Gluga, R., Kay, J., Lister, R., Teague, D.: On the reliability of classifying programming tasks using a neo-piagetian theory of cognitive development. In: Clear, A., Sanders, K., Simon, B. (eds.) ICER 2012, pp. 31–38. ACM, Auckland University of Technology, Auckland (2012)
10. Szabo, C., Falkner, K., Falkner, N.: Experiences in course design using neo-piagetian theory. In: Simon, Kinnunen, P., (eds.) The 14th Koli Calling International Conference, pp. 81–90 (2014)

11. Piaget, J.: Science of Education and the Psychology of the Child. Orion Press, New York (1970)
12. Morra, S., Gobbo, C.: Cognitive Development: Neo-Piagetian Perspectives. Lawrence Erlbaum Associates, New York (2007)
13. Dagiene, V.: Information technology contests: introduction to computer science in an attractive way. Inform. Educ. **5**(1), 37–46 (2006)
14. Dagienė, V., Futschek, G.: Bebras international contest on informatics and computer literacy: criteria for good tasks. In: Mittermeir, R.T., Sysło, M.M. (eds.) ISSEP 2008. LNCS, vol. 5090, pp. 19–30. Springer, Heidelberg (2008). https://doi.org/10.1007/978-3-540-69924-8_2
15. Tomcsányiová, M., Kabátová, M.: Categorization of pictures in tasks of the Bebras contest. In: Diethelm, I., Mittermeir, R.T. (eds.) ISSEP 2013. LNCS, vol. 7780, pp. 184–195. Springer, Heidelberg (2013). https://doi.org/10.1007/978-3-642-36617-8_16
16. Carney, R.N., Levin, J.R.: Pictorial illustrations still improve students' learning from text. Educ. Psychol. Rev. **14**(1), 5–26 (2002)
17. Hubwieser, P., Hubwieser, E., Graswald, D.: How to attract the girls: gender-specific performance and motivation in the Bebras challenge. In: Brodnik, A., Tort, F. (eds.) ISSEP 2016. LNCS, vol. 9973, pp. 40–52. Springer, Cham (2016). https://doi.org/10.1007/978-3-319-46747-4_4
18. Keller, J.M.: Motivational Design for Learning and Performance. Springer, Boston (2010)
19. Ruf, A., Berges, M., Hubwieser, P.: Types of assignments for novice programmers. In: Proceedings of the 8th Workshop in Primary and Secondary Computing Education, pp. 43–44. ACM, New York (2013)
20. Ruf, A., Berges, M., Hubwieser, P.: Classification of programming tasks according to required skills and knowledge representation. In: Brodnik, A., Vahrenhold, J. (eds.) ISSEP 2015. LNCS, vol. 9378, pp. 57–68. Springer, Cham (2015). https://doi.org/10.1007/978-3-319-25396-1_6
21. Mayring, P.: Qualitative Content Analysis. Basic Procedures and Software Solution. Social Science Open Access Repository. Theoretical Foundation, Klagenfurt (2014)
22. Mayring, P.: Qualitative content analysis. Forum Qual. Sozialforschung/Forum: Qual. Soc. Res. **1**(2), 1–10 (2000). Qualitative methods in various disciplines i: psychology
23. von Eye, A.: An alternative to cohen's k. Eur. Psychol. **11**(1), 12–24 (2006)
24. Merrill, M.D., Twitchell, D.: Instructional Design Theory. Educational Technology Publications, Englewood Cliffs (1994)
25. Sweller, J.: Cognitive load during problem solving: effects on learning. Cogn. Sci. **12**(2), 257–285 (1988)
26. Chandler, P., Sweller, J.: Cognitive load theory and the format of instruction. Cogn. Instr. **8**(4), 293–332 (1991)

The Second Decade of Informatics in Dutch Secondary Education

Nataša Grgurina[1(✉)], Jos Tolboom[2], and Erik Barendsen[3,4]

[1] Teaching and Teacher Education, University of Groningen, Groningen, The Netherlands
n.grgurina@rug.nl

[2] Stichting Leerplanontwikkeling, Enschede, The Netherlands
j.tolboom@slo.nl

[3] Radboud University, Nijmegen, The Netherlands
e.barendsen@cs.ru.nl

[4] Open University, Heerlen, The Netherlands

Abstract. In 1998, informatics was introduced as an elective subject for all students in the upper grades of senior general secondary education and pre-university education in the Netherlands. Rather than focusing on digital literacy or the use of office applications, it focuses on informatics as a scientific discipline. In its first decade, it faced growing pains while fighting for recognition and necessary facilities from the stakeholders: students, parents, school administrators, politicians and the general public. In 2007, the curriculum was slightly streamlined but not updated. In its second decade, informatics reached adulthood with established teacher training programs and a new curriculum which is to be introduced in 2019. In this paper we describe the events and processes that led to the renewal of the curriculum, the curriculum itself with the principles it is based on and its aims, the current process of teaching material development, the related research, the teacher training, curriculum reform in primary and lower secondary education, and the current situation of informatics as an upper secondary school subject, together with the challenges it still faces.

Keywords: Secondary informatics · Curriculum development
Country report

1 Introduction

In 2008, in our article The First Decade of Informatics in Dutch High Schools [11] we described the introduction of informatics in secondary education in the Netherlands as an elective subject in grades 10 and 11 of the senior general secondary education spanning grades 7 through 11 (in Dutch: HAVO) and in grades 10 through 12 of the pre-university education spanning grades 7 through 12 (in Dutch: VWO). We reported about its position in the secondary school curriculum, its objectives, teacher training, teaching practices, the discussions taking place around it and problems and challenges it faced. We concluded by remarking,

S. N. Pozdniakov and V. Dagienė (Eds.): ISSEP 2018, LNCS 11169, pp. 271–282, 2018.
https://doi.org/10.1007/978-3-030-02750-6_21

> *"During the first decade of Informatics in Dutch high schools, the objectives outlined in the 1990s do seem to have been achieved. What Informatics will look like in its second decade depends on the outcome of the discussions about the introduction of a national exam and whether to make it a compulsory subject, as well as on the repercussions from the fact that many Informatics teachers are not licensed and/or adequately trained. Furthermore, it is not yet clear whether the government intends to reform education in the upper grades of high school again, and if so, what consequences this will have for Informatics. And, last but not least, we believe that clearing up the misconceptions surrounding Informatics and bringing proper attention to bear on its significance would contribute to a bright(er) future for Informatics education."*

Now, ten years later, we report on the second decade of informatics in Dutch secondary education: it did not become compulsory and no national exam was introduced. However, there was a informatics curriculum reform, new technologies have changed our lives in ways unforeseen ten years ago and these developments have led to a whole new set of discussions and challenges surrounding informatics.

This paper focuses on the events that led to the curriculum reform, the curriculum itself, the current situation of informatics, and on other developments related to informatics such as an advised introduction of a foundational module in lower secondary education [19] focusing on digital literacy. In the Netherlands, digital literacy is considered to consist of four skills: basic ICT-skills, media literacy, information literacy and computational thinking [22].

2 Second Decade

2.1 Situation in Practice

In this chapter, we describe the present situation of informatics in the Netherlands. Beginning with the most recent figures from 2017, we present the results of the 2014 research project charting the actual situation in schools, describe the events leading to the new 2019 curriculum and finally we discuss the newest developments.

Schools, Students and Teachers

Looking at the numbers of schools offering informatics and numbers of students following it, we see that during the period 2002–2006, out of about 474 independent schools, the percentage of schools that do offer informatics was fairly constant at around sixty percent with about ten percent of students following it [21], cited in [11]. In the period 2011–2017 out of approximately 500 schools, the percentage of schools offering informatics dropped from 55% to 47%, while the proportion of students following it remained fairly constant at around 11% for HAVO and around 12% for the VWO type of school [8].

In 2013, the government commissioned an inquiry and a report by the Netherlands Institute for Curriculum Development (in Dutch: Stichting leerplanontwikkeling, SLO) to explore the teachers' ideas about the necessity to change the informatics curriculum. In this section we present the data that were collected concerning the teachers and their ideas about desired curriculum changes. and in the section on the curriculum, we report extensively about the results of this inquiry [23]. Regarding the teachers themselves, 89% are male and 11% are female. Almost two out of three are the sole informatics teachers in their schools, with 31% of schools having two teachers and 4% having three teachers. The majority—55%—teaches another subject as well, both in science (mostly mathematics) and in humanities and other subjects (e.g. geography, history, economy, arts and languages). When teaching informatics, almost two-thirds of them cooperate with the teachers of other subjects, mostly physics, mathematics and business, but also from other sciences, humanities and, notably, arts. Most of the teachers—62%—have been teaching informatics for more than six years. Concerning education they attended to qualify them to teach informatics, 52% of the teachers said they attended the CODI in-service program (described in our earlier paper [11]), 18% followed an university educational master, and 36% did something else. Since these numbers add up to more than 100%, we suspect that a number of teachers took several educational routes. Most teachers actively engage in staying up-to-date by following in-service training courses (67%), participating in teacher networks (65%), reading professional literature (81%) and engaging in other activities (39%). Still, most of them—62%—find the in-service training courses offered to be insufficient and see that as a problem threatening the quality of informatics as a school subject [23].

When it comes to teaching materials they use, we see that the online books offered by the three publishers are often combined with each other and with other teaching material, either found elsewhere or written by the teachers themselves [23]. Competitions have made their way into the classroom too: The Informatics Olympiad[1] including CodeCup[2] and the international Bebras competition [7].

When asked about their opinion on the informatics curriculum, 7% of the teachers said they were not familiar with it. One out of four teachers did not find it useful, 38% would like it to contain less or other learning objectives, and 36% were satisfied with it. When asked what learning objectives to strike from the curriculum, almost half of the teachers—45%—said none but added that they would like the curriculum to offer more guidance. Other teachers, those wishing to strike some learning objectives, most often mentioned those related to business aspects of informatics (organizations and information flow) and information analysis. When asked what they were missing in the curriculum, they most often mentioned (more) programming, social and professional aspect of informatics, security aspects, and networks and communication [23].

Teacher Training

Eight years after the introduction of informatics in secondary education, regular pre-service teacher training was established first at the University of Groningen in 2006, and then another four universities followed. As pre-service university teacher training for other subjects, this is a two-year educational master. Specifically, for informatics, only students with a university bachelor degree for informatics (or an equivalent) are admitted. During this master, the students both deepen their subject matter knowledge and learn about teaching through extensive internships at school and accompanying theoretical underpinnings concerning informatics didactics, pedagogy and educational science [4]. For those who already possess a master's degree in informatics, a one-year program is available. The number of students obtaining this degree and thus becoming

[1] http://www.informaticaolympiade.nl.

[2] http://www.codecup.nl/intro.php.

qualified informatics teachers in the years 2008–2013 was nation-wide six on average; in 2014 and 2015 there were four, and in 2016 there were three. These numbers do not come anywhere near the perceived need: the expected unfulfilled vacancies are estimated to be 36 in 2018, 52 in 2020 and rising to 86 in 2025—implying that roughly a third of schools offering informatics might not be able to find qualified teachers [3].

While the number of regular university students interested in becoming teachers is tiny, every year in the meetings of informatics teachers' educators from the five universities involved, we hear about dozens of professionals with a background in IT industry who show interest in becoming informatics teachers. However, due to the strict requirements, only a few get admitted to the teacher training straight away.

To help people with university degrees in technology or science to meet the teacher training admission requirements, in 2015 the beta4all[3] project was started for chemistry (chem4all), and in 2016 physics (natk4all) and informatics projects were added: inf4all[4]. Beta4all project is a result of a cooperation of universities offering teacher training (i.e. educational master) where a number of courses are offered to interested candidates as well as to interested teachers, in the form of specifically tailored courses of 6 ECTS each. For informatics, these courses are Foundations, Algorithms, Advanced Object Oriented Programming, Networks, Databases and Information Retrieval; Media, Games and User experience; Artificial Intelligence, and finally, Internet of Things. The courses are taught biweekly during one semester in the form of three-hour lectures on Fridays in Utrecht, in the center of the Netherlands, thus allowing people from all over the country to participate.

The admission procedure is then as follows: a candidate interested in becoming an informatics teacher approaches the university of their choice where their educational background and relevant professional experience are assessed. In case the candidate is not admissible yet, a tailored plan is put together consisting of appropriate inf4all courses (and possibly other courses taught at the university itself) to be taken in order to fulfill the admission requirements for the educational master.

2.2 Curriculum Reform and Curriculum

Here we describe the events leading to the informatics curriculum reform and the new curriculum itself.

The Royal Netherlands Academy of Arts and Sciences Report (KNAW Report)
Ever since the late 2000's, in the Netherlands, just like in the international field of experts [9], several stakeholders have been expressing concerns about outdated curriculum and position of informatics as a school subject in general and advocated a curriculum revision. However, the government refused to draw consequences from periodic evaluations [21] and the Ministry of Education, Culture and Science maintained that there was no apparent need for a curriculum reform since there were no complaints "from the field". In 2012, triggered by serious concerns expressed by a number of influential informatics education specialists, The Royal Netherlands

[3] http://www.beta4all.nl.

[4] http://www.beta4all.nl/prog_inf4all.htm.

Academy of Arts and Sciences (in Dutch: Koninklijke Nederlandse Akademie van Wetenschappen, KNAW) formed a committee to investigate the situation of informatics in secondary education. This committee wrote a critical report containing five recommendations aimed at improving informatics education in general, reaching far beyond the scope of the current informatics course. The report recommends to "Completely overhaul the optional subject informatics in the upper years of HAVO and VWO" and suggests to make it modular and flexible, relevant and attractive to all students. Furthermore, it recommends to "Introduce a new compulsory subject Information & communication in the lower years of HAVO and VWO" and goes on to make recommendations about encouraging "interaction between these subjects and other school subjects", adequately training teachers, instructing higher education to collaborate in this regard and, finally; to "promote instruction in digital literacy" to help achieve the goals set in the nation's ICT policy concerning innovation and economic development [19].

Even though this report was received with great enthusiasm by the informatics field, the government was still reluctant to initiate a curriculum reform, without exactly knowing the concerns of the secondary informatics teachers.

The Netherlands Institute for Curriculum Development Report

In 2013, under pressure from the stakeholders, the government commissioned an inquiry and a report by the Netherlands Institute for Curriculum Development (in Dutch: Stichting Leerplanontwikkeling, SLO) in order to assess (1) what is needed to realize a modern and attractive informatics education in upper grades of senior secondary education and pre-university education and (2) in case it turns out that a change of curriculum is required, what should that change entail. The Institute appointed a team of three researchers for this job. First, they conducted a literature study about the importance of informatics education, both nationally and internationally. Then they invited Informatics teachers to fill in an online questionnaire about their current informatics teaching practice and about their wishes and suggestions concerning possible changes in the Informatics curriculum. Subsequently, they conducted in-depth interviews with a small number of these teachers. Finally, they consulted a large number of informatics experts, not all of them involved in secondary informatics education.

This investigation resulted in early 2014 in a report containing three recommendations and a description of four factors playing a decisive role in subsistence of informatics in secondary education. First of all, the report recommends to design a new informatics curriculum aimed at a diverse student population, varied enough to be relevant and attractive to all students. The second recommendation instructs to design a curriculum containing a limited number of compulsory learning objectives and a number of objectives from which a student can choose. Finally, it recommends to keep the assessment as it is (ie. at the school level only, rather that introducing a national final exam which most other subject have). Furthermore, the report lists four critical factors which need to be addressed in order to make and keep informatics a viable school subject:

1. quality of the assessment (with no national final exams, there is no quality control across different schools);

2. development of modular teaching material in order to provide for rapid advances of the discipline;
3. in-service training of the teachers;
4. training of adequate numbers of new teachers [23].

Within weeks of the publication of this report, the government appointed a committee of nine members—teachers, informatics specialists, experts from higher education, and curriculum and assessment specialists—to redesign the informatics curricula for the HAVO and VWO types of schools, that was formulated as follows:

- The committee's task is to design a new curriculum for the elective course informatics in the upper grades of HAVO and VWO types of school.
- The purpose of the new curricula is to enhance the quality of this course by updating and modernizing the its learning objectives.
- The curricula need to be formulated globally: for the teachers it needs to be clear what the curricular goals are, while at the same time the schools keep sufficient room for their own interpretation.
- There is sufficient distinction between the HAVO and VWO curricula without them being two separate curricula.
- Each curriculum contains a number of compulsory core components and elective components. The elective components are related to the educational tracks the students follow (either one of the two humanities tracks or one of the two science tracks), yet they are within reach of all the students choosing informatics, regardless of the track they actually follow.
- The curriculum design is to follow the context-concept approach.

Furthermore, when formulating the new curriculum, the committee needs to take into account the following requirements: The assessment should remain as it is, consisting of a school exam only and no national exam. This curriculum is to be aligned with the curricula in lower secondary and primary education, which are to be developed in the near future. The study load needs to remain the same. The curriculum should not be overloaded and it must be possible to implement it within the available time. The curriculum does not favor any particular didactical approach; it describes the "what" and not the "how". The new curriculum needs to be able to count on the wide support of the teacher community. The textbook publishers need to be kept informed on the progress in order to enable them to prepare the teaching materials in time [1].

Lorentz Workshop

At the same time when The Netherlands Institute for Curriculum Development inquiry took place in 2013, but independently of it, a number of leading Dutch scholars proposed to organize a Lorentz Workshop[5]. By the time the workshop took place in September 2014, the committee for the reform of the informatics curriculum had already been appointed.

[5] "The Lorentz Center is an international center that coordinates and hosts workshops in the sciences, based on the philosophy that science thrives on interaction between creative researchers." http://www.lorentzcenter.nl/aim.php.

The aim and goal of the Lorentz workshop were described as follows: "secondary education on informatics and digital literacy urgently needs thorough improvement. The workshop intends to develop a contemporary design for the discipline, following and learning from similar efforts in other countries." The attendees were international experts from Belgium, France, Germany, Israel, Lithuania, UK and USA and Dutch computer scientists, teachers, education specialists, students and policy makers. During the five-day workshop, the international experts presented their country reports and various topics were discussed in focus groups:

- Definition: what comprises an ideal curriculum for a "digital literacy" course in the lower grades of secondary education and an "informatics" course in the upper grades;
- Sustainability: how to make "the curriculum sustainable in a rapidly developing field";
- Concepts and contexts: context-based teaching approach similar to the one adopted for other science subjects;
- Diversity: catering to the needs of students with different educational backgrounds and interests;
- Integration with other subjects in secondary education;
- Teacher training [2].

On the final day, the results of the workshop were presented and discussed in a meeting with a representative of the Ministry of Economic affairs, a member of parliament specialized in education, a representative of the Dutch informatics teacher association[6], representatives from higher professional education and universities, a CEO from industry and the chairman of the KNAW committee who authored the KNAW report [19].

2.3 The New Informatics Curriculum

Design Principles

The new curriculum is based on a number of design principles intended to make it modern and robust, and to cater to the needs of all those involved in its use. To ensure the relevance of the new curriculum in the long term, the curriculum committee decided to follow the so-called concept-context approach—a pedagogical principle that was already applied to several science subjects, for example chemistry [6]. The fundamental concepts—that were described concretely—were separated from the contexts described generically. In order to deal with the diversity of students, stemming from their varying interest in informatics, the educational track they follow (science or humanities), and the fact that division into HAVO and VWO type of school is not always reflected in students' achievements for informatics, it was decided to divide the curriculum into a core curriculum that is mandatory for all students, and a number of elective themes. Furthermore, as many see informatics as a constructive discipline where one engages in

[6] http://ieni.org.

creation of artifacts, 'design and development' is positioned as a central skill in the new curriculum. Finally, in order to balance guidance and freedom experienced by the informatics teachers, the committee drafted comprehensive learning objectives: 30 of these are in the core curriculum and the other 34 in the elective themes, thus allowing the schools to shape their informatics educations according to their preferences [4, 5].

Learning Objectives

The learning objectives of the new curriculum are organized in six compulsory domains forming the core curriculum and twelve elective themes from which a HAVO student needs to choose two and a VWO student four. The domains forming the core curriculum are: (A) Skills, (B) Foundations, (C) Information, (D) Programming, (E) Architecture, and (F) Interaction. The elective themes are: (G) Algorithms, computability and logic, (H) Databases, (I) Cognitive computing, (J) Programming paradigms, (K) Computer architecture, (L) Networks, (M) Physical computing, (N) Security, (O) Usability, (P) User Experience, (Q) Social and individual impact of informatics, and (R) Computational Science [4].

2.4 Teaching Materials for Elective Themes

In this section we describe the project in which teacher teams develop teaching materials for the elective themes. We first provide the general description of this project and then focus on one particular team—the one working on Computational science.

Teacher Teams Developing Teaching Materials

The curriculum specifies only high-level learning objectives and does not provide further details about them, nor about the instruction or assessment. In line with the Dutch tradition, this is left to the educators and authors of teaching materials, usually employed by publishing companies. In the Netherlands, there are three publishers of teaching materials for informatics. With 11 to 12% of the students in HAVO and VWO schools electing to take this course [8], the market for the publishers is rather small. This situation, combined with the fact that elective themes in the new curriculum will inevitably be chosen by even smaller numbers of students, means that the publishers have no financial incentive to develop teaching materials for the elective themes and are only interested in developing teaching materials for the core domains. To alleviate this problem, the Ministry of education provided financial means and asked the Netherlands Institute for Curriculum Development (SLO) to coordinate a project where teams of teachers would develop teaching materials for elective themes. SLO developed a procedure describing the participants and stakeholders in the project, the guidelines outlining the process they engage in, and finally, the products to be delivered. In accordance with this procedure, for each of the twelve elective themes a team should be formed, consisting of at least two informatics teachers, an expert and a teacher educator specialized in didactics of informatics. First, the team writes a global description of the module they work on, which specifies the intended learning outcomes, target audience, planning and other relevant details. Then they engage in the actual writing of the module which needs to satisfy the following criteria:

- suitable for self-study because not all teachers are expected to possess adequate expertise for that particular domain
- embed the intended learning outcomes in rich and relevant contexts
- incorporate at least one of the three basic skills in the curriculum, namely: design and development, using informatics as a perspective, and finally, cooperation and interdisciplinarity
- suitable for both the HAVO and the VWO students, yet provide for their differences
- suitable to be published online
- accompanied by teachers' instruction and a suitable form of assessment (e.g. a test or a practical assignment).

When a module is finished, it should be tested in at least two schools. The feedback from the teachers and their students who engage in testing of a module should then be collected, and a new version of a module should be written. The final version of the module should be presented to an external expert and a certifying body for final approval. This certification serves as quality control in multiple ways, not the least to partly compensate the lack of a national exam and corresponding lack of quality control and lack of ways to compare students' achievements across different schools.

Development of Teaching Materials for Computational Science
We will illustrate this process with the example of teaching materials being developed for the elective theme R: Computational Science where the first author of this paper leads the teacher team. In the new curriculum, the learning objectives of this theme are described as "Modeling: The candidate is able to model aspects of another scientific discipline in computational terms" and "Simulation: The candidate is able to construct models and simulations, and use these for the research of phenomena in that other science field." [4] In the context of a larger research project on teaching Computational Science in informatics in Dutch secondary education, we investigate pedagogical aspects and teachers' pedagogical content knowledge (PCK) about modeling. Following Magnusson et al. [20], we distinguish four elements of content-specific pedagogy: (M1) goals and objectives, (M2) students' understanding and difficulties, (M3) instructional strategies, and (M4) assessment. First, we refined the CSTA definition of computational thinking (CT) [14], made initial explorations of teachers' PCK [15, 16], and of the computational modeling process [13]. We then obtained an operational description of the intended learning outcomes of the learning objectives of Computational science—thus focusing on Magnusson's element M1, observed students working on modeling tasks—focusing on Magnusson's element M2, established what data sources were suitable for assessment—Magnusson's element M4 [17], investigated teachers' initial pedagogical content knowledge on modeling and simulation [12], and finally, explored the characteristics of the assessment instrument for the measurement of the intended learning outcomes for computational science [10]. The results of this research, supplemented with the decision to employ the 4C-ID instructional design [18], form the starting points for the teams and thus insure that the teaching materials, accompanying assessment instruments and teachers' manuals will be set up upon solid theoretical foundations. All aspects of the implementation in schools will be monitored closely and will form the input for further research into the teaching and learning of computational science.

2.5 Research

During the last decade, informatics education research in the Netherlands was given a new impulse with the appointment of the first full professor in informatics education. He set up a nation-wide research group conducting research on various aspects of teaching and learning of informatics in primary, secondary and tertiary education. The research topics in secondary education include programming, design-based informatics education, assessment, context-based teaching and learning of fundamental concepts including algorithms, and finally, computational science (i.e. modeling and simulation)—the research project described in the previous section where the first author engages in. In all of the research projects mentioned here, specific attention is given to the teachers and their pedagogical content knowledge (PCK).

We consider this as a special and a beneficial situation when aiming at research-based informatics curriculum development.

2.6 Informatics Curriculum Reform in Primary and Lower Secondary Education

One of the recommendations of the 2013 report by The Royal Netherlands Academy of Arts and Sciences [19] was to introduce digital literacy into the Dutch lower secondary education. The report led to the chain reaction described earlier in this paper, thus mainly focused at what already existed in the curriculum: informatics in upper secondary education. Nevertheless, both primary and secondary schools started experimenting with integrating digital literacy in their school-based curriculum. Very interesting initiatives emerged, deployed by creative and innovative teachers at primary and secondary schools. While experimenting, the question arose at schools, from teachers, students and parents: is what we are doing now aligned with the formal national curriculum? The answer to this question was: yes, but only because in this formal curriculum—outside upper secondary education—the relevant learning objectives are global and non-specific.

The somehow strange situation – where educators were asking for guidelines that did not exist—was resolved in March 2018, when the curriculum.nu[7] project was started: design teams consisting of selected teachers started to rethink the whole of the curriculum. One of the domains to be inspected is digital literacy. A national system for feedback was implemented in order to facilitate revision of and wide support for the vision (April 2018), big ideas (June 2018) and curricular brick stones (October 2018) as deliverables from the design team. This project is planned to end in May 2019 with an advice by the design team on how to revise the Dutch primary and secondary curriculum with respect to digital literacy. This may lead to the introduction of learning goals with respect to digital literacy in primary and lower secondary education.

We see that informatics, now clearly visible in the upper secondary education, has gained that much momentum, that it could possibly contribute to reforms in the Dutch educational system.

---

[7] https://curriculum.nu.

3 Conclusion and Discussion

In this paper we described the present situation of the elective subject informatics in upper secondary education in the senior general secondary education and the pre-university education in the Netherlands, the informatics curriculum reform together with the events leading to it and we sketched the developments related to teaching informatics in primary and lower secondary education. We see that on one hand, significant progress has been made with five universities offering regular teacher training, a nation-wide research group performing research of international relevance and a grassroots movement with parents, teachers, headmasters and other stakeholders demanding more, earlier and broader informatics education. On the other hand, the teacher population forms one of the weak spots in the informatics ecosystem: many teachers are underqualified, far too few new informatics teachers are being trained, and it is not clear who should teach informatics or digital literacy if it gets introduced into primary and lower secondary education. Some stakeholders see the informatics curriculum reform as a missed opportunity to make informatics a mandatory subject or for the introduction of a national exam. Finally, it is not clear yet what will happen with the desire and all the initiatives employed to introduce informatics, in whatever form, into the primary and lower secondary education.

References

1. Opdracht vernieuwingscommissie informatica 2014–2015 (2014)
2. Lorentz Worksop (2015)
3. Adriaens, H., Fontein, P., den Uijl, M., de Vos, K.: De toekomstige arbeidsmarkt voor onderwijspersoneel po, vo en mbo 2015–2025; Update November 2016. CentERdata, Tilburg (2016)
4. Barendsen, E., Tolboom, J.: Advisory report (intended) curriculum for informatics for upper secondary education. SLO, Enschede (2016)
5. Barendsen, E., Grgurina, N., Tolboom, J.: A new informatics curriculum for secondary education in The Netherlands. In: Brodnik, A., Tort, F. (eds.) ISSEP 2016. LNCS, vol. 9973, pp. 105–117. Springer, Cham (2016). https://doi.org/10.1007/978-3-319-46747-4_9
6. Bennett, J., Holman, J.: Context-based approaches to the teaching of chemistry: what are they and what are their effects? In: Gilbert, J.K., De Jong, O., Justi, R., Treagust, D.F., Van Driel, J.H. (eds.) Chemical Education: Towards Research-Based Practice, pp. 165–184. Kluwer, Dordrecht (2002)
7. Dagiene, V., Stupuriene, G.: Bebras-a sustainable community building model for the concept based learning of informatics and computational thinking. Inform. Educ. **15**(1), 25 (2016)
8. DUO: Leerlingen in het voortgezet onderwijs, 13 June 2018
9. Gander, W., et al.: Informatics education: Europe cannot afford to miss the boat. Report of the Joint Informatics Europe & ACM Europe Working Group on Informatics Education, (2013)
10. Grgurina, N., Barendsen, E., Suhre, C., van Veen, K., Zwaneveld, B. Assessment of Modeling Projects in Informatics Class. In Anonymous (2018, in press)
11. Grgurina, N., Tolboom, J.: The first decade of informatics in Dutch high schools. Inform. Educ. **7**(1), 55–74 (2008)

12. Grgurina, N., Barendsen, E., Suhre, C., van Veen, K., Zwaneveld, B.: Investigating informatics teachers' initial pedagogical content knowledge on modeling and simulation. In: Dagiene, V., Hellas, A. (eds.) ISSEP 2017. LNCS, vol. 10696, pp. 65–76. Springer, Cham (2017). https://doi.org/10.1007/978-3-319-71483-7_6
13. Grgurina, N., Barendsen, E., van Veen, K., Suhre, C., Zwaneveld, B.: Exploring students' computational thinking skills in modeling and simulation projects: a pilot study. In: Anonymous Proceedings of the Workshop in Primary and Secondary Computing Education, pp. 65–68. ACM (2015)
14. Grgurina, N., Barendsen, E., Zwaneveld, B., van de Grift, W., Stoker, I.: Computational thinking skills in Dutch secondary education. In: Anonymous Proceedings of the 8th Workshop in Primary and Secondary Computing Education, pp. 31–32. ACM (2013)
15. Grgurina, N., Barendsen, E., Zwaneveld, B., van Veen, K., Stoker, I. Computational thinking skills in Dutch secondary education: exploring pedagogical content knowledge. In: Anonymous Proceedings of the 14th Koli Calling International Conference on Computing Education Research, pp. 173–174. ACM (2014)
16. Grgurina, N., Barendsen, E., Zwaneveld, B., van Veen, K., Stoker, I.: Computational thinking skills in Dutch secondary education: exploring teacher's perspective. In: Anonymous Proceedings of the 9th Workshop in Primary and Secondary Computing Education, pp. 124–125. ACM (2014)
17. Grgurina, N., Barendsen, E., Zwaneveld, B., van Veen, K., Suhre, C.: Defining and observing modeling and simulation in informatics. In: Brodnik, A., Tort, F. (eds.) ISSEP 2016. LNCS, vol. 9973, pp. 130–141. Springer, Cham (2016). https://doi.org/10.1007/978-3-319-46747-4_11
18. Kirschner, P.A., Van Merriënboer, J.: Ten steps to complex learning a new approach to instruction and instructional design. In: Anonymous (2008)
19. KNAW: Digitale geletterdheid in het voortgezet onderwijs. Koninklijke Nederlandse Akademie van Wetenschappen, Amsterdam (2013)
20. Magnusson, S., Krajcik, J., Borko, H.: Nature, sources, and development of pedagogical content knowledge for science teaching. In: Gess-Newsome, J., Lederman, N.G. (eds.) Examining Pedagogical Content Knowledge, pp. 95–132. Kluwer, Dordrecht (1999)
21. Schmidt, V. Vakdossier 2007 informatica. Technical report, SLO, Stichting Leerplanontwikkeling, Enschede, The Netherlands (2007)
22. Thijs, A.M., Fisser, P., van der Hoeven, M.: Digitale geletterdheid en 21e eeuwse vaardigheden in het funderend onderwijs: een conceptueel kader (draft). SLO, Enschede (2014)
23. Tolboom, J., Kruger, J., Grgurina, N.: Informatica in de bovenbouw havo/vwo: Naar aantrekkelijk en actueel onderwijs in informatica. SLO, Enschede (2014)

The Bebras Contest in Austria – Do Personality, Self-concept and General Interests Play an Influential Role?

Andreas Bollin, Heike Demarle-Meusel, Max Kesselbacher(✉), Corinna Mößlacher, Marianne Rohrer, and Julia Sylle

Alpen-Adria-Universität Klagenfurt, 9020 Klagenfurt, Austria
{Andreas.Bollin,Heike.Demarle-Meusel,Max.Kesselbacher,
Corinna.Moesslacher,Marianne.Rohrer,Julia.Sylle}@aau.at
https://www.aau.at/en/informatics-didactics

Abstract. The Bebras (Beaver) contest aims at testing of and motivating for Informatics and Computer fluency, and as such it is designed to be a contest for all pupils between 8 and 19. But, does it really attract and favor all types of children likewise? This paper takes a closer look at different types of personality, self-concept and interests of the winners of the Bebras contest in Austria and discusses those factors that might contribute to a successful participation. It concludes with some recommendations that might help in increasing the number of participation at the event.

Keywords: Bebras contest · Personality · Self-concept

1 Motivation

It is a big challenge for society to foster interest in computing as a 21st century skill among children and adolescents. A single definition on what should be taught at school is hard to give, and this is the responsibility of the respective ministries of each country. However, in the future, the need on skilled workforce to meet the requirements of the industry 4.0 will increase. Thus, it gets more and more important for the education sector to honor this evolution. There are already initiatives on different levels in place to foster competences and interests in informatics, e.g. from ministries or other organizations up to private groups like CoderDojo (more examples were shown by Grandl and Ebner [9]). In the field of informatics, the Bebras (Beaver) Contest (described by Dagienė and Futschek [7]) has a competitive character to motivate pupils of different ages with the aim to make them familiar with informatics concepts and computational thinking. On the one hand it fosters basic skills in informatics, but it also can, and according to the key driver behind the contest it also should, attract all different types of pupils for this field of science.

S. N. Pozdniakov and V. Dagienė (Eds.): ISSEP 2018, LNCS 11169, pp. 283–294, 2018.
https://doi.org/10.1007/978-3-030-02750-6_22

Participants have to be nominated by schools and cannot register individually. There are both advantages and disadvantages to this approach. Pupils that did not consider participating might get in touch with informatics and their interest may be aroused, but on the other hand interested individuals rely on the willingness of their school to be part of this competition. This causes a broad range of levels of interest, from high to low attentiveness. But, very little is known about the personalities and structure of interests of the participants, especially the differences between winners and unsuccessful contestants. Relevance to gain greater knowledge on this issues is obvious, having the requirements of the 21st century in mind. Tailor-made offers to attract children and adolescents to informatics can help to avoid skills shortage in this field. To obtain satisfactory effects, it is important to intervene at an early age.

For this reason, the objective of this paper is to take a closer look at the different types of personality, the self-concept and the interests of the winners of the Bebras contest in Austria and to discusses those factors that might contribute to a successful participation. The results are additionally compared to two other populations: two school classes who participated at the Bebras Contest without winning, and a set of teenagers who successfully took part at an international (and quite demanding) coding contest – as we also wanted to check for pronounced differences.

The rest of the paper is structured as follows: Sect. 2 provides background information about related work and summarizes the tests used during our study. Section 3 presents the details of the study, introduces the hypotheses and summarizes the results. Section 4 then reflects on the findings and Sect. 5 concludes with a summary and an outlook.

2 Background

2.1 Testing the Masses

Contests for testing students in their abilities in certain subjects and topics have been developed and implemented in many countries. However, the number of studies looking at criteria, ability and skills determining whether someone is among successful students is very low.

In the field of informatics and computational thinking, the probably widest-known contest is the Bebras Contest [7]. In the meantime, Bebras turned into a diverse event, where individuals or teams are competing to each other at various settings and levels of difficulty. The tasks in the Bebras Contest are developed considering a set of criteria (some have to be and some should be fulfilled by all tasks), e.g. 'Good tasks are related to informatics, computer science or computer literacy'. The criteria provide general information about the development of the tasks (topics, representation of the tasks, no previous knowledge required). Some of the criteria consider the abilities of the students: The tasks 'have a difficulty level (3 levels)', 'are adequate for the age of the contestants (3 age groups)' and 'are independent from any curriculum'. The difficulty levels have a range from 'all pupils of the target group should be able to solve' to 'only the best can solve these tasks'. A revision to these criteria was stated in 2014 by Vaníček [16]. Amongst others, the acceptance of tasks that require no(!) pre-knowledge is recommended. A rich and still ongoing discussion about good tasks can be found on the web-site of the Bebras contest [4].

A comparable contest in the field of mathematics is the International Mathematical Kangaroo [2]. A study by Applebaum looking at the results of the Mathematical Kangaroo showed that the achievements of mathematically motivated students in tasks that require spatial abilities correlate with their achievements in non-standard problems [3]. This study links a cognitive skill, the spatial ability, with the achievements in mathematics of this student.

The perception of learning activities is an issue for different studies. Theodoropoulos et al. performed a study in Greek schools to assess the relationship of certain students' personality structures (the cognitive styles) and the students' attitude (the students' quality of learning experience) towards the game-based programming activities of code.org. The study shows that specific cognitive styles differed by the Myers-Briggs Type Indicator (MBTI) correlate with higher achievements in the provided tasks. Therefore a more balanced and personalized approach is recommended [15].

2.2 Personality, Self-concept and General Interests

Psychological theories, like the theory of work adjustment by Dawis [8] and the RIASEC theory of careers by Holland [10] assume, that individual needs and skills become relative stable between the age 14 and 24 (as shown by Nerdinger et al. [13]). Individual needs is a generic term and includes motives, personality, interests and social values, which are essential for successful professional careers. Influencing variables on the career choice are vocational interests, intelligence and personality (shown by Ackermann and Beier [1]). Career choice is a conscious decision; people try to find a job with the highest match between personality structure and the job profile (person-job-fit). When there is a good fit between the personality type and environmental requirements, people are much more satisfied and successful in their jobs [10]. Holland formulates six interest dimensions: Realistic (R), Investigative (I), Artistic (A), Social (S), Enterprising (E), and Conventional (C). The dimensions are presented hexagonal in the order of RIASEC. Dimensions of interests are more similar to each other, the closer they are presented at the Hexagon. Example giving, Realistic and Investigative have much more in common, than Realistic and Social. Bergmann and Eder presented a list to identify fields of study or careers consistent with the individual interest dimensions [5]. Each profession is assigned a three-letter code. Informatics and information management is allocated to the code CIS (Conventional, Investigative and Social). There are some code variations depending on the vocational specifications, e.g. ICE for business informatics. The dimensions Conventional and Investigative seem very important for a good fit to the field of informatics.

Interests play an important role in the career finding process and far beyond in the success and satisfaction within the job. So the question is, how to foster these interests in an early stage. Building up opportunities for the mainstream to get in touch with concepts of informatics and computational thinking – like the Bebras – is a practicable way. Such experiences may foster a positive subject-specific self-concept. The self-concept gives an assessment about individual strength and weaknesses. A positive self-concept has an influence on the learning process. It influences the decision, which learning objectives and tasks pupils set. Results from PISA demonstrate a positive correlation between self-concept and results [14]. The development of the self-concept is affected from self-observation and feedback, e.g. from teachers or success in competitions. A positive self-concept will be built up by experience.

3 The Study

3.1 Setting

In order to assess influences of personality, academic self-concept and general interest on Bebras participation, a survey was employed to collect these factors from different groups. The survey was conducted in paper form as well as in the online environment KAUA[1], and contains the following data fields:

Demographic data: Sex (male/female/other), age

General interests: Six Likert items for the six dimensions of interests (RIASEC) following Holland [10]. Two variants of formulations are used, depending on the age of the participants. Survey participants older than 14 receive the standard formulation (scale with 9 items) of the general interests test [5]; others receive a re-formulation for children (scale with 3 items). The results per dimension are grouped in three equally sized brackets: not interested, partly interested, very interested.

Personality: Two Likert items (scale with 13 items) for two dimensions (Dominant/Easy-Going, Formal/Informal) of the Five-Factor and Stress Theory [12,17]. Two variants of formulations are used, depending on the age of the participants. Survey participants older than 14 receive the standard formulation; others receive a re-formulation for children.

Academic self-concept: A set of questions for verbal as well as mathematical self-concept is surveyed. Each consists of three statements[2] regarding the respective self-concept, on a scale with 4 items between disagreement and agreement, which are also included in PISA surveys [11]. Moreover, for both

[1] KAUA is an online survey system with support for anonymous, longitudinal studies, designed for and implemented at the Department of Informatics Didactics, Alpen-Adria-Universität Klagenfurt.

[2] V_1: I am hopeless in German classes. V_2: I learn things quickly in German classes. V_3: I get good marks in German. M_1: I get good marks in mathematics. M_2: Mathematics is one of my best subjects. M_3: I have always done well in mathematics.

German (the medium of instruction in Austria) and Mathematics, the last received school grades and the self-given grades are surveyed (*VGrade*, verbal, and *MGrade*, mathematical).

The data was collected for three groups to compare the different factors:

Bebras winner group: 43 Austrian Bebras winners (20 males, 23 females, mean age 11.57 ± 2.13) were surveyed in paper form during the Bebras 2018 award ceremonies.

Bebras control group: 36 non-winning Austrian Bebras participants (12 males, 21 females, 3 others, mean age 12.08 ± 0.84) were surveyed in online form to provide a means of comparing winner and non-winner participants.

School Coding-contest group: 20 male participants of the Catalysts School Coding Contest[3] 2018 in Klagenfurt (mean age 17.80 ± 0.62) were surveyed in online form to provide another control group of computer science interested students.

Two sets of hypotheses are evaluated for the collected data:

H1-H2: Bebras winners statistically differ significantly in personality, academic self-concept and general interests from the control group (H1) and the coding-contest group (H2).

H3-H5: Factors of personality (H3), academic self-concept (H4) and general interests (H5) contribute to winning the Bebras contest in Austria.

Hypotheses H1-H2 are evaluated with the help of U-test statistics, and analysis of correlations and plots. Hypotheses H3-H5 are evaluated with the help of mean value comparisons, t-test statistics, correlation analysis and linear regression.

Table 1. Mean values for: Six dimensions of interest (range $[-1, 1]$, from *not interested* to *very interested*), two personality dimensions (range $[-6, 6]$), agreement to six statements of academic self concept (V_i and M_i, range $[1, 4]$ from *disagreement* to *agreement*), actual and self-given grades in the subjects German and Mathematics (*VGrade*/*MGrade*, range $[1, 5]$).

Group	R	I	A	S	E	C	Easy-Going	Informal
Winner 1	0.26	0.64	3 0.45	3 0.56	0.39	0.12	2 1.791	0.002
Control 2	0.27	0.39	0.22	3 0.61	0.39	0.11	1,3 −1.500	−0.417
School-CCC 3	0.33	0.68	1 −0.13	1,2 0.19	0.29	0.15	2 0.800	−0.250
Group	V_1	V_2	V_3	VGrade Actual / Self	M_1	M_2	M_3	MGrade Actual / Self
Winner 1	1.71	2 3.14	3.21	1.88 / 1.74	2 3.58	2 3.31	2 3.41	1.72 / 1.57
Control 2	1.94	1 2.75	2.81	2.39 / 1.94	1 3.19	1 2.75	1 2.94	2.08 / 1.81
School-CCC 3	1.60	2.90	3.15	2.10 / 2.00	3.55	3.25	3.15	1.75 / 1.65

[3] More information: https://register.codingcontest.org/.

3.2 Results

This section contains descriptive result tables summarizing the data, and tables and plots of additional analysis. The results are discussed in the next section.

Table 1 shows a summary of the data for the three surveyed groups of students. Mean values for the different dimensions of data are reported. Questions regarding the areas of interest are answered on a scale of three items (winner and control group) or nine items (School-CCC group) ranging from *not interested* to *very interested*, and are encoded numerically in the range $[-1, 1]$. The middle interpretation *partly interested* is encoded as 0 on the coarse scale and in the range $[-0.25, 0.25]$ in the more fine-grained scale. Negative values of personality indicate the first personality types (Dominant and Formal), positive values indicate the second personality types (Easy-Going and Informal). For brevity, only the positive ones are written. The questions regarding the academic self-concept (V_i and M_i) are answered on a scale of four items ranging from disagreement to agreement, encoded from 1 to 4. Low values indicate a weak self-concept, high values indicate a strong self-concept. This is true for all items but V_1, which is an inverse item. Furthermore, the students were asked to report their last received grades and the grades they would give themselves in the subjects German and Mathematics, encoded from 1 to 5; lower numbers indicate better grades.

Table 1 also shows significant differences between groups. Shapiro-Wilk tests with significance level $p < .05$ were used to test for the null hypothesis of normal distribution. For most of the data columns, the null hypothesis could not be rejected. Therefore, significant differences were found employing non-parametric Mann-Whitney-U-Tests with significance level $p < .05$. Significant differences are marked with subscript row numbers signifying the relationships (1 for differences to the winner group, 2 for differences to the control group, 3 for differences to the School-CCC group), and are marked symmetrically.

Table 2 shows statistical analysis results employed on the combined groups of all Bebras participants (winner+control). A binary variable *winner* with value 0 for non-winners and 1 for winners was introduced. For this variable, all significant correlation scores are reported in the table (significance level $p < .05$, linear and rank correlation was examined, Kendall results are omitted as they are the same as Spearman results). Moreover, a linear regression model was fitted for the response variable *winner*, with iterative backward selection and significance level $p < .05$. The table reports all significant variables with their estimated prediction factors, and reports the regression scores measured as multiple and adjusted R^2. *SexM* and the not significant *SexF* are binary auxiliary variables introduced with value 1 for participants of the respective sex and 0 for others. The Spearman correlation scores between the significant factors of linear regression are also reported for the winner and control group.

Figure 1 shows the distribution of the surveyed students in a plane with the personality dimensions Dominant/Easy-Going and Formal/Informal. Each point corresponds to one student, distinct points may overlap. For each group, the mean personality values are included in the plane, together with a circle representing the 33% percentile of data points nearest to the mean for the resp. group.

Table 2. Statistical analysis of binary variable *winner*, computed for both Bebras groups ($n = 79$). Factors and correlations significant at $p < .05$ are marked bold. Results show significant correlation scores for the variable *winner*, linear regression model fitted with iterative backward selection for the response variable *winner*, and spearman correlation scores between regression factors.

Correlations for *winner*

Correlation	Easy-Going	V_2	VGrade Actual	M_1	M_2	M_3
Pearson	**0.46**	**0.23**	**-0.22**	**0.24**	**0.26**	**0.25**
Spearman	**0.46**	**0.23**	-0.20	**0.23**	**0.29**	**0.25**

Linear Regression for *winner*

Feature	Intercept	SexM	Artistic	Social	Easy-Going	M_3
Estimated Factor	-0.147	**0.529**	**0.217**	**-0.161**	**0.089**	**0.147**
Multiple R^2	0.4909		Adjusted R^2	0.4560		

Spearman Correlations for Regression Factors
Top half winner ($n = 43$), bottom half control ($n = 36$)

Control \Winner	SexM	Artistic	Social	Easy-Going	M_3	
SexM	1	**-0.57**	**-0.49**	**-0.53**	0.16	
Artistic	**-0.74**	1	**0.51**	0.20	**-0.32**	
Social	-0.16	0.27	1	**0.56**	0.05	
Easy-Going	**-0.72**	**0.54**	0.10	1	-0.04	
M_3	0.18	0.16	0.05	**-0.42**	1	

Figure 2 show scatter plots between the variable *winner* and four of the significant factors of correlation and linear regression analysis shown in Table 2. Figure 3 shows the distribution of the responses for each area of interest for the winner and control groups. For the students, it is possible to choose the same level of interest for multiple areas.

3.3 Discussion

Concerning **interests**, differences were uncovered between the groups. According to the RIASEC test (see Table 1 and Fig. 3), Bebras winners are more investigative (mean 0.64 compared to 0.39) and more artistic (mean 0.45 compared to 0.22) than the control group. The result is not statistical significant, but Fig. 3 also shows that winners are, with the exception of the social dimension, in general more interested in all the other fields of interest. Bebras winners (and coding contest participants) seem to be more curious and open to explore new things. It is notable that the School-CCC participants are less interested in the social dimension (the smaller number-labels in Table 1 indicate that this observation is also statistical significant to the winner and control group).

In some sense this tells us that Bebras participants are quite comparable to the control group, they just show a bit higher interest in everything and are more interested in the artistic field. The type of Bebras questions (which are quite often very creative and try to be out of different domains) seems to

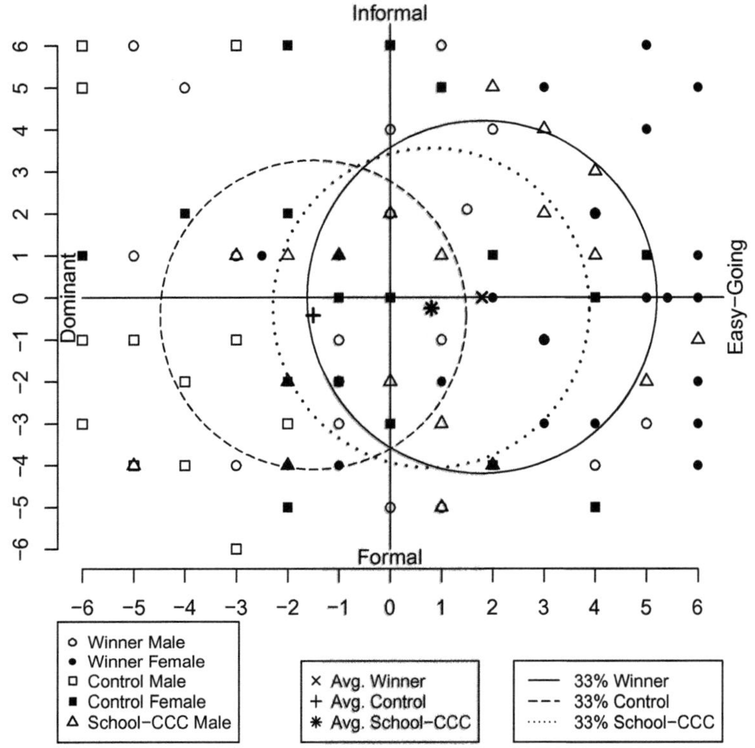

Fig. 1. Distribution of the students of the different groups in the plane of the two personality dimensions Dominant/Easy-Going and Formal/Informal.

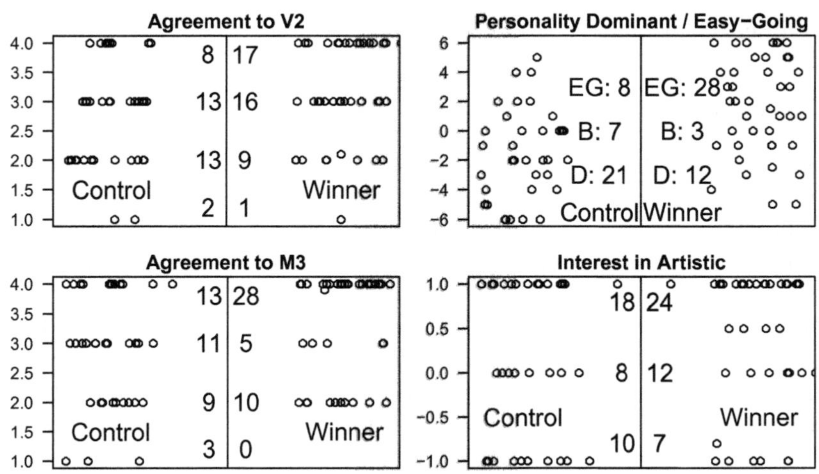

Fig. 2. Scatter plots for four of the significant factors of Table 2 against the binary variable *winner*. The x-axes contain jitter for the *winner* variable to avoid point overlap, the y-axes plot the respective factor.

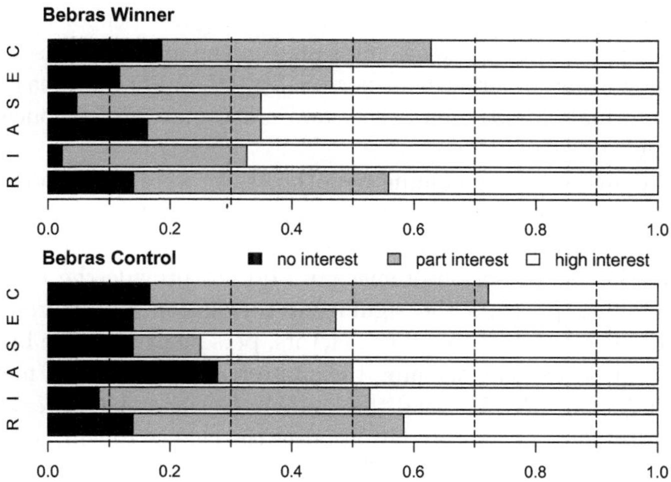

Fig. 3. Areas of interests of the Bebras participants.

support them in some sense. On the other hand, School-CCC participants might already have developed their own set of interests and have less interest in some dimensions: they are older with a mean age of 17.80 compared to the mean ages of 11.57 (winner) and 12.08 (control).

Concerning **personality**, there is a big (statistically significant) difference between the winner and the control group. Winners (and to some extent also the coding contest group) are more easy-going, neither formal nor informal, and not really dominant. Figure 1 shows this difference with mean values and quantile areas. Additionally, there is an observable difference between Bebras Winner and School-CCC participants. The latter are less easy-going than Bebras winners.

In some sense, this observation contradicts the myth that for being good in computational thinking one needs to be quite formal. Formality might be useful in some contexts, but not in the case of the Bebras contest.

Concerning **self-concept**, there are again observable differences. Bebras winner have better grades in German (so, in their mother tongue) and in Mathematics, and they also have a higher self-concept in both of the fields compared to the control group. The differences between winner and control groups are significant, and it indicates that Bebras winners do have a higher verbal and mathematical self-concept. To some sense this is not so surprising as mathematical thinking, reading and text comprehension are helpful in understanding and solving Bebras tasks. Lastly, School-CCC participants are comparable to Bebras winner, with lower verbal self-concept and grades, but still higher than the control group. To conclude, we can answer Hypotheses H1 and H2 in the following way.

(H1) Bebras winners significantly differ from the control group in respect to personality and verbal/mathematical self-concept. They are a bit more easy-going, have better grades and a stronger self-concept. They also show some differences in respect to the interests dimension.

(H2) Bebras winners significantly differ from the School-CCC group in respect to interests. They are more interested in the artistic and social domain. They also show some differences in personality (they are more easy-going and a bit more informal). Also, their verbal and mathematical self-concept and the grades are slightly better.

In order to answer the remaining hypotheses, we were taking a closer look at the correlations between the different factors and compute a regression formula, eliminating all the factors that are not contributing to the result (of winning the Bebras contest). Due to reason of space, we do not provide the full correlation tables, but Table 2 presents the significant correlation and regression factors ($p < 0.05$). It turns out that, of all the factors, personality has the highest (i.e. a medium-size) influence onto winning the contest. The verbal and mathematical self concept (V_2, M_1, M_2, M_3) and the grade in German ($VGradeActual$, lower grades are better, a negative correlation raises the chance to win) also have some influence. The regression consists of five factors for predicting a winner.

$$\begin{aligned} Winning \approx &-0.147 + 0.529 \cdot SexM + 0.217 \cdot Artistic \\ &- 0.161 \cdot Social + 0.089 \cdot EasyGoing + 0.147 \cdot M_3 \end{aligned}$$

It is notable that $SexM$ (of being a man) is part of the formula. Table 1 shows that $SexM$ and being *artistic* or *easygoing* are highly correlated, so $SexM$ is somehow a corrective factor in the formula to fit both, male and female winners.

A power test was used to describe the power of the employed correlation test. For the combined Bebras participants group ($n = 79$) and a significance level of 0.05 and a test power of 0.95, a correlation score of 0.3895 has sufficient power [6]. Therefore, only the correlation to the personality factor (Easy-Going) statistically holds with the given parameters. This does not mean that the other factors do not have any influence, and so we extended our analysis by scatter plots to look for correlations. Figure 2 summarizes the plots for four of the significant factors of Table 1 against the binary variable winner. As can be seen (data points in the area), in all the 4 plots, winners have a slightly higher verbal and mathematical self-concept, and interest in the artistic field. To conclude, we now can answer Hypotheses H3 to H5 in the following way.

(H3) The factor of personality contributes to winning the Bebras contest. The more easy-going a participant is, the higher the chance to win.

(H4) The academic self-concept contributes to winning the Bebras contest in some sense. A strong verbal self-concept and mathematical skills raise the chance to win.

(H5) General interests have some influence on winning the Bebras contest. Interests in the artistic dimension seem to help in winning the contest.

3.4 Threats to Validity

As basically all Bebras winners were at the award ceremony in Klagenfurt in 2018, we had a unique chance to reach the full population. However, the results of the study have to be taken with some care. First, the size of the population is still quite small. Even though some of the findings are statistically significant, some others are, up to now, of anecdotal evidence. Secondly, the results might not be transferable to other countries. There also is no guarantee that the findings hold for the next contests. Being aware of that, we included the coding contest group to get an even better picture, and the results seem comprehensible.

Some of the data has been collected in written form, so there might have been errors during data-transfer. However, we checked all the data several times, following a four-eye-principle. The statistical analysis has been done with the R framework, so, we assume the data and the results to be valid.

4 Recommendations

In the light of the results we now dare some prudent recommendations, with the objective to even raise the chance to win a Bebras contest in the future.

At first, it is apparent that Bebras winner are interested in a lot of different domains, they are artistic, social, and are good and feel confident in their mother tongue and in Mathematics. The winners are also a bit more of an ease-going personality and of an investigative nature. At the beginning we raised the question if the Bebras contest is attractive to everybody. In the light of the results we can give a defensive "Yes" as an answer. The differences to the control group are not that big, and it is the creativity in the Bebras tasks and the social event (often the whole class takes part) that is a strong argument for its attractiveness.

Now, in order to raise the chance of being a Bebras winner, educators should try to do the following: (a) keep pupils interested and open-minded, (b) support social activities whenever possible, (c) try to provide more incentives to also attract dominant pupils, and finally, (d) try to increase the mathematical and verbal self-concept whenever possible.

5 Summary and Outlook

In this paper we took a closer look at different types of personality, self-concept and interests of the winners of the Bebras contest in Austria and compared them with a control group and group of pupils taking part at a programming contest. It turned out that (in our setting) there is a significant difference between the Bebras winners and the control group in the personality, self-concept and interest dimensions. We also looked at factors predicting winning the contest, and it turned out that a strong verbal self-concept and mathematical skills, as well as artistic interest and an easy-going personality have a positive influence.

Due to the small group sizes there are for sure many more things to learn, and so we are currently working on making the KAUA platform more popular and continue collecting RIASEC, personality and general interest data, and we also plan to repeat the study for the next and upcoming contests.

Acknowledgement. We want to express our deepest thanks to all the participants of the study and to all the colleagues that helped us in gathering the data. A big Thank

You goes to Max Kesselbacher for implementing (maintaining) the KAUA platform and for investing countless hours in dealing with the data used in this study.

References

1. Ackerman, P.L., Beier, M.E.: Intelligence, personality, and interests in the career choice process. J. Career Assess. **11**(2), 205–218 (2003)
2. AKSF: Kangourou Sans Frontieres. http://www.aksf.org/. Accessed 15 June 2018
3. Applebaum, M.: Spatial abilities as a predictor to success in the Kangaroo contest. J. Math. Syst. Sci. **7**, 154 (2017)
4. Bebras Webpage - Publications. https://www.bebras.org/?q=publications. 06 Aug 2018
5. Bergmann, C., Eder, F.: AIST-R. Allgemeiner Interessen-Struktur-Test mit Umwelt-Struktur-Test (UST-R) - Revision. Manual. Hogrefe, 1 edn. (2005)
6. Cohen, J.: Differences between Correlation Coefficients. In: Cohen, J. (ed.) Statistical Power Analysis for the Behavioral Sciences, pp. 109–143. Academic Press (1977)
7. Dagienė, V., Futschek, G.: Bebras international contest on informatics and computer literacy: criteria for good tasks. In: Mittermeir, R.T., Sysło, M.M. (eds.) ISSEP 2008. LNCS, vol. 5090, pp. 19–30. Springer, Heidelberg (2008). https://doi.org/10.1007/978-3-540-69924-8_2
8. Dawis, R.V.: Work adjustment theory and person-environment-congruence counselling. In: Brown, D., Brooks, L. (eds.) Career Choice and Development, pp. 75–120. Jossey-Bass Publishers (1996)
9. Grandl, M., Ebner, M.: Informatische Grundbildung - ein Ländervergleich (2017). https://www.medienimpulse.at/articles/view/1069. Accessed 15 June 2018
10. Holland, J.: Exploring careers with a typology - what we have learned and some new directions. Am. Psychol. **51**(4), 397–406 (1996)
11. Kunter, M., et al.: PISA 2000: Dokumentation der Erhebungsinstrumente. Materialien aus der Bildungsforschung, vol. 72 (2002)
12. Mujkanovic, A., Bollin, A.: Improving learning outcomes through systematic group reformation - the role of skills and personality in software engineering education. In: 2016 IEEE First International Conference on Connected Health: Applications, Systems and Engineering Technologies (CHASE), pp. 97–103 (2016)
13. Nerdinger, F.W., Blickle, G., Schaper, N.: Arbeits- und Organisationspsychologie. Springer-Lehrbuch (2001)
14. OECD: Organisation For Economic Co-Operation And Development. PISA 2006: Naturwissenschaftliche Kompetenzen für die Welt von morgen. OECD Publishing, Paris and W. Bertelsmann Verlag, Germany (2008)
15. Theodoropoulos, A., Antoniou, A., Lepouras, G.: How do different cognitive styles affect learning programming? Insights from a game-based approach in greek schools. Trans. Comput. Educ. **17**(1), 3:1–3:25 (2016). https://doi.org/10.1145/2940330, http://doi.acm.org/10.1145/2940330
16. Vaníček, J.: Bebras informatics contest: criteria for good tasks revised. In: Gülbahar, Y., Karataş, E. (eds.) ISSEP 2014. LNCS, vol. 8730, pp. 17–28. Springer, Cham (2014). https://doi.org/10.1007/978-3-319-09958-3_3
17. Yamada, Y., et al.: The impacts of personal characteristic on educational effectiveness in controlled-project based learning on software intensive systems development. In: 2014 IEEE 27th Conference on Software Engineering Education and Training (CSEE&T), pp. 119–128. IEEE, April 2014

Gender Differences in Graph Tasks - Do They Exist in High School Bebras Categories Too?

Lucia Budinská(✉), Karolína Mayerová, and Michal Winczer

Department of Informatics Education,
Comenius University in Bratislava, Bratislava, Slovakia
{lucia.budinska,mayerova,winczer}@fmph.uniba.sk

Abstract. This paper explores gender differences across the abilities of Junior (15–17 year old) and Senior (17–19 year old) students in terms of solving graph problems. As a basis to our assessment, we look at the graph tasks from the Slovak Bebras competition in 2012 to 2017 across both Junior and Senior categories. In our earlier research on this topic, we introduced a new method of categorising graph problems. This was based on an in-depth analysis of the various problem types aimed at 8–15 year old students, whereby a set of indicators were defined to predict whether a task was more likely to be successfully solved by girls or boys. In this paper, we apply the new categorisation onto graph tasks aimed at Junior and Senior students with an aim to verify whether the same predictors of girls' and boys' success remain valid. A qualitative analysis indicates that our categorisation of graph tasks is suitable for Junior and Senior categories with minor adaptation only. As a result of a subsequent quantitative analysis, we find a significant difference in the solution success rates between girls and boys in 38 out of 65 analysed graph tasks. In 35 tasks boys were significantly more successful and these were tasks with an overall lower success rate. Furthermore, a few tasks with contradictory results concerning girls' and boys' solution success were identified. We selected one of these tasks where a higher error tendency in older students was apparent, and further analysed it together with the students themselves (15–19 years old) in order to better understand the methods used by them while solving this task. Our findings can be used to enable authors of task sets and lesson plans to define problems in a manner that will minimize gender success differences such as the ones described in this study.

Keywords: Bebras · High school · Graph tasks · Gender differences

1 Introduction

The Bebras international competition in Informatics was held in Slovakia in 2017 for the 11th time, with a total of 74 216 students and pupils from 992

S. N. Pozdniakov and V. Dagienė (Eds.): ISSEP 2018, LNCS 11169, pp. 295–306, 2018.
https://doi.org/10.1007/978-3-030-02750-6_23

schools taking part. Our aim is to keep continuously improving the contents of the contest which attracts a relatively broad spectrum of students from various educational backgrounds and is by no means limited to a small population of gifted students with strong academics. The growing number of participants year on year motivates us to create new and better problems for the future rounds of the competition. As part of the preparation of the problems for the Bebras competition, we are concerned both in terms of the content as well as the formal definition of the tasks. To do this more effectively, results from prior years are extensively analysed. In doing so, we wish to better understand the relationship between students' solution success rates and the content and form of the tasks introduced in the Slovak competition.

In our previous research we focus on participant categories concerning students aged 8–15 years, i.e. Little Beavers, Benjamins and Cadets. In [1] our initial data sample covers the Little Beaver category (7–9 years old) during the 2012–2017 period. Based on a qualitative analysis of the problems presented to the contestants, a new task categorization is defined, distinguishing between 'programming', 'logical', 'algorithmic' and 'user' tasks. An indication of gender differences in terms of solution success rates is observed within a subset of the 'logical' task category where graphs in any form were present. However, as the overall number of problems in this category was low, we expand our sample to also include the Benjamin (10–12 years) and Cadet (13–14 years) categories. Our findings confirm significant differences in problem solutions depending on gender [2]. Specifically, we are able to identify a set of criteria which allows one to predict whether a given task is more likely to be successfully solved by boys as opposed to girls or vice versa. Identification of gender differences allows us to adopt a better informed problem setting strategy with a view to make the contest equally accessible and enjoyable for both girls and boys, which was the main motivation behind this study. The results can also help teachers lecturing on graph structures and/or algorithmic problem solving, as both of these thematic areas are part of the Slovak Informatics curriculum.

Other research [3,4] suggests that boys tend to be generally more successful than girls in solving the Bebras tasks. We argue that these findings can be further expanded on by encompassing task-specific considerations, i.e. accounting for commonalities between some of the contest problems. The attractiveness of Bebras tasks to girls is studied in [3], indicating that "girls perform better in a certain task if three conditions of Keller's ARCS Model of Motivation are met: the tasks have to be visually appealing to attract the attention of girls, they have to represent a situation relevant to real life, and they have to be comparably easy to solve." Valentina Dagiene [5] further states that "(a) boys and girls show different results when it comes to problems that require spatial thinking. It takes them the same amount of time to solve the task, but boys do it better. (b) Pupils' performance in terms of contest problem solving increases with age, but boys of lower grades have almost equal results as girls of upper grades. (c) Guessing is frequent in multiple-choice questions: about 10% of contestants try to guess the right answer, with boys doing this more frequently." There is a vast array of literature [6,7] focusing on estimating the difficulty of contest problems, however the success of these methods is only moderate.

Furthermore, there are studies aimed at delving into the differences and similarities between genders [8]. However, the goal of this paper is not to focus on a specific feature of one of the genders or to try enforcing their success in the competition. Our aim is to understand how to set contest tasks in a way that makes them equally attractive and solvable for both genders, and as a next step, help teachers overcome the issues that boys or girls may have when solving specific types of problems. Ilomaki [9] also agree that it is extremely important and entirely possible to set problems in a manner that would entice girls' motivation and thus make graph tasks more attractive to girls. We believe this may be crucial in order for girls not to lose interest in Informatics.

2 Graph Tasks

In previous research we studied graph tasks in primary and lower secondary school participant categories. We consider a task to be a graph task when there is a graph data structure (contains vertices and edges). Graphs can be represented as a diagrams or tables or even text. As a graph task we count diagrams representing actions or relationships, quadratic grids in which orientation and adjacency of cells is relevant.

2.1 Categories of Graph Tasks

Based on a qualitative analysis [10] of tasks that we considered to be graph tasks from participant categories Little Beaver, Benjamin and Cadet, we used the following criteria to assign tasks to specific categories.

- **Type of structure:** tree, quadratic grid, directed or undirected graph, etc.
- **Method of how the task is solved:**
  - *Reading the graph:* gathering information from the structure.
  - *Creating the graph:* creating or adapting the graph according to the instructions.
  - *Transformation of the graph:* changing the graph representation (e.g. from diagram to a table).
- **Type of algorithm used:** set only if the assignment required using the algorithm (e.g. finding the shortest path, vertex cover, backtracking, traversing of the graph).
- **Interactivity:** choosing from four possibilities or interactive task.

Based on previous criteria we established five categories of methods/strategies that we assume students have used to solve the problems. These are:

- **Developing the strategy:** to solve the task one needs to choose a strategy for traversing or modifying the graph, or simply to reduce the number of possibilities that have to be examined.

- **Discovering the strategy:** a hint concerning the strategy is included in the text of the assignment or in the examples, and hence the student only needs to discover it and use it appropriately.
- **Graph search with certain constraints:** one has to account for the constraints set within the assignment or the constraints that are given by the graph structure (e.g. direction of the edges or their values).
- **The "look and see" method:** to solve the task one simply needs to grasp the graph structure and read the answer from it.
- **Try all possibilities:** in these problems there is usually a small number of possibilities (4–6). Students can try all of them and realize which one is the correct one. The possibilities can be set directly, or one has to identify them.

As part of the qualitative analysis we were also considering the length of the assignment text and the type of pictures.

2.2 "Girls"' and"boys"' Tasks

In previous research, chosen graph problems from categories Little Beavers (7–9 years), Benjamins (10–12 years) and Cadets (13–14 years) were further examined based on the associated participants' solution success rates. With the use of statistical methods three groups of tasks were obtained: (1) group in which girls and boys were equally successful, (2) group in which boys were substantially more successful and (3) group in which girls were more successful than boys. The type of problems in the latter group (3), i.e. the "girls" tasks, contained complex structures (e.g. automata, labyrinths, graphical representation of multilist, directed and undirected graphs and trees) however the used operations were quite simple (reading directly from the graph or evaluation of a small number of possibilities) and the beginning of the solution within the graph structure was marked or visible in a straight way. The assignment text for these problems was shorter as the pictures of the actual graph structures contained more information (often with labelled vertices and/or edges). Hence one could say the tasks were less abstract. On the other hand, the "boys" tasks had longer text, but the structures were simpler (quadratic grid, undirected graphs) than the ones observed in the "girls" tasks. Pictures in the text assignments were more abstract and one cannot immediately see the starting vertex. Many of the tasks had a large number of potential (sometime even correct) solutions and therefore one had to use a certain strategy or algorithm to obtain the right solution. With this type of problems, the students either developed their own strategy or performed a graph search with some constraints to reach the solution. A huge portion of "boys" tasks had an overall low success rate and were categorised as hard.

3 Research Methods

The research presented in this paper had several research goals. The first goal was to validate if our problem categorization mentioned in Sect. 2.1 can be applied to tasks relating to older participant categories or if it needs be redefined (and if so, then how). The second but equally important goal was to establish as to what extent the observed solution success rate differences between boys and girls were dependent on age. Can we find the same differences among older students too? At first, we tried to apply our categorisation on problems from the Junior and Senior participant categories. We chose qualitative research [11] whereby a method of coding was used to apply our categorisations to all tasks in both categories across years 2012 to 2017. 65 graph tasks were selected, consisting of 35 Senior tasks and 31 Junior tasks (one used in both categories).

To answer our second research goal, we used quantitative data analysis to determine if we can predict the success of girls and/or boys in the tasks across the two secondary school participant categories according to the same rules that were used for the primary school (Little Beavers, Benjamins and Cadets) task analysis. Based on the data available we analysed how students proceeded with solving the selected tasks. There were three possible outcomes: correct, incorrect and not solved. These are by definition categorical data and hence we used a test described in [12–14]. The data used was based on anonymized results of all participants in the actual contest. In each year there were about 10 000 students in both categories. Detailed numbers including gender specifics can be found in Table 1.

Table 1. Numbers of participants in both categories

		12–13	13–14	14–15	15–16	16–17	17–18
Senior	Girls	1150	1206	1439	1633	1392	1698
	Boys	3006	2793	3106	2921	2962	3018
	All	4156	3999	4545	4554	4354	4716
Junior	Girls	2334	2542	2935	3648	3385	3181
	Boys	4132	4066	4138	4988	4794	4594
	All	6466	6608	7073	8636	8179	7775

Considering the categorical nature of our data we used a contingency table. We observe gender: female or men, $r = 2$ and success in solving a given task: correct, wrong and do not solve, $c = 3$. Therefore a 2×3 ($r \times c$) contingency table was used and the hypothesis H_0: gender and success in solving the task are independent, H_1: gender and success in solving the task are dependent, were tested. We used Pearson chi-square test of independence (in contingency tables). The testing criterion is

$$\chi^2 = \sum_{i=1}^{2}\sum_{j=1}^{3} \frac{(n_{ij} - \frac{n_i n_j}{n})^2}{\frac{n_i n_j}{n}},$$

where n_{ij} is value in row i and column j in contingency table, n_x sum of all values in row/column x and n sum of the whole table. If $\chi^2 > \chi^2_{(1)(2)}(\alpha)$, (obtained from statistical tables) we did not accept H_0 at level α. In case of rejecting H_0 we examined standardized Pearson residuals.

4 Results

In contrast with categories for younger students (7–14 years) we observed a different ratio of girls' and boys' tasks across the categories for older students. In our analysis of 65 graph tasks, girls were more successful than boys in only 3 tasks, 27 tasks were neutral (no statistically significant difference between genders) and in 35 tasks boys were more successful. (Part of the results can be seen in Table 2.) Thus, we can argue that boys (15–19 years old) are significantly more successful in solving graph problems than girls in the same age group. Similar results were obtained in [5]. All three girls' tasks do not show significant common attributes. One task contained finite automaton and the other two tasks were about a family tree, whereby in one it was shown as a picture and in the second one only a table description was given.

Our analysis of the contest problems indicates that tasks which were considered girls' tasks in younger categories (shorter text in assignment, concrete picture of graphs, one should do simple transition in graph or examine a small number of possibilities, or the answer is observable) were mostly neutral in categories for older students.

Abstract structures, discovering and mainly developing a strategy together with optimization tasks are usually boys' tasks, the same as it was in categories for younger students. However, such tasks are much more frequently used in categories for older students. Most of boys' tasks contained some graph algorithm (e.g. vertex cover, minimal spanning tree, graph search) or the starting point of the solution was not clearly shown and it was necessary to use a certain strategy (there were usually too many possibilities and it was inevitable to eliminate them

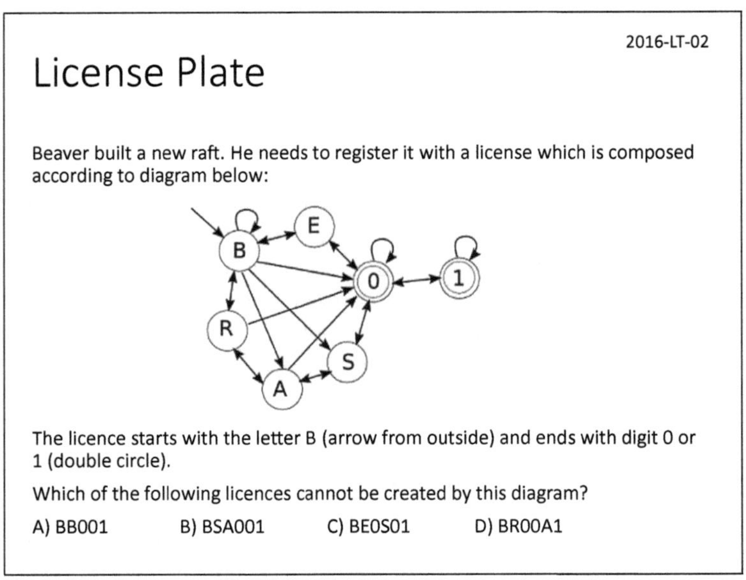

Fig. 1. Girls' task – Senior (17–19 years old), year 2016/17, girls' success rate: 82%, boys' success rate: 77%

or to go through them in a systematic way). Sample tasks can be seen in Figs. 1, 2, 3 and 4.

2012-FR-07

Beaver's teritory

The territory of Beaver is defined by the area he can reach from his home in less than 5 minutes.

The diagram below represents Beaver's home (the red circle), and the surrounding area. Every minute, Beaver can move from his current square to the squares above, below, to the left or to the right of his current square, but he cannot move into black squares.

Color every square of Beaver's territory, by clicking on all the squares he can reach within 5 minutes of his home. To help you keep track, you can change color by clicking on the rectangles on the right. Once a square is colored, you can click again on it to cancel.

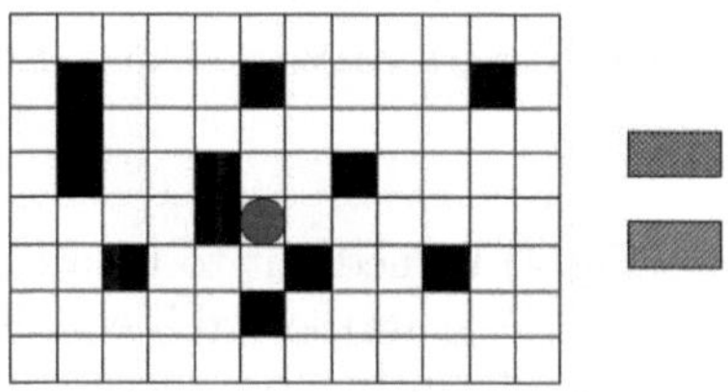

Fig. 2. Boys' task – Senior (17–19 years old), year 2012/13, girls' success rate: 23%, boys' success rate 42%

2016-PL-01

E-Friends

Friendship of 5 animals is shown in the picture and in the table below. The lines show which animals are friends with each other. The table records how many friends each animal has.

Animal	Number of Friends
beaver	4
rabbit	2
hedgehog	2
squirrel	1
skunk	1

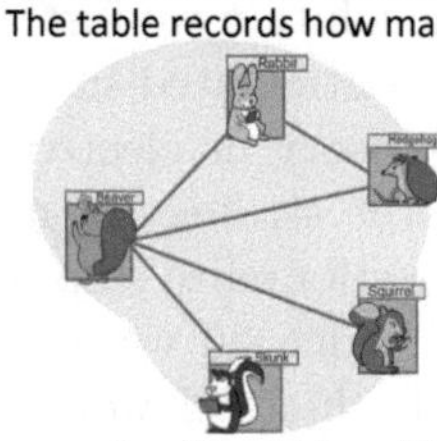

Which of the following **cannot** be the table recording friendships of 5 other animals?

A)

Animal	Number of Friends
fox	4
groundhog	2
chipmunk	2
turtle	1
snake	1

B)

Animal	Number of Friends
fox	4
groundhog	2
chipmunk	2
turtle	1
snake	1

C)

Animal	Number of Friends
fox	4
groundhog	2
chipmunk	2
turtle	1
snake	1

D)

Animal	Number of Friends
fox	4
groundhog	2
chipmunk	2
turtle	1
snake	1

Fig. 3. Neutral task - Senior (17–19 years old), year 2016/17, girls' success rate: 46%, boys' success rate: 46%

Table 2. Example of three neutral, boys' and girl' tasks. Columns girls and boys show task success rate. Pearson residuals are from left to right for boys' correct answer, boys without answer (not solved) and boys' incorrect answer. (Residual table is 2×3. Residuals for girls are the opposite numbers.)

	Task	Girls	Boys	Pearson residuals		
Neutral	2013-TW-04	45%	44%	−0.26	−0.273	0.43
	2015-IL-01	76%	76%	0.049	−0.979	0.43
	2016-PL-01	46%	46%	0.118	0.981	−0.56
Boy's	2012-FR-07	23%	42%	11.42	−2.698	−9.88
	2013-UA-01	47%	57%	5.513	−0.265	−5.67
	2017-RO-06	46%	56%	8.39	0.974	−8.6
Girl's	2016-LT-02	82%	77%	−3.13	1.353	2.84
	2012-HU-06	84%	82%	−2.16	0.695	2.05
	2011-IT-01b	53%	51%	−1.45	−1.944	2.45

The task Text Machine (Fig. 4) turned out to be a contradictory one as our analysis goes. Girls and boys (15–17 years) solved it equally successfully, however older boys (17–19 years) were significantly more successful than girls in the same age group. We are not able to explain this discrepancy, as this was not supposed to be a boys' task according to our criteria classification.

We were interested in understanding the reasoning behind this paradox. Hence, a slightly modified assignment (we changed the input word and re-drew the picture) was prepared and submitted for solving to high school students via an electronic questionnaire form. We shared the link to the questionnaire with a group of teachers that we collaborate with as part of our other research activities. Alongside the problem solution we further asked students to specify their grade, gender, whether they participated in the Bebras competition and if they have Informatics as a compulsory or elective module at their school. Students were also asked to describe the strategy or method they used to solve the problem.

We received 178 questionnaire responses, with 93 falling under the 15–17 age group (Junior) out of which 36 were girls, and 85 falling under the 17–19 age groups (Senior) out of which 44 were girls. 131 students answered correctly - the detailed solution success rates can be found in Table 3. The results show the same trend as what was previously observed from the data from the actual competition. Younger girls and boys had similar solution success rates. There were more incorrect answers among older girls. Based on their answers, younger students tried all possibilities whereas older students attempted to find a "better" strategy and (maybe therefore) often made a mistake. Some of the younger boys and older girls specified that they were guessing the correct answer. Usually these guessed answers were provided by students attending an Informatics module due to it being compulsory at their school and who have not taken part in the Bebras competition in the past. Hence we may conclude that these were

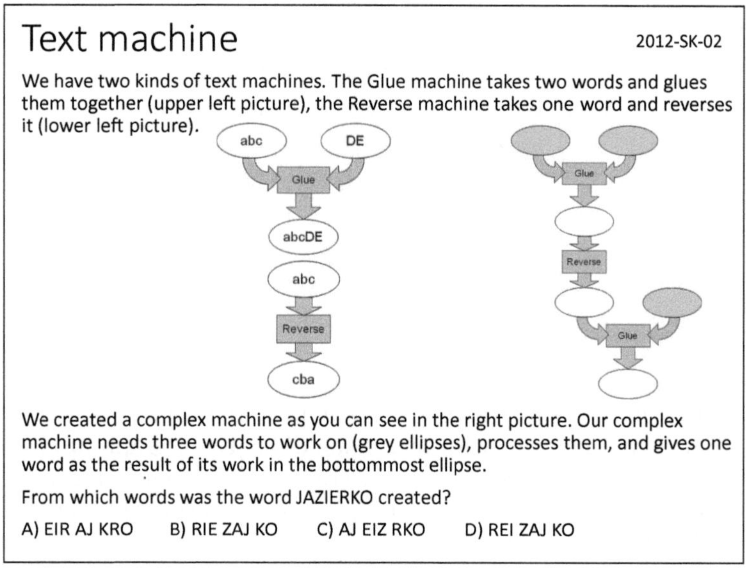

Fig. 4. "Contradictory task" - Junior and Senior (15–19 years old), year 2012/13, Junior girls' success rate: 60%, Junior boys' success rate: 59%, Senior girls' success rate: 60%, Senior boys' success rate: 65%

students with a lower interest in Informatics as a subject. Considering the results of the questionnaires we did not find a statistically significant difference between boys' and girls' solutions, however there was a significance in difference between Juniors' and Seniors' solutions in favour to Juniors, Pearson residual was 2.57.

5 Discussion

We have identified a few potential areas of weakness in relation to our study. We acknowledge that there may have been an instance of imprecision during the task coding process with a risk of an incorrect category being assigned to a given task. This may stem from an expansion of the research team, whereby new members were applying categories to the graph problems, however they did not partake in the creation of these categories. On the other hand, we see this as a form of verification of the criteria clarity. It was shown that criteria are applicable to tasks in the 15–19 years categories with minor adjustments only. Certain more complex data structures, graph problems and graph traversing algorithms (e.g. the Eulerian path, Hamiltonian path and articulation points), which would naturally be too advanced for younger students, were added to the sample as these were relevant with the higher competition category.

From the results it is strongly evident that boys are significantly more successful than girls as we see from 35 boys' tasks vs. 3 girls' tasks. The reasoning behind this discrepancy can be only assumed. Nevertheless, our criteria are still valid

Table 3. Answers of questionnaire

		Correct	Wrong
15–17 year	Girls	83,33% (30)	16,67% (6)
	Boys	80,70% (46)	19,29% (11)
	All	81,72% (76)	18,28% (17)
17–19 year	Girls	56,82% (25)	43,18% (19)
	Boys	73,17% (30)	26,83% (11)
	All	64,71% (55)	35,29% (30)

for some subsets of the tasks. While analysing the possible reasons behind such a large imbalance in successful solving of graph problems among boys versus girls, we came to a conclusion that with increasing difficulty of graph problems, girls' success in identifying a correct solution decreases. This occurred in younger student categories too, which further strengthens our belief that this hypothesis may be true. In [15] the author finds that girls "sought a deep, conceptual understanding of mathematics" and in latter work [16] she adds that girls need to know how, when and why methods work and without this understanding they can lose interest and motivation to complete the task. Even though the problems analysed in this paper are not purely mathematical (graph theory is mostly considered interdisciplinary), similar reasons could be causing girls' underachieving in harder tasks (which often required to create or uncover strategy, and thus involved methods which could not have been known by secondary school students).

Another potential explanation of our results could be the fact that the Junior category appears to be a significant step-up in terms of difficulty in comparison with the categories below. As part of their feedback to the organizers, contestants in the Junior category often mention lack of time as a constraint for completing the full set of tasks. Furthermore, motivation elements (e.g. fun story, pictures, etc.) are used less in assignments for Juniors and Seniors than they are in the lower categories. All of the aforementioned may cause a decreasing number of female participants in the higher categories of the competition, as well as a potentially decreased motivation to solve the tasks successfully. These findings serve as a strong incentive for us to ensure that in future rounds of the competition, we set tasks so that the motivational aspect or the formal assignment of the tasks does not discourage girls from partaking or adversely affect their results in the contest.

Based on a further analysis of the questionnaires we assume that the source of a lower success rate in higher categories could also be caused by the students' ambition to discover strategies that will enable them to reach the solution much faster than trying all of the possibilities. In these cases, students often choose a wrong answer possibly due to a combination of distractors among the four possible answers which tend to include some of the most frequent solution misconceptions.

The authors of this paper have personal experience teaching students of this age group and they have empirically observed that girls tend to be more often interested in subjects other than Informatics, and some of them get enrolled into the competition without any particular intrinsic motivation.

6 Conclusion

The main aim of our research was to apply our own categorization of graph tasks for pupils aged 7–14 years to tasks from categories Junior and Senior (students aged 15–19 years). Our intention was to verify the usability of our previous graph tasks categorization and we were also interested in finding out if the factors determining the gender relative task success from the lower categories could be applied to the higher categories. We analysed 65 graph tasks from Junior and Senior categories. Only a few new data structures and algorithms were necessary to add as subcategories, otherwise the categorization stayed identical. The methods/strategies students used in solving these tasks also remained largely the same and these mostly showed dependence with gender performance.

Out of the 65 analysed tasks, there were 3 tasks identified where girls' solution success rate was significantly higher, 27 tasks with no differences in success rates of girls and boys (we call this group neutral) and 35 task where boys where significantly more successful. It can be concluded that criteria for boys' tasks (i.e. tasks with significantly higher success rate in boys) are the same as for the lower competition categories that we studied before. Boys' tasks include abstract pictures, require good understanding of the given structure, however the structures may be relatively simple. On the other hand, girls' tasks and neutral tasks (in which there was no significant difference between boys and girls, but girls had slightly better results) show graphs with relationships, vertices or edges and are often labelled with real world objects. These properties are the same as properties of girls' tasks in the lower competition categories.

The big discrepancy between the numbers of girls' and boys' tasks could be explained by mostly boys' motivation being used in tasks. In lower categories the graph tasks were generally posed as easy, whereas in categories Junior and Senior graph tasks were usually posed as medium to hard, thus having lower overall success rate. Understanding differences between solution success rates of boys and girls at a deeper level could help us uncover possible weak spots in the Bebras competition. Therefore, we plan to further study the differences between boys and girls task success rates, specifically focusing on how task formulation could make the task success rate of girls and boys more alike.

As graph theory is an essential part of computer science, and many of its problem are posed as logical puzzles to secondary school students, we consider many of the analysed tasks applicable in school Informatics lessons. Therefore, the presented results can also help Informatics teachers create better materials, as setting only boys' tasks can demotivate girls and vice versa. We also plan to perform a further in-depth study of students' solution process in relation to graph problems, aiming to gain an even better understanding of why some problems are harder for girls or for boys, and perhaps going as far as identifying the source of their error tendency. We believe that with the right approach all individuals should be able to successfully solve graph problems and experience the beauty of graph theory.

Acknowledgement. We would like to thank referees for their comments on this paper. This research was supported by the VEGA 1/0797/18 and the UK/249/2018 grants.

References

1. Budinská, L., Mayerová, K., Veselovská, M.: Bebras task analysis in category little beavers in Slovakia. In: Dagiene, V., Hellas, A. (eds.) ISSEP 2017. LNCS, vol. 10696, pp. 91–101. Springer, Cham (2017). https://doi.org/10.1007/978-3-319-71483-7_8
2. Budinská, L., Mayerová, K.: Graph tasks in Bebras contest: what does it have to do with gender? In: Proceedings of the 6th Computer Science Education Research Conference, pp. 83–90. ACM (2017)
3. Hubwieser, P., Hubwieser, E., Graswald, D.: How to attract the girls: gender-specific performance and motivation in the Bebras challenge. In: Brodnik, A., Tort, F. (eds.) ISSEP 2016. LNCS, vol. 9973, pp. 40–52. Springer, Cham (2016). https://doi.org/10.1007/978-3-319-46747-4_4
4. Hubwieser, P., Mühling, A.: Playing PISA with Bebras. In: WiPSCE 2014. ACM, Berlin (2014)
5. Dagien, V., Pelikis, E., Stupurien, G.: Introducing computational thinking through a contest on informatics: problem-solving and gender issues. Informacijos Mokslai/Inf. Sci. **73**, 55–63 (2015)
6. Vegt, W.: Predicting the difficulty level of a Bebras task. Olympiads Inf. **7**, 132–139 (2013)
7. Vaníček, J.: What makes situational informatics tasks difficult? In: Brodnik, A., Tort, F. (eds.) ISSEP 2016. LNCS, vol. 9973, pp. 90–101. Springer, Cham (2016). https://doi.org/10.1007/978-3-319-46747-4_8
8. Shibley Hyd, J.: The gender similarities hypothesis. Am. Psychol. **60**(6), 581–592 (2005)
9. Ilomaki, L.: The effects of ICT on school: teachers' and students' perspectives: Ph.D. thesis, University of Turku (2008)
10. Švaříček, R., Šed'ová, K.: Kvalitativní výzkum v pedagogickéch vědách. Portál, Praha (2014)
11. Creswell, J.W.: Educational Research: Planning, Conducting, and Evaluating Quantitative and Qualitative Research, Enhanced Pearson eText with Loose-Leaf Version-Access Card Package (2015)
12. Chráska, M.: Metody pedagogického výzkumu. Grada (2007)
13. Agresti, A.: Categorical Data Analysis. 2nd edn. Willey (2002)
14. Wimmer, G.: Štatistické metódy v pedagogike. GAUDEAMUS, Hradec Králové (1993)
15. Boaler, J.: Paying the price for "Sugar and Spice": shifting the analytical lens in equity research. Math. Thinking Learn. **4**(2–3), 127–144 (2002)
16. Boaler, J.: Mathematical Mindset – Unleashing Students' Potential Through CreativeMath, Inspiring Messages and Innovative Teaching. Jossey-Bass (2016)

Differences Between 9–10 Years Old Pupils' Results from Slovak and Czech Bebras Contest

Lucia Budinská[1(✉)], Karolína Mayerová[1], and Václav Šimandl[2]

[1] Comenius University, 842 48, Bratislava, Slovakia
{lucia.budinska,mayerova}@fmph.uniba.sk
[2] University of South Bohemia, 371 15 České Budějovice, Czech Republic
simandl@pf.jcu.cz

Abstract. The education system in Czechia and the education system in Slovakia are very similar but while in Slovakia the education reform (together with the reform of the curriculum for Informatics) was implemented some years ago, in Czechia it is currently being prepared. Informatics in Slovakia is taught from primary school, unlike in Czechia where it only appears in some types of high school. Nevertheless, both countries organise the Bebras challenge - the international Informatics contest. Therefore, we were interested in the achievement of pupils from the two countries, expecting Slovakian contestants to be more successful. We analysed the results from both competitions, focusing on the age category Little Beavers/Mini, which includes younger primary school pupils. This paper presents a case study, in which we compare Year 4 contestants (9 to 10 years old) from the two countries. Their results from 15 tasks with the same form and wording (to minimise the influence of other factors) were studied. As it results from the study, Slovakian Year 4 pupils are more successful in digital literacy tasks and in algorithmic tasks and they are slightly more successful in statement logic tasks and in programming tasks. In logic tasks dealing with graph theory no significant differences between among Year 4 pupils in Slovakia and Czechia were revealed. For each from the 15 tasks' results, gender differences were also analysed - dividing tasks into three groups (girls' tasks, boys' tasks, neutral tasks), with almost the same distribution for both countries.

Keywords: Bebras contest · Informatics education
Slovakia vs. Czechia · Computer science · Gender differences
Country comparison

1 Introduction

Czechia is preparing to reform the provision of informatics by beginning to teach algorithms and programming in primary schools. This new teaching approach is very different from the current concept of teaching informatics at primary/lower

S. N. Pozdniakov and V. Dagienė (Eds.): ISSEP 2018, LNCS 11169, pp. 307–318, 2018.
https://doi.org/10.1007/978-3-030-02750-6_24

secondary level. Contrarily, a similar reform had already been introduced in Slovakia several years ago, first in 2008. The breadth and depth of informatics and its content is currently set out in the Innovated National Curriculum [1]. It requires schools to teach a minimum of 1 lessons of informatics a week in two years at primary level[1] and 1 lesson a week in four years at lower secondary level. Hence, informatics focuses not only on the teaching of digital literacy but also on the teaching of computational thinking and computer science basics from the earliest age groups.

At the moment, the informatics section of the Czech national Curriculum for primary and lower secondary schools completely fails to take into account computational thinking, including algorithms and programming [2]. Table 1 shows that schools are required to teach a minimum of one lesson per week throughout the primary level [2]. However, schools can decide to increase this number by using extra lessons they have at their disposal.

According to the curricular documents mentioned above, there are clearly great differences in the teaching of computational thinking at primary/lower secondary schools in the two countries. What unifies both countries in this respect is their participation in the Bebras contest, which aims to support computational thinking at all levels of education. Both countries organize the contest in several age categories, ranging from primary school pupils to high school students in their final year, for primary and lower secondary school categories see Table 1. In the past, the two countries have worked together to compare results from the contest [3,4]. The authors faced problems with implementation and incoherency of data, having compared data from the school years 2007/8 and 2008/9. Finland, Lithuania and Sweden also attempted to carry out an international comparison of results from this contest [5]. Their findings indicate that there was a slight mismatch between the difficulty level of the tasks used in the contest and students' actual abilities, as some tasks were too difficult. Their results also show that there is no difference in performance between boys and girls in this age group. A German research [6] reveals that there is no significant difference between the performance of girls and boys in younger age group in

Table 1. Differences between informatics in school in Slovakia and Czechia, together with respective Bebras categories

<table>
<tr><td colspan="2">Typical age:</td><td>6-7</td><td>7-8</td><td>8-9</td><td>9-10</td><td>10-11</td><td>11-12</td><td>12-13</td><td>13-14</td><td>14-15</td></tr>
<tr><td colspan="2"></td><td colspan="5">primary school</td><td colspan="4">lower secondary school</td></tr>
<tr><td colspan="2">Year:</td><td>1.</td><td>2.</td><td>3.</td><td>4.</td><td>5.</td><td>6.</td><td>7.</td><td>8.</td><td>9.</td></tr>
<tr><td colspan="2">Czech categories in Bebras contest</td><td colspan="3"></td><td colspan="2">Mini</td><td colspan="2">Benjamins</td><td colspan="2">Cadets</td></tr>
<tr><td rowspan="2">Number of years of informatics</td><td>Czechia</td><td colspan="4"></td><td>1</td><td colspan="4">1</td></tr>
<tr><td>Slovakia</td><td colspan="2"></td><td>1</td><td>1</td><td>1</td><td>1</td><td>1</td><td>1</td><td></td></tr>
<tr><td rowspan="2">Slovak categories in Bebras contest</td><td>until 2016</td><td colspan="2"></td><td colspan="2">Little Beavers</td><td colspan="3">Benjamins</td><td colspan="2">Cadets</td></tr>
<tr><td>from 2017</td><td></td><td colspan="2">Mini</td><td colspan="2">Little Beavers</td><td colspan="2">Benjamins</td><td colspan="2">Cadets</td></tr>
</table>

[1] Primary level in Slovakia includes Years 1 to 4 only.

this contest. However, the differences increase dramatically with the age of the contestants [6].

In the run-up to a reform in Czechia, it would be of benefit to ascertain to what extent and in which areas the competences of Slovakian primary pupils differ from the competences of Czech pupils in the same year group and if the differences in gender performance could be caused by informatics education. We assume the Czech and Slovakian versions of the Bebras contest could provide a suitable platform for such research, measuring pupils' results achieved in comparable tasks. The two countries have a very similar culture, both having very similar sets of values, a similar education system and school curriculum. It can therefore be expected that school teaching will be the real cause of particular differences in pupils' competences. Another reason for selecting this platform is the large number of participants.

2 Research Aims

Our main research aim is thus to ascertain whether there are differences in Czech and Slovakian primary pupils' achievement in the Bebras contest and, if so, in which areas of informatics. The impact of informatics teaching on Slovakian pupils as compared to Czech pupils, who are not taught informatics to such an extent, will be of interest to us. We are aware that this research problem should have a clear answer that the teaching of informatics positively influences contestants' achievement in Slovakia. However, this was not unanimously confirmed by some of the results of the pilot study examining this issue. For that reason, we decided to investigate this in more detail.

As stated above, there is no significant difference in boys' and girls' overall achievement in the Bebras contest in this age group. However, among older pupils, boys are more successful than girls. Therefore, our additional research aim is to ascertain whether informatics education influences the difference in boys' and girls' achievement in some task group from the Bebras contest. It is possible that informatics teaching has a significant positive impact on achievement of one gender while the other gender is not influenced to such an extent. The impact of informatics teaching on differences in Slovakian girls' and boys' achievements as compared to differences in Czech girls' and boys' achievements will be of interest to us.

Two hypotheses were created and tested using analysis of gathered data:

1. *Slovakian Year 4 pupils' achievement in identical tasks in the Bebras contest is statistically significantly higher than that of Czech pupils of the same age in identical tasks in the Bebras contest.*
2. *Differences in Year 4 boys' and girls' achievement in identical tasks are the same in both countries.*

3 The Bebras Contest

Both Czechia and Slovakia take part in the international Bebras contest, aimed at informatics and computational thinking [7]. This contest is designed for primary/lower secondary pupils and high school students and is organised into several age categories[2]. The contest is called *Bobřík informatiky* in Czechia and *iBobor* in Slovakia. Both countries base their contests on the common Bebras core but they differ in partial decisions. Take the list of tasks used in the contest for example - despite a database of contest tasks being available to be accessed by all countries, each country is entitled to use its own subset of tasks [3].

3.1 Primary Level Contest Categories

Category Mini is designated for pupils in year 4 and 5 in the Czech version of the Bebras contest and in the Slovakian version this includes Benjamin and Little Beavers categories. Year groups which each category is designated for can be found in Table 1. Regarding our research aim, it appears to be most convenient to compare the results of pupils in the Mini (CZ) and Little Beavers (SK) categories. These categories focus on the competences of primary pupils (as opposed to the Benjamins category, which could include tasks verifying the competence of lower secondary pupils) and have been running in the contest for several years (category Mini (CZ) since 2012 and Little Beavers (SK) since 2011). The following part provides a comparison of the characteristics which the categories Mini (CZ) and Little Beavers (SK) have in common and those they differ in.

3.2 A Comparison of Categories Mini (CZ) and Little Beavers (SK)

Category Mini (CZ) and category Little Beavers (SK) have the same 30 min time limit for solving 12 tasks. There are three types of tasks in both categories: (a) multiple choice with four possible answers, (b) short-answer tasks (e.g. the contestant enters a certain number), (c) interactive tasks, where the contestant e.g. might drag cards with pictures to designated positions.

Tasks in both categories are divided into three levels of difficulty - easy, medium and hard. Contestants receive a certain number of points for a correct answer, whereas points are subtracted for an incorrect answer. The contestant's score remains unchanged if he leaves the question blank [8,9].

There are differences between the contests as well, though. One of them concerns interactive tasks. In the Slovakian category Little Beavers, interactive tasks often have a lower success rate. Interactivity offers pupils more possible answers, thus making it more difficult. The conception of interactive tasks in the Czech category Mini is to use them more as a help and they may even comprise answer checks, increasing their success rate as opposed to the Slovakian ones. Another difference is also linked to answering. Although contestants in both

---

[2] http://bebras.org/?q=structure.

countries have the right to decide whether to answer a question or not, the way of leaving a question blank differs. In the category Mini (CZ), the contestant can check a special box *Leave blank*, whereas he can cancel his choice by pressing a *Delete answer* button in the category Little Beavers (SK). Results indicate that this is a significant difference and Czech contestants decide to leave a question blank much more often than Slovakian contestants. Another difference between the categories is in the way contestants register for the contest. In the Mini (CZ) category, contestants register for the contest themselves just before the contest is about to start by using a so-called school code provided by the contest's school coordinator. This code is common for all contestants in one school. In the Little Beavers (SK) category, the school coordinator registers a contestant for the contest. The selection of contestants is left to the coordinator and often depends on the school's capacity possibilities. If the school does not have a sufficient number of computers available, coordinators must select pupils who will compete.

4 Research Method

4.1 Choice of Comparable Tasks in the Mini and Little Beavers Categories

Tasks that were mutually comparable or the same were selected for research from the Czech Mini category and the Slovakian Little Beavers category. The selection of such tasks was carried out qualitatively. As each task is named differently in the Czech and Slovakian version, task content had to be compared. Comparison was done by means of qualitative coding [10] of the wording of the assigned task. Tasks were analysed by each researcher separately then jointly discussed. We focused on task type, wording of answer choices including incorrect answers (so-called distractors) and accompanying graphics. Tasks were not compared only within one year of the contest but throughout the duration of the contest from 2012 to 2017. By doing this, 15 tasks were identified as seeming to be fully comparable and being used in both the Czech Mini category and the Slovakian Little Beavers category. Along with them, another 9 tasks were identified as seeming to be comparable to a certain extent, differing only slightly (for example different distractors or different question). Particular care needs to be taken in interpreting comparisons of contestants' achievement and for that reason these 9 tasks will not be used for further analysis. Only the 15 identical tasks will be explored.

4.2 Data Processing

The Bebras contest already has its own task categorization, but we have formed our own categorization during the last year, based on tasks from Slovakian contest, to suit our research [11]. In the first phase of this research, i.e. during the qualitative phase, tasks were placed into individual categories from our own categorization. A brief description of the categories follows:

- **Digital literacy** tasks – focusing on verifying knowledge and skill that prove a good software or hardware understanding;
- **Logical** tasks subdivided into:
  - **graph** tasks – pupils work with a graph structure (net, binary tree, etc.), carrying out complicated or less complicated operations on it;
  - **statement** tasks – by examining statements, pupils have make judgements as to which answer is correct. Statements may be in the form of text or picture.
- **Algorithmic** tasks – pupils observe a procedure, algorithm or set of instructions to guide them to find the result of operating with objects or information. It is usually a matter of dynamic action.
- **Programming** tasks – pupils either create or interpret a program in the form of simple commands, cards or icons.

4.3 Sample of Participants

Having identified appropriate tasks, the second part of the research was approached. This was of a quantitative character. The sample of research participants was made up of contestants from the Mini(CZ) and Little Beavers(SK) categories, i.e. Year 4 primary school pupils. This is the only primary year group that competed in the same category in both Slovakia and Czechia. From the Czech Mini category, all contestants who had not been explicitly excluded by the school coordinator of the contest (for example due to cheating) and had registered themselves as Year 4 pupils became participants. It can be said that this is a case of nonprobability sampling, more specifically convenience sampling [12]. In the Slovakian Little Beavers category, it was all the contestants from Year 4 who had responded to at least one task. This was close to double the number of participants than in the Czech contest. Numbers of contestants are given in Table 2.

Table 2. Number of Year 4 girls and boys in Slovak and Czech competition for each analysed year

Contest year	Mini (CZ)		Little Beavers (SK)	
	Boys	Girls	Boys	Girls
2017	2 407	2 157	4 714	4 309
2016	3 037	2 714	4 280	3 940
2015	1 719	1 568	4 267	3 923
2014	1 503	1 348	3 794	3 288
2013	1 040	901	3 597	3 186
2012	1 152	470	3 020	2 697

4.4 Data Analysis

Data needed for the analysis were gained from databases. Although both countries use their own database, differences between them are not significant for data analysis. Table 2 indicates the considerable differences in numbers of Year 4 pupils, i.e. our research participants. For that reason, we searched for a statistical method that would take the differing sample sizes into account and prove to be suitable for comparing the two distinct groups. For each task there was created contingency table with two nominal variables, country (SK or CZ) and answer (correct, incorrect, none) and we seek to find out if the results in the task is dependent on the participants' country. Therefore, we decided to use the Chi square test of independence [13,15] for each task which we identified as fully comparable. While chi-square test provides little information about the nature of the association [15], Pearson residuals were also computed. See example in Table 3[3]. If there turned out to be significant differences in the zero response option between Slovakian and Czech Year 4 pupils, we decided to analyse only the number of correct and incorrect responses, excluding pupils who had not completed the task from the analysis.

Table 3. Example of country differences statistical analysis in task 2016-SK-10

2016-SK-10	Correct answer	No answer	Incorrect answer	Total
CZ pupils	1 833	559	3 359	5 751
	(1 943)	*(347)*	*(3 461)*	
	(−3.98)	*(15.27)*	(−3.58)	
SK pupils	2 886	285	5 049	8 220
	(2 776)	*(497)*	*(4 947)*	
	(3.98)	(−15.27)	*(3.58)*	
Total	4 719	844	8 408	13 971

Our null hypothesis for each of the 15 observed tasks was: There is no difference in the response given for the chosen task between Year 4 pupils at Czech and Slovakian primary schools. This was set at level $\alpha = 0.025$, providing χ^2 was smaller than 5.02 (according to statistical tables for $(2-1)(2-1) = 2$ degrees of freedom) [14]. In other instances, we dismissed the hypothesis, because test showed a strong evidence of an association (i.e. results of contestants are dependent on a country they come from).

In the analysis of differences by gender, we examined the differences separately for each country, which means there were two nominal variables – gender (boys, girls) and answer (correct, incorrect, none) and the same method as above was used. We investigated if answer is independent of gender of Year 4 pupils separately for each of the identical tasks. The Pearson residuals [15] were used

[3] Second column contains estimated expected frequencies for testing independence, third column contains standardized Pearson residuals.

to enable us to identify the level of significance the differences occurred at. If the score was between 1.96 and 2.93, the difference was at level $\alpha = 0.05$. If it was between 2.93 and 3.3, it was at level $\alpha = 0.01$. If it was higher than 3.3, the significance of the difference was at level $\alpha = 0.001$.

5 Results

Thanks to appropriate statistical methods, we were able to work with an unequal number of participants, Slovakia having involved many more Year 4 primary school pupils than Czechia. Presumably, this is related to the compulsory teaching of computational thinking in Slovakian primary schools. Despite such a disproportion, pupils from both countries achieved the same results in several tasks, even considering their decision not to answer a question, something which Czech pupils would have been more likely to do otherwise. In several tasks, however, statistically significant differences between countries in the number of correct and incorrect answers were disproved, but there were statistically significant differences in non-response. All these tasks shall be considered as tasks with the same result in both countries.[4]

5.1 Differences Between Countries

The results of the analysis show that there is no statistically significant difference between Czech and Slovakian contestants' answers in 5 tasks. On the contrary, there is a statistically significant difference in 10 tasks (Czech pupils having done better in 1 of them). It follows that Slovakian pupils' achievement in most tasks is statistically significantly higher than that of Czech pupils. To better understand what categories of tasks these statistically significant differences came up in (or did not come up in), the tasks were split into categories from our task categorization, see Fig. 1.

As Slovakian Year 4 primary school pupils (as opposed to Czech pupils in the same year group) had informatics lessons, the observed results can lead us to assume that the teaching of informatics in Slovakian primary schools: (1) is likely to influence digital literacy competences, algorithmic competences and programming abilities of Year 4 primary school pupils, (2) has a possible influence on pupils' statement logic ability, (3) is unlikely to have influenced pupils' graph logic abilities.

5.2 Differences by Gender

The quantitative analysis described in Sect. 4.4 enabled us to observe the statistically significant difference to determine whether girls or boys had achieved better results in each particular task. If a common characteristic can be identified in certain tasks in this respect, it is stated. The analysis shows that the

[4] Complete results of all analysed tasks can be obtained from www.edi.fmph.uniba.sk/~budinska/issep2018-appendix.pdf.

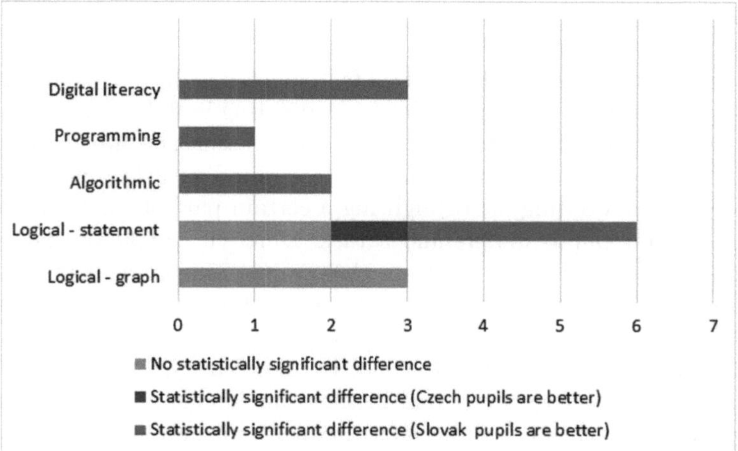

Fig. 1. Numbers of tasks by category and existence of statistically significant difference in answers

outcome of 10 tasks out of 15 was the same in both countries, as far as gender is concerned – i.e. either boys achieved better results in both countries; or girls did; or boys and girls achieved the same results in both countries. It follows that differences in boys' and girls' achievement in most tasks are the same in both countries. More precisely it can be stated that:

- In both countries:
  - boys achieved better results in two tasks;
  - girls achieved better results in four tasks (those four tasks being from the Statement logic category);
  - girls and boys achieved the same results in four tasks.
- boys and girls achieved the same results in 5 tasks in one country, while either girls or boys achieved better results in the other country (each option occurred).

In addition to the above mentioned findings, the following facts were also observed: (1) there were more significant differences between boys and girls in Slovakia, (2) tasks where pupils achieved the same results in both countries had differences in results according to gender, (3) tasks in which either Slovakian pupils or Czech pupils did better had the same outcome as far as gender is concerned.

Observed result did not show some trends or tendencies that gender performance is dependent on task category (apart from 4 aforementioned girls' tasks). Ten tasks with same results can lead us to assume that the teaching of informatics in Slovakian primary schools does not influence the differences in boys' and girls' competencies.

6 Discussion

The qualitative analysis revealed several factors among the Slovakian and Czech tasks that may have led to very similar tasks differing in difficulty. These include different wording of tasks, different distractors, different accompanying graphics and different ways of formulating answers. Despite a task leading to the same outcome, different wording or highlighting a certain part of the task may cause differences in how pupils understand a task. Different distractors may confuse several pupils if they contain answers that pupils are often misled by. If the distractors do not reflect such behaviour, the correct answer can often be revealed by way of trial and error. The use of varying task types is also related to this, where multiple choice tasks might be set in one country, but interactive tasks may be set or short answers required in the other. In some short-answer tasks, there were cases where one of the most frequent wrong answers was not even included in the four available options. The most visible differences were in tasks with accompanying graphics. The Crispy Cake task (see Fig. 2) is one example where signposts providing links to the next ingredient in the recipe made the Slovakian version more user-friendly than the Czech one, which only displayed pictures with a different background.

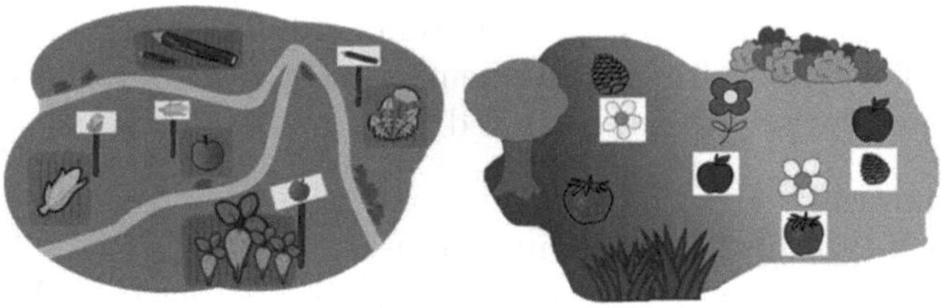

Fig. 2. Comparison of graphics for the same task in the Slovakian version (on the left) and the Czech version (on the right)

The research participants themselves are another factor which could have influenced the results of our research. Bearing in mind that computational thinking is not to be taught at primary schools as part of the Czech National Curriculum for informatics, it could be assumed that primary school pupils often enter the contest in Czechia due to their enthusiastic teachers. This might be a lower secondary informatics teacher (who does not usually teach at primary level and therefore does not directly influence primary pupils' abilities) or it could be the primary teachers themselves whose enthusiasm leads to pupil involvement. To distinguish these two cases, we traced how many Czech schools took part in only the Mini category of the Bebras contest (which is intended for primary school pupils). According to the findings for years 2012 to 2017, there are always around a quarter of schools which only took part in the Mini category; the remaining three quarters of schools that took part in the Mini category also competed in the Benjamin and Cadet categories, which are intended for lower secondary pupils. On the other hand, teachers in Slovakia can, due to capacity problems, enroll only pupils with better school results or high intrinsic motivation.

Pupils' achievement in the statement logic category may have been influenced by mathematics education in both countries, while in Czechia there are more schools that use different, non-traditional ways of teaching mathematics.

Our research could be considered to have been limited by the low number of quantitatively analysed tasks, of which there were only 15. The low number of analysed tasks was a result of efforts to eliminate the influence of differing task difficulty, which has been discussed above. For that reason, only tasks that were fully comparable were included in our quantitative research. To generalize the results, more task should have been studied.

7 Conclusion

The aim of our article was to ascertain whether and in which areas of informatics there are differences in Czech and Slovakian primary school pupils' achievement in the Bebras contest. We compared the success rate of Slovakian and Czech pupils in those contest tasks that were identical in both countries. 15 such tasks were found in 2012 to 2017 contests. Due to differences in targeted age groups in primary school contest categories in the two countries, we narrowed the analysis of results down to Year 4 primary school pupils. Our own form of categorisation was then carried out on the analysed tasks [12]. Slovakian Year 4 pupils are more successful in digital literacy and algorithmic tasks, slightly more successful in statement logic and programming tasks. In tasks involving graph logics, there is no difference between Czech and Slovakian Year 4 pupils. The question here is to what extent graph logics should be included in an appropriate scope and form in the primary school informatics curriculum, this area having turned out to be the weakest of the areas researched in both countries.

If we are to focus on difference by gender, 10 tasks out of 15 had the same outcome in both countries, i.g. either boys did better in both countries; or girls did; or boys and girls achieved the same results in both countries. Slovakian pupils' results showed significant differences in the number of right and wrong answers, whereas these differences were mainly in right answers in Czech pupils' results.

We find the recommended improvements for the creators of contest tasks useful. They are to look more closely at the wording of tasks in Slovakian or Czech and harmonize the wording of tasks in both countries. It would also be possible to prevent double translation from English by arranging to cooperate on the translation, Czech and Slovakian syntax being much more similar as compared to English.

At the very end, let us state that the teaching of informatics in Slovakia is perceived positively by us, both from the point of view of achievement in the contest and in terms of the number of contestants. However, we believe that Czech pupils will also manage to achieve similar or even better results after the informatics teaching reform has been implemented.

Acknowledgement. We would like to thank all referees for their comments on this paper. This research was supported by grant VEGA 1/0797/18 and grant UK/249/2018.

References

1. Innovated National Slovak Curriculum: Informatics (2014). http://www.statpedu.sk/sites/default/files/dokumenty/inovovany-statny-vzdelavaci-program/informatika_nsv_2014.pdf. Accessed 29 May 2017
2. Framework education program for elementary education in CZ. www.nuv.cz/uploads/RVP_ZV_2017_verze_cerven.pdf. Accessed 12 June 2018
3. Tomcsányi, P., Vaníček, J.: Implementation of informatics contest Bebras in Czechia and Slovakia. In: Mechlov, A., Valcha, A. (eds.) Information and Communication Technology in Education (2009)
4. Tomcsányi, P., Vaníček, J.: International comparison of problems from an informatics contest. In: Proceedings of the Information and Communication Technology in Education, pp. 219–223 (2009)
5. Dagiene, V., Mannila, L., Poranen, T., Rolandsson, L., Stupuriene, G.: Reasoning on children's cognitive skills in an informatics contest: findings and discoveries from Finland, Lithuania, and Sweden. In: Gülbahar, Y., Karataş, E. (eds.) ISSEP 2014. LNCS, vol. 8730, pp. 66–77. Springer, Cham (2014). https://doi.org/10.1007/978-3-319-09958-3_7
6. Hubwieser, P., Hubwieser, E., Graswald, D.: How to attract the girls: gender-specific performance and motivation in the Bebras challenge. In: Brodnik, A., Tort, F. (eds.) ISSEP 2016. LNCS, vol. 9973, pp. 40–52. Springer, Cham (2016). https://doi.org/10.1007/978-3-319-46747-4_4
7. Bebras competition. http://www.bebras.org. Accessed 14 April 2018
8. Competition rules in SK. http://ibobor.sk/pravidla-Bobrici.php. Accessed 14 April 2018
9. Competition rules in CZ. https://www.ibobr.cz/o-soutezi/23-pravidla-souteze. Accessed 14 April 2018
10. Švaříček, R., Šedová, K.: Kvalitativní výzkum v pedagogických vědách. Portál, Praha (2014)
11. Budinská, L., Mayerová, K., Veselovská, M.: Bebras task analysis in category little beavers in Slovakia. In: Dagiene, V., Hellas, A. (eds.) ISSEP 2017. LNCS, vol. 10696, pp. 91–101. Springer, Cham (2017). https://doi.org/10.1007/978-3-319-71483-7_8
12. Creswell, J.W.: Educational Research: Planning, Conducting, and Evaluating Quantitative and Qualitative Research, Enhanced Pearson eText with Loose-Leaf Version-Access Card Package (2015)
13. Chráska, M.: Metody pedagogického výzkumu. Grada (2007)
14. Values of the Chi-squared distribution. MedCalc Software. https://www.medcalc.org/manual/chi-square-table.php. Accessed 1 May 2018
15. Agresti, A.: Categorical Data Analysis, 2nd edn. Willey, Hoboken (2002)
16. Recommended curriculum for class 4. http://www.vuppraha.cz/wp-content/uploads/2011/03/Doporucene-ucebni-osnovy-predmetu-CJL-AJ-a-M-pro-zakladni-skolu.pdf. Accessed 1 May 2018

Problem Solving Olympics: An Inclusive Education Model for Learning Informatics

Roberto Borchia[1], Antonella Carbonaro[2(✉)], Giorgio Casadei[2], Luca Forlizzi[3], Michael Lodi[2,4], and Simone Martini[2,4]

[1] Istituto Tecnico Industriale "Q. Sella", Biella, Italy
antonella.carbonaro@unibo.it
[2] Dip. di Informatica–Scienza e Ingegneria, Università di Bologna, Bologna, Italy
[3] Dip. di Ingegneria e Scienze dell'Informazione e Matematica, Università dell'Aquila, L'Aquila, Italy
[4] INRIA Sophia-Antipolis, Valbonne, France

Abstract. The paper presents the *Olimpiadi di Problem Solving*, a mild and inclusive competition aimed to promote computational thinking and general problem-solving in Italian schools. We describe motivation, teaching strategies behind the initiative, as well as its structure, organization and give some sample of the problems proposed to students. We also present some data that show the broad participation of Italian schools to the initiative, and a preliminary analysis of the results obtained by the students in the last 5 editions, which suggests that the competition fosters deep learning of computational thinking knowledge and skills.

Keywords: Inclusive competitions · Computational thinking Problem-solving

1 Introduction

The *Olimpiadi di Problem Solving - Informatica e pensiero computazionale nella scuola dell'obbligo* ("Problem Solving Olympiad - Informatics and computational thinking in compulsory education") (henceforth: OPS) is an initiative of the Italian Ministry of Education, University and Research (henceforth: MIUR), to foster both problem-solving and team-working skills in a single action.[1]

Usually in the education world the expression "Olympics of X" means a competition aimed to single out and promote exceptional skills at the individual level in the age of 16–18. However:

- OPS are mainly training activities: the core of OPS are the training contests, followed by two rounds of competitive contests (regional and national);
- OPS are mainly team-work activities;

[1] The project guide is entrusted to the Directorate-General for Education Guidelines (*D.g. per gli ordinamenti scolastici e per l'autonomia scolastica*) of MIUR.

S. N. Pozdniakov and V. Dagienė (Eds.): ISSEP 2018, LNCS 11169, pp. 319–335, 2018.
https://doi.org/10.1007/978-3-030-02750-6_25

- OPS are aimed at all the compulsory education age range; activities are organized at three *levels*: the last two years of primary school (4–5 grade), lower secondary school (6–8 grade), the first two years of upper secondary school (9–10 grade);
- OPS are aimed to reach all students, and not only exceptional ones: each school is encouraged to participate with as many teams as possible (for each level);
- OPS are gender neutral: each team is required to have people of both genders.

It was noted by Nobel laureate Carl Wieman [11] that competitions outside of school fail to improve STEM education; since 2008 MIUR has promoted OPS as training/competition *within* the school system to pave the way for a more widespread introduction of Informatics in curricula and to foster the learning of effective competences for general problem-solving.

The remainder of this paper is organised as follows. Section 2 discusses the variety and diffusion of contests focusing on Informatics organized worldwide in the last decades. Section 3 describes main features and goal of OPS, and the structure of the competitions. Furthermore, it proposes some examples of standard problems and presents how the training and the contests, at the different levels, are organized. Section 4 presents some data about participation in the initiative and a preliminary analysis of the results obtained by the students in the last editions, to evaluate the training effect on students on their problem-solving skills. Section 5 proposes the question of digital gender gap and evaluates the involvement of girls and boys in OPS. Finally, some considerations close the paper.

2 Promoting Informatics Through Competitions

Several contests focusing on Informatics have been organized worldwide in the last decades. They vary in design, difficulty levels, and type of audience they cater to.

Such events mainly result from two attitudes of mind: one focused in selecting particularly talented students and another one aimed at spreading the basic concepts of the discipline to a vast audience of students. This section only shares a few examples to show the variety and diffusion of such events. See [1] and [8] for recent reviews about contests, classification criteria and a selection of existing online programming contests.

ACM International Collegiate Programming Contest (ICPC)[2] is the most sought after programming competition in the world. Every year, the ICPC contests include contestants from over 2000 universities and colleges from across the world. The contestants receive problems that they have to solve, providing a program written in a widespread programming language such as C, C++ or Java.

[2] https://icpc.baylor.edu/.

IEEE also proposes a contest, namely the IEEEXtreme Programming Competition[3], which lasts 24 h and is dedicated to teams of students. All the teams receive a set of programming problems and as for ACM-ICPC, they have to solve the greatest number of problems.

Among the events targeted to secondary school students, the International Olympiad in Informatics (IOI)[4] is the most popular worldwide. Like in ICPC, contestants are challenged to provide, in few hours, programs written in mainstream programming languages that solve problems of algorithmic nature. Unlike ICPC and IEEEXtreme Programming Competition, IOI is an individual contest. A lot of countries do have online programming contests to make the selection for their national team to be sent to the IOI. Just to mention some of them: USA Computing Olympiad (USACO), Italian Olympiad in Informatics, France-IOI, Indian Computing Olympiad (ICO), French-Australian Regional Informatics Olympiad (FARIO). All those contests are following the same philosophy as the IOI, encouraging young talent from high schools to programming challenges.

The Bebras contest [4] is a competition organized on an annual basis in several countries since 2004. In the past few years, the number of the Bebras participants has been notably growing. The contest has been spreading over 40 countries involving various activities, e.g. several rounds of the contest, discussion on Informatics topics, task solving seminars, teacher workshops, and task developing events. The Bebras challenge has been developed for all primary and secondary school pupils. The second full week of November is the official time for the Bebras challenge (first round) in participating countries. Several countries have established a second round of the Bebras challenge, usually at the end of January or beginning of February, and it is dedicated for the best participants of the first round challenge.

It is a well-known consensus in the community around Informatics contests that the difficulty of these contests progressively increases, as observed, for example, by Verhoeff et al. in [10]. Kelevedjiev and Dzhenkova [6] mention that in many countries the age at which children start with programming is already as low as ages 11 to 12. Thanks to this early start, the set of topics used in contest tasks is growing. Kiryukhin in [7] describes the development of the Russian Olympiad in Informatics: since 1995 the focus in programming contests started to shift from “implement a correct algorithm” towards the much harder “implement a correct algorithm that is as efficient as possible”. As a result, and even more so than previously, only the best students are involved in these kind of competitions. All the other students lose the opportunity to develop, in an engaging way, fundamental problem-solving knowledge and skills required for living and working in our society, having applicability in the entire sphere of economic, social, political and cultural life. The dissatisfaction with this state of affairs motivated MIUR, back in 2008, to start OPS with the goal to spread problem-solving and computational thinking across all the compulsory

[3] https://www.ieee.org/membership/students/competitions/xtreme/index.html.

[4] http://ioinformatics.org/index.shtml.

education age range, which in Italy goes up to grade 10. Moreover, OPS are aimed to reach all students, and not only exceptional ones.

3 OPS: An Inclusive Education Model for Learning Informatics/Computational Thinking

3.1 Main Features and Goals

The main goal of OPS is to disseminate problem-solving skills and computational thinking [12] in Italian education.

Since no explicit provision of problem-solving teaching is present in the Italian guidelines for primary and secondary education (while *computational thinking* has been recently introduced, for the moment only as a transversal competence), OPS promote activities in this area with a trans-disciplinary approach, trying to captivate teachers of various disciplines. Being activities directly offered to classes as contests, they are appealing and have an immediate impact on the participating youngsters [3]. However, no real successful participation is possible without support and training from local teachers. This implies that teachers should develop and promote curiosity, interest and consensus in their own classes. Teachers themselves are therefore stimulated to engage in the game even if skills and competences needed are foreign, at least explicitly, even for them.

The collaboration is recognized as one of the most effective means of spreading problem-solving skills and also allows for significant motivational and relational benefits. For this reason, the OPS foster collaboration by offering mainly team work activities. In designing the teaching strategy for OPS we have taken into account the dual nature of team competition (competitive and collaborative); actually this strategy offers many possibilities when facing a heterogeneous group of student [9].

Problem-solving as interpreted in OPS is intended as one of the most effective paths to the acquisition of computational thinking attitudes. For this purpose, one component of OPS is the ability to understand simple formal structures (such as terms, lists and graphs), and to follow, simple (and less simple) algorithms expressed in semi-formal languages, thus forming the background on which an explicit teaching of programming and Informatics may be based. This component is further strengthened (in grades 9 and 10) by administering some problems that require the execution of (easy) calculations to be repeated a number of times so large to make the solution infeasible unless one writes and executes a program.

Another important feature of the OPS, which differentiates it from most of the similar initiatives, is the fact that they favor incremental learning by offering explicit training sessions for both students and teachers during every entire school year. After each training session, the scientific committee of the OPS releases the solutions and the comments to the solutions for the various exercises proposed. Both the involved students and the teachers judge in a very positive way the usefulness of the solutions for the incremental acquisition of skills.

We may therefore summarize the main goals of OPS:

- offer explicit problem-solving training to students at the compulsory education age range (including team-working skills);
- involve the teachers in such a way that they also acquire and consolidate the needed skills (to use in their everyday teaching);
- use semi-formal setting and pseudo language to embed problem solving in the context of computational thinking with the perspective of (eventually) acquiring programming skills;
- offer training sessions during the entire school year to both students and teachers.

3.2 Joining the OPS

Participation is on a voluntary basis. Italian teachers are expected to participate in "additional activities" as well as to teach their discipline. MIUR promotes various initiatives that qualify as additional activities: OPS is one of them. In September/October, MIUR issues the annual bylaw for OPS, with the dates of the contests. Since participation in the project is the responsibility of the scholar institution, teachers have to negotiate adhesion with the principal.

Involved teachers (often in mathematics, but also in other disciplines) form teams within their classes; again participation of the students is voluntary, but very often discussion about OPS problems, assignment of exercises and study of problem-solving techniques are extended to the whole class and are not limited just to the team(s): this fact is the main added value of OPS.

3.3 Structure of Competitions

At the beginning, OPS were exclusively based on contests where students receive problems that are asked to solve in a well-defined time frame. Students participating to contests of this kind are divided in three *levels*: (i) grades 4–5; (ii) grades 6–8; (iii) grades 9–10.

In the first editions, OPS consisted in three series of *team contests*, one for each level. Each team is made up of 4 students, possibly with gender equality. In the last few years two more series of contests of the same nature have been added, for individual students of the second and third levels. In each OPS edition, all series have the same number of contests, usually six (see Table 1). All the contests except the last two are *training contests*, which means that the score achieved by a team (or an individual) is only provided as a feedback. The last two contests are *competitive*: the first one is used to select, for each series, the best teams (or individuals) of each Italian region, while the final one decides the winners.

The team contests consist of 12 problems: the amount of work to be done in the allotted time (120 min for the training contests and 90 min for the competitive ones) to solve them largely exceeds the effort that can be expected from a single participant; hence planning, collaboration, specialization and team-working are necessary. The individual contests consist in 8 slightly simpler problems, in the same amount of time (120 and 90 min).

The given problems are prepared by means of a controlled process, with a strict time schedule, which involves two committee: the *problem editors* (mainly university researchers with experience in computer science education) define the problems and write texts and commented solutions, while the *problem reviewers* (mainly selected teachers with experience in the OPS topics) check for errors and difficulty.

More recently, along with the above "classic" OPS, that remain the core contests of the competition, other team contests have been added as "side" activities:

- *Coding* (grades 1–5 and 6–8), where students engage with creative programming activities, realizing a project on a topic chosen by the committee, with suitable environments (e.g. Scratch);
- *Programming* (grades 9–13), where students solve a complex programming task (e.g. implement a graph algorithm);
- *Making* (grades 1–5, 6–8, 9–13) where student realize a physical project using electronic boards (e.g. Arduino) on a topic chosen by the committee.

In the following we refer only to "classic" OPS, with particular focus on team contests, the original and distinguishing contests of the OPS.

3.4 Topics

OPS proposes at the three levels the same kinds of problems, with differences (among the levels) in size or abstractness. Each year five o six topics are chosen: from these, "standard" problems come up. In the last school years the chosen topics where: formal deduction from a set of rules, paths in a maze or in a chessboard, knapsack, hierarchies, graph covering, graph traversal, cryptography, subsequences and reading/tracing of procedures written in a pseudo-code.

A semi-formal syntax about terms, lists, strings is used in problems and answers. Additional topics are comprehension of a text (in Italian) and non "standard" problems, each time of a new kind (and often formulated in English), to stimulate creativity and the ability to deal with new situations.

3.5 Examples of Standard Problems

Examples of a "standard" problem are shown in Appendix - Figs. 4, 6 and 8 (originally in Italian, translated for this work).

The first problem was part of the second training for primary school: problems, on the same subject (graphs), in following contests were gradually more complex, and the solution had to be chosen among up to a dozen of paths. The second problem was part of the fifth training for secondary school. The third problem was part of the final contest for lower secondary school: as you can see it involved a lot of programming structures (e.g. variable assignments, vectors, while loops, if-then-else), introduced gradually during the training contests.

3.6 Commented Solutions

A key feature of the OPS is that, along with the solution to each problem, after each contest, "comments" are provided; often this section makes up an outline for the in-depth study and analysis that teachers are invited to follow along with the students. In this way, knowledge and skills are spread among teachers and students. As you can see in the examples in Appendix, as the level and the difficulty grows, the comments become much longer and elaborate.

3.7 The Training Contests

In a training contest, on a fixed date, problems are proposed on a secure web platform and are accessible for a suitable interval of time (e.g. 9:00 – 17:00). Schools connect to the platform when they deem suitable (within the given interval of time) and, under the supervision (and the guarantee of fairness) of local teachers, the teams and the individual students participate to the contest. Problems are administered and their solutions should be entered within 120 min from the first access. During the contest each team/individual is allowed to use any additional material as it sees fit (books, notes, additional PCs, browsing the Internet, etc.), the ability to quick retrieve and organize relevant information being one of the key components of effective problem-solving. When the access to problems is closed, correct solutions and comments are made available; then answers are evaluated and teams ranked.

Three to five different training contests are organized in this way from November to March: the difficulty of the problems is gradually increasing. Then, for each level, each school selects teams and individual students for a regional competition; the winning teams and individual students of each region (20) meet in Cesena for the final competition.

3.8 The Final Contest

The final contest is a fierce competition; around twenty teams and twenty individual contestants for each level are invited in Cesena. The final contest takes place in the Department of Computer Science and Engineering, University of Bologna, under control of a Jury and with strict rules.

1. Each team has the same type of workplace available, which includes one workstation.
2. Teams are allowed to bring books, notes and an extra PC.
3. Participants are not allowed to communicate with other persons during the contest, except with members of their own team and the Jury.
4. Use of hardware other than watches, medical equipment, the PC and the provided workstations is not allowed.
5. A team can be disqualified for any activity that jeopardizes the contest.
6. When a team presume that a problem is ambiguous or incorrect, the team can ask a clarification to the Jury. The Jury will respond and if the answer is relevant to all teams, the Jury will communicate the answer to all teams.

The Jury determines the final team ranking as follows.

- Teams are sorted by the number of accepted solutions, in non-increasing order.
- When two or more teams have the same number of accepted solutions, these teams will next be sorted by total time, in ascending order. The total time is the time passed between the start of the contest and the time at which the last solution was submitted.
- There is no penalty for unsolved problems.

4 Participation and Results

OPS were proposed, organized and developed with the guidance of several "working hypotheses", among which those that participation to OPS: (i) fosters and develops problem-solving skills, both at the personal and the class level; (ii) enhances the success level in standardized performance tests, like Italian INVALSI, or OECD's PISA; (iii) is an effective way to induce computational thinking habits in the students; (iv) facilitates the introduction of explicit, disciplinary teaching of computer science. Although we have qualitative indicators confirming these hypotheses (especially the feedback from instructors who have proposed OPS for more than 10 years), available data are not sufficient to discuss here all these far-reaching goals. We report only on the first one.

The first 10 editions of the OPS have recorded a noteworthy participation, both in terms of students and teachers involved, as shown in Table 1. These data show that the OPS are among the most successful initiatives, in terms of participation, for the diffusion of computational thinking in Italy.

Table 1. Participation to the first 10 editions of the OPS

School year	Number of rounds	Teachers	Students
2008/2009	3	550	10200
2009/2010	5	500	9850
2010/2011	6	400	7400
2011/2012	6	630	11400
2012/2013	4	880	16500
2013/2014	6	400	15100
2014/2015	7	500	12000
2015/2016	6	830	16700
2016/2017	6	850	23357
2017/2018	6	730	22225

4.1 First Results

The comparative impact of OPS on participants is difficult to establish due to a selection effect: in fact, participation in OPS is voluntary, so we expect that the best and most innovative teachers are better represented among those participating in OPS. Moreover, we cannot rule out that participating teams are made up of some of the smarter students in their classes. This selection bias is difficult to asses and avoid in data analysis; a comparison of the educational careers of those who have participated in OPS and students from another sample is an extremely delicate task (see Sect. 6).

On the other hand, the training effect on students is clearly visible, especially because problems, from contest to contest, become progressively more difficult. Some examples can be given, by considering the average scores obtained by the teams who participated in the project during the last 5 editions[5] on algorithmic problems, which are the most indicative of computational thinking competencies. For grades 4–5 (see Fig. 1) the trend, in each edition, has no marked fluctuations. This, related to the progressive increase in the difficulty of the problems, indicates a development of the problem-solving skills of the pupils. It can be noted that in the second or third contest there is often a slight lowering of the performances, which corresponds to the introduction of problems that are considerably more difficult than those proposed in the first contest of each edition.

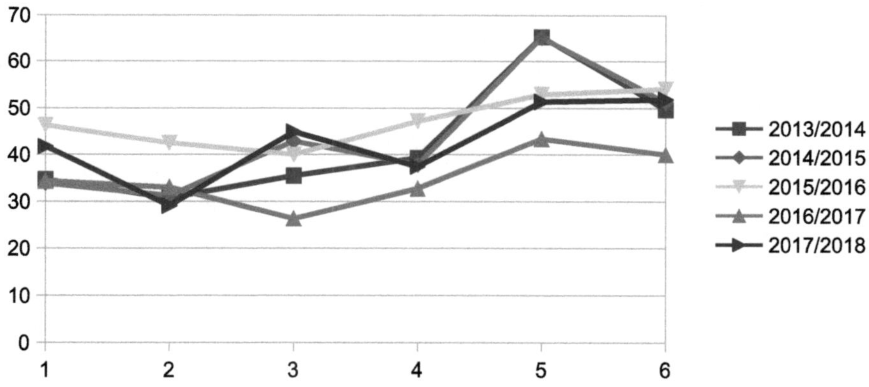

Fig. 1. Average score in algorithmic problems for grades 4–5

Data for grades 6–8 (Fig. 2) highlight, in most of the editions, two contests in which the scores decrease, which is explained by a more rapid increase in the difficulty of the problems in this level. The trend, however, remains positive and strong growth in the two competitive contests.

At the third level (Fig. 3) we register more differences between one edition and another. This can be explained by the fact that the set of problems proposed

[5] These editions are comparable since all of them had 6 rounds, with the only exception of 2014/15. For that specific school year, we noted that two consecutive intermediate rounds had very similar results at all levels, so we normalized it to 6 rounds too.

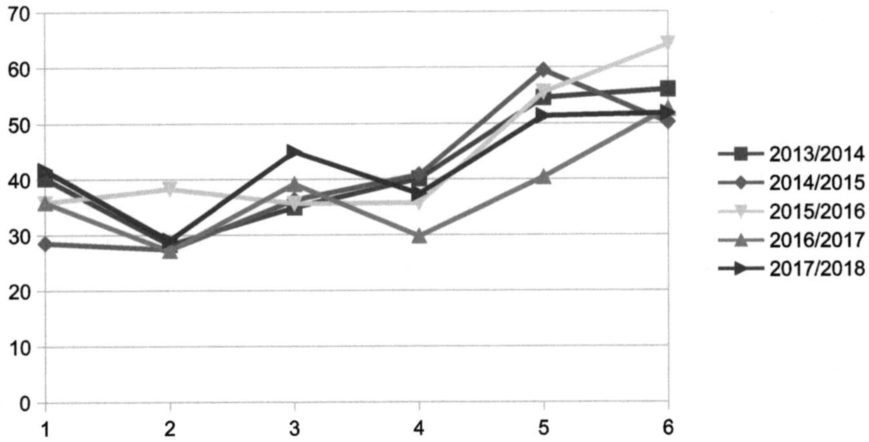

Fig. 2. Average score in algorithmic problems for grades 6–8

at this level changes more from year to year. In any case, the trends are similar to those shown in the other levels, with a more marked improvement in correspondence with the competitive contests, typical of the greater commitment that students to this level of maturation can profuse.

Another impact difficult to assess is on teachers; it was noted that the competitions (at least in computer science) encourage teachers to learn more to support their students; currently, besides a qualitative confirmation, it does not seem possible to measure this effect.

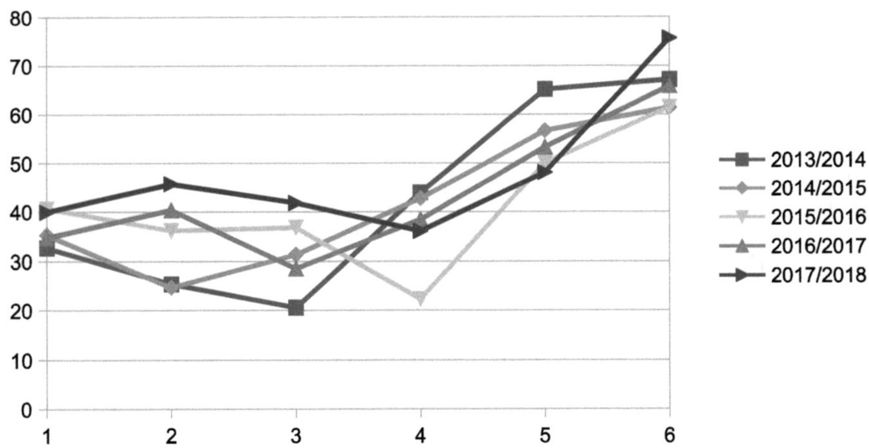

Fig. 3. Average score in algorithmic problems for grades 9–10

5 OPS and Gender

A recent European Parliaments Policy Department for Citizens Rights and Constitutional Affairs study attempts to reveal the links between the different factors which prevent women from having equal access to digital technology [5]. While ICTs are recognised as having the potential to promote gender equality and womens empowerment, a digital gender divide has been identified, whereby women access and use ICTs less than men. Increasing the number of women in ICT-related education could be a policy consideration. Women may also have more to gain from ICT than men, in time, freedom and opportunities. Addressing the underlying causes of digital gender disparities is vital, as dealing with the symptoms without fighting the causes would lead to superficial measures.

We attempted to evaluate the involvement of girls and boys in OPS by calculating the number of participants per gender on the three school levels. The goal is to try to understand at what time the disinterest of the girls towards the computer disciplines occurs, so as to suggest the best time to propose remedies. We evaluated the numerical participation of girls and boys on the three levels of school. It is almost equal in elementary school; then the number of girls involved in competitions concerning first and second grade of secondary school drastically decreases. These results are similar to those found in another, independent MIUR initiative to promote Informatics and computational thinking [2].

Based on our experience, the measures that can be taken to combat digital gender gap must be implemented in the early years of elementary schools. Doing it later can be useless because the factors that cause the digital gender gap have already pushed away the female component.

6 Conclusions

We presented OPS, an Italian initiative to disseminate problem-solving skills and computational thinking activities with a trans-disciplinary approach. OPS are targeted at all the compulsory education age range and are aimed to reach all students, and not only exceptional ones. In the past few years, the number of participating students and teachers has been notably growing, as a testament to the validity of the initiative.

Among the advantages of the OPS approach we may cite: interactivity, collaborative work inside the group, active participation, challenge versus duties, and motivation for the students to explore their own topics, on problem-solving skills and computational thinking, to support the challenges. The best feedback obtained is probably the feeling of the involved students and teachers.

Preliminary data show an increase in scores of algorithmic problems from the first contest to the last in each school year, at all levels. Given that the difficulty of problems increases from one context to the next, this may indicate an increase in algorithmic problem solving skills in pupils.

Large direct feedback from the teachers involved in OPS makes evident a positive correlation between participation to OPS and general performance of students (as measured in standard tests, like PISA). This has been a working hypothesis of our work since the firsts editions of OPS. Turning this hypothesis into a scholarly acceptable evaluation is one of the main directions of our current work on the evaluation and assessment of OPS.

Appendix

See Figs. 4, 5, 6, 7 and 8.

PROBLEM

In a map there are towns and roads between them: this situation can be abstracted with a *graph* in which *nodes* represent cities and the *arcs* represent roads. An arc (road) of the graph can be described by a term like:

arc(n4,n8,5)

which means that there is an arc between node n4 and node n8 and its length is 5.

Two nodes connected by an arc are said *adjacent*.

A *path* is (described by) a list of adjacent nodes. A *simple* path does not contain repeated nodes.

Consider a graph described by the following list of terms:

arc (n1,n5,3) arc(n3,n1,6) arc(n2,n4,2)
arc(n6,n3,6) arc(n5,n2,5) arc(n4,n6,1)

Draw the graph and determine:

1. the list L1 describing the *shortest* path between n1 and n6 and calculate its length K1;
2. the list L2 describing the *longest* simple path between n1 and n6 and calculate its length K2.

Enter your answer in the following table.

L1	
K1	
L2	
K2	

Solutions:

L1	[n1, n5, n2, n4, n6]
K1	11
L2	[n1, n3, n6]
K2	12

COMMENTS TO THE SOLUTION

After a few attempts the graph can be drawn in such a way that the arcs do not intersect, as in the following figure.

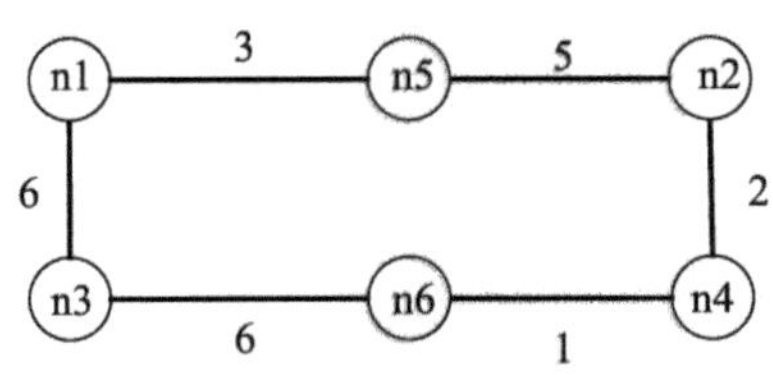

Note that a major difficulty lies in drawing the graph so that the arcs do not intersect; it is necessary to proceed by trial and error, by placing nodes in various ways until the drawing is satisfactory; *this can be done in many ways*.

Note also that the lengths that appear in the terms (that represent roads) are *not* proportional to those of the arcs of the graph (that are "*symbolic*" straight line segments).

The graph describes a "circuit" and it is easy to see that the possible paths between n1 and n6 and the relative lengths are:

path	length
[n1, n5, n2, n4, n6]	11
[n1, n3, n6]	12

Fig. 4. Example of a standard problem (team contest, primary school, grades 4–5, second training contest

PROBLEM

A *deduction rule* can be described by a term like

rule(3,[a,b],c)

which means that the rule (number) 3 permits to deduce **c** from (that means knowing) **a** and **b**; **c** is said *consequent*; **a** and **b** are said *antecedents*.

Rules can be chained for complex *deduction procedures*; a deduction procedure can be described by a list of rule numbers.

Consider the following rules:

rule(1,[f,g],h)	rule(2,[q,f],b)	rule(3,[p,q,c],a)	rule(4,[m,p],q)
rule(5,[a,b,c],d)	rule(6,[m,p],f)	rule(7,[p,h],c)	rule(8,[m],p)
rule(9,[e,f],c)	rule(10,[f,b],i)	rule(11,[c,e],r)	rule(12,[f,s],e)
rule(13,[e,t],b)	rule(14,[a,u],f)	rule(15,[e,b],v)	rule(16,[u,d],t)

Determine:

1. the list L1 that describes the shortest procedure to deduce **a** knowing **c**, **m**;
2. the list L2 that describes the shortest procedure to deduce **c** knowing **m**, **g**;
3. the list L3 that describes the shortest procedure to deduce **d** knowing **m**, **g**;

Criterion for the lists. List the (numbers of the) rules in the order that corresponds to the sequence of application of the rules: the first element (from the left) of the list must be the number that corresponds to the first rule to be applied; if there are several rules that apply at the same time, give priority to the one with lower number.

L1	
L2	
L3	

SOLUTION

L1	[8,4,3]
L2	[8,6,1,7]
L3	[8,4,6,1,2,7,3,5]

COMMENTS TO THE SOLUTION

To solve the problem, you can use the backward (or top-down) method, that is start from the unknown and try to find a rule to derive it. If there is a rule whose antecedents are all known (the data), the solution is found; otherwise you look for a rule whose antecedents are not *all known* and you continue to look for rules to derive the unknown antecedents (that appear in the rule).

For the first question, it is immediate to check that **a** appears as consequent only of rule 3 which has as its antecedent **p**, **q** and **c**: the first two are unknown, the last is given; **p** is deductible only by the rule 8 directly from **m** (given); **q** is deductible only with rule 4 from **m** (given) and **p**, just deduced. The procedure is illustrated by the tree in the figure below. The list L1 is [8,4,3].

For the second question, we immediately verify that **c** appears as the consequent in the rules 7 and 9. The rule 9 has antecedents **e** and **f**, both unknown; **e** is deductible by the rule 12 which has antecedents **f** and **s**: the latter can not be deduced with any of the given rules. Therefore, to deduce **c**, only rule 7 is usable; this rule has antecedents **p** and **h** both unknown; **p** is deductible only with rule 8 directly from **m** (given); **h** is deductible only with rule 1 from **f** (unknown) and **g** (given). At the end **f** is deductible by rule 6 from **m** (given) and **p** (already deducted) or by rule 14 from **a** and **u** (both unknown): it is clear that we must choose the first alternative. The proceedings is illustrated by the tree in the figure below. The list L2 is [8,6,1,7].

Fig. 5. Part A

To answer the third question, we immediately verify that d appears as a consequent only in rule 5 that has antecedent **a**, **b** and **c** all the unknowns:

- to deduce **a** can be used partially what was said for the first question; rule 3 has antecedent **p**, **q** and **c**: **p** is deductible only by rule 8 directly from **m** (given); **q** is deductible only by rule 4 from **m** (given) and **p**, just deducted. **c** is deductible by the rule 7 or by rule 9: the first should be applied because of the two antecedents, **p** and **h**, one has already been deducted; **h** can be deducted only by rule 1 that has antecedents **f** (unknown) and **g** (given); **f** is deductible only by rule 6 that has antecedents **m** (given) and **p** already deducted;
- **b** can be deducted only by rule 2 which has antecedent **q** and **f**: both already deducted;
- **c** has already been deducted .

The overall process is illustrated by the tree to the right of the figure below. The list L3 is [8,4,6,1,2,7,3,5]: to build it is essential to keep in mind the criterion for the list given in the problem.

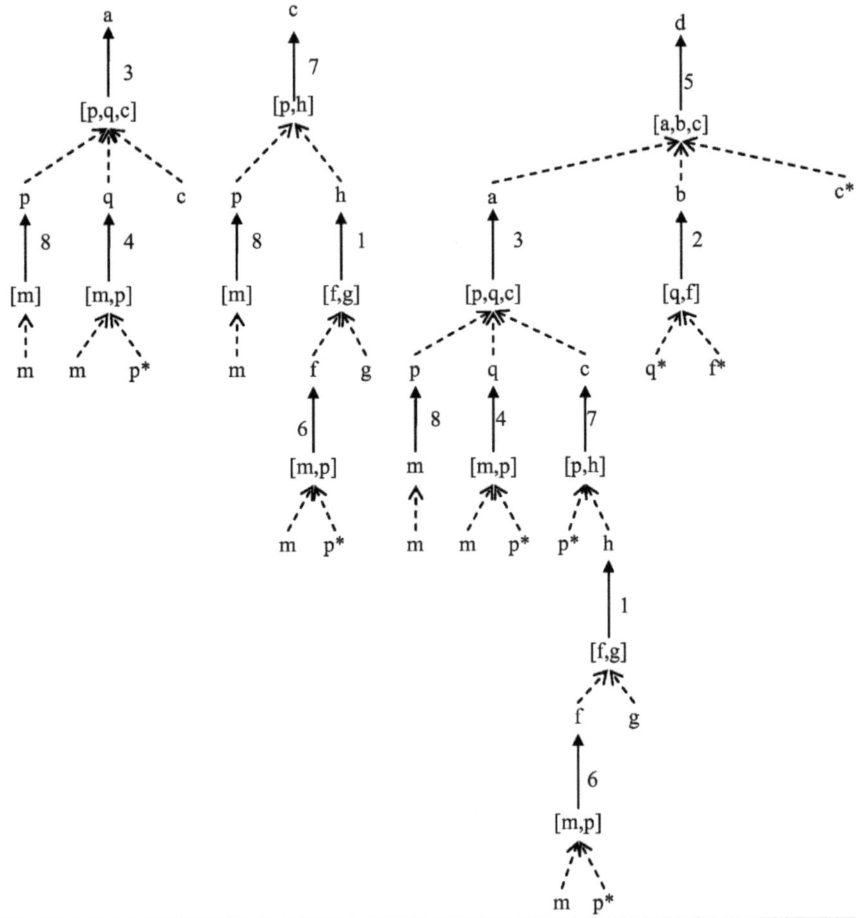

Fig. 6. Part B. Example of a standard problem (secondary school, grades 9–10, fifth training contest)

PROBLEM

Consider the following procedure ALFA.

```
procedure ALFA;
variables I, N, K, S integer;
variables A(1:8) vector of integer;
A ← [1,12,23,34,45,56,67,78]
I ← 1;
N ← 50;
K ← 0;
S ← 0;
T ← 0;
while K = 0 do;
        if A(I) < N
                then   S = S + A(I);   I = I+1;
                else   K = I;
        endif;
endwhile;
while K = 0 do;
        T ← T + A(K);
        K ← K + 1;
endwhile;
output I, K, S, T;
endprocedure;
```

Determine the output values of I, K, S, T and enter them in the following table.

I	
K	
S	
T	

SOLUTION

I	6
K	9
S	115
T	201

Fig. 7. Part A

COMMENTS TO THE SOLUTION

The program calculates in S the sum of the values of the vector A that are lower than N, and in T the sum of the values greater (or equal) to N. The variable I will indicate the index (the position) of the first value greater than or equal to N in the vector.

The values of I, K, S before the first while loop and after each of the iterations of the (body of) cycle are shown in the following table.

	Value of I	Value of K	Value of S
before the loop	1	0	0
after the first iteration	2	0	1
after the second iteration	3	0	13
after the third iteration	4	0	36
after the fourth iteration	5	0	70
after the fifth iteration	6	0	115
after the sixth iteration	6	6	115

The values of K and T before the second while loop and after each of the iterations of the (body of) cycle are shown in the following table.

	Value of K	Value of T
before the loop	6	0
after the first iteration	7	56
after the second iteration	8	123
after the third iteration	9	201

Fig. 8. Part B. Example of a standard problem of pseudo-code reading (lower secondary school, grades 6–8, national final contest

References

1. Combéfis, S., Wautelet, J.: Programming trainings and informatics teaching through online contests. Olymp. Inform. **8**, 21–34 (2014)
2. Corradini, I., Lodi, M., Nardelli, E.: Computational thinking in Italian schools: quantitative data and teachers' sentiment analysis after two years of "programma il futuro". In: Proceedings of 2017 ACM Conference on Innovation and Technology in Computer Science Education, ITiCSE 2017, pp. 224–229. ACM, New York (2017). http://doi.acm.org/10.1145/3059009.3059040
3. Dagienė, V.: Sustaining informatics education by contests. In: Hromkovič, J., Královič, R., Vahrenhold, J. (eds.) ISSEP 2010. LNCS, vol. 5941, pp. 1–12. Springer, Heidelberg (2010). https://doi.org/10.1007/978-3-642-11376-5_1
4. Dagienė, V., Futschek, G.: Bebras international contest on informatics and computer literacy: criteria for good tasks. In: Mittermeir, R.T., Sysło, M.M. (eds.) ISSEP 2008. LNCS, vol. 5090, pp. 19–30. Springer, Heidelberg (2008). https://doi.org/10.1007/978-3-540-69924-8_2
5. Davaki, K.: The underlying causes of the digital gender gap and possible solutions for enhanced digital inclusion of women and girls. Technical report, Policy Department for Citizen's Rights and Constitutional Affairs - European Parliament's Committee on Women's Rights and Gender Equality (2018)

6. Kelevedjiev, E., Dzhenkova, Z.: Tasks and training the youngest beginners for informatics competitions. Olymp. Inform. **2**, 75–89 (2008)
7. Kiryukhin, V.M.: The modern contents of the Russian national olympiads in informatics. Olymp. Inform. **1**, 90–104 (2007)
8. Raman, R., Vachharajani, H., Achuthan, K.: Students motivation for adopting programming contests: innovation-diffusion perspective. Educ. Inf. Technol. (2018). https://doi.org/10.1007/s10639-018-9697-3
9. Verdú, E., Lorenzo, R.M., Revilla, M.A., Regueras, L.M. (eds.): A New Learning Paradigm: Competition Supported by Technology. CEDETEL, Sello Editorial, Madrid (2010)
10. Verhoeff, T., Horváth, G., Diks, K., Cormack, G.: A proposal for an IOI syllabus. Teach. Math. Comput. Sci. **4**(1), 193–216 (2006)
11. Wieman, C.: Applying new research to improve science education. Issues Sci. Technol. **29**(1), 25–32 (2012). http://www.jstor.org/stable/43315691
12. Wing, J.M.: Computational thinking. Commun. ACM **49**(3), 33–35 (2006). http://doi.acm.org/10.1145/1118178.1118215

Socio-psychological Aspects of Teaching Informatics

Evaluation of Learning Informatics in Primary Education
Views of Teachers and Students

Johannes Magenheim[1(✉)], Kathrin Müller[1], Carsten Schulte[1], Nadine Bergner[2], Kathrin Haselmeier[3], Ludger Humbert[3], Dorothee Müller[3], and Ulrik Schroeder[2]

[1] University of Paderborn, Paderborn, Germany
{johannes.magenheim,kathrin.mueller,carsten.schulte}@uni-paderborn.de
[2] RWTH Aachen University, Aachen, Germany
{bergner,schroeder}@cs.rwth-aachen.de
[3] University of Wuppertal, Wuppertal, Germany
{khaselmeier,humbert,dmueller}@uni-wuppertal.de

Abstract. How does learning about informatics in primary education unfold in the eyes of teachers and their students? We report on the evaluation results from a distributed project in Germany (North Rhine-Westphalia) and some implications of these findings for future improvements. Three modules for informatics in primary education and a corresponding concept for teacher training were developed collaboratively by researchers and practitioners. The project was assessed with methods of formative and summative evaluation. The first results indicate that teaching and learning of informatics in primary education are possible. It is regarded overall as rewarding and exciting, but it was difficult for primary school students and teachers as well to discern the bigger picture of informatics education and thus to relate the topics taught and learned to everyday experiences.

Keywords: Informatics education · Teacher training
Primary education

1 Introduction

Informatics Education at primary level gets increased attention in the last years, see e.g. recent publications at this and related conferences. In general, these publications give the impression that it is possible to teach about informatics at this level. Discussion unfolds on topics like e.g. unplugged approaches, teacher education, and other issues. Tim Bell et al. suggest that one issue for teachers

Supported by North Rhine-Westphalia Ministry of Education.

S. N. Pozdniakov and V. Dagienė (Eds.): ISSEP 2018, LNCS 11169, pp. 339–353, 2018.
https://doi.org/10.1007/978-3-030-02750-6_26

is discerning the so called Bigger Picture. In [1] they give an example of the missing big picture:

> For example, in some of the professional development with the teachers using black and white cards to represent binary values, teachers have asked which colour is used for 0 and 1. The real concept is that some sort of convention must be agreed on, rather than rote-learning a rule about this particular abstraction.

The quote hints at a general problem for teachers, who usually are not trained in the subject, to teach informatics: Their own limited or even wrong conceptualization of the subject, leading to shallow approaches to teaching and learning, like rote-learning isolated rules. Even if they were aware of the relevance of the rule, the problem probably would persist, as teaching in primary education should not only be construed as introduction to an academic field of study, but linked to everyday experiences – like everyday actions or problems children might encounter, or in connection to informatics systems they get in touch with – but how should children be able to link topics learned at school to these experiences if teachers aren't aware of them? In this paper we report on experiences from a distributed, three years lasting (2016–2018) project, with three universities, 30 primary schools and 37 primary school teachers from the state of North Rhine-Westphalia (Germany) and about 450 students involved. Three modules and corresponding materials for teacher training were developed, covering three different topic areas: data representation; robotics and programming; cryptology. They were taught mainly according to a CS-unplugged learning approach. The article presents the project, evaluation methods and initial evaluation results obtained with qualitative methods (content analysis of teachers' answers) and quantitative methods (factor analysis of ratings) in students' answers. The first results indicate that teaching and learning about informatics in primary education are possible. It is regarded overall as rewarding and exciting, but it was difficult for primary school students, and teachers as well, to discern the bigger picture of computing education and thus to relate the topics taught and learned to everyday experiences. Based on the findings we discuss implications for teacher education and future initiatives to support informatics education in primary schools.

2 Project Overview

The project started in 2015 for three years in cooperation of three universities and the local ministry of education. Main goal of this R&D-project was to investigate the implementation of informatics in primary schools. For this purpose, scientists and active teachers developed general informatics skills, which are already supposed to dominate primary school children. Using an unplugged teaching approach, informatics can be (initially) taught independent from technical equipment of schools (computers, tablets, software). Supplementary materials will also make use of computing technology for optional later transfer. The modules cover the three different topic areas: (1) data representation, (2) robotics and programming and (3) cryptography. Furthermore, a corresponding concept for teacher training was developed and put into practice with the teachers involved in the project.

The modules are based on a curricular model for informatics [2] which need to be adapted for students in the age of 8–10 to define a proper competence model for primary level. The underlying constructivist didactic concept supports discovering learning with hands on materials which relate to everyday experience of the students. The instructional design is influenced by various existing projects such as CS unplugged [5] which specifically relates enactive, iconic, and symbolic representations and allows for action-based learning. The didactic design is based on findings of primary education. The modules pick up aspects of the children's lifeworld and answer children's questions.

The main goals of the project are

- to form a concept of breaking down principles in informatics to describe competencies to be acquired by students of primary education,
- to develop teaching materials and guidelines for the prototypical lessons, and
- to model further education for teacher training regarding primary teachers.

The topics of the modules are independent from each other and can be taught in any sequence. Each module will cover 6–8 lessons. At each site the concepts, materials and teaching guidelines were developed by scientists and primary teachers who contributed with their experience in primary school didactics, and also pre-tested the first versions in their classes. Based on the feedback from the first test runs, the modules were iteratively improved. All teachers tested the modules developed at the other locations and provided comprehensive feedback. Alternatives regarding the didactical and methodological design were developed.

In a second phase, teachers from about 30 schools were trained, and tested the modules with their students. Thus, along with the teaching concepts and materials one and a half day seminars for primary teachers were developed for each module. During these seminars primary teachers acquired the core aspects of informatics, the required technical as well as pedagogical knowledge and competences for teaching each of the modules. Through these trials under different conditions, further improvements and alternative implementations were created. All three modules were thus revised several times and expanded with new ideas. Overall, the concepts and materials are well transferable to other schools.

In the following you find a short description of the three modules.

2.1 Module 1: Digital World

It is the goal for this module to enable primary school teachers to explore the digital world together with their students and understand the principles on which it functions. The use of data should be understood by primary students to at least a rudimentary degree. Typical everyday questions like "How can a computer save thousands of photos?" and "How does a video fit through a cable?" are answered. Abstract concepts in informatics like digitalization are visualized through lightbulbs (on and off). Binary numbers build the baseline for digital data storage and transfer, as well as error detection and thus 0 and 1 make the connecting element of this module.

2.2 Module 2: How Does a Robot Work?

Main focus of this module is on first programming concepts. Students learn that robots work with commands and that these commands have to be exact. They "program" a paper robot with simple commands and control it over a playground. As an enactive support commands are printed on jigsaw pieces as in block based programming languages like Scratch. During their work with a research journal the students become familiar with parameters and simple control structures. Another focus of this module is the fundamental working principle of a robot as an interplay of sensors, actors and a program (IPO-principle).

2.3 Module 3: I Have a Secret

Using the example of cryptology, in this module a central topic area is opened up for primary school students. The module provides an introduction to the basic standard algorithms of encryption, based on primary school didactics and informatics pedagogy. Under the headline "I have a secret" the teaching framework around the well-known protagonists Alice, Bob and Eve offers an attractive scene for historical secrecy, code usage and symmetric encryption. Two basic encryption concepts are made accessible to the children: transposition and substitution. They are approached without the use of computer systems, just by using enactive and haptic material like, for example, wooden sticks, paper and pencil.

3 Evaluation Setup

For the setup of the evaluation it is important to have the overall project structure in mind: It was a distributed project with three universities as core development hubs. Each facility had also a group of assorted teachers from local schools, and administered short teacher trainings to their groups before the teachers then tested the developed teaching concepts and materials in their classes. While each project partner was responsible for one module (including the teacher training material), each partner was also responsible for teacher training and observing the trials of the imported modules from the other two partners.

In a cyclic development and evaluation approach the materials and concepts were refined in a cyclic approach. First, each site developed a teaching unit together with local teachers. These were then locally tested; e.g. tried in a classroom. Then also locally a corresponding teacher training and supplementary material for the teachers about the unit was developed. Then feedback on these materials from the other two sites were included. Second, the teacher trainings were distributed to the other sites, so that each site tried the two external teacher trainings and the local teachers then taught all three modules in their classrooms (ideally, not all teachers could incorporate all modules, but only one or two). In a third phase the experiences were used to refine the teaching material, and then the refined units were again tested (the first phase is not ended by the time of writing).

Although this overall project structure is aligned to cyclic educational design research as proposed and described by e.g. [3], the systematic collection of feedback data was challenging, in part because resources for the evaluation of the project were granted only after beginning of the project, so that the approach and the infrastructure for data collection had to developed just in time. A concept for the formative evaluation of the project was therefore difficult to implement and was only available in principle in a late project phase.

A more systematic approach to data collection and formative assessment was possible only for the three project phases highlighted in the enumeration above. This was done by observing and note-taking by the local partners who collected feedback from the local teachers on their experiences with teaching the material developed in the project. In addition, teachers filled out a feedback-questionnaire developed as part of the evaluation concepts. For summative evaluation a set of questionnaires for students was developed:

1. General Pre-Test: Interests, motivation, attitudes
2. Specific Post-Test for each module: Module-specific interests and comprehension
3. General Post test: Interests, motivation, attitudes (some comprehension questions)

The questionnaires contained general items for motivation, self-efficacy, and interest in informatics topics, as well as test items for students learning success. The questionnaires for teachers mainly focus on their classroom experience in teaching informatics and their evaluation of teacher training

Since the approved test instruments for the general pre-test were only available relatively late, they were used at different times at the specific locations, possibly only during or after the first run of the module. In this paper we present first results of the data obtained at students level. These data are related to students interests and attitudes towards general aspects of informatics and to their thematic motivation as well as to their module-specific interests and their content-related comprehension. Furthermore, results of the evaluation of the teacher survey by means of qualitative data are presented, which focus on the teachers' reflection on the three modules after completion of their lessons as well as on their further training in the project and their perceived qualification needs.

4 Evaluation – Students' Results

4.1 Students Attitudes, Interests and Motivation

A total of 450 data records were evaluated, 207 of them female, 222 male and 21 not specified. The average age is 9.15 years. 61 students are in the second class, 110 in the third class and 138 of them in the fourth class. 141 participants of the survey haven't entered the class level. The data were entered partly with paper questionnaires distributed in the classroom and partly directly from the classroom online by the students. To assess the students' learning interests, motivation and attitudes, we applied statements with a five-level Likert scale. Some selected results of the assessment are presented here. The statement "I am interested in informatics because..." (Fig. 1 was evaluated with the reasoning of the following Likert Items (1 = do not agree at all; 2 = hardly agree; 3 = agree about; 4 = agree pretty much; 5 = agree very much).

(A) ...I find it exciting (M = 4.1; sd = 0.9)
(B) ...I want to know more about computer science (M = 4.0; sd = 1.0)
(C) ...we did it in class (M = 4.0; sd = 1.2)
(D) ...my friends find it exciting (M = 2.7; sd = 1.3)
(E) ...my parents want me to. (M = 2.4; sd = 1.4)

The data show that the items A and B, which are aimed at intrinsic motivation and interest in content, are rated significantly higher by the students than the items which represent rather extrinsic aspects. Students take part in computer science lessons mainly out of interest in the subject and topic-related motivation. The same tendency also shows the students' assessments about their computer science lessons. The following ratings were given for the corresponding Likert items:

(A) The computer science classes are fun. (M = 4.3; sd = 1.0)
(B) I look forward to the computer science classes. (M = 4.1; sd = 1.0)
(C) The computer science classes are exciting. (M = 4.1; sd = 1.0)

The students of primary school age perceive their computer science lessons in the three modules as predominantly exciting and motivating and also state that they most enjoy them. Regarding the students' interests or value beliefs (see comparable items from [4]) towards the importance of computers for their future, the evaluation of the following Likert items was instructive:

(A) I find it useful to be able to use the computer. (M = 4.3; sd = 0.9)
(B) Most professions will need computer knowledge in the future (M = 4.2; sd = 1.0)
(C) It is important to me to be able to use computers better and better (M = 3.9; sd = 1.2)
(D) It is important to me to know a lot about computers (M = 3.7; sd = 1.1)

Here, too, there is a clear interest of the students in computer science (computers), which is accompanied by the assessment of the high importance of computers in a future professional activity. These items represent the computer value belief scale from [4], who found that boys had slightly higher value beliefs then girls. In our data overall values are a little lower (3.7 compared to 4.1 in the study from Vekri et al.), but now differences between boys and girls.

The students are flexible towards the computer as a learning medium in informatics lessons and are open to both 'plugged' and 'unplugged' methods. However, the analysis of the individual statements shows that there is a clear tendency to learn with computers.

(A) I want to use a computer for learning (M = 4.4; sd = 1.0)

(B) I want to work with and without a computer (M = 3.8; sd = 1.3)
(C) I want to learn without a computer (M = 2.2; sd = 1.3)

A factor analysis of the students' interest in computer science and their assessment of the teaching of computer science with these and other items led to the extraction of three relevant factors that can clarify 55% of the total variance.

Factor 1: Intrinsic motivation (interest in using, knowing and programming IT systems; f-ld: 3.34)
Factor 2: Extrinsic motivation (participation in class because of friends and parents; f-ld: 1.65)
Factor 3: PC as medium for learning (function of the PC in informatics learning: f-ld: 1.61)

The results of the factor analysis also show that the students' attitudes to computer science learning are primarily shaped by intrinsic motivation and an interest in learning more about computers. This result is also supported if one compares the assignment of persons in a two-dimensional orthogonal coordinate system, which is spanned by 2 factors. Thus, it can be revealed that rather lower values on factor 2 accompany high values on factor (number of persons with factor 1 > 0.5 and factor 2 < 0.5: 75%). This group of students also shows a certain preference for learning with computers in informatics lessons.

4.2 Module-Specific Results: Digital World

For the first module "Digital World", 224 data sets were evaluated, 94 of which were female, 113 male and 17 without information. The average age is 8.95 years. Of the students, 44 are in the second grade, 106 in the third grade and 61 in the fourth grade, 13 students did not make an entry in the grade level.

After the module, the children solved some informatics tasks. Some tasks had already been worked out in the classroom before, others required a transfer. The results of selected tasks are explained below. Table 1 shows the distribution of points.

At the beginning, the children answer the MC-question "What happens if a key is pressed on the computer?". This question was not explicitly discussed in the classroom and yet answered by nearly 40% of the students correctly.

In the second task the children should mark and describe three IT-systems in a big picture. This task has not been practiced before. Through their everyday experiences, 60% of the students could recognize three IT-systems and describe their function correctly

The next two tasks dealt with converting from binary to decimal and vice versa. This was explicitly practiced in class. Accordingly, almost half of the children have solved all four tasks correctly. Nevertheless, a quarter of the children could not solve the task at all.

Also very close to the lesson was the fifth task to calculate the transmitted binary number from switched on and off light bulbs and read off the corresponding letters using a table. 48.7% of the children were able to solve this complex task without any errors.

Table 1. Results of module-specific questions - module 1: Digital World

	Question	Score					
		Max	0	1	2	3	4
1	Technical understanding (keystroke)	1	60.7%	39.3%			
2	Recognition of computer systems	3	14.7%	10.7%	13.8%	60.7%	
3	Converting from binary to decimal	4	21.0%	7.6%	8.9%	21.4%	41.1%
4	Converting from decimal to binary	4	29.5%	8.0%	3.6%	19.2%	39.7%
5	Bulbs message	1	51.3%	48.7%			
6	IPO-principle: drinks machine	1	22.3%	77.7%			
7	IPO-principle: tablet	3	71.4%	13.8%	13.8%	0.9%	
8	How computers work	2	25.0%	46.9%	28.1%		
9	Error detection - one-dimensional	1	54.0%	46.0%			
10	Error detection - two-dimensional	1	90.6%	9.4%			

Two other tasks asked for an understanding of the IPO-principle. In this case, the children should correctly assign the input, processing and output of a drinks vending machine and a tablet. The majority of the students (77.7%) were able to correctly reproduce the IPO-principle using the example of a drinks machine. However, the transfer to a tablet succeeded only a few students.

In the eighth tasks, the students should recognize how computers work. There was an MC-question with two correct answers. 63 out of the 224 students interviewed responded with both correct answers. Another 105 kids ticked one of the two correct answers.

The last topic of the module was the error detection. There were two tasks for this: application and transmission. Almost half of the students were able to apply the learned method of error detection correctly. The transfer of the learned one-dimensional process to a two-dimensional process was achieved by 21 of the 224 Kids.

4.3 Module Specific Results: How Does a Robot Work?

In addition to general questions of interest, the questionnaire for the robotics module focuses on recognizing robots as IT systems, the IPO-Principle and programming. Here we present the results of 178 data sets (85 female, 83 male, 10 not specified). The average age was 8.87 years. The evaluation results are very different with regard to the different foci of the questionnaire. A total of 17 points were achieved in the area of content, which no participant achieved. Nevertheless, the results of most participants are in the upper midfield (median 11 points) as shown in Table 4.

Table 2. Results of specific questions

Question	Max score	Score			
		0	1	2	3
Which picture shows a robot?	2	9,5%	43,3%	47,2%	
Which object is equipped with a computer?	3	5,1%	27,5%	20,8%	46,6%
Which object can be used to control a robot?	3	3,9%	30,4%	21,3%	44,4%
Assign Items to IPO-Principle	1	48,3%	51,7%		
How can a robot understand you?	1	10,1%	89,9%		
Understand simple program	1	50,6%	49,4%		
Understand program with loop	1	94,4%	5,6%		
Understand program with loop and condition	1	84,8%	15,2%		

The results for interesting questions are shown in Table 2 and named in the following: The children could easily identify robots between other objects. In addition, they were able to identify the objects that are equipped with a computer. In the context of how a robot works, the IPO-Principle was well understood and the children understood that robots need clear commands. With regard to programming, it became clear that simple programs could be easily understood by the children With the constructs condition and loop, however, the evaluation results show difficulties in understanding. The poor results of the evaluation in context of the constructs condition and loop led to a revision of the working sheets for the children. The children now only have to understand the constructs condition and loop and no longer have to program them themselves. We hope that this will make it easier for the children to develop an understanding of these constructs.

4.4 Module Specific Results: I Have a Secret

A factor analysis on students' interests in the contents of the module 'Cryptology' shows that they have a great need for knowledge on both the subject-related and the application-related aspects of the subject area. The factor analysis reveals two factors that clarify a total of 49% of the variance. Factor 1 Technical knowledge of cryptology (encryption and decryption; hiding information, decrypting messages; f-load: 1.99). Factor 2 Cryptology in everyday life (encryption on the PC, codes in everyday life, use of encryption tables; f-load: 1.90). The technical terms of the module must be introduced, explained and justified very well in order to understand the underlying informatics principles. The materials addressed the following content aspects: encryption, decryption and algorithms as a comprehensive aspect. In order to test to what extent the students have understood algorithmic concepts of cryptology, several respective test items were included in the test-instruments. For example, the students had to assess whether listed elements are to be classified as algorithms or not. Out of

Table 3. Results of module-specific questions - module 3: I have a secret

	Question	Score							
		Max	0	1	2	3	4	5	6
1	Knowledge of encryption	3	43.7%	34.5%	19.5%	2.3%			
2	determine algorithm	6	16.7%	17.8%	24.1%	27.6%	10.3%	3.4%	0%
3	Operation principle for the caesar disc	3	20.7%	29.3%	24.1%	25.9%			
4	Recognize correct order of an algorithm	1	21.9%	78.1%					
5	Correct flowchart for scytale-decryption	1	67.0%	33.0%					
6	Importance of encryption	4	7.5%	9.2%	21.3%	31.6%	20.5%		

six possible correct answers, they recognized an average of 1.4 items as an algorithm and none of them could correctly identify exactly six algorithms. When the terms were clearly and child-friendly introduced, the students had little difficulties. The following table shows the evaluation points of the module (Table 3):

The data allow different interpretations: On the one hand, the students had too little time to put the foreign words into an everyday context and then, provided with a concept, to anchor them in their personal knowledge memory. On the other hand, primary school teachers do not have the necessary specialist knowledge and are therefore unable to introduce the terms with the necessary accuracy. They cannot highlight the overarching aspects of their teaching and make them available to pupils. Furthermore, there is the possibility that the children can act very well algorithmically, but their linguistic ability falls behind their practical ability. The historical perspective on cryptology, combined with the prospect of writing "secret messages", offered an attractive framework for dealing with cryptology. The great interest in the topic led, among other things, to the fact that the difference between transposition and substitution could be reconstructed historically and evaluated with regard to its relevance. Questions on data security and copyright could not be answered sufficiently within the framework of the module and form central elements of the further development. Finally, it can be stated that cryptological concepts were well understood, but that the comprehensive informatics concept "Algorithms" was predominantly action-oriented and that the big picture must be significantly further developed and sharpened.

5 Evaluation – Teachers' Results

The following results of the evaluation and reflection of teachers' teaching experience in the project are based, on the one hand, on observations made during the training and, on the other hand, on feedback forms filled in by teachers for each module. The results of the feedback forms were obtained inductively using MaxQDA. Frequently mentioned aspects were summarized to common content categories, and on this basis, a quantification of the statements was conducted. These categories are based on feedback to the contents, their didactic processing and the competences to be achieved; feedback to the material and the equipment at school, to differentiation possibilities and didactical social forms, additionally to the target group and their previous educational experience, and last, but not least to the time factor and the perceived overload of the curriculum. The observed diffuse expectations of the teachers at the beginning of the training series gave a hint that even these voluntary participants, selected as interested, do not have a differentiated picture of informatics. A classification of the modules' informatics content into a bigger picture, therefore cannot succeed. Rather, there was a surprise effect, since the modules are designed unplugged, i.e. they refer more to the informatics idea than to a technical implementation. Exemplary statements from the training context were: "So this is informatics?", That's not what I had in mind underneath. In the course of the training, it also became clear that the teachers involved were initially unsure why it was precisely these topics that were to be taught. Hence they could only gradually develop an idea of why the selected module contents were relevant to informatics, indeed central. Although the diffuse expectations could be somewhat structured by the real training, the overall view on the topics of informatics could not be structured and sharpened in the context of the training as the feedback results show.

The close orientation to the material made it possible for the teachers to develop their own informatics ideas and to communicate them to the students in a very closely guided manner. The bottom line, however, is that the handling of informatics ideas is very complex and difficult, which means that students' further questions and considerations cannot always be answered competently by the teachers. This promotes uncertainty in the classroom and there is a risk that this uncertainty will be transferred to the students. The teachers have an increasingly urgent desire to understand the world of informatics, but a still missing bigger picture shows that further training is highly needed.

Nevertheless, the teachers involved have gone through the training courses and tested the materials in their lessons. 15.9% of the participants changed, expanded, modified or reduced the material and adapted it to their learning group. In summary, it can be said that material creation is very time-consuming and a offered material package should be helpful (28.6% indicate this). However, 20.6% of the teachers involved would like to concentrate on fewer contents and smaller goals. Further feedback allows conclusions to be drawn regarding the necessary school equipment.

Due to inadequate equipment in schools, 57.1% of the teachers surveyed stated that although it is possible to use computers for half class sizes on average per school, they work too slowly or are not connected to the Internet at all. There are massive problems as to whether the systems are ready for use and whether programs may be installed on the systems, so that this infrastructure is hardly usable for a technical deepening of the informatics contents with digital media. Nevertheless, a total of 12.7% of teachers would like digital media to be available to convey the content and to be implemented with suitable programs. They not only expect to have a direct connection of the learning materials to the everyday world of children (27%) but also see the need to address the ideas of computer science in a technical realization, especially for programming a robot or dealing with QR codes. The results of the evaluation show that both, the teachers and the students involved, have an interest in transferring their acquired knowledge into a computer-based learning environment and respective software applications. This step cannot be taken by the teachers without training. The follow-up project is therefore to be devoted to this task.

The conviction of the necessity of informatics education leads teachers to the assessment that the complexity of the topic must be met by intensive training and further education offers in order to be able to deal competently with the content and the available material, to modify it, to differentiate it and to process it for their own learning group. The focus is on linguistic accuracy, the definition of terms and the description of the underlying informatics concepts. In addition, the classification in the overall context must be comprehensible and relevant for teachers and students.

6 Discussion of Results

When looking at the results for teachers', it's probably no surprise that they closely stick to the material, and had problems with the so-called bigger picture. We found two aspects interesting: First, that this also resulted in problems of understanding the relevance of the material; and second that at the same time some of the teachers' nevertheless reworked and adapted the material for their classes.

Probably, for future initiatives teacher workshops should focus more on discussing the bigger picture, to help teachers to be able to adapt the materials to their classes - but in the direction of a suitable bigger picture.

When looking at the material and evaluation more closely, we found four strands for such a bigger picture at least implicitly in our three modules: These are organized around the four themes: understanding and perceiving technical systems as informatics systems; comprehend the IPO-principle of those systems; understanding simple algorithms ideas; get an idea of coding and (programming) languages.

In future teacher trainings such underlying principles could be discussed more explicitly, in order to give teachers a better understanding how the different topics are connected to an overall big picture of informatics education. When we write big picture of informatics education, and not big picture of informatics, we want to hint at another issue for discussion and further work: What is a suitable big picture to be taught and learned in primary schools? This questions also deserves a closer look in the future.

Further issues for teacher training, as based on the teacher feedback, are the role of technology-based teaching and the needed prerequisites to so. As mentioned already above, this question also needs further attention, as currently the teaching technology installed at schools does not work out of the box (at least in the perception of our teachers).

The inclusion of technology-based teaching is also an issue from the students' point of view. The overwhelming majority of our students want to learn at least also with technology. Based on our results we think that including technology should not only be used as motivator or as teaching aid for the topics taught, but also as a means to foster understanding the big picture. On the one hand finding informatics principles in technology at school could foster the applicability and the transfer to everyday experiences – on the other hand including technology might lead to mis-perceptions of the nature of informatics (in the form of e.g. informatics is the science of using computers or similar misconceptions). So this is another issue for future work.

With regard to the specific content related results we learned that the three main themes are realistic goals to pursue in primary education, but the more abstract themes quickly become difficult to grasp; see e.g. the results in the three modules.

A Tables and Figures

See Figs. 2 and 3.

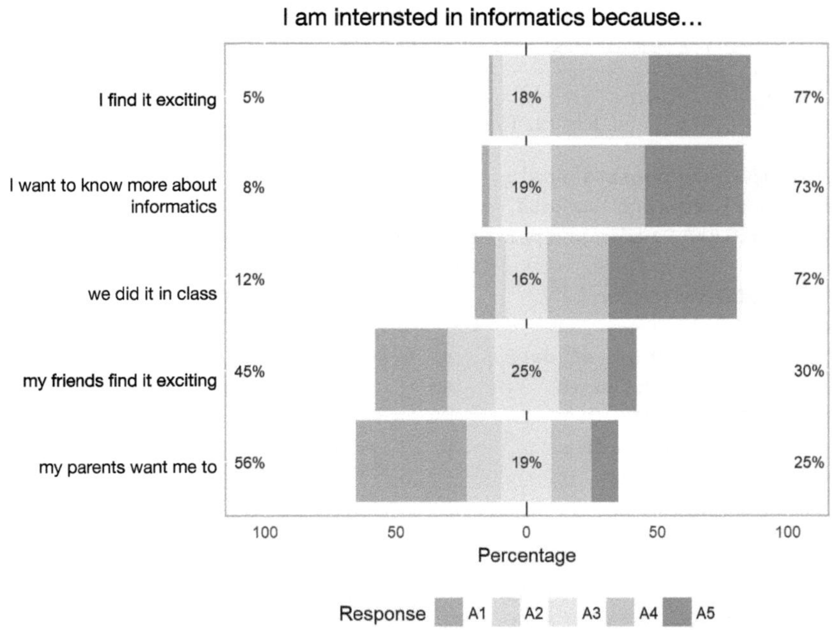

Fig. 1. Interests in informatics

Table 4. Results of the participants for module robotics

Score	0	3	4	5	6	7	8	9	10	11	12	13	14	15	16
Number of children	3	3	3	5	12	15	14	10	17	30	23	20	14	8	1

```
## Principal Components Analysis
## Call: principal(r = skala, nfactors = 3)
## Standardized loadings (pattern matrix) based upon correlation matrix
##                                      item  RC1   RC3   RC2   h2   u2 com
## Applying Informatics Systems (IS)       8 0.80              0.65 0.35 1.0
## Knowing what IS is able to do           9 0.75              0.60 0.40 1.1
## Excited about informatics               1 0.71              0.53 0.47 1.1
## Know how to program                     7 0.71              0.50 0.50 1.0
## Know about informatics                  2 0.69              0.50 0.50 1.1
## Parts of a PC                           6 0.63              0.42 0.58 1.1
## Friends are excited about informatics   3       0.84        0.72 0.28 1.0
## Parents want me to do so                4       0.81        0.66 0.34 1.0
## was a compulsory course                 5                   0.28 0.72 1.9
## Learning without PC                    11             0.84 0.71 0.29 1.0
## Use of a PC                            10            -0.70 0.58 0.42 1.4
## Learning with and without PC           12             0.59 0.45 0.55 1.6
##
##                        RC1  RC3  RC2
## SS loadings           3.34 1.65 1.61
## Proportion Var        0.28 0.14 0.13
## Cumulative Var        0.28 0.42 0.55
## Proportion Explained  0.51 0.25 0.24
## Cumulative Proportion 0.51 0.76 1.00
##
## Mean item complexity =  1.2
## Fit based upon off diagonal values = 0.89
```

Fig. 2. Results cluster analysis 1

```
## Principal Components Analysis
## Call: principal(r = skala, nfactors = 2)
## Standardized loadings (pattern matrix) based upon correlation matrix
##                            item  RC1  RC2    h2   u2 com
## Types of encryption           4 0.78      0.682 0.32 1.2
## Hiding data                   1 0.73      0.532 0.47 1.0
## De- and encryption of data    5 0.69      0.510 0.49 1.1
## Encryption of Messages        6           0.074 0.93 1.9
## Encryption at PC              7      0.79 0.631 0.37 1.0
## Encryption real life          8      0.76 0.619 0.38 1.2
## Codes in real life            3      0.63 0.546 0.45 1.6
## Use of code charts            2           0.288 0.71 2.0
##
##                        RC1  RC2
## SS loadings           1.99 1.90
## Proportion Var        0.25 0.24
## Cumulative Var        0.25 0.49
## Proportion Explained  0.51 0.49
## Cumulative Proportion 0.51 1.00
##
## Mean item complexity =  1.4
## Fit based upon off diagonal values = 0.82
```

Fig. 3. Cluster analysis module cryptography

References

1. Duncan, C., Bell, T., Atlas, J.: What do the teachers think?: introducing computational thinking in the primary school curriculum. In: Proceedings of the Nineteenth Australasian Computing Education Conference, pp. 65–74. ACM, New York (2017)
2. Brinda, T., Puhlmann, H., Schulte, C.: Bridging ICT and CS: educational standards for computer science in lower secondary education. ACM SIGCSE Bull. **41**, 288–292 (2009)
3. Plomp, T., Nieveen, N.: Educational Design Research. Part A: An Introduction. SLO Netherlands Institute for Curriculum Development (2013)
4. Vekiri, I., Chronaki, A.: Gender issues in technology use: perceived social support, computer self-efficacy and value beliefs, and computer use beyond school. Comput. Educ. **51**(3), 1392–1404 (2008)
5. Bergner, N., et al.: Zieldimensionen informatischer Bildung im Elementar- und Primarbereich. In: Stiftung Haus der kleinen Forscher (Hrsg.) Frühe informatische Bildung Ziele und Gelingensbedingungen fr den Elementar- und Primarbereich. Berlin (2018)

How an Ambitious Informatics Curriculum Can Influence Algebraic Thinking of Primary School Children

Francesca Agatolio[1(✉)], Fabio Albanese[2], and Michele Moro[1]

[1] University of Padova, Padua, Italy
francesca.agatolio@phd.unipd.it, michele.moro@unipd.it
[2] Collegio Pio X, Treviso, Italy
fabio.albanese@fondazionecollegiopiox.org

Abstract. In this paper we describe the special case of an informatics curriculum implemented in a primary school, and the observed learning outcomes. The particularity of this curriculum is based on both the variety of the contents and on their apparent complexity. The children experienced different programming languages, including one text-based, and became confident with many educational robotics kits such as Lego WeDo, MBot and Arduino. During this path, children appeared strongly involved also in dealing with complex challenges and seemed to have developed their mathematical thinking. In particular, even if they had never worked with the formal structures of algebra during the math classes, children appeared confident with the concept of variable found in programming. For this reason, we decided to investigate whether these competencies applied even to mathematics, using a well-known national test developed to gauge the level of skills and selecting some questions related to algebra and designed for 8th grade students. The results that emerged were encouraging, suggesting that informatics could be useful in reinforcing algebraic thinking and introducing some mathematical concepts particularly complex for many students, such as variables.

Keywords: Education in informatics · Informatics curriculum
Algebraic thinking · Computational thinking

1 Introduction

Since its first mention by Wing [27], *computational thinking* (CT) is a successful expression that incorporates several meanings in itself. In particular, Wing emphasizes the mental process activated by searching an interpretable and not ambiguous solution of a problem, i.e. a computational solution, which in general terms involves humans and machines. Literature provides other designations such as algorithmic thinking [4] but we think that the frequent major association with computer programming skills proofs rather reductive. Actually CT can be classified as a kind of analytical thinking: this is why it is easy to find

S. N. Pozdniakov and V. Dagienė (Eds.): ISSEP 2018, LNCS 11169, pp. 354–365, 2018.
https://doi.org/10.1007/978-3-030-02750-6_27

relations with mathematical thinking (problem solving, abstraction), engineering thinking (design and evaluation of complex systems connected with real environments), scientific thinking (understanding computability, intelligence, the mind and human behavior) [28]. In [7] the authors present a survey of the core concepts and skills related to CT they found in some fundamental works in literature. They also provide an interesting addendum of dispositions/attitude/attributes such as persistence, collaboration, and others, which, together with knowledge and skills, form the essence of competences. Moreover, this work reminds us that CT is not simply digital literacy because it goes beyond the objective to prepare competent and safe users of digital tool, trying to make them aware of what is "behind the curtain". Abstraction, problem-solving, programming and debugging skills, collaborative attitudes are all considered relevant components of the CT process and its outcomes. This means that there is a general consensus on the valuable transversal impact that promoting CT at curricular level may have within an innovative education [19,24]. There are several practical ways to "feed" CT, depending on the level of school, but teaching programming and practicing coding is considered the central engine to this purpose [4]. Among these, Educational Robotics (ER) is a powerful approach to introduce programming in a way which is attractive, rewarding and enforced by the building of "intelligent" artefacts [1]. Actually ER has proved as one of the powerful tool to stimulate and guide CT from kindergarten to University [3]. Like CT, ER is denoted as supporting STEM teaching-learning but more recently it has been related to the wider spectrum of STREAM disciplines which includes also Reading-writing and Arts [9]. As far as the multidisciplinary power of CT is concerned, we can expect positive effects on single disciplines, either in form of a reinforcement of an already evident attitude, particularly in presence of a special talent, or, maybe more interestingly, making the student previously in difficulty more confident and less frightened by a certain discipline. In this paper we would focus on the declination of CT as mathematical and algebraic thinking and its impact on affordable mathematical competences. Literature shows that the strict relationship between CT and Mathematical thinking (MT) comes from the analytic perspective and the degree of abstraction applied in mathematical problem-solving [21]. The relevance of MT does increase due to the rapid evolution in professional fields which are related to mathematics and sciences, from which the necessity of a more realistic view is actually required to better prepare students for pursuing careers in these fields [25]. In [26] Wilkerson et al. underlines the relationship between CT/MT and the ability of building precise models able to support innovative investigations and to provide predictive data so important in the XXI centrury information society. "Immaginative programming" is also another expression used to explain that through CT Mathematics is brought to life [5]. The paper aims to show, dealing with a direct experience in a primary school Italy that includes ER, the validity of the abovementioned principles with special attention to mathematical skills. In Sect. 2 we would argue on how the teaching-learning of CS and programming can support the introduction of mathematical concepts and abilities at this level. Our specific experience is presented in Sect. 3 and the paper is concluded by a final discussion and possible future developments.

2 Algebraic Thinking

Algebraic thinking refers to a set of cognitive processes involved in using algebra that have a lot in common with CT. In K-12 education (i.e. by the end of the usual secondary education), algebra can be described as [16]:

- manipulation and transformation of symbolic statements;
- generalizations of laws about numbers and patterns;
- the study of structures and systems;
- rules for transforming and solving equations;
- learning about variables, functions and expressing change and relationships;
- modelling the mathematical structures of situations within and outside mathematics.

In all these aspects the role of variables and symbolization in general is fundamental. Although it is possible to introduce many algebra's aspects since early age through the use of a pre-algebric approach [14] (i.e. without using letters), the symbolization becomes essential as soon as the more formal aspects are introduced. For many students, this is a watershed point in the learning of mathematics. In fact, the literature reports the frequent difficulties that can arise over the transition from an arithmetic to an algebraic form of reasoning: in particular, students struggle to imagine a letter as standing for a range of numbers or as representing an object rather than a number and they have great difficulty operating on unknowns [8,13]. This transition in the italian education happens just around the 7th grade (12 years old), but the literature suggests that many mechanism of the algebraic thinking can be introduced much earlier [8] so that the students can familiarize with some concepts before they appear in the secondary grades. To achieve this objective, computer-based tools are good allies. In the literature, the use of modern technologies to support the learning of mathematics and mathematical thinking in general is well documented [11]. In particular two kinds of approach emerge: the first one concerns the use of technological tools explicitly aimed to enhance the learning of some mathematical concepts, such as graphic calculators or specific environment (e.g Geogebra, Bebras) [10]. In the second approach, instead, informatics, and in particular programming, is used to implicitly promote this [6,15]. The curriculum we are going to describe uses this second approach that follows essentially the Seymour Papert theories: in fact, in [17] Papert guessed that "children could also benefit, [...], from the way in which computer models seemed able to give concrete form to areas of knowledge that had previously appeared so intangible and abstract." The outcomes observed at the end of the three years course described here, show that this idea is effective, and that the cognitive transfer between the two concepts of variable - as it appears in programming, and as it is taught in mathematics - is possible. We consider this hypothesis as representative of overall educational value of artifacts as "comfortable" vehicles of various mathematical skills.

3 Curriculum

The informatics curriculum hereby described is an anomaly within the italian primary school. What makes it different from the ordinary informatics teachings in Italy is primarily the richness of the contents and of the tools involved in the pattern (Fig. 1), combined with the apparent complexity of some topics covered, if compared to the age of the students (8–10 years old). The curriculum was implemented in a class of 27 students of a private school. The time employed was about two hours per week. In the following sections we describe the contents addressed during the 3rd, 4th and 5th grade programs, discussing the main applied methodologies and the conditions that had made it possible.

3.1 Contents

The contents addressed during the three years dealt with different areas of computer science. In the Table 1 we briefly present these topics, divided into five categories partially inspired to the "Scheme of Work for Computing" designed by the CAS community (https://community.computingatschool.org.uk/resources/2119/single). Because of the great importance given to educational robotics, we choose to create a specific category reserved to this topic. The sixth category,"Connection to real world" underlines the great importance given to the applications and to multidisciplinarity.

(a) Educational robots

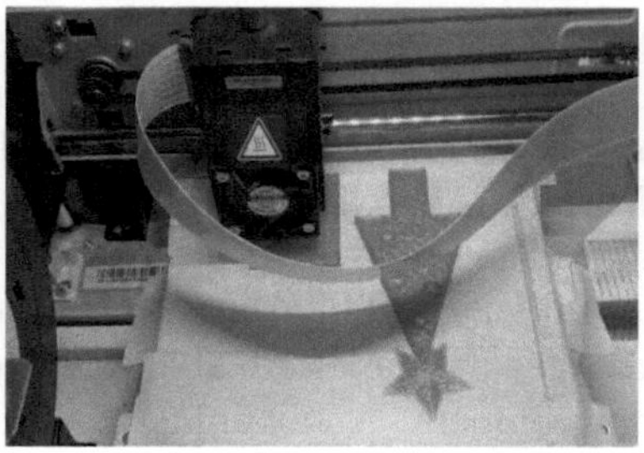

(b) 3D printer

Fig. 1. Examples of technological tools used in the activities

3.2 Activities Examples

3rd Grade: Pinocchio Digital Story. During this activity children reproduced the Pinocchio fairy tale using Scratch (scratch.mit.edu). Digital storytelling is often used to introduce programming [12], but the particularity of the experience described here relies on the technological tools employed. After seeing the Pinocchio movie, the teacher split the students into groups and required from each of them to reproduce a scene from the cartoon using Scratch. The children had to keep in mind two constraints: each scene should have lasted 120 s, and the scenes of the different groups should have been mutually consistent. The second request aimed to enhance communication among the groups. After that, the teacher sequenced all the scenes and the students had the possibility to dub them with the collaboration of the music teacher and thanks to the presence in the school of an apposite small voice-acting room.

4th Grade: App + Robotics Animation + Videogame. During the first part of the year, the students increased their programming skills through the creation of videogames and apps. They were introduced to educational robotics with the Lego WeDo robot. In the second part of the year the teacher proposed the "App + robotics animation + videogame" activity with the aim to strengthen the acquired competencies and to enhance the students' autonomy, increasing their sense of responsibility. The students were divided into groups of 4–5 members each and they were required to create a videogame, a little project using Lego WeDO and an interactive app. They had four months and they were left the choice to distribute tasks among themselves or to face each step together one at a time: collecting the information, designing the app's structure, providing for the script, etc., all in complete autonomy.

5th Grade: Create a 3D Lighted Sign with Arduino. Arduino (arduino.cc) has been introduced after some lessons dedicated to the study of electricity and energy. Therefore, after they have met Arduino, children were able to recognize physical concepts such as the electrical current, the resistance, the voltage and the relationship among those physical quantities - i.e. the Ohm law. Although these contents were introduced in a simplified way, students showed to understand their general meaning. For this purpose, the teacher used also technical instruments (e.g. the multimeter); to program the hardware, students used the MBlock environment. The reasons behind this choice were two: the first one is that MBlock is very similar to Scratch, which children already knew; the second is that MBlock allows an immediate automatic translation from graphical to textual language. This way students could have a taste of the C++ language and, as a result, they were able to write very simple programs using the Arduino IDE environment. An example of such activities is the creation of a lighted sign using Arduino and the 3D printer. Students designed the physical structure using the TinkerCad software, then they added some LEDs controlled by Arduino. In doing this, they applied some theoretical physics concepts to build a tangible artifact, such as the LED polarization. The aim was to make them aware of the applicability of the knowledge transmitted by school.

3.3 The Guiding Principles

The curriculum aimed to develop and to reinforce three main aspects.

The Development of Computational Thinking. CT had a wide space in the curriculum, firstly because the students were continuously involved in programming. Therefore, for all the time they were required to solve problems traducing them in a language understandable by a computer. Moreover, thanks to the wide

Table 1. The contents addressed in the curriculum

	Algorithms	Programming & development	Data & Representation	Hardware & processing	Educational robotics	Connection with real world
3th grade	Use of instructions' sequences to create stories; sprites' temporal synchronization	Programming with Scratch using only simple commands (e.g. movements, dialogues)	Strings and numbers	Computer general structure based on Von Neumann architecture. Introduction of the concepts of CPU, RAM, ROM, input and output peripheral devices		Creation of simple cartoon in the form of digital storytelling
4th grade	Use of more advance commands such as loop, if/else and logical operators. Sprites synchronization using the broadcast commands	Creation of videogames in Scratch. Creation of personalized blocks. Introduction of the routine concept. Programming Lego WeDo using Scratch	Variable concept in informatics. Introduction of the data types. Concept of digitalization	Study of simple network architectures. Information binary representation. Building simple logical circuits using Logic Lab software (Fig. 2)	Introduction to educational robotics through Lego WeDo	Solving mathematical problems in Mblock through generalized algorithms (es. Creation of a program to calculate the perimeter of a regular polygon)
5th grade	Deepening of the if/else statement associated to the use of sensors	Programming robots such as MBot and Arduino using Mblock environment. Introduction of a textual programming environment for Arduino (IDE)	Instances of digitalization techniques for text, images and sounds. Transmission of the binary information	Sensors and actuators concepts. Introduction to the 3D printing	Implementation of simple projects with Arduino using LEDs and buttons. Study of a smart home model based on Arduino	Comparison between the virtual environment and the real one. Introduction to simple physical concepts using MBot (es.friction, speed, electric current, battery, Ohm law)

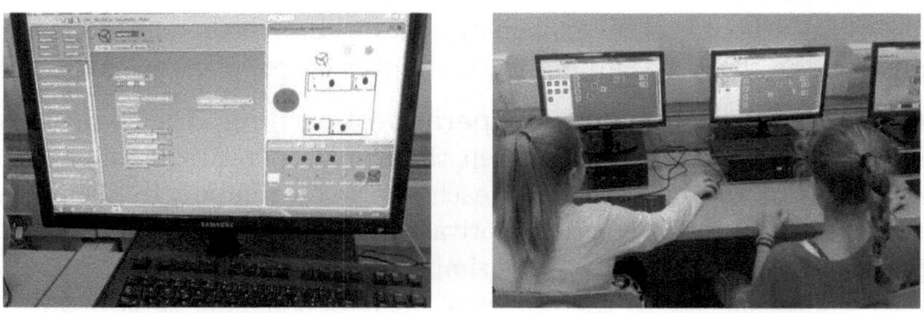

(a) An app (work-in-progess) (b) Logic Lab

Fig. 2. Examples of activities

set of technological tools employed, children had the opportunity to face problem of different kinds that required diverse strategies to be solved. For instance, the two tasks of designing components with the 3D printer and of creating an app with Scratch both needed to translate an idea in a form consistent with the used software even if radically different. Furthermore, with educational robotics the children had to take into account also new issues related to the real environment. An aspect we consider fundamental in the development of CT, is the "white-box" approach adopted by the teacher: he tried to make students aware of the functioning of the technologies they were using, for example showing the internal components of a computer or discussing with them the physics principles at the basis of some devices, such as the battery or the ultrasonic sensor (see also section below). Behind this approach, there was the idea that the understanding of how thing works is a fundamental step to realize something new.

Connection with the Real World and Multidisciplinarity. The importance to make a didactic tied to reality is well-known in literature [23]. In fact, this bond allows to motivate children to accept in a good mood even the more complex challenges. Educational robotics is particularly useful for this purpose, because the activities it proposes are inspired to day-to-day issues [3], such as, for example, the study of a smart home with Arduino, an activity covered during the K5 year; moreover, the usage of robots such as MBot prompted them to rethink about the differences between the virtual environment they met using Scratch and the physical world, with its laws and imperfections: for example, the movements of the robot can be used to introduce the concepts of physical error and of forces like friction but also to treat advanced concepts, such as the motion laws, in a simple and understandable way. One of the key aspects of the curriculum has been, in fact, the intention to make students engaged and aware of a wider perspective about the school subjects - perspective that allowed them to perceive the teachings of each subject as an "unicum", giving them an anticipated, if partial, knowledge of the future contents. This approach is guided by the deep conviction that this anticipation is fundamental to give students an idea of the structure of the surrounding world, and to help them to understand the role of the school both in explaining the world to them, and to make them prepared to face the same subjects with a higher degree of complexity.

Sense of Responsibility and Cooperative Learning. The students' sense of responsibility proceeds step by step through cooperative learning; in fact, the awareness of the importance of each one's contribution to the collective effort was a key factor in creating motivation and self-esteem in students [20]. Moreover, most of the activities were simply presented by the teacher, with the concrete realization left to the students' creativity, hoping to stimulate their resourcefulness.

3.4 The Applied Methodology

Constructionism, as described by Seymour Papert, was the guiding methodology. As stated by Papert in [18], the presence of computer and other computer-based tools "shifts the balance between transfer of knowledge to students and the production of knowledge by students". The students were actively involved in the learning process, also thanks to the great importance given to the creation of physical artifacts. The word "artifact" here had a double meaning: on the one hand it was the cognitive tool by which to apply the acquired knowledge and build a new one (e.g. computer, robot, 3D printer); on the other hand it is the results of a learning creative process to which the students put their effort. As a result "children might come to want to learn it because they would use it in building these models" [18] and this happens also when complex abstract concepts are involved. Also the teacher acted following the constructivist perspective: he did not work as a traditional teacher - transferring ready knowledge to students - but rather acted as an organizer, coordinator and facilitator. He gave the guidelines of the activity, provided to students with many materials for thoughts and observed their learning process. His presence was very discrete and his help was be offered only when necessary [2].

3.5 The Effects on Algebraic Thinking

At the end of the three years, observing the meaningful goals reached by the children, we tried to investigate whether this path had an impact on their mathematical thinking. In particular we were interested in evaluating if they were able to understand the use of symbolization in the representation of mathematical problems after they have experienced something similar in programming. For this purpose, we used INVALSI (http://www.invalsi.it/invalsi/index.php), that is a national test developed to gauge the level of the students' skills in some specific years of their education (2nd, 5th, 8th and10th grades). We chose four questions from the 8th and 10th grade questionnaires. In fact the 5th grade test does not contain references to the use of symbolization since, in italian education, it is introduced just around the 7th grade. The Fig. 3 reports the selected questions (Q1, Q2 and Q4 come from the 8th grade level, while Q3 belongs to the 10th grade level). In all the questions we replaced the words "formula","expression" and "equation" with the term "option" in order to make it understandable to the children.

In the Table 2 there are reported the results performed by the students, compared with the national percentage of correct answers; the students who took the test was 25 over 27.

The positive students' performance in the questions 1,3 and 4 indicates that the most part of them was able to identify the algebraic model of a problem, recognizing the symbolical representation both of the numbers and of the relationships among them. We think their experience with variables in programming provided them of an intuitive interpretation of the use of variables in mathematics. Moreover, the scientific approach grown during the three years, could have make them familiar with the mathematical way of describing a problem. Indeed, many of the addressed activities called for solving a problem translating it in a programming language, a process that has a lot in common with the mathematical one. The lower performance in Q2 could be explained by the graphical

QUESTION 1

a) When Paola runs, she consumes 60 kilocalories for each kilometer. Fill the table with the missing values

kilometers (n)	kilocalories (c)
1	60
3	...
5	...

b) If **n** is the number of the travelled kilometers, which of the following expressions allows calculating how many kilocalories Paola consumed when she runs?

- k = 60 * n
- k = 60 : n
- k = n : 60
- k = n + 60 +60

QUESTION 2

Observe the scheme:

53

x 3 x

Which option represents the scheme?

- 3 * 2x = 53
- x + 3x = 53
- 2x + 3 = 53
- 3 + x2 = 53

QUESTION 3

To join the swimming pool, you have to pay a membership of EUR 10 and EUR 7 for each entry. William can spend EUR 100, at most. Which of the following options describes the William's number of entries? n stands for the number of entries.

- (10 + 7)*n ≤ 100
- 10*n + 7 ≤ 100
- 10 + 7*n ≤ 100
- 10 + 7*n ≥ 100

QUESTION 4

Luisa and Joanna use a different number of laundry pegs when they hang out the sheets, as shown in the figure.

Luisa

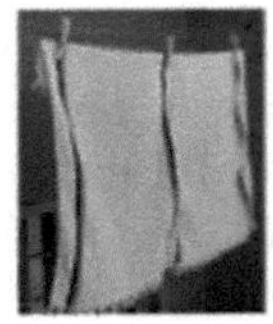

Joanna

a) Complete the following table:

Number of sheets	Luisa's number of laundry pegs	Joanna's number of laundry pegs
2	4	3
3	6	4
4	8	5
6	...	...
...	20	...
...	...	20

b) Which of the following options does describe the numbers of laundry pegs that Joanna uses to hang out n sheets?

- n - 1
- n + 1
- 2*n – 1
- n + 2

c) Luisa and Joanna hang out the same number of sheets. Joanna uses x laundry pegs. Which option allows calculating the number of laundry pegs used by Louisa?

- (x – 1) *2
- 2*x – 1
- x + 1
- x : 2 + 1

Fig. 3. The math test: questions from INVALSI test

representation of the question: students may not have identified the variable x with a part of the segment in the figure or they may had difficulties in understanding that the length of the entire segment was 53. In fact, they didn't met such kind of representation within programming. Surely, there are some limitations: the use of closed-ended questions does not allow observing the cognitive

Table 2. Percentage of correct answers. The national results refer to 8th grade and 10th grade levels.

	Our students' performance	National performance
Q1 (8th grade)	(a) 84%, (b) 88%	(a) 90%, (b) 85%
Q2 (8th grade)	24%	49%
Q3 (10th grade)	60%	56%
Q4 (8th grade)	(a) 44%, (b) 60%, (c) 56%	(a) 50%, (b) 57%, (c) 52%

processes involved; moreover, selecting the correct answer from among a range of options, is easier than asking students to discover their own a formula. Nevertheless, the collected data provided us with several points of consideration for further development.

4 Further Development and Conclusion

In this paper we described an advanced informatics curriculum implemented in a primary school and we discussed about its impact in the students' algebraic thinking. Although, the concept of variable in computer science is not exactly the same than in mathematics [22], the emerged data suggest that, through programming, children can be introduced to the use of symbolization so that a variable appears quite familiar when it is used within the mathematical context. Of course, we are not saying that our students acquired the same knowledge of students in 8th or 10th grade, but the results seem to indicate that programming is an effective way to anticipate mathematical concept that are particularly tricky for the students. Somehow we can assume that the variable concept, apparently so unnatural for many students, lies instead in a sort of Vygotskian "zone of proximal development" since the primary school. Therefore, the computer, under the teacher's guidance, acted as a"bridge" between the arithmetic reasoning and the algebraic one. In the future work we aim at further investigating the obtained results asking students to find their own algebraic representation of a certain problem, in order to discover how deep and well-structured is their understanding of variables. Finally, all the questions we selected aimed at evaluating a specific aspect of algebra that is the modelling of problems through the mathematical language - the same process at the base of computational thinking. The affinities existing between the algebraic thinking and the CT, suggest that the evaluation of the first could be used, at least partially, to assess the second. We plan to organize further investigations to obtain a stronger evidence of our hypothesis though the obtain results are in our opinion already encouraging.

Acknowledgement. We thank the school "Collegio Pio X" and all the students from class "5 Attivamente" that cooperated eagerly in this study.

References

1. Agatolio, F., Moro, M.: A workshop to promote Arduino-based robots as wide spectrum learning support tools. In: Merdan, M., Lepuschitz, W., Koppensteiner, G., Balogh, R. (eds.) Robotics in Education. AISC, vol. 457, pp. 113–125. Springer, Cham (2017). https://doi.org/10.1007/978-3-319-42975-5_11
2. Alimisis, D.: Exploring paths to integrate robotics in science and technology education: from teacher training courses to school classes. IJREA: Int. J. Robot., Educ. Art **2**(2), 16–23 (2012)
3. Alimisis, D.: Educational robotics: open questions and new challenges. Themes Sci. Technol. Educ. **6**(1), 63–71 (2013)
4. Ambrosio, A.P., Almeida, L.S., Macedo, J., Franco, A.H.R.: Exploring core cognitive skills of computational thinking. In: Psychology of Programming Interest Group Annual Conference 2014 (PPIG 2014), pp. 25–34 (2014)
5. Barr, V., Stephenson, C.: Bringing computational thinking to k-12: what is involved and what is the role of the computer science education community? ACM Inroads **2**(1), 48–54 (2011)
6. Benton, L., Hoyles, C., Kalas, I., Noss, R.: Building mathematical knowledge with programming: insights from the scratchmaths project. Suksapattana Foundation (2016)
7. Bocconi, S., Chioccariello, A., Dettori, G., Ferrari, A., Engelhardt, K., et al.: Developing computational thinking in compulsory education-implications for policy and practice. Tech. rep, Joint Research Centre (Seville site) (2016)
8. Carraher, D.W.: Early algebra and algebraic reasoning. Second Handbook of Research on Mathematics Teaching and Learning, pp. 669–705 (2007)
9. Eguchi, A.: Educational robotics for promoting 21st century skills. J. Autom. Mob. Robot. Intell. Syst. **8**(1), 5–11 (2014)
10. Ferrara, F., Pratt, D., Robutti, O., et al.: The role and uses of technologies for the teaching of algebra and calculus. In: Handbook of Research on the Psychology of Mathematics Education. Past, Present and Future, pp. 237–274 (2006)
11. Hoyles, C., Lagrange, J.B.: Mathematics Education and Technology: Rethinking the Terrain. Springer, Boston (2010). https://doi.org/10.1007/978-1-4419-0146-0
12. Kelleher, C., Pausch, R.: Using storytelling to motivate programming. Commun. ACM **50**(7), 58–64 (2007)
13. Kieran, C.: Research on the learning and teaching of algebra. In: Handbook of Research on the Psychology of Mathematics Education: Past, Present and Future, pp. 11–49 (2006)
14. Linchevski, L.: Algebra with numbers and arithmetic with letters: a definition of pre-algebra. J. Math. Behav. **14**(1), 113–120 (1995)
15. Noss, R.: Constructing a conceptual framework for elementary algebra through logo programming. Educ. Stud. Math. **17**(4), 335–357 (1986)
16. Nunes, T., Bryant, P., Watson, A.: Key Understandings in Mathematics Learning. Nuffield Foundation, London (2009)
17. Papert, S.: Mindstorms: Children, Computers, and Powerful Ideas. Basic Books, Inc. (1980)
18. Papert, S., Harel, I.: Situating constructionism. Constructionism **36**(2), 1–11 (1991)
19. Qualls, J.A., Sherrell, L.B.: Why computational thinking should be integrated into the curriculum. J. Comput. Sci. Colleges **25**(5), 66–71 (2010)

20. Slavin, R.E.: Synthesis of research of cooperative learning. Educ. Leadersh. **48**(5), 71–82 (1991)
21. Sung, W., Ahn, J., Black, J.B.: Introducing computational thinking to young learners: practicing computational perspectives through embodiment in mathematics education. Technol. Knowl. Learn. **22**(3), 443–463 (2017)
22. Usiskin, Z.: Conceptions of school algebra and uses of variables. Ideas Algebra, K-12 **8**, 19 (1988)
23. Vallerand, R.J., Fortier, M.S., Guay, F.: Self-determination and persistence in a real-life setting: toward a motivational model of high school dropout. J. Pers. Soc. Psychol. **72**(5), 1161 (1997)
24. Voogt, J., Fisser, P., Good, J., Mishra, P., Yadav, A.: Computational thinking in compulsory education: Towards an agenda for research and practice. Educ. Inf. Technol. **20**(4), 715–728 (2015)
25. Weintrop, D., et al.: Defining computational thinking for mathematics and science classrooms. J. Sci. Educ. Technol. **25**(1), 127–147 (2016)
26. Wilkerson, M.H., Fenwick, M.: Using mathematics and computational thinking. In: Helping Students Make Sense of the World Using Next Generation Science and Engineering Practices, pp. 181–204 (2017)
27. Wing, J.M.: Computational thinking. Commun. ACM **49**(3), 33–35 (2006)
28. Wing, J.M.: Computational thinking and thinking about computing. Philos. Trans. R. Soc. Lond. A Math. Phys. Eng. Sci. **366**(1881), 3717–3725 (2008)

Computer Tools in Teaching and Studying Informatics

Gamification of Problem Solving Process Based on Logical Rules

Fedor Novikov(✉) and Viktor Katsman(✉)

St. Petersburg Polytechnic University, St. Petersburg, Russia
fedornovikov51@gmail.com, vikto9494@gmail.com

Abstract. One of the main elements of the modern educational process in the field of IT is the solution of logical-combinatorial problems. When solving such problems, learners need to build a new solution based on the set of basic operations studied before being combined according to certain rules. To consolidate these skills, leaner need to solve a reasonable number of problems that leads to need of verification of a huge number of solutions.

Many systems allow us to automate the verification of solutions. In most cases, these systems check pure answer only, but not the progress of the solution itself. Such a method of verification does not exclude the possibility of obtaining the correct answer and the credited task with an incorrect or inconsistent solution.

We propose a method for verifying the solution of problems, based on search of valid transformations, or stepwise refinements, similar to search for proof in logical calculi. This means that, the system at each step effectively sorts out all possible transformations, trying to find one that the learner applied. In this case, the system not only can find an error in the solution, but also indicate the source of this error, which is wrong transition between steps.

In addition to automatically verifying the solutions, this approach allows us to generate tasks that require the application of specific rules. Also the application of the rules can be interpreted as "moves" in the intellectual game. Then the solution of the problem turns into a game process, and the correct solution corresponds to a sequence of steps leading to the victory in the game.

The proposed approach was tested on students of the junior courses and showed good results. Namely, in the conducted experiments the efficiency of the teacher's work when checking solutions increased more than 4 times.

Keywords: Education · Problem solution · Learning automation
Logical rules · Stepwise refinement

1 Introduction

To date, automation is one of the most effective, and therefore widespread ways to increase productivity. In particular, automatic learning environment systems become much more popular. Such systems are able to perform part

S. N. Pozdniakov and V. Dagienė (Eds.): ISSEP 2018, LNCS 11169, pp. 369–380, 2018.
https://doi.org/10.1007/978-3-030-02750-6_28

of the teacher's work or significantly simplify it, allowing teachers to concentrate on the most important and interesting aspects of their work. More routine things can be performed by machines, which will not get tired or annoyed, unlike live teachers. Teachers are required to thing only once, but very carefully what exactly has to be done and how to do it. After that machines will work and their work is much easier to scale, and the quality of their work does not depend on their mood and personal circumstances, but only on the original algorithm inherent in them [1,2].

Different aspects of the teachers functions could be automated: the presentation of new material, discipline maintenance during classes, checking solutions and answers, and others. Automation of many of these aspects is already actively used, for example, during the lesson some part of the teacher's instruction is replaced by a video recording. In online learning systems, video recording allows the teacher to replicate their instruction. Such automation requires the teacher only one-time qualitative preparation of the video recording, instead of having to repeat recorded instruction time and time again.

It is much more difficult to competently automate the work of a teacher in situations where an individual approach to the learner is required, as well as understanding of his or her psychology, mood, and level of knowledge. After initial instruction, it is necessary to consolidate it, which is achieved by means of solving a large number of tasks.

It is desirable to select the tasks individually for each learner so that to solve them, he or she would be required to apply the newly acquired skills, as well as their poorest skills from the recent training course. In addition to selecting tasks for learners it is also necessary to check their response and solutions. It is desirable that when receiving the results of the test, the learner could understand where exactly he or she could have made a mistake, and, perhaps, could also get a clue how this error should be corrected.

The opportunity to generate tasks and check their answers and solutions automatically, taking into account the requirements described in the previous paragraph, opens a lot of prospects in the field of teaching. In particular, it reduces the time that the teacher takes to check solutions. In addition to the diversity of full-time education and the development of distance learning, this opportunity also helps to turn the learning process into a game, which significantly increases the learners motivation and makes the hole process of learning more engaging.

In this article, we describe a method that allows generating tasks and checking their solutions automatically, as well as the opportunities for the learning process to be gamified based on the proposed method. The method is particularly well suited for tasks in Computer Science and Discrete Mathematics in the areas of set theory and combinatorics and has been repeatedly tested by us on the junior students of the Peter the Great Saint-Petersburg Polytechnic University.

The paper is organized as follows. Section 2 provides an overview of the existing methods that allow generating task conditions and verifying their solutions. The Sect. 3 describes the basis of the proposed method. Section 4 covers the opportunities of using this method, and, also, for the gamifying of the learning process. The final Sect. 5 contains the results of experimental verification of the effectiveness of the method.

2 Existing Methods Exercises Automation

To date, the verification of the answer is a common method of automated verification of the solution of the problem. In this case, the teacher manually sets the condition of the problem and the correct answer criteria, which will determine the correctness of the answer given by the learner. Accordingly, the task is counted for the learner if and only if his or her answer meets the criteria set by the teacher.

Criteria for the correctness of the answer are different. The simplest criterion for the correct answer is the correct answer itself. In the field of IT, it is usually a number or some sequence of symbols, for example, corresponding to the result of the work of some algorithm. If the answer can be written in different ways, for example, with different precision or different symbolic expressions, then you can either supplement the condition with the rules for formulating an answer or allow the learner to pick one of the multiple choose options. Both options theoretically allow the teacher to test the answer in any Computer Science task and are widely used in both Computer Science exams and distance learning, for example, on the Coursera [3], Stepic [4], WebWork [5], Moodle [6] and many others.

Nevertheless, in many cases, these methods significantly increase the routine component of the problem-solving process. For example, if the learner is asked to choose the right program from the suggested ones, he or she will be required to read all the suggested programs, including those which will not lead to the desired result. This is because the skills necessary to construct the learners own program differ significantly from the skills necessary to read and understand existing ones. Also, the answer can be guessed by chance, and the skill will not be mastered.

In some cases, answers recorded in different ways can also be unambiguously compared. For example, the equality of two symbolic expressions could be checked automatically if these expressions contain only natural numbers and variables that are linked with addition, subtraction and multiplication. Tarski's algorithm allows us to verify the truth of closed arithmetic formulae of the first order with variables for real numbers, that is, with a finite set of real numbers [7]. But for most problems there are no simple checks: for example, the impossibility of automatically checking the equivalence of two programs by their code follows from Rice's theorem [8]. The impossibility of automatically verifying the equality of symbolic expressions using rational numbers and the operations of exponentiation follows from Richardson's theorem [9].

Thus, we cannot verify the correct answer in all cases given the single value only. For example, consider the answer in a form of symbolic expression that contains variables: $(x+1)/x = 1+1/x$. Which form should be considered as the only right one?

In many cases, the problem of the ambiguity of the answer form is solved by testing. The method involves in comparing the learner's answer with the correct one by performing a series of computational experiments, in each of which the result obtained by the learner at certain values of the parameters is compared to the correct answer. If in all computational experiments the learner's answer coincides with the correct one, the solution is considered correct, otherwise, you can give the learner a counterexample.

Such a verification method is probabilistic, since an incorrect answer can be interpreted as correct if the test coverage is not complete. Thus, the selection of the values of the parameters for which it is required to perform computational experiments (test cases) becomes the key factor. The teacher needs either to conduct it manually - to work out the tests, or to provide an algorithm for this selection - to design the automatic tests generation. Both methods require a serious effort. Nevertheless, this method of verification is widely used in distance learning systems, especially for software testing. For example, when creating online courses in the Stepic system, you can ask the learners to write programs, and you can use automatic tests as a test criterion [10].

For example, when testing the expression "$a+b = a*b$", the test "$a = b = 2$" passes, and the test "$a = b = 3$" does not.

In addition to the chance of interpreting the wrong answer as correct, such testing has another drawback, namely the lack of form verification. However, the form of the answer is often important. When programming it is important to follow the style of coding. When specifying a symbolic expression in an answer, it is desirable to simplify it. Sometimes it is required to verify if the learner has or has not applied a certain operation in his or her solution.

In most school tasks in Computer Science, the methods listed above make it possible to automatically verify the correctness of the answer, and sometimes to show the learner where he or she made a mistake. But all these methods allow you to check only the final result without analyzing the way in which the learner has obtained it. In fact, it often happens that learners come to the right answer by chance, without taking into account a number of important things. If you check not only the value of the answer, but the solution itself, you can help the learner find the point from which his or her reasoning became erroneous.

Another important aspect is the automatic task generation. This aspect seems less important since it is required to check the solution of problems much more often than to draw up tasks. In addition, in most cases, you can find ready-made tasks, rather than inventing your own. Therefore, the main research is carried out in the field of automatic distribution of tasks already prepared by the teacher among the learners, depending on their individual progress.

This issue is usually solved due to the detailed manual categorizing of tasks by their complexity, topics and manual setting of the rules for the learners transition between tasks, depending on the tasks already solved by them and their feedback on how difficult it was to solve these tasks. Similar adaptive learning approaches are used in many distance learning systems, for example, in NeuroRehabLab [11], Coursera [3] or Stepic [4].

Nevertheless, the compilation or even the selection of tasks also requires a significant effort from the teacher, and in many cases it is a routine work. For example, in situations where a large number of similar tasks are required, for instance, different options for different learners in order to combat the learner's cheating. In this case, the teacher can be helped by an approach that allows you to create a task template, and then on this template automatically generate tasks individually for learners. This approach is implemented, for example, in the WebWork system, where the task template is a text in which special variables and expressions can occur. When generating each variable, a random value is assigned to it, which then replaces all occurrences of this variable [5].

The approach proposed in the article significantly expands the prospects both for automated verification of solutions and for generating tasks.

3 Rule-Searching Method

In the process of solving a typical problem, the learner, first of all, reads and interprets the condition of the problem. After that, step by step he or she begins to derive corollaries from the condition and it continues until the next deduced consequence leads them to the solution of the problem. As a solution to the problem, the learner presents a sequence of transformations (steps). Such a sequence corresponds to the process of solving the problem after understanding its condition and is the only information that the teacher receives for verification. That is, when verifying a written solution, the teacher can check only the correctness of the sequence presented by the learners without any chance to trace the course of the learner's reasoning when interpreting the condition. The teacher can check only the final result: the expressions and formulae, not the learners thoughts.

The process of creating a sequence of transformations by the learner can be divided into steps: each step corresponds to the derivation of a new consequence based on the condition and the consequences already deduced from previous steps. The consequences are deduced with the help of previously learned rules describing arithmetic-logical transformations (operations). The step taken according to these rules is considered correct. If the entire solution consists of correct steps, and the required result is found, then the solution should be considered correct.

If it is impossible to find the rule by which the step was taken, then the step must have been either incorrect or too complicated, that is too many rules might have been applied at once. Both of these two cases should be the subject of criticism: in the first case the step itself contradicts the theory, in the second case the learner made an unclear, vague transition: learner could have guessed it or could have missed an important detail. That is, we consider reasonable the behavior of the verification system if in those cases when no suitable rules are found, it will give a message about the incomprehensibility of the transition.

A design which allows you to use the method of rule-searching to verify the correctness of the steps performed by the learner in the process of solving the problem is as follows:

1. The teacher once sets the rules adequate for the solution of problems, corresponding to the theory and the level of the learners knowledge, so that each rule is an elementary and fully understandable step for the learner. Also, according to the level of the learners, the teacher can set the weight to the rules and the upper limit to the total weight of rules that can be applied simultaneously, in one step. The step should be split into several steps if it has too large weight.
2. The learner prepares the solution of the problem step by step in a special format, understood by the checking system.
3. The checking system sequentially follows the steps taken by the learner and at each step it sorts out the rules set by the teacher. If for some step no rules are found, permitting to take this step from the previous ones, the system gives a message: 'the transition to such a step is not valid'. Afterwards, the learner can correct the decision of a problem and submit it again for checking.

This design is well extensible, some additions to the method give a very significant increase in speed and ease of solution of problems for the learner. For example, in addition to the steps of the solution, the learner can be allowed to derive new rules based on the existing ones, and then use them as the existing ones. That is, if there is a rule that is too complicated for one step, which the learner wants to use repeatedly, he or she can once derive this rule out of existing rules, and then use it in one step. This is analogous to using auxiliary lemmas in a long derivation.

Consequently, the proposed method allows us to check the problem solutions that can be described by the rules, for the formulation of which it will be possible to create a language. The ideas of the method are very close to the physics of the process of problem solution verifying and therefore one can expect that this method will be easy for both students and teachers to understand.

4 Method Application in School Combinatorics

The rules of school combinatorics are simple and well known. To apply the method, it is necessary to specify the language or notation interpreted by the learner and the automatic checking system, and also to specify the rules describing the transformations permitted in the school combinatorics.

By the problems of school combinatorics, we mean the problems of proving and solving equations in which, in particular, the following combinatorial numbers can be used:

1. $U(m, n) = m^n$ - number of placements with repetitions
2. $A(m, n) = m!/(m - n)!$ - number of placements
3. $P(n) = n!$ Is the number of permutations

4. $C(m, n) = m!/n!/(m - n)!$ - number of combinations
5. $V(m, n) = (m+n-1)!/(m-1)!/n!$ - number of combinations with repetitions

To write a solution, the learner uses the common text notation for recording arithmetic transformations of numbers, variables, and functions similar to programming languages such as C++ or Java. Complex constructs, such as the sum or product of n expressions, are introduced as functions in combination with the rules for converting them. The learner can put additional rules inside square brackets and annotate the application of the transformation to both sides of the equation - in curly brackets.

Let's consider some features of the proposed notation on the example of solving a specific problem: "solve the equation: '$C(v + 1, v) = k$' relative to the variable 'v''.

1. $v =$ [// unknown
2. $C(v + 1, v) = k$; // initial equation, C - number of combinations
3. $k = C(v + 1, v) = (v + 1)!/v!/(v + 1 - v)! = (v + 1)!/v!/1! = (v + 1)!/v! = (v + 1) * v!/v! = v + 1$; // the expansion and simplification of C (v + 1, v)
4. $v + 1 = k; -1$; // the subtraction of 1 from both parts is announced
5. $v = k - 1$ // the rule derived from the initial equation
6.] $= k - 1$ // answer: the derived rule immediately gives an expression for v

The system splits the solution of the problem into steps and checks for each pair of steps whether there is a conversion rule between them. For example, in line 3 the learner consecutively applied the rules for expanding the number of combinations, reducing terms, eliminating 1! and similar constants, expanding the factorial, reducing fractions.

In order for the system to be able to test tasks on combinatorics, in addition to the standard rules for converting arithmetic expressions, it is required to specify the transformation rules used for solving combinatorial numbers, as well as transformations of the sum and product of n expressions.

As rules for transforming arithmetic operations, we have taken the rules that correspond to the basic properties of these operations: commutativity, associativity and distributivity, and, also, the well-known algebra rules (for example, rules for removing parenthesis when rearranging the exponent of a sum and difference of powers). It can be suggested that the sum and product of n expressions be transformed by dividing it into two parts and omitting the summation sign in trivial parts whose upper limit coincides with the lower one. The rules of transformations of combinatorial numbers correspond to their definitions. Additional rules, for example, expressing some combinatorial numbers through others, learners, if they need, can derive by themselves.

4.1 Automated Check of Solutions to Tasks

The method can be used to check combinatorial problems of solving equations and the proof of identities. In solving problems of proof, it is required that the learners sequence of transformations bind the left and right sides of the identities to be proved. When solving equations, it is required to check that expressions for all the unknown variables are derived from the condition and that the unknown variables themselves are not used in these expressions.

The second section describes how to apply a method to verify the correctness of the transformation sequence. Accordingly, when verifying the proof, it is required to verify that the learner has deduced a sequence of equivalent transformations that connects both the left and the right sides of the statement that had to be proved. This means that the right and the left sides of the statement must be found among the consequences of one sequence. Checking the equivalence of the transformation will automatically follow from the equivalence of the rules by which it was carried out, that is, not only the result of applying the rule follows the initial statement, but also vice versa: the result of its application follows the original statement.

4.2 Automated Task Generation

The idea of representing problem solving process in the form of consecutive steps, following one another according to specified rules, makes it possible to generate tasks that require the application of precisely those rules that the learner knows the worst. Statistics on the mastering of the rules can be obtained automatically when checking previously solved problems. Thus, the learning process can be individually adjusted to the learner as accurately as possible if a sufficient bank of various tasks is collected.

The parameters of task generation are set on the basis of the generating grammar, the rules of which correspond to the meaningful rules of transformations in the conferred area. In addition, these rules can be weighed by scales in accordance with their complexity for the learner. Then, the generation of tasks can occur as follows: an assertion or expression is generated randomly, which is then becomes the left-hand side of the statement you need to prove or to find. Then this statement or expression is transformed by chosen at random rules, and at that the rules the worst mastered by the learner are chosen with the most weight. The result of the transformations becomes the right-hand side of the statement that the learner has to prove or the initial condition in the equation.

For example, a learner has difficulties in transforming the number of combinations with repetitions $V(m,n)$. Then the basic formulation of the condition "$m * C(m-1, n-1) = n * C(m, n)$" can be transformed with a high probability into the following: "$m * C(m-1, n-1) = n * V(m-n+1, n)$".

4.3 Gamification Based on Rule Search

Teaching games can pursue two tasks: developing the learner's skills of rules manipulation when solving a problem and, also, remembering the permissible transformation rules themselves. The skills of rule manipulation are extremely wide: it is assumed that the learner, in possession of a goal and the rules, can achieve the goal using these rules, at least in the area under study. The memorization of rules also occurs when they are repeatedly applied.

To date, there are many games to memorize the rules, in which the conversion rules are simply to be written, composed of characters, choose the right one and many others. To win this game you need either to memorize the rules or to thoroughly understand their logic. On the basis of the method proposed, it is possible to build games in which the main emphasis is not on memory training, but on the skills of constructing a solution or proof based on acquired rules.

For example, the player at any given time sees on the screen some formula and a set of rules that can be applied to this formula. The player can select a rule and drag it to a specific place in the formula. If the rule is applicable to this place of the formula, the formula automatically changes according to this rule, and then the new formula and a new set of rules applicable to it appear on the screen. The purpose of the game is to derive a new formula from the given one. Besides the new formula being determined by an expression, it can also be predetermined by some criteria. The first case corresponds to the problems of identity proof. The second can correspond to the problems of solving equations.

In addition to standard interest boosters, such as shooting formulae in the direction of the place of substitution or modern graphics with inspiring music, the game may contain specific additions appropriate to the tasks of the educational process. For example, a task may be reach the goal in the least number of steps, that is, with minimum applications of rules. If weighed rules are used, the task may be to apply rules with the largest average weight.

Besides, a serious symbolic significance can be attached to the transition to a new level of complexity. It can correspond to a profound familiarization of the learner with the ways of applying all the rules at this level and the emergence of the new ones, without which the tasks at the new level cannot be solved. The new tasks at the level can be generated in such a way that to solve them the learner is required to use the rules used at this level the least often.

The range of gamification possibilities is not limited to combinatorics. It can also be successfully applied for the purpose of developing the learners' skills of logical transformations and their memorization in almost any field if the theory is described by the rules. The work of the teacher when creating and configuring such games is minimized: just as for verifying the solution of problems, the teacher is required to specify the permissible transformation rules only. If the game consists of several levels and other additions, the teacher may need to adjust the parameters of these additions, for example, set the new rules introduced at the new levels in a logical sequence for learning.

Thus, the proposed method can be used not only for automatic generation and verification of problem solutions, but also for creating a class of games applicable for studying the fields of knowledge which are described by rules. At the same time, the application of the method requires minimal expenses from the teacher, incomparably less time, which is spent on manual creating and checking solutions of numerous tasks (Fig. 1).

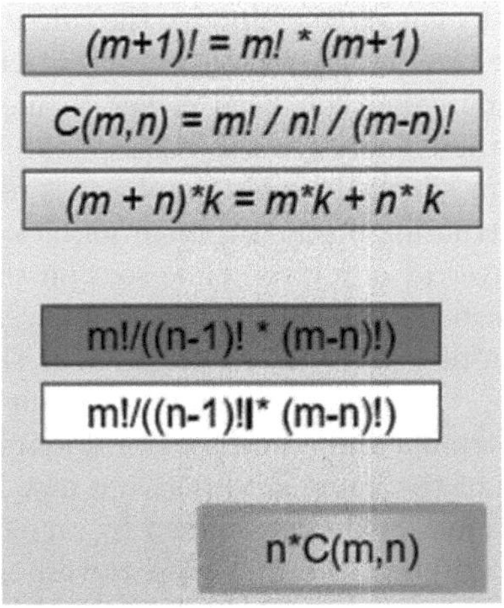

Fig. 1. The player receives the original expression (in the center) and the target expression (in the bottom right-hand corner) to which it should be reduced. At the top of the screen, possible transformations are displayed. With each step the player selects one of them and drags it to the original expression, which is modified according to the transformation. This happens until the original expression is converted to the target expression. To pass the level, you have to reach the goal for a certain number of steps.

5 Experiments

The experiments were carried out to make sure that the proposed method is applicable not only for teachers but for learners as well. Namely, it is necessary to verify that the notation and rules proposed for writing expressions can be quickly mastered, that the problem solving will take approximately the same time to put it into the computer as it takes to write the solution on paper, and that the results obtained by automated verification of solutions will be close to the results deduced by the teacher.

So far we have already managed to conduct experiments on 2 groups of 2nd-year students of the Polytechnic University within the framework of the course "Discrete Mathematics" in 2017 and 2018. Over the past year, the testing program has been slightly improved: some bugs were fixed and logic was improved, but the overall concept of experiments has not been changed. In the framework of experiments, first the learners were briefly explained the principles of the system, and then they were asked to solve a number of problems in combinatorics, set theory, and logical calculi. During the solution process, students had possibilities to run automatic checking for current version of solution, to see the checking results with information about exact place where the error was made and to correct the solution. After deadline the final versions of students's solutions were automatically verified by the system.

The results show that students are able to quickly absorb the new rules for recording solutions. There was only one learner in two groups who could not solve any problem at all. The problem solving speed on the computer on average turned out to be about one and a half times less than the speed of solving problems on paper. It is possible to increase the speed of recording the solution by means of significant improvements in notation and interface.

Another goal of the experiment was to get an idea of how much time the teacher saves due to automated verification. It took about an hour to compile the rules (one-time routine), another half-hour took was spent on bringing together of the results of the automated verification. Manual verification of solutions of the same tasks for the reference group of students took more than 6 h.

Thus, the conducted experiments confirm the possibility and relevance of using the proposed expression method for automated verification of solutions of standard problems.

6 Conclusion

The proposed method significantly expands the prospects for generating tasks in informatics and verifying their solutions. The results of using this method substantially depend on the degree of ease with which the learner perceives the recording of problem solutions, which should also be understood by the checking system.

The language used for combinatorics problems seems to be acceptable for use, but there are possibilities for significant improvements we keep working in this direction. We also carry on working on creating languages for tasks from other subject areas, including logical transformations of sets, logical calculi, coding, and some others.

References

1. Vene, V.: Comparing different styles of automated feedback for programming exercises. In: Proceedings of the 17th Koli Calling International Conference on Computing Education Research, Koli Calling 2017, pp. 183–194 (2017). https://doi.org/10.1145/3141880.3141909
2. Tirronen, M., Tirronen, V.: A framework for evaluating student interaction with automatically assessed exercises. In: Proceedings of the 16th Koli Calling International Conference on Computing Education Research, Koli Calling 2016, pp. 180–181 (2016). https://doi.org/10.1145/2999541.2999568
3. Coursera Homepage. https://ru.coursera.org/. Accessed 19 May 2017
4. Stepik Homepage. https://welcome.stepik.org/en. Accessed 19 May 2017
5. WeBWorK Homepage. https://webwork.elearning.ubc.ca/webwork2/. Accessed 19 May 2017
6. Moodle Homepage. https://moodle.org/. Accessed 19 May 2017
7. Rogers, H.: The Theory of Recursive Functions and Effective Computability. MIT Press (1987). ISBN: 0-262-68052-1; ISBN: 0-07-053522-1

8. Rice, H.: Classes of recursively enumerable sets and their decision problems. Trans. Am. Math. Soc. **74**(2), 358 (1953). https://doi.org/10.2307/1990888
9. Richardson, D.: Some unsolvable problems involving elementary functions of a real variable. J. Symb. Log. **33**(4), 514–520 (1968). https://doi.org/10.2307/2271358
10. Stepik Code Lesson. https://stepik.org/lesson/9173/step/1?course=Epic-Guide-to-Stepik&unit=1718. Accessed 19 May 2017
11. NeuroRehabLab Homepage. https://neurorehabilitation.m-iti.org/TaskGenerator/. Accessed 19 May 2017

Music Computer Technologies in Informatics and Music Studies at Schools for Children with Deep Visual Impairments: From the Experience

Irina Gorbunova[1(✉)] and Anastasia Govorova[1,2]

[1] Herzen State Pedagogical University of Russia, 48, emb. river Moika, 191186 St. Petersburg, Russia
gorbunovaib@herzen.spb.ru

[2] Children's Art School "Okhta Center for Aesthetic Education", 8 "A", Marshal Tukhachevsky st., 195253 St. Petersburg, Russia

Abstract. Music computer technologies (MCT) open up wide opportunities for blind students to more effectively study the diverse content and methods of presentation of educational material in Informatics, contributing to the achievement of positive learning outcomes in a shorter time. This is especially important for children who study in children's music schools. Mastering of MCT by children with profound visual impairment has a number of characteristic features, which are most clearly manifested in the initial period of studying Informatics. With the help of contemporary computer technologies (speech synthesizers, Braille displays, etc.), as well as due to the possibility of using "hot keys" blind students quickly master many MCT-programs.

The main objectives of the lessons on musical informatics are: to study the basic concepts related to the receipt and use of information, both in school and in everyday life; to obtain skills in working with a computer and some peripherals. In the program considered by the authors of the article it is supposed to study the basic concepts and acquire the skills included in the existing programs in informatics, taking into account the fact that all tasks in informatics are based on materials related to music.

The program is designed in such a way that it is possible to perform the proposed tasks not only with the help of a computer keyboard and "hotkeys", but also with the help of MIDI-keyboard. This is achieved by the connection between the actual music and informatics.

The authors also propose to consider the application software – a tool that would be accessible to the sighted and blind and would not cause difficulties in working with him/her both in some and in others: the exchange of information between the teacher and the blind student or vice versa - the blind teacher and the ordinary/seeing pupil.

Keywords: Inclusive education · Informatics · Music computer technologies Visual impairment pupil

S. N. Pozdniakov and V. Dagienė (Eds.): ISSEP 2018, LNCS 11169, pp. 381–389, 2018.
https://doi.org/10.1007/978-3-030-02750-6_29

1 Introduction

The development of computer technology in the late 20s – early 21st century has significantly expanded the ways of obtaining information. High-tech information educational environment requires the search for new approaches and fundamentally new systems of education in the School of the Digital Age. "The ICT revolution brings along an increased potential for inclusion and participation, but also risks for exclusion and thus the responsibility for implementing eAccessibility. It provokes a growing number of challenging research questions. Old boundaries of concepts dissolve, new approaches and fresh thinking are formed: not only in technical terms, but also in social, economic, pedagogic and other terms" – G. Kouroupetroglou, General Chair of the 16th International Conference on Computers Helping People with Special Needs ICCHP-2018 (July 11–13, 2018, Linz, Austria) said [9].

Innovative pedagogy of music and informatics at the present stage is associated with the use of music computer technologies (MCT), it is a contemporary and effective means of improving the quality of teaching the art of music and informatics at all levels of the educational process [5].

MCT is a unique technology for the implementation of inclusive pedagogical process in teaching children with disabilities.

Possibilities of MCT for inclusion and participation in the information society strive for better Assistive Technology "for support, enhancement and restoration of resources for people with disabilities and compensating limitations of standardized Human Computer Interaction (HCI)". These opportunities still gains "more importance due to the ongoing ICT revolution (Internet/ Web of Things/ Ubiquitous computing/ Cloud based services)" [9].

It should be noted that the consequent application of MCT in inclusive pedagogy still remains little known among the contemporary pedagogical approaches.

Nevertheless, there are some remarkable premises for forming and developing the methods constituting this approach. These premises have been discussed by the authors of the article with colleagues in Hungary, including Prof., Dr. N. Maczelka, Pianist, Head of the Arts Institute and the Department of Music Education Faculty, Prof., Dr. T. Csendes, Head of Department of Computational Optimization University of Szeged, Prof., Dr. M. Benedict, Department of Theoretical Physics, some colleagues from the Eszterhazy Karoly University (Eger) and Eötvös Loránd University (ELTE), Budapest, - as well as with Dr. I. G. Alieva, Baku Musical Academy named after U. Hajibaili, Azerbaijan.

All of them have marked that MCT are able to make a significant contribution to the improvement of the life of pupil with disabilities.

2 MCT as New Creative Educational Medium

The authors were guided by the general principles that had been developed at the Educational and Methodical Laboratory 'Music Computer Technologies', Herzen State Pedagogical University of Russia (Saint Petersburg). Sphere of interests of its members includes the problems of interrelation of natural and technical sciences and humanities, as well as the possibilities of applying the results of such interrelation for the purposes of music education and upbringing. Scientific group of the Laboratory also take part in working out the specialized software for computer music devices and in application of this software in pedagogical processes.

Research activities of the members of Laboratory including such directions as:

- MCT in professional musical education (as a means to expand creative opportunities),
- MCT in general musical education (as one of the means of education),
- MCT as a means of rehabilitation of people with disabilities,
- MCT as the new direction in preparation of specialists of humanitarian and technological profile,
- MCT in the field of digital arts,
- MCT in information technology, psychoacoustics and musical acoustics.

Developments and researches in the field of musical pedagogics and musicology, music computer science (musical informatics), computer modeling of processes of musical creativity, timbre programming, art of performing skill and arrangement on electronic musical instruments, creative work in the field of computer music, mathematical methods in musicology, etc. – all these directions in its totality allow to work up the methodological principles and pedagogical approaches to the use of MCT in inclusive education (as part of eInclusion) for children with profound visual impairment. (See: [4, 5, 10] a.o.)

3 From the Experience

3.1 Psychological and Pedagogical Features of Teaching MCT for the Visually-Impaired

The process of teaching the MCT to people with profound visual impairments is related to the following main points. First of all, the computer facilitates a blind person's access to information of all kinds, but at the same time people with LHO on vision have a complex set of mental reactions that the teacher needs to keep in mind when giving classes.

The specificity of the training of blind MCT is also in the fact that this contingent of students is heterogeneous in the type of visual pathologies available, in the form of visual impairments, etc. at the same time, each group of people with LHO in vision, combined on the basis of the severity of visual pathology, is characterized by the presence of certain mental features that must be taken into account in the organization of the educational process. A significant role in the development of the blind basic computer skills play their visualization. A comprehensive study of this problem is being carried out by Y. Krivodonova (Ural State Pedagogical University, Ekaterinburg, Russia) and A. Voronov (Educational and Methodical Laboratory 'Music Computer Technologies', Herzen State Pedagogical University of Russia, Saint Petersburg). According to contemporary scientists, vision provides a person with about 90% of information. The image analysis allows us to study the spatial structures of the object, and the distribution of optical densities and colors reflects the most important information about the properties of both real and virtual objects of the world. Thus, we can say that visualization is of great importance in the process of development of the blind people, because it is thanks to the ability of a person to create a certain imaginary picture in the study of a computer program he has an adequate idea of their own actions; this “forms <…> the image of themselves as a figure, able to understand certain things, in certain computer programs” [11, p. 255].

Visualization plays a particularly important role in the development of the blind; it is objectively more difficult to study the basic, MCT-programs. It should be noted that each person who has an LHO on vision, regardless of the time of the onset of damage to the visual analyzer and the degree of its severity, the visualization is purely individual. This phenomenon is caused by a complex of various factors and largely depends on the strategy of family education, on the method of formation of a blind child or an adult who has lost his sight, “the ability to dream – visualize, to attract the desired images of certain objects to his/her imagination” [10, p. 256]. It should be emphasized that the development of MCT people with LHO on vision ability of a particular person to visualize often becomes a powerful mechanism that allows him/her to master a particular music program.

Thus, to achieve the best results in teaching people with LHO on vision, the teacher of the MCT should take into account the above features. The teacher, first of all, should form the ability of blind students to correlate the real image that appears in the process of mastering certain knowledge with the imaginary one. In this case, close attention should be paid to the individual characteristics of each individual student. For example, it should be borne in mind that the visualization of people with congenital blindness has an important distinctive feature: the image that arises from them in the study of a particular material is initially created on the basis of tactile sensation, and then can be endowed with visual elements. The teacher should be given material based on the method of visualization of a particular student. In particular, if a person with born blindness is given material based only on visual information, he/she will not be able to understand a lot, and if the same information is given out taking into account the peculiarities of his/her perception, the result will be noticeable immediately.

In addition, it is necessary to pay attention to the fact that in recent years, people with visual impairments are increasingly found in so-called “comorbidities”, that is, along with deep visual impairment, there are concomitant diseases, often associated with the defeat of the central nervous system. These diseases are mainly responsible for difficulties in assimilating the information offered, which greatly complicates the successful implementation of the learning process. In this regard, the same information should be presented by the ICT-teacher in different ways, taking into account the whole complex of psychophysical characteristics of a particular person. At the same time, for people with concomitant diseases, the work should be dosed, so as not to harm their health. It is noted that such people are not recommended to work permanently in the headphones, listening to the voice synthesizer programs JAWS (Job Access With Speech) or NVDA (NonVisual Desktop Access), because sounding headphones and voice synthesizer cause the rehabilitant increased feelings of fatigue.

We also note that all of the above psychological and pedagogical features of MCT training for students of specialized music schools and music classes for children with profound visual impairment determine the need for an individual approach, taking into account the state of health and psychological characteristics of a particular person, which is the basic principle of working with blind people of any age.

3.2 The Use of MCT in Teaching Informatics for Children with Deep Visual Impairment

For musicians with profound visual impairment, the use of a musical computer (MC) is of a particular importance [10]. First of all, the MC is for them a means of contact with the "outside world", however, it helps in the realization of their creative potential and adaptation in the modern social environment. MCT opens up a lot of opportunities for blind musicians to more effectively study a variety of content and methods of presentation of educational material, contributing to the achievement of positive learning outcomes in a shorter period of time [7]. However, the development of MCT by musicians with profound visual impairment has a number of characteristic features that are most clearly manifested in the initial period of training [3, 4].

First of all, it should be noted that with the help of contemporary computer technologies (speech synthesizers, Braille displays), as well as the possibility of using "hot" keys, blind people can master many MCT programs. Nevertheless, the specifics of teaching the ICT to people with profound visual impairment, is that the professional development of the ICT programs involves the presence of blind students' basic skills of a PC user. Getting skills to work with a "talking" computer is a time-consuming process that requires special training not only from students but also from their teachers. This is due to the widespread use of MCT by people with profound visual impairment, mainly in the field of secondary and higher music education, while at present, MCT is actively used at the early stages of education, including inclusive education (when working with children with hearing impairment, muscle-skeleton disorder).

One of the types of computers – a laptop – blind, like no other, is actively used, justifying in the literal sense the translation of its name: the laptop for them was not just a notebook, as well as a library, recorder and organizer. And for blind musicians, the computer has become even more of an assistant: with the advent of screen access programs, people with visual impairment were able to create, process, record and edit music on their own.

In training, we faced a shortage of Braille notes. And this fact helped us to look at the problem more broadly and deeply. After all, the problem is not in the notes or books themselves with these notes, but in the interaction of the teacher and the student. Exchange of information between a teacher and a blind student, or vice versa – a blind teacher and an ordinary student. The most important thing is to convey the information so that this information is correctly (adequate) interpreted. At this stage, there are many difficulties with different conventions: for the blind student, a teacher with specific knowledge is needed, and the blind teacher needs to explain to the sighted student certain symbols and styles of various signs, to be able to set new material, a new play.

3.3 The Use of Special Software in Teaching Informatics and Music for Schoolchildren with Visual Impairments

In the process of overcoming these difficulties, the idea was born to create an application software with which to solve these difficulties and overcome the barrier in the transmission of training information. To create a tool that would be accessible to the sighted and blind, and would not cause difficulties in working with it, both in some and in others. (In particular, we examine the concepts constituting the bases of education technologies that has earlier been used in inconsistent and contradictory ways.)

Of course, this software will be presented with certain requirements: full access from the keyboard, both in the set of the score, and in the management of all functions of this application; full information output through the speech synthesizer and Braille display; printout on solid media; the adequacy of the information displayed on the display.

This program should have the following properties and meet the following parameters:

1. The program should represent music notation editor with which possible to have a seamless set of notes or revision of the scores.
2. An important condition is the ability to enter notes and other necessary characters, as well as other manipulations and commands from the keyboard. Due to the fact that the blind person can't see the mouse, he/she performs the usual for the sighted person standard tasks using keyboard shortcuts (hot keys). In order for a blind person to fully use this program, the hot keys of this program should not coincide with the hot keys of the operating system, and simultaneously running programs.
3. The program must be "readable" using a speech synthesizer through screen access programs such as NVDA or JAWS. A screen access program is a special program for blind or visually impaired people, which performs the following functions: displays information from the computer monitor by means of sound (speech synthesizer) or tactile output to the Braille line. Often we are faced with a situation where the program is developed without taking into account the features of the interaction with the program screen access. In the future, at the request of the blind community, they try to adapt the interface of the already developed program for the needs of people with visual impairment. Our idea is that we initially take into account all the features of the screen access programs.
4. Adequate visualization of the interface. Quite often, special programs for the blind are developed without the correct graphical interface. For example, there is a situation when the program for the blind meets all the specifics of the work of people with visual impairment, but the computer monitor can be either a blank screen without images or a contour image, which is an inconvenience for the seeing users. In the development of our music editor, we aim to make *this software* available for everyone, both visually and with a full sound output.
5. Ability to import and export a music text to files of popular extensions. There are many music editors that save a music text in files with their extensions. Accordingly, there are many scores written in these extensions. Or another situation: the user either does not want to learn a new editor, or wants to use the familiar editor.

One of the tasks of our development is the fact that our software allows you to import files with various extensions into your environment. With *this software* property we want to achieve easier interaction between the sighted and the blind musician.

6. Ability to convert scanned scores to available formats. One of the known disadvantages of the screen access programs is the need to convert graphic images (graphic information is not readable or requires a certain recognition system). To date, there is no adequate Converter of a music text with access for blind users. This proposal is also due to the fact that there are a lot of scanned scores on the Internet, but, as due to the lack of screen access program mentioned above, blind people do not have access to these materials.

It should be that teaching materials on teaching informatics include: a set of materials for the teacher; a set of computer tasks for the pupil; a set of tasks in workbooks; a set of tasks for active logical and creative games using musical material.

4 Conclusions and Future Work

It is possible to solve the problems of information education for schoolchildren with deep visual impairments using specific software.

This application can be used in various fields of activity of blind musicians:

1. When teaching music to blind students of children's musical schools and children's schools of arts, this application will expand the available material. This program can be used in the process of teaching such disciplines as solfeggio, harmony, music theory, music literature, analysis of musical works, a special instrument, etc. The teacher can give a pre-prepared music text to the blind student, while he/she does not own Braille. And most importantly, from our point of view, the universal property of this program – the blind teacher has the opportunity to teach a sighted student, giving material through this program, which will contribute to the development and implementation of inclusive education.
2. Today there is a fact that the number of blind musicians is increasing. This circumstance is due to two main factors: firstly, children deprived of vision, by definition, possess acute hearing, which "takes over" partial replenishment of information about the outside world, and, secondly, the development of Information Technology (IT), in general, and MCT, in particular, open up unique prospects for people with visual impairment to provide and obtain musical information in almost full [1, 2, 6]. With the use of specially developed technologies, blind people are able to access all kinds and ways of transmitting information about music; all this gives blind people the opportunity to get a profession of a contemporary musician, corresponding to their interests and abilities. In this regard, our application will be useful and in demand for many, because it, for example, gives the opportunity to a trained musician to write a work and to share his/her work without anybody's assistance.
3. Thanks to the appearance of such an instrument as a music editor, the blind musician has the opportunity to become a full member of the creative group, to join

on stage, because in the process of work he/she can freely type music texts to exchange music and other materials.

We also propose to consider the application software – a tool that would be accessible to the sighted and blind and would not cause difficulties in working with him/her both in some and in others: the exchange of information between the teacher and the blind student or vice versa – the blind teacher and the ordinary/seeing student.

With the appearance of such an instrument, blind musicians have wide horizons: free exchange of a music text, free transfer of the material to the sighted musician, the possibility of full and unhindered cooperation between musicians [8].

This application software is now being worked up.

The results of the methodological principles and pedagogical approaches concerning the use of MCT in informatics and music studies at schools for children with deep visual impairments, worked out by the authors of the article, were presented at the Russian-Hungarian Education Forum, February 17, 2017 (Hungarian Cultural, Scientific and Information Centre, Moscow), at the annual International Research and Practical Conference 'Contemporary Musical Education' (2015, 2016, 2017, Saint Petersburg, Russia), and at the 16th International Conference on Computers Helping People with Special Needs, July 11–13, 2018 (Linz, Austria). The participants of the conferences have estimated these results as having good perspectives.

In the future, the developed software will become a multitasking tool for blind musicians in working with a music text, which will open up more horizons for musical creativity and allow the blind musician to work in a team with sighted people on an equal basis, without experiencing difficulties in reading and editing musical material. The application, developed on the basis of the latest achievements in the field of MCT, may become one of the essential elements of inclusive music education in the future [5] in various directions of its implementation.

References

1. Gorbunova, I.B.: Computer science and computer music technologies in education. Theory Pract. Soc. Dev. **12**, 428–432 (2015)
2. Gorbunova, I.B.: Information technology in music and music education. World Sci. Cult. Educ. **63**(2), 206–210 (2017)
3. Gorbunova, I.B.: Music computer: modeling the process of musical creativity. World Sci. Cult. Educ. **4**(65), 145–148 (2017)
4. Gorbunova, I.B.: Music computer technologies and digital humanities. In: Contemporary Musical Education – 2015, Proceedings of the 14th International Research and Practical Conference, vol. 1, pp. 29–34. Publishing House "The Herzen State Pedagogical University of Russia", St. Petersburg (2015)
5. Gorbunova, I.B.: Musical-computer technology: the laboratory. Mediamusic, no. 1, pp. 5–7 (2012). http://mediamusic-journal.com/Issues/1_5.html
6. Gorbunova, I.B., Chibirev, S.V.: Music computer technologies and the problem of modeling the process of musical creativity. In: Regional Informatics "RI-2014", Proceedings of the XIV St. Petersburg International Conference, pp. 293–294 (2014)

7. Gorbunova, I.B., Govorova, A.A.: Music computer technologies as a means of teaching people with visual impairment musical art. Theory Pract. Soc. Dev. **11**, 298–301 (2015)
8. Hargreaves, D.J., MacDonald, R., Miell, D.: How do people communicate using music. In: Miell, D.E., MacDonald, R.A.R., Hargreaves, D.J. (eds.) Musical Communication, pp. 1–26. Oxford University Press, Oxford (2005)
9. Kouroupetroglou, G.: Welcome to ICCHP 2018! (2012) http://www.icchp.org/welcome-chair-18
10. Voronov, A.M., Gorbunova, I.B., Kameris, A., Romanenko, LYu.: Music computer technologies in the digital age school. Proc. Irkutsk. State Tech. Univ. **5**(76), 256–261 (2013)
11. Voronov A.M., Krivodonova J.E.: Psychological and pedagogical features of information technology with visual impairment people. In: Child in the Modern World: Proceedings of the International Scientific Conference, pp. 251–256. Publishing House “The Herzen State Pedagogical University of Russia”, St. Petersburg (2013)

Computer Modeling of Secretary Problem and Its Interesting Results

Olga Starunova, Valeriia Nemychnikova(✉), and Anna Dronzik

Moscow South-Eastern School named after Marshal V.I. Chuikov, Moscow, Russia
sooobus@gmail.com

Abstract. A methodics of composing research work in programming for middle school students (1–2 years of programming experience) is offered in this article. This methodics is demonstrated using one interesting problem: secretary problem, or marriage problem. This problem is too complex to be theoretically solved in school and comprises probability theory and calculus. However it can be easy modeled using programming and it allows many modifications that can be invented by students. Moreover, results of such computer modeling allow to make non-trivial practical conclusions about decision making and optimal of choice strategies.

Keywords: Project-based approach · Secretary problem
Numerical simulation · Monte-Carlo method · PascalABC

1 Introduction

It is often believed that school students, especially schoolchildren of middle (not high) school, achieve success and new results in research on mathematics only in exceptional cases. Therefore, the programming courses for middle school students are often constructed as a cycle of short algorithmic problems with pre-known answers. Along with the undoubted effectiveness of this approach for the development of programming techniques, it is useful to educate students about the programming as laboratory of mathematics. In particular, to offer them mathematical problems, maybe inaccessible to them for a theoretical solution, but useful for a numerical simulation. In such experiments, students can understand how scientists work, and as a side effect new or little-known, but beautiful results are possible. One of the examples of work on this problem is described in detail in this article.

2 Formulation of Problem

Secretary problem is known also as marriage problem, sultan's dowry problem, etc. [1]. It firstly appeared in the middle of 20 century and is formulated (in terms of marriage) below [3]:

S. N. Pozdniakov and V. Dagienė (Eds.): ISSEP 2018, LNCS 11169, pp. 390–394, 2018.
https://doi.org/10.1007/978-3-030-02750-6_30

Fig. 1. Illustration for the problem

A bride invites N grooms in random order (ill. Fig. 1).

Each groom has a measure of quality—how good he is. The bride does not know this number beforehand, but after a meeting with each groom she can compare him with any of the previous ones and say which one is better (the grooms can theoretically be sorted by quality in strict growing order). After talking with one of them, she either chooses him, and he becomes her husband, and the process stops, or rejects him, he leaves and can not be returned. The bride wins if the groom she chose as a result is the best of all. Otherwise, she loses. Question: what should be the optimal strategy of the bride to ensure maximum probability of winning? What is the probability of winning with the optimal strategy?

This task has a fascinating solution: it turns out that the optimal strategy is to skip N/e of grooms, remember the best among them, and then choose the next one that outperforms him in quality. Following this strategy, the bride maximizes the probability of winning, and this probability is $1/e$.

Methodical sense of using this task on programming lessons is the following.

Theoretical solution of this problem is understandable by a high school student, if he or she is familiar with the theory of probability and material analysis. Computer simulation of this task (and many of its modifications) is not difficult and is available even for a sixth-grade student after 1 year of programming in any algorithmic language. In addition, this problem gives a wide scope for the computational experiment: there are many parameters in the condition, that can be changed to create new sub-problems. Since the middle of the 20th century more than 2000 articles [2] have been written on this subject, but interest in the problem does not stop, more and more results are obtained [2,5].

In 2018, we tried to offer this task to a group of two school students who finished the sixth grade. Pupils spent two years programming in Pascal. The task was given within the framework of the after-hours project. The students were asked to simulate the problem in a classical formulation, then to come up with variations of the experiment and ask their own questions to research. It was interesting to find out what tools they would try to apply and in what direction the research would go, and in addition—how they would interact inside the team.

3 Results

Firstly (approximately during the first two days of work), the students managed to model the condition of the problem and conduct a numerical experiment, writing a program in PascalABC (about 300 lines). Figure 2 shows the graph of the percentage of winning brides depending on strategy. "Strategy" here is defined as the number of the groom, up to whom the bride rejects everyone, remembering the current maximum. Here the number of candidates is $N = 100$, the "quality" of each is a random non-repeating number from 1 to 100, each strategy was tested by a group of 100,000 brides, for each group the percentage of the winners was calculated.

The result of the calculations matches the theory: the optimal is the strategy in which the brides miss $100/e$ 37 candidates and then choose the one who is better than the best of this group. At the same time, approximately 37% brides won.

One should noted that at this stage group work has appeared. One student was responsible for graphically displaying the results on the screen, a graphical interface and explanatory descriptions, the other was responsible for the direct implementation of the experiment. Both parts of the work were critically important for obtaining the result. In school group projects it is not always possible to successfully split the task into two independent parts, but here it was possible.

Then the question arose: where to go next? Students offered quite obvious, but for them a nontrivial thought: what if the bride wins not only choosing the best, but choosing one of the k best grooms? (For example, for $k = 3$ this means that the bride wins by choosing the groom with a quality of 100, 99 or 98). How the graph Fig. 2 changes depending on k?

The next day schoolchildren obtained an empirical answer to this question.

They made plots for different k (see Fig. 3) and realized that if the bride's requirements for grooms were reduced, the proportion of those who won with the optimal strategy is growing, and the optimal strategies tend to letting go less and less grooms when choosing one of the best.

The next natural question was: how does the probability of winning change depending on k, provided that all brides act optimally? In other words, what happens to the probability of winning if we gradually relax the requirements for the quality of winning grooms and the bride will be considered the winner if she chooses a groom with a quality of not less than $101 - k$?

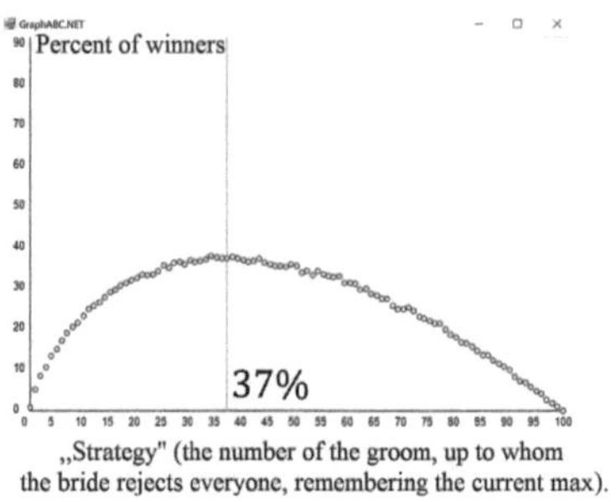

Fig. 2. Numerical simulation of the problem. Function of winning probability depending on a number of groom (see explanation in the text). Parameters: N = 100 grooms with "quality" 1 to 100, each strategy was tested by 100000 brides

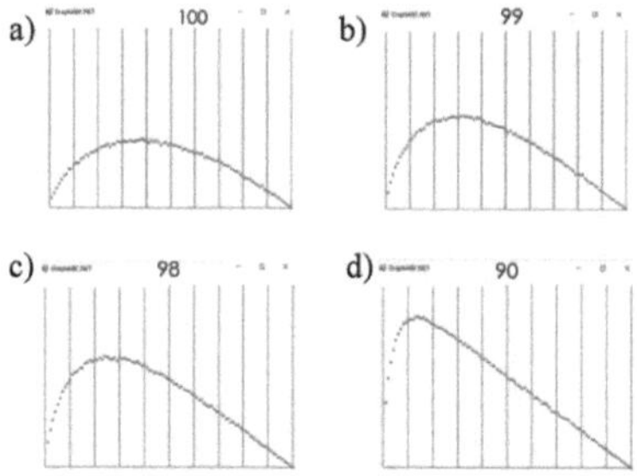

Fig. 3. Comparing of plots of percentage of winning brides depending on strategy. (a) Bride wins only when chooses a groom with quality 100. (b) she wins when chooses 99 or 100. (c) 98–100 (d) 90–100

This pattern was revealed by students at the end of a week's work on the project. From the graph shown in Fig. 4 one can draw several mathematical, practical and worldview conclusions.

Firstly, it can be seen from the graph that only slightly weakening the requirements for the groom, the bride greatly increases her chances of winning. For example, by agreeing not for the best, but to one of the two best grooms, the bride increases her chances of winning from 37% to 52%. And by agreeing to one of the top ten, it raises the chances of 82%. It would be useful to invite students to come up with other examples from real life, when the same effect works: a slight decrease in the requirements for the candidate dramatically increases the chances of success.

Secondly, it can be seen from the graph that too much reduction of requirements does not lead to any noticeable increase in the chance of winning. If the bride agrees to the groom from the best 33%, her chances of winning are equal to 92%, if she greatly reduces the requirements and agrees to the groom from the best half, her chances of winning are 95%, the difference in chances is not great compared with the price of victory.

Thirdly, it is useful to think about the other paramaters of the problem that can change the shape and properties of this graph. What processes in real life have a different type of sensitivity to changing requirements for candidates?

4 Discussion

The main pedagogical result of the work on this problem is that students were able to conduct their own small research on a small scale. It had many characteristic features of this scientific research: an open-ended problem with an unobvious solution, a great degree of freedom in questions and experiments.

It must be said that the results of numerical experiments related to the secretary problem are published in serious scientific journals at the moment [5].

In addition, there is a whole direction of setting not computer, but real experiments with real users, which are modifications of this problem. One of the

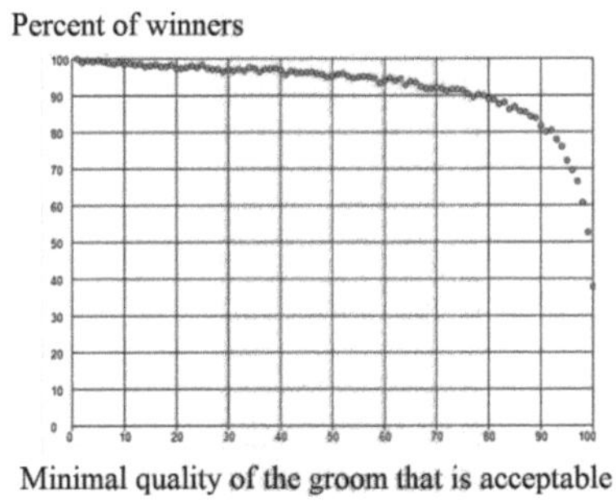

Fig. 4. Percentage of winning brides depending on quality requirements. X axe shows minimal quality of the groom that is acceptable

ways to develop this work for school students can be the development of a web application for studying the training of real people for an optimal strategy, just as it was done in [5], but with a different formulation of the question.

5 Conclusion

There is a wide range of research tasks available for middle and high school students. Frequently, in problems where the students lack the mathematical technique for the analytic solution because of age, there is room for numerical modeling. In this area, students can achieve successful and sometimes even scientifically new personal results.

References

1. Secretary problem formulation. https://en.wikipedia.org/wiki/Secretary_problem#cite_note-2
2. Goldstein, D.G., et al.: Learning in the Repeated Secretary Problem. Microsoft Research (2017). arXiv:1708.08831v1 [cs.GT]
3. Ferguson, T.S.: Who solved the secretary problem? Stat. Sci. **4**(3), 282–289 (1989)
4. Freeman, P.R.: The secretary problem and its extensions: a review. Int. Stat. Rev. **51**(2), 189–206 (1983)
5. Bearden, J.N.: A new secretary problem with rank-based selection and cardinal payoffs. J. Math. Psychol. **50**, 58–9 (2006). https://doi.org/10.1016/j.jmp.2005.11.003

Author Index

MIX
Papier aus verantwortungsvollen Quellen
Paper from responsible sources
FSC® C105338

If you have any concerns about our products,
you can contact us on
ProductSafety@springernature.com

In case Publisher is established outside the EU,
the EU authorized representative is:
Springer Nature Customer Service Center GmbH
Europaplatz 3, 69115 Heidelberg, Germany

Printed by Libri Plureos GmbH
in Hamburg, Germany